America's Public Philosopher

America's Public Philosopher

Essays on Social Justice,
Economics, Education, and
the Future of Democracy

John Dewey

Edited and with an introduction
by Eric Thomas Weber

Columbia University Press

New York

Columbia University Press
Publishers Since 1893
New York   Chichester, West Sussex
cup.columbia.edu

Copyright © 2021 Columbia University Press
All rights reserved

Library of Congress Cataloging-in-Publication Data
Names: Dewey, John, 1859–1952, author. | Weber, Eric Thomas, editor.
Title: America's public philosopher : essays on social justice,
economics, education, and the future of democracy / John Dewey ;
edited and with an introduction by Eric Thomas Weber.
Description: New York : Columbia University Press, [2020] |
Includes bibliographical references and index.
Identifiers: LCCN 2020022538 (print) | LCCN 2020022539 (ebook) |
ISBN 9780231198943 (hardcover) | ISBN 9780231198950 (trade paperback) |
ISBN 9780231552882 (ebook)
Subjects: LCSH: Philosophy. | Political culture.
Classification: LCC B945.D41 W43 2020 (print) |
LCC B945.D41 (ebook) | DDC 191—dc23
LC record available at https://lccn.loc.gov/2020022538
LC ebook record available at https://lccn.loc.gov/2020022539

Cover image: John Dewey, © Everett Collection Inc. / Alamy Stock Photo
Cover design: Chang Jae Lee

Contents

Acknowledgments ix

Introduction: Democratic Faith and Education in Unstable Times, by Eric Thomas Weber   1

PART I
Democracy and the United States

1. Democracy Is Radical   19

2. Address to National Negro Conference   24

3. A Symposium on Woman's Suffrage   27

4. The Challenge of Democracy to Education   30

5. America in the World   40

6. Our National Dilemma   44

7. Pragmatic America   49

8. The Basic Values and Loyalties of Democracy   55

9. Creative Democracy—The Task Before Us   59

PART II
Politics and Power

10. Politics and Culture   69

11. Intelligence and Power   78

12. Force, Violence, and the Law   83

13. Why I Am Not a Communist   88

14. Dualism and the Split Atom   93

15. Is There Hope for Politics?   98

16. A Liberal Speaks Out for Liberalism   105

17. Future of Liberalism   112

PART III
Education

18. What Is a School For?   117

19. Dewey Outlines Utopian Schools   121

20. Industrial Education—A Wrong Kind   127

21. Why Have Progressive Schools?   133

22. Can Education Share in Social Reconstruction?   143

23. Nationalizing Education   148

24. The Teacher and the Public   156

25. Democracy and Education in the World of Today   161

PART IV
Social Ethics and Economic Justice

26. Capitalistic or Public Socialism?   173

27. Does Human Nature Change?   185

28. The Ethics of Animal Experimentation   193

29. Ethics and International Relations   200

30. Dewey Describes Child's New World   211

31. The Collapse of a Romance   217

32. The Economic Situation: A Challenge to Education   223

33. The Jobless—A Job for All of Us   231

PART V
Science and Society

34. The Influence of Darwinism on Philosophy   237

35. Science, Belief and the Public   249

36. Social Science and Social Control   255

37. Education and Birth Control   260

38. The Supreme Intellectual Obligation   263

39. The Revolt against Science   270

PART VI

Philosophy and Culture

40. The Case of the Professor and the Public Interest   277

41. Social Absolutism   282

42. Some Factors in Mutual National Understanding   289

43. The Basis for Hope   299

44. Art as Our Heritage   303

45. The Value of Historical Christianity   308

46. What Humanism Means to Me   314

....

References   *319*

Index   *323*

Acknowledgments

I began working on this collection of John Dewey's public writings in 2011. Along the way, many people were essential in the development of this project. At the time, I was teaching at the University of Mississippi, in which my department chair, Dr. Robert Haws was immensely supportive. I am also grateful to Dr. Doug Sullivan-Gonzalez, dean of the Sally McDonnell Barksdale Honors College at the University of Mississippi, for the support that work with his college provided me over the years. Those funds enabled me to hire two undergraduate research assistants, Christine Dickason and Elizabeth Lococo, who deserve key thanks for their work on this project. By 2013, I had narrowed my selections down to just over sixty essays from Dewey's vast corpus as candidates for inclusion in this volume. The following year, I enlisted Christine's and Elizabeth's help as they were two of the most talented undergraduate students I have had the privilege to hire as research assistants. They read through all of the essays that I had selected, letting me know which they found to be the most compelling, where they found matters to be needing more introduction or prefacing, and more. Their thoughts on the initial selection of essays enabled me to trim the collection down to the most powerful and timely essays for readers today. Their reactions were invaluable for my editorial work and writing aimed at introducing and explaining the essays included here.

This collection would have been impossible without the mentorship that I was fortunate to receive from Dr. Larry A. Hickman, former director of the Center for Dewey Studies and professor emeritus at Southern Illinois University Carbondale, in Carbondale, IL. Furthermore, I am one of the lucky few to have more than one mentor. Dr. John Lachs of Vanderbilt University has guided me countless times at all stages of my career, including with respect to this project. I am grateful to John and Larry both for being my guiding examples.

Angela Moore-Swafford of Southern Illinois University Press was supportive and kind in the process of checking and procuring the permissions to republish Dewey's essays included in this volume. I am thankful to her and to SIU's board of trustees for permission to use Dewey's essays, as well as for Angela's help and support.

Dr. Tibor Solymosi has long been a good friend and colleague and for this volume generously offered me editorial feedback on my selections and introductions to the essays. The collection is significantly stronger than it would have been without his help. I am also grateful to the blind reviewers whose feedback helped me to strengthen the organization of these essays.

My colleagues in the Department of Educational Policy Studies and Evaluation in the University of Kentucky's College of Education have been a great source of support and encouragement as well. I am grateful to my colleague Dr. Beth Goldstein, who advised me on matters relating to the publication of this collection. Dr. Kelly Bradley has been an ideal department chair, and her encouragement has meant a great deal to me. Dr. John Thelin, my senior faculty mentor in the department, is an exemplar of the publicly engaged scholar whom I hope to emulate. In addition, I am excited that my college's new dean, Dr. Julian Vasquez Heilig, has shown already both in words and deeds, in his career and here in our college, that he champions publicly engaged scholarship, the kind of spirit which animates this volume.

I also owe thanks to John W. Wright, of the John W. Wright Literary Agency, who encouraged me to submit this project to Columbia University Press. My editor, Wendy Lochner, of the press has been wonderful to work with and has been understanding and supportive at every step.

Without question, I am most grateful to my family, especially to my brilliant wife, Dr. Annie Davis Weber, who has been my strongest supporter. My parents, Drs. Collin and Dominique Weber, have also been proud of my work in philosophy from the beginning. And my in-laws, Dr. Paul and Jane Davis, have been kind and supportive at every turn. I am truly, deeply fortunate and am grateful to each of these people and many more beyond them.

In the spirit of John Dewey, I must thank all of the many students I have worked with, who have inspired me with their thoughts and questions throughout nearly two decades of teaching in higher education. I hope that this collection of essays honors all that these many people have taught me and shares with others the inspiration that drew me in to philosophy and its dialogue with life and policy.

America's Public Philosopher

Introduction

Democratic Faith and Education in Unstable Times

It is hard to find a basis for hope in the world today. Gains in the struggle for women's historic equality are eroded when politicians' demeaning stances toward women and dismissal of their testimony about sexual assault become commonplace and accepted.[1] Progress in civil rights is met with explosive growth in privatized prisons disproportionately populated by minority citizens, police brutality commonly resulting in no indictments of officers, and even angry white mobs bearing torches in defense of Confederate monuments.[2] The United States elected a champion of anti-intellectualism and unfettered capitalism who raises concerns of fascism.[3] And his challengers are charged with being in the pockets of finance capitalism and having rigged primary elections.[4] The potential for war is heightened at a time when the most powerful politician in the world speaks loosely about the use of nuclear weapons.[5] The national organization of public education is also under threat, and the head of the U.S. Department of Education is rolling back regulations intended to protect and address the interests of students with educational-accessibility needs and vulnerabilities.[6] Nearly a third of American voters polled genuinely believe today in the potential for another civil war, all while favoring protectionist economic policies that are hurting the very people they were intended to help.[7] And Americans have elected a president who has fought to hide the findings and release of a national climate assessment in which more than a dozen federal agencies warn of "substantial damages" and climate effects that are "intensifying across the country."[8]

Americans today desperately need guidance in intellectual and moral leadership. As I hope that this book will make clear, John Dewey was an exemplary public philosopher who sought to provide Americans and lovers of democracy around the world with a vision for living intelligently and creatively together. Dewey's work can help us find a basis for hope about democracy and education even in troubled times. Dewey did not have all the answers, but he offered a crucial democratic attitude and outlook, rooted in a cautious but reasoned faith in human potential. That faith was not naïve. Dewey was born in 1859, just two years before the start of the American Civil War. His lifetime spanned the period of the dissemination and explosion of Darwin's influence on the biological and social sciences, two world wars, the Great Depression, and the lead-up to McCarthyism. Dewey's life of ninety-two years, ending in 1952, witnessed the arguments for different approaches to the still new universal public education, including the debates about what schools are for. He was an advocate for women's suffrage and democratic equality. He called attention, furthermore, to the contradictions in Americans' criticisms of Germany's prejudices and iniquities while people in the United States were committing injustices against women and black, Asian, and Jewish Americans at the same time. Dewey challenged the growing nationalism, isolationism, and anti-immigrant sentiment of his time, all while resisting the idea that the United States was the world's police officer.

It is essential that we look to Dewey today because our world needs voices like his and because it looks more like his world than anyone would care to admit. We throw around words like "fascist," "Nazi," or "communist," while in Dewey's day these terms were frequently used without exaggeration. These were the real terms of real people working in his time to pursue allegedly democratic aims, but by authoritarian and often cruel means. Time and again, Dewey noted the ways in which people often made the mistake of trying to pursue democratic goals by means of dictatorships and violence. "Democratic ends require democratic means," he argued. The white supremacists who are presently growing more visible and vocal like to suggest that the Black Panthers were aggressive and equivalent to their aims but for persons of African descent. The claim that one is entitled to self-defense and to arms for that purpose should not be translated as threats to others, no more so than "Don't tread on me," at least. Self-defense is justifiable, for Dewey, but the idea of intending to harm others for the sake of democratic means is not. At the same time, the demands of democracy would represent a radical shift from unjust present practices. Dewey wrote, for instance, that "any system that cannot provide elementary security for millions has no claim to the title of being organized in behalf of liberty and the development of individuals."[9]

In his own day, Dewey was considered "foremost among educators in the country," and the editors of the *New York Times* referred to him in his front-page obituary, above the fold, as "foremost philosopher of his time."[10] It is difficult today to imagine that the general public might know American philosophers by name. Highly educated circles often know Peter Singer, Martha Nussbaum, or Michael Sandel. And some philosophers have local followings or are rising stars, but Dewey became well known all while being generally a mild-mannered and humble professor of philosophy, one who nevertheless often addressed the public in writings and speeches. Dewey's soft-spoken good character was familiar, but the relation between his philosophical ideas and his consequent motivation to be publicly engaged as a writer and speaker has gone underappreciated, including by prominent, self-proclaimed Deweyans like Richard Rorty.[11] While general audiences will benefit from a return to Dewey's wisdom and example, scholars in the academy stand to learn a great deal, including about a possible path forward for a new movement of engaged public scholarship that is still only burgeoning, even now. It would be especially valuable if this volume were to inspire administrators and leaders in higher education to make meaningful in reality, practice, and policy their generally empty statements and vague allusions to valuing publicly engaged scholarship.[12]

John Dewey was born in Burlington, Vermont, on October 20, 1859, to Archibald and Lucina Dewey. He studied at the University of Vermont, graduating in 1879, and then taught for three years, first at the high school level in Oil City, Pennsylvania, until 1881, and then at the elementary level in Charlotte, Vermont, until 1882. His time in Oil City left some lasting impressions on him, given that it was an industrial-age town at its prime. In addition, he had a vague but powerful "mystic experience," a "supremely blissful feeling" that led him to abandon his earlier worries about the need for adequate prayer to a supernatural being and to focus on experience and his relation to other people.[13] Dewey attended Johns Hopkins University, where he earned his Ph.D. in 1884. As a student, he participated in and gave presentations before the Metaphysical Club, the subject of Louis Menand's 2002 Pulitzer prize–winning book on American philosophers.[14] Upon earning his doctorate, he accepted a position as instructor at the University of Michigan, where two years later he was appointed assistant professor of philosophy in 1886. That year, he married Harriet Alice Chipman, and the next year he published his *Psychology*, which gained little academic attention. In 1888, he accepted an offer from the University of Minnesota, only to be courted back to the University of Michigan in 1889 to become chair and professor of philosophy. The same year, he published "The Value of Historical Christianity," included in this volume. In that essay, he noted the moral benefits of certain Christian principles and teachings, which he saw as residing in human beings' concerns for one another, as well as the joining of the divine in humanity, which Jesus embodied. In this essay, we find an early expression of Dewey's democratic faith, which would continue to mature in his lifelong appreciation of democratic values, especially the ideas that all people matter and that there is a supreme importance in how we approach human relations to one another. Later in life, Dewey would more squarely be considered a humanist, but his concern for all fellow human beings lived on, and the idea of the divine as an implicit ideal in human experience carried forward to his powerful short book *A Common Faith*.[15] Dewey remained at the University of Michigan until 1894, before moving to the University of Chicago.

While in Ann Arbor, Dewey was profoundly influenced by William James's magisterial, 1,300-page work, *The Principles of Psychology*. In the year of its release, Dewey taught a seminar on James's *Principles* and later raved to James about the work in a letter.[16] It is commonly recognized in the literature on the philosophical pragmatists that William James was a great inspiration for Dewey, but less often is it noted that Dewey was an inspiration for James, a claim I have argued.[17] In particular, Dewey wrote to James a year after the *Principles* was published, in 1891, about his encounter with a journalist, Franklin Ford, of Bradstreet, who caught Dewey's interest in his thinking about the relationship between ideas and their practical value for real life, such as in the selling of information as a business. Dewey related to James the intriguing question of how free ideas are from the constraints of the world, as well as the question of how information and intelligence can be disseminated. All of these questions were inspired by journalism, yet in them Dewey saw real philosophical questions worth exploring. For even if ideas are believed to have value in the abstract, he thought, the real test of their meaning and worth must have some bearing on life. Dewey's appreciation for the scientific attitude resonated with William James's scientific approach to psychology, and James praised Dewey's lectures and essays in a number of letters.[18] The explosion of the sciences at the time and the revolutionary influence of Darwin's *On the Origin of Species* all seemed to be pointing, according to Dewey, away from the European rigidities and classical patterns of thought through which past thinkers sought to interpret scientific discoveries. Dewey's championing of the scientific outlook and of seeing the meaning of ideas in relation to their bearing on the world demonstrated the crucial importance of education for empowering people and reflected the democratic faith that knowledge and wisdom can come from anywhere.

From 1894 to 1904, Dewey chaired the University of Chicago's philosophy department, where he was inspired by Jane Addams and his experience of the Pullman strikes. Upon arriving in Chicago, he founded the famed Laboratory School at the university and served as director of the School of Education. A year later, his son Morris died of diphtheria. While in Chicago, Dewey published some of his greatest work in psychology, including the technical yet highly influential scholarly essay "The Reflex Arc Concept in Psychology,"[19] which challenged the oversimplified "stimulus/response" outlook in psychology, one of the remnants of problematic thinking in James's *Principles*, as well as in other psychological works. That important essay noted that we cannot separate stimulus and response in the way that tradition had done, for when you consider looking at an object, the eye engages in a kind of searching that focuses, selecting things seen, in a way, or at least as a part of the functioning of sight. Similarly, a child's attention could be on a ball, music in the background, or any number of things in his or her environment. In the beginning, in a sense, is the selectivity of attention, something that Dewey saw as the germination of human personality. When you watch babies jerk their arms and legs in odd ways, it is as if they are probing, searching the environment or feeling their bodies first and foremost, before reaching out for anything in particular. In this rich psychological idea, we can identify a source of Dewey's valuing of the interests of the child or the pupil in his or her studies. Recognizing the activity inherent in observation or listening was revolutionary at the time, as young people were thought to be empty vessels or blank slates, the tabula rasa, into which schooling was to be poured or onto which wisdom transcribed. There are many reasons today to think that educational practices are still stuck in the old model, as we see in the emphasis on high-stakes testing and standardization of curricula, rather than the cultivation of individuals' powers. Dewey's thinking was groundbreaking. James noted Dewey's inspiration in having founded a genuine school of philosophy at Chicago.[20] In connection with his influence in philosophy and psychology, Dewey also wrote extensively on education and the child, publishing works like *School and Society* in 1899 and *The Child and the Curriculum* in 1902.

Dewey moved to Columbia University in New York City in 1904 and also that year lost a second son, Gordon, to typhoid. In his time at Columbia, Dewey was highly active beyond the university, including with the Society for Ethical Culture. He participated in organizational meetings for the National Association for the Advancement of Colored People (NAACP). Around that time, he advocated for universal suffrage. In addition, he published his most popular work, *Democracy and Education*, in 1916. A few years later, he had the opportunity to travel and lecture in Japan in 1919 and then in China from 1919 to 1921. The experience was amazing for Dewey, who believed in democracy and resisted some of his contemporaries' isolationism and anti-immigrant sentiment. In 1922 he published *Human Nature and Conduct*, in which he explained how human beings and our norms have evolved over time, much like other species. Understanding humanity in terms of the insights of evolution, we can see that at certain times norms arose in ways that then seemed necessary and useful and that over the generations, new problems and opportunities have emerged and past threats have receded. This way of thinking helps to explain how norms change over time and how human beings adapt.

Dewey often commented on the affairs of his day. Even though Rorty suggests that what Dewey said to colleagues in philosophy bore little relation to his public pronouncements,[21] if we look back to Dewey's letter to James about Franklin Ford, we see that Dewey all along was animated by the belief that our abstract ideas are to be tested objectively in the real world, that their meaning is to be understood in application. It is easy to imagine, for instance, that his ideas in *Human Nature and Conduct* were at work in his progressive attitude toward universal suffrage and the need to advance the conditions of African Americans of his day, as in the NAACP. Several related essays on these subjects are included in this volume. His shift, furthermore, from an early Christianity to his later humanism is clearly related to his belief in the importance of adaptation and letting go of past habits of thought and practice that present encumbrances to new developments. In my own lifetime, attitudes toward homosexuals went from mockery, marginalization, and murder to equal rights and the opening up of the tradition and policies concerning marriage to same-sex couples. Were Dewey alive today, I believe that he would draw a clear connection between Darwin's insights and the eventual need for a change in historically contingent and oppressive attitudes about sexuality between consenting adults.

I have argued that one of Dewey's most important essays on the relationship between his scholarly work and his public engagement was the address he delivered in 1933 before the American Association for the Advancement of Science, titled "The Supreme Intellectual Obligation," included in this collection.[22] In that essay, Dewey argues powerfully that the chief obligation for intellectuals is to ensure that inquiry and its products are to benefit humanity, the masses of people. That obligation implies, he explains, that insights inaccessible to the public nevertheless can be made relevant to people's lives and made to benefit them, whether or not average people can understand them. In addition, many of the advancements of the sciences and technology can come with great costs to human beings, as we witnessed in 2016 with cybercrime, hacking, and the manipulation of people in the lead-up to the presidential election.[23] Amazing and powerful handheld devices make our lives better in many ways but also cause deep and troubling problems, such as in the harms that come from too much screen time for kids and the devices' effects on our brains and on our democracy.[24] For Dewey, the consequences of the fact that new technologies and insights come both with benefits and costs had two parts. First, inquiry should ensure that benefits are secured and that inquiry continue into the study of how to alleviate the harmful effects of new developments. It benefited people to drive cars rather than only horse and carriage, for example, but wind was uncomfortable. Windshields addressed the problem of wind, but caused terrible injuries when people were cut on glass in car accidents. Now our windshields shatter into small, dull bits, sandwiched between plastic. The development of seatbelts and airbags is all a consequence of inquiry into how to address the harms that came from earlier technological innovations. Fewer unnecessary deaths are an example of the ways that human beings can benefit from inquiry. The example also shows that inquiry does not happen only in colleges and universities but also in industry and among people beyond the academy. After all, companies sometimes try hard to listen to their customers' complaints, addressing them in newer models, or else their competitors will and gain advantage.

The second consequence for Dewey of the supreme intellectual obligation has to do with those developments and insights that require participation of masses of people for their benefit to be felt and to spread. For those, it is essential that the wider public develop the scientific attitudes and habits of mind necessary to appreciate wisdom and to put it to use. In his address, Dewey was explaining, among other things, the importance of science education, understood broadly, for the elementary curriculum and in subsequent schooling. The right attitudes are essential for the development of good inquirers, for people to be able to put insights to use for making their lives better.

The problem, as Dewey saw it, in things like academic jargon and impenetrable technical language was that they were often not necessary. When it is necessary, we can have specialists translate for the rest of us. We call them opinion leaders in everyday language. At the same time, there are many matters that need not be inaccessible. Often in the academy, the task of rendering ideas accessible is given the label of "popularizing" or "dumbing down." Einstein comes to mind, however, in the phrase often attributed to him: "If you can't explain it simply, you don't understand it well enough." It is more difficult, not easier, to explain complex ideas simply. Scholars are so used to the formalization of the academic context that we feel insecure when our ideas are explained simply. I have heard many scholars apologize to their peers for public statements or essays for general audiences. They call others to refer to this or that impenetrable text for their more precise renditions of complex matters. Scholars are also insecure in making ideas accessible because, all of a sudden, their ideas can be critiqued by a far larger audience, some of whom may not apply the tradition of academic charity in interpretation. Given that, ultimately Dewey calls on scholars to be courageous. Timidity leads writers to be abstract, technical in style, and irrelevant to public concerns. Often arrogance masks their irrelevance and puts down the audiences and purposes of publicly engaged scholars in relation to their own elevation above the unwashed masses. Dewey rejected these attitudes outright and proclaimed the opposite to be the scholar's "supreme intellectual obligation." Despite the example and insights of great figures like Dewey, critics have rightly pointed out that colleges' and universities' policies and practices do not match their rhetoric about public engagement.[25]

Dewey retired from Columbia University in 1930 at the age of seventy, after several celebrations of his work around the time of his birthday in 1929. Dewey's retirement did not slow him down, however. In fact, he became highly vocal and publicly engaged at that time, just as the country was falling into the Great Depression. In 1930, Dewey published "What Humanism Means to Me,"[26] included in this volume. A few years later, he signed the "Humanist Manifesto" in 1933, a document that declared belief in the "universe as self-existing and not created" as well as in "man as part of nature . . . that . . . has emerged as a result of a continuous process." The manifesto also claims that "the time has passed for theism, deism, modernism, and the several varieties of 'new thought.'"[27] Dewey's early religious inclinations underwent a kind of evolution, maintaining what he believed to be the important moral aspects of historical religions while letting go of those characteristics that he believed no longer were needed for the benefit of humanity. The manifesto continues, for example, proclaiming that "in the place of the old attitudes involved in worship and prayer the humanist finds his religious emotions expressed in a heightened sense of personal life and in cooperative effort to promote social well-being." These ideas share key sentiments that Dewey had expressed over forty years earlier in his essay on the value of historical Christianity.

The 1930s were an active time for Dewey's writings, especially given the economic collapse. He was deeply concerned about the incredible levels of unemployment, which reached 25 percent in 1933. It was 3.8 percent in 2019. Dewey wrote for general audiences in powerful pieces titled "The Jobless—a Job for All of Us" and "The Collapse of a Romance," referring to a kind of romance with laissez-faire capitalism. Both essays are included in this collection.[28] Dewey wrote often for the *New Republic* and advocated in many writings for the "need for a new party." An essay by that name could have been included in this collection, but another more succinct and powerful statement was published in *Scribner's* magazine, titled "Is There Hope for Politics?"[29] As noted from the outset, today it can be difficult to feel hope. I believe little can be more inspiring than Dewey's answer to such a challenge that he published in 1931, with the Great Depression worsening rapidly. His answer related to the ideas mentioned here already, that solutions sometimes must come through letting go of outmoded ways of thinking. Americans have long felt stuck in two-party politics, and many feel disconnected from both parties. It is perhaps true to a greater degree now than in Dewey's day, given how much polarization has grown.[30] Dewey believed at the time what some still think today, that both major parties are in the pocket of Wall Street, of the rich, and not sufficiently concerned about laborers and the unemployed.[31]

In his day, Dewey was a towering figure in the academy, yet shortly after he died, his great fame and favor turned hard against his moral and publicly engaged approach to philosophy. Dewey had argued for a reconstruction of philosophy, away from outmoded ways of looking for timeless, absolute truths and toward a frame of mind broadly understood as scientific. He resisted unquestioned first principles and favored following the evidence where it leads. He also advocated for starting from real problems for real people, not from abstract first principles assumed to be correct. He believed that the scholars and authors who took the opposite approach were continuing traditions that had been built up during elitist periods, when the majority of people lived in slavery or near-slavery. The democratic world, he believed, demands empowerment for all people and a radical reorientation of social structures to align them with the benefit of all. The consequent democratic approach to education that he developed and for which he is best known starts with recognizing power and activity in all individuals and is referred to in everyday language as "learning by doing."

The essays in this volume each highlight one or a few of the central themes in Dewey's body of work. Many more of his public writings and addresses were first gathered, reviewed, and evaluated along a set of criteria for inclusion in this collection. The first criterion was that the essay be accessible, either understandable for general audiences today or with the potential to be, with the help of an editor's introduction. One or two essays are more challenging than the rest but are of such importance with respect to Dewey's thinking or to public matters that they merit inclusion, I believe, for appreciating his great contributions. Further criteria included the potential of his then-timely writings to continue to speak to readers now about matters that remain important. They also had to be some of his best examples of clear philosophical thinking that reveals the importance of philosophy for life and policy. As noted in the acknowledgements to this volume, three readers reviewed the essays and my introductions, considering my criteria, and helped guide the selection of essays as well as how they needed to be introduced. The categories into which his essays are organized include "Democracy and the United States," "Politics and Power," "Education," "Social Ethics and Economic Justice," "Science and Society," and "Philosophy and Culture."

For Dewey, the United States was a special place of experimentation in the world. Europe symbolized for him an old place, stuck in longstanding habits of thought and practice. These included what philosophers call "dualisms," the hard distinction between two extremes of a difference, which often fail to appreciate the significant middle ground or alternatives of thought to them. The United States' pioneer mentality and ingenuity was well suited for learning from Darwin's insights about adaptation, even if still today 38 percent of Americans doubt the lessons of the evolutionary sciences.[32] It was also a place that aspired to far-reaching ideals, though falling far short of them. In pursuing ambitious goals and experimenting with new systems and practices, furthermore, Dewey advocated many times against confusing means to a goal for the goal. Today in education it often appears as though administrators confuse the tools we use for evaluating learning for the goals of education, for example. Such mistakes sadly impoverish schooling and create high-stakes focus on matters that students struggle to value. Dewey's democratic spirit rings throughout this collection, including in the section "Science and Society," in which he clearly and powerfully argues for the importance of science and the intellectual attitudes and habits that it requires while avoiding absolutist outlooks on truth. He believed that philosophers could reconstruct our habits and practices, letting go of outmoded ways of thinking and keeping the problems of our day front and center in our minds. This attitude was central to his fundamental belief in the obligation of the intellect to improve people's lives, to inquire and act for the benefit of humanity.

Many current defenders of democracy are wondering whether civility is still truly called for.[33] Should we not punch neo-Nazis, for example?[34] Dewey was an outspoken advocate for free democratic communication, yet he also referred to hatred as treasonous to democracy, such as in essays like "Democracy Is Radical" and "Creative Democracy—the Task Before Us," both included in this volume.[35] This tension is challenging to navigate yet is at the heart of his democratic cosmopolitanism. The United States was and remains a very diverse society, one that cannot be characterized without compound terms. There is no pure American, Dewey thought, separate from the African American, the Irish American, and so on. It is of utmost importance, he thought, to see the fact of our common existence in the country as a quality we share. The United States is a nation of many cultures, all participating in creating a larger one together yet without "melting," as the saying goes in the famous metaphor. Instead, like each different instrument playing in a complex orchestra, ringing different notes, none must lose its special character, and in fact such differences enrich the resulting sound.

Today perhaps the most powerful force advancing conformity and undercutting the enrichment of democratic difference is the push of commercialism and materialism, Dewey would likely think. In his own day, he mused about what education would look like in utopian schools, in an essay also included in this collection. He argued that our assumptions in the real world include the monotonous refrain that education is primarily a means to economic ends, which are in turn only means to the endless accumulation of things. Commercialism has only increased, perhaps radically, since his day. The purpose of study or education is presently treated as though it were only to get a job, not to enrich one's life culturally. To sum up what might be Dewey's most important contributions for the public, I suggest that they are that wisdom is meant to be for everyone and can come from anyone and that learning and education should be thought of as lifelong, for real education is much more than schooling. It is democratic life itself. This project is meant to offer general readers inspiration in Dewey's causes for hope and in the methods he recommends for its fulfillment. It also is meant to speak to scholars and administrators, calling them to task when their claims about valuing public engagement are but hollow slogans. The reconstruction of philosophy and education that Dewey championed has yet to take hold widely, and the world still needs it now. Its achievement will never be complete but always understood as approaching an ideal. Coming closer to it would represent a deep and meaningful shift in the public and political culture, to make it more philosophical and more humane.

NOTES

1. Jessica Bennett, "The 'Tight Rope' of Testifying While Female," *New York Times*, September 28, 2018, https://www.nytimes.com/2018/09/28/us/politics/christine-blasey-ford-testimony-testifying-while-female.html.
2. Rina Palta, "Why For-Profit Prisons House More Inmates of Color," NPR, March 13, 2014, https://www.npr.org/sections/codeswitch/2014/03/13/289000532/why-for-profit-prisons-house-more-inmates-of-color; See Waseem Abbasi, "Jason Stockley Verdict Shows How Rare Officer Convictions Are in Police Shootings," *USA Today*, June 17, 2017, https://www.usatoday.com/story/news/nation/2017/06/17/convictions-rare-officers-police-shootings/102947548/; Cassandra Chaney and Ray V. Robertson, "Armed and Dangerous? An Examination of Fatal Shootings of Unarmed Black People by Police," *Journal of Pan African Studies* 8, no. 4 (September 2015): 45–78; Eugene Scott, "President Trump, 'Angry Mobs,' and 'Very Fine People,'" *Washington Post*, October 8, 2018, https://www.washingtonpost.com/politics/2018/10/08/president-trump-angry-mobs-very-fine-people/.
3. See Peter Beinart, "Is Trump a Fascist?," *New York Times*, September 11, 2018, https://www.nytimes.com/2018/09/11/books/review/jason-stanley-how-fascism

-works.html; Noah Berlatsky, "Is Trump a Fascist? Learning About How Fascism Works Can Help Prevent Its Spread in America," *NBC News*, September 3, 2018, https://www.nbcnews.com/think/opinion/trump-fascist-learning-about-how-fascism-works-can-help-prevent-ncna905886.

4. Andrew Prokop, "What Hillary Clinton Told Wall Street Bankers in Private, According to Leaked Emails," *Vox.com*, October 7, 2016, https://www.vox.com/2016/10/7/13206882/hillary-clinton-wikileaks-speeches-goldman; Ezra Klein, "Was the Democratic Primary Rigged?," *Vox.com*, November 14, 2017, https://www.vox.com/policy-and-politics/2017/11/14/16640082/donna-brazile-warren-bernie-sanders-democratic-primary-rigged.

5. See Tim Kaine, "Don't Let Trump Go to War with Iran," *The Atlantic*, July 13, 2018, https://www.theatlantic.com/ideas/archive/2018/07/dont-let-trump-go-to-war-with-iran/565082/; Steve Holland and Parisa Hafezi, "Trump, Iran's Rouhani Exchange Threats, Insults on U.N.'s World Stage," *Japan Today*, September 26, 2018, https://japantoday.com/category/world/wrapup-9-trump-iran's-rouhani-exchange-threats-insults-on-u.n.'s-world-stage; Aaron Blake, "Trump's Loose Talk on Nuclear Weapons Suddenly Becomes Very Real," *Washington Post*, October 11, 2017, https://www.washingtonpost.com/news/the-fix/wp/2017/10/11/trumps-loose-rhetoric-on-nuclear-weapons-has-become-a-very-real-concern/.

6. See Scott Sargrad, "Rolling Back Rights for Students," *U.S. News and World Report*, March 7, 2018, https://www.usnews.com/opinion/knowledge-bank/articles/2018-03-07/betsy-devos-education-dept-to-roll-back-help-for-students-with-disabilities; Moriah Balingit, "DeVos Rescinds 72 Guidance Documents Outlining Rights for Disabled Students," *Washington Post*, October 21, 2017, https://www.washingtonpost.com/news/education/wp/2017/10/21/devos-rescinds-72-guidance-documents-outlining-rights-for-disabled-students/.

7. Ryan W. Miller, "Poll: Almost a Third of US Voters Think a Second Civil War Is Coming Soon," *USA Today*, June 27, 2018, https://www.usatoday.com/story/news/politics/onpolitics/2018/06/27/civil-war-likely-voters-say-rasmussen-poll/740731002/; Daniel J. Mitchell, "Tariffs Are Harming the American Workers They're Supposed to Protect," Foundation for Economic Education, June 22, 2018, https://fee.org/articles/tariffs-are-harming-the-american-workers-theyre-supposed-to-protect/, Mark J. Perry, "Backfire Economics—Trump's Tariffs Are Hurting US Farmers and Workers and Putting the Entire Economy at Risk," *AEIdeas*, July 9, 2018, http://www.aei.org/publication/backfire-economics-trumps-protectionism-is-hurting-farmers-and-putting-us-jobs-at-risk/; and Dany Bahar, "Trump's Trade Policy: Protecting American Workers at the Expense of American Consumers," *Brookings*, January 6, 2017, https://www.brookings.edu/blog/up-front/2017/01/06/trumps-trade-policy-protecting-american-workers-at-the-expense-of-american-consumers/.

8. Juliet Eilperin and Toluse Olorunnipa, "'He Gets to Decide': President Escalates His Fight Against Climate Science," *Washington Post*, March 3, 2019, https://www.washingtonpost.com/politics/he-gets-to-decide-trump-escalates-his-fight-against-climate-science-ahead-of-2020/2019/02/28/6e12dbbc-3aa3-11e9-a2cd-307b06d0257b_story.html.

9. John Dewey, "A Liberal Speaks Out for Liberalism," *New York Times Magazine*, February 23, 1936, 3, 24, reprint, LW.11.282–89 and chapter 16 in this book.
10. Editors of the *New York Times* introducing Dewey's contribution, "What's a School For?," *New York Times*, March 18, 1923, 3; editors, "Dr. John Dewey Dead at 92; Philosopher a Noted Liberal," *New York Times*, June 2, 1952, 1.
11. Even one of the best-known Dewey scholars and "neo-pragmatists," Richard Rorty, challenged the relevance of what philosophy departments do. In an interview he gave to Phillip McReynolds, Rorty explained that "I don't think you can find much of a connection between what Dewey said to the philosophy professors and what he said to the general public. The questions that he took up in response to people like [Bertrand] Russell or [Josiah] Royce are just too remote from politics for one to claim that the one presupposed or entailed the other. In general, I don't think there's much connection between the kinds of things that philosophy professors talk about with their colleagues and the kinds of things that they talk about when they play a role in public affairs. Philosophical ideas are confined to one percent of the population and they tend to be cosmopolites." At the same time, Dewey explicitly called for a "reconstruction" of philosophy, which would entail a reorientation of philosophy to make just such a connection. See Richard Rorty and Phillip McReynolds, "Richard Rorty on John Dewey," in "American Philosopher," October 2, 2013, YouTube video, https://www.youtube.com/watch?v=MVPPprXDETQ. See also Phillip McReynolds, *The American Philosopher: Interviews on the Meaning of Life and Truth* (Lanham, MD: Lexington, 2015), 18.
12. Audrey Williams June, "Do Universities Value Public Engagement? Not Much, Their Policies Suggest," *Chronicle of Higher Education*, October 8, 2018, https://www.chronicle.com/article/Do-Universities-Value-Public/244748.
13. David Hildebrand, *Dewey: A Beginner's Guide* (Oxford: Oneworld, 2008), 184.
14. Louis Menand, *The Metaphysical Club* (New York: Farrar, Straus, and Giroux, 2002).
15. John Dewey, *A Common Faith* (New Haven, CT: Yale University Press, 1934), reprint, LW.9.1–58.
16. Ignas K. Skruplekis and Elizabeth M. Berkeley, eds. *The Correspondence of William James*, vol. 7, *1890–1894* (Charlottesville: University Press of Virginia, 1998), 162–63 (1894). Hereafter this collection will be referred to as James, *Correspondence*.
17. Eric Thomas Weber, "James, Dewey, and Democracy," *William James Studies* 4 (2009): 90–110.
18. As noted in my essay "James, Dewey, and Democracy," James wrote in July of 1896 to Alice Howe Gibbens James, recounting that "I heard a lecture by John Dewey at 2.30, & another by Bryan . . . both very good. Unfortunately Dewey has already left—I should have stayed on indefinitely to hear more of his lectures," in *The Correspondence of John Dewey, 1859–1952*, 2nd ed., gen. ed. Larry A. Hickman, ed. Barbara Levine, Anne Sharpe, and Harriet Furst Simon (Charlottesville, VA: InteLex, 2001), July 23, 1896 (09530).
19. John Dewey, "The Reflex Arc Concept in Psychology," *Psychological Review* 3, no. 4 (1896): 357–70; reprint, EW.5.96–110.
20. James, *Correspondence*, vol. 10, *1902–1905*, 324.

21. Again, see Rorty and McReynolds, "Richard Rorty on John Dewey," in "American Philosopher," October 2, 2013, YouTube video, https://www.youtube.com/watch?v=MVPPprXDETQ; and McReynolds, *The American Philosopher*, 18.
22. Eric Thomas Weber, "Lessons from America's Public Philosopher," *The Journal of Speculative Philosophy* 29, Issue 1 (2015): 118–35; John Dewey, "The Supreme Intellectual Obligation," *Science Education* 18 (February 1934): 1–4, reprint, LW.9.96–102.
23. See Eric Lipton, "The Perfect Weapon: How Russian Cyberpower Invaded the U.S.," *New York Times*, December 13, 2016, https://www.nytimes.com/2016/12/13/us/politics/russia-hack-election-dnc.html; Adam B. Ellick and Adam Westbrook, "Operation Infektion, Russian Disinformation: From Cold War to Kanye," *New York Times*, November 12, 2018, https://www.nytimes.com/2018/11/12/opinion/russia-meddling-disinformation-fake-news-elections.html.
24. See Victoria L. Dunckley, "Gray Matter: Too Much Screen Time Damages the Brain," *Psychology Today*, February 27, 2014, https://www.psychologytoday.com/us/blog/mental-wealth/201402/gray-matters-too-much-screen-time-damages-the-brain; Mark Tschaepe, "Undermining Dopamine Democracy Through Education: Synthetic Situations, Social Media, and Incentive Salience," *Pragmatism Today* 7, no. 1 (2016): 32–40; Tibor Solymosi, "We Deweyan Creatures," *Pragmatism Today* 7, no. 1 (2016): 41–59; Tibor Solymosi, "Dewey on the Brain: Dopamine, Digital Devices, and Democracy," *Contemporary Pragmatism* 14, no. 1 (2017): 5–34; and Tibor Solymosi, "Affording Our Culture: 'Smart Technology' and the Prospects for Creative Democracy," *Eidos* 4, no. 6 (2018): 46–69.
25. Again, see June, "Do Universities Value Public Engagement?"
26. John Dewey, "What Humanism Means to Me," *Thinker* 2 (June 1930): 9–12, reprint, in LW.5.263–67, and included here as chapter 46.
27. American Humanist Association, "The Humanist Manifesto I," *New Humanist* ([1933] 1973), https://americanhumanist.org/what-is-humanism/manifesto1/.
28. John Dewey, "The Jobless—a Job for All of Us," *Unemployed*, February 1931, 3–4, reprint, in LW.6.153–56, and here as chapter 33; Dewey, "The Collapse of a Romance," *New Republic* 70 (April 27, 1932): 292–94, reprint, in LW.6.69–75, and here as chapter 31.
29. John Dewey, "Is There Hope for Politics?," *Scribner's* 89 (May 1931): 483–87, reprint, in LW.6.182–90, and here as chapter 15.
30. John Laloggia, "Republicans and Democrats Agree: They Can't Agree on Basic Facts," *Pew Research Center*, August 23, 2018, http://www.pewresearch.org/fact-tank/2018/08/23/republicans-and-democrats-agree-they-cant-agree-on-basic-facts/.
31. Jeff Bukhari, "Wall Street Spent $2 Billion Trying to Influence the 2016 Election," *Fortune*, March 8, 2017, http://fortune.com/2017/03/08/wall-street-2016-election-spending/.
32. Art Swift, "In U.S., Belief in Creationist View of Humans at New Low," *Gallup News*, May 22, 2017, https://news.gallup.com/poll/210956/belief-creationist-view-humans-new-low.aspx.
33. Elizabeth Bruening, "The Left and the Right Cry Out for Civility, but Maybe That's Asking Too Much," *Washington Post*, October 16, 2018, https://www.washingtonpost.com/opinions/the-left-and-the-right-cry-out-for-civility-but

-maybe-thats-asking-for-too-much/2018/10/16/3866a8a6-d16f-11e8-b2d2-f39722 7b43f0_story.html.
34. Liam Stack, "Attack on Alt-Right Leader Has Internet Asking: Is It O.K. to Punch a Nazi?," *New York Times*, January 21, 2017, https://www.nytimes.com/2017/01/21 /us/politics/richard-spencer-punched-attack.html.
35. John Dewey, "Democracy Is Radical," *Common Sense* 6 (January 1937): 10–11, reprint, in LW.11.296–300, and here as chapter 1; Dewey, "Creative Democracy—the Task Before Us," in *John Dewey and the Promise of America*, Progressive Education Booklet No. 14 (Columbus, Ohio: American Education Press, 1939), 12–17, from an address read by Horace M. Kallen at the dinner in honor of Dewey in New York City on October 20, 1939, reprint, in LW.14.224–31, and here as chapter 9.

PART I
Democracy and the United States

I

Democracy Is Radical

—

(1937)

EDITOR'S INTRODUCTION

In 1937, Japan was at war with China and was working to dominate Asia. World War II is generally said to have started in 1939, but war was already spreading, and nations were arming for it when, two years earlier, Dewey wrote one of his most elegant essays, "Democracy Is Radical." At the time, the communist movements of the world said that they were the embodiment of true democracy. Germany's growing fascist regime said that its own efforts were for democratic ends. Nations around the world were violent and militant in their alleged pursuit of democracy. The means they undertook, however, struck Dewey as clearly undemocratic. He believed that this mismatch was madness.

In this essay, Dewey is especially critical of those on the political Left for the error of mismatched ends and means, claiming to pursue democratic goals through authoritarian steps. He was also critical of those on the Right for narrowly emphasizing the interests of those engaged in manufacturing and commerce. The latter criticisms are quick in this essay, but the context of his remarks is important to recall. In 1937, the Great Depression had endured for seven years. The United States reached its peak unemployment in 1933, at nearly 25 percent.[1] It was uncontroversial at the time to say that a meaningful liberalism had to be more than the simple protection of the interests of manufacturers and finance capitalists.

In characteristic fashion, Dewey pursued a middle-ground outlook that aimed to avoid the errors of both opposed political extremes. This is not to say that any outlook on the Left or Right is equally extreme as any given position on the opposing side. Dewey argued that we should seek radically democratic ends, however, caring about the poor and unemployed, but we must achieve them through the use of democratic means. For Dewey, therefore, democracy demands a radical departure from existing conditions, yet the pursuit of it by undemocratic means is wrongheaded and self-defeating. The former point captures the sense in which he believed that democracy is radical. It is radical to aim for serious democratic respect for all, given how much change such an aim would require. It is also radical to depart from the long-standing tradition of decision making driven by power and violence rather than by democratic, communicative, and collaborative intelligence.

There is comparatively little difference among the groups at the left as to the social ends to be reached. There is a great deal of difference as to the means by which these ends should be reached and by which they can be reached. This difference as to means is the tragedy of democracy in the world today. The rulers of Soviet Russia announce that with the adoption of the new constitution they have for the first time in history created a democracy. At almost the same time, Goebbels announces that German Nazi-socialism is the only possible form of democracy for the future. Possibly there is some faint cheer for those who believe in democracy in these expressions. It is something that after a period in which democracy was scorned and laughed at, it is now acclaimed.

No one outside of Germany will take seriously the claim that Germany is a democracy, to say nothing of its being the perfected form of democracy. But there is something to be said for the assertion that the so-called democratic states of the world have achieved only "bourgeois" democracy. By "bourgeois" democracy is meant one in which power rests finally in the hands of finance capitalism, no matter what claims are made for government of, by and for all the people. In the perspective of history it is clear that the rise of democratic governments has been an accompaniment of the transfer of power from agrarian interests to industrial and commercial interests.

This transfer did not take place without a struggle. In this struggle, the representatives of the new forces of production asserted that their cause was that of liberty and of the free choice and initiative of individuals. Upon the continent and to a less degree in Great Britain, the political manifestation of free economic enterprise took the name of liberalism. So-called liberal parties were those which strove for a maximum of individualistic economic action with a minimum of social control, and did so in the interest of those engaged in manufacturing and commerce. If this manifestation expresses the full meaning of liberalism, then liberalism has served its time and it is social folly to try to resurrect it.

For the movement has definitely failed to realize the ends of liberty and individuality which were the goals it set up and in the name of which it proclaimed its rightful political supremacy. The movement for which it stood gave power to a few over the lives and thoughts of the many. Ability to command the conditions under which the mass of people have access to the means of production and to the products that result from their activity has been the fundamental feature of repression of freedom and the bar to development of individuality through all the ages. It is silly to deny that there has been gain to the masses accompanying the change of masters. But to glorify these gains and to give no attention to the brutalities and inequities, the regimentation and suppression, the war, open and covert, that attend the present system is intellectual and moral hypocrisy. Distortion and stultification of human personality by the existing pecuniary and competitive regime give the lie to the claim that the present social system is one of freedom and individualism in any sense in which liberty and individuality exist for all.

The United States is the outstanding exception to the statement that democracy arose historically in the interest of an industrial and commercial class, although it is true that in the formation of the federal constitution this class reaped much more than its fair share of the fruits of the revolution. And it is also true that as this group rose to economic power it appropriated also more and more political power. But it is simply false that this country, even politically, is merely a capitalistic democracy. The present struggle in this country is something more than a protest of a new class, whether called the proletariat or given any other name, against an established industrial autocracy. It is a manifestation of the native and enduring spirit of the nation against the destructive encroachments of forces that are alien to democracy.

This country has never had a political party of the European "liberal" type, although in recent campaigns the Republican party has taken over most of the slogans of the latter. But the attacks of leaders of the party upon liberalism as one form of the red menace show that liberalism has a different origin, setting and aim in the United States. It is fundamentally an attempt to realize democratic modes of life in their full meaning and far-reaching scope. There is no particular sense in trying to save the word "liberal." There is every reason for not permitting the methods and aims of democracy to be obscured by denunciations of liberalism. The danger of this eclipse is not a theoretical matter; it is intensely practical.

For democracy means not only the ends which even dictatorships now assert are their ends, security for individuals and opportunity for their development as personalities. It signifies also primary emphasis upon the means by which these ends are to be fulfilled. The means to which it is devoted are the voluntary activities of individuals in opposition to coercion; they are assent and consent in opposition to violence; they are the force of intelligent organization versus that of organization imposed from outside and above. The fundamental principle of democracy is that the ends of freedom and individuality for all can be attained only by means that accord with those ends. The value of upholding the banner of liberalism in this country, no matter what it has come to mean in Europe, is its insistence upon freedom of belief, of inquiry, of discussion, of assembly, of education: upon the method of public intelligence in opposition to even a coercion that claims to be exercised in behalf of the ultimate freedom of all individuals. There is intellectual hypocrisy and moral contradiction in the creed of those who uphold the need for at least a temporary dictatorship of a class as well as in the position of those who assert that the present economic system is one of freedom of initiative and of opportunity for all.

There is no opposition in standing for liberal democratic means combined with ends that are socially radical. There is not only no contradiction, but neither history nor human nature gives any reason for supposing that socially radical ends can be attained by any other than liberal democratic means. The idea that those who possess power never surrender it save when forced to do so by superior physical power, applies to dictatorships that claim to operate in behalf of the oppressed masses while actually operating to wield power against the masses. The end of democracy is a radical end. For it is an end that has not been adequately realized in any country at any time. It is radical because it requires great change in existing social institutions, economic, legal and cultural. A democratic liberalism that does not recognize these things in thought and action is not awake to its own meaning and to what that meaning demands.

There is, moreover, nothing more radical than insistence upon democratic methods as the means by which radical social changes be effected. It is not a merely verbal statement to say that reliance upon superior physical force is the reactionary position. For it is the method that the world has depended upon in the past and that the world is now arming in order to perpetuate. It is easy to understand why those who are in close contact with the inequities and tragedies of life that mark the present system, and who are aware that we now have the resources for initiating a social system of security and opportunity for all, should be impatient and long for the overthrow of the existing system by any means whatever. But democratic means and the attainment of democratic ends are one and inseparable. The revival of democratic faith as a buoyant, crusading and militant faith is a consummation to be devoutly wished for. But the crusade can win at the best but partial victory unless it springs from a living faith in our common human nature and in the power of voluntary action based upon public collective intelligence.

NOTES

First published in *Common Sense* 6 (January 1937): 10–11, reprint, in LW.11.296–300.
1. Robert E. Lucas and Leonard A. Rapping, "Unemployment in the Great Depression: Is There a Full Explanation?," *Journal of Political Economy* 80, no. 1 (1972): 186–91.

2

Address to National Negro Conference

(1909)

EDITOR'S INTRODUCTION

In 1909, a generation had passed since the Civil War ended, yet profound resistance remained to the mixing of races in the professional, religious, and social spheres. Objections rested on the idea that black Americans were biologically different beyond matters of skin color, in ways that had to do even with behavior. In the background of such beliefs was the notion that behavioral characteristics learned in life, such as in the habits of thought and action developed over several generations' lifetimes of enslavement, were passed down and distilled in descendants. This way of thinking was an excuse for believing that people's social disadvantage was, if not natural, then at least caused by the behavior or conditions of their parents. Therefore, when discrimination or tiers of citizenship, opportunity, and education existed, they were thought to be justified by the facts of the world: that some people were biologically inferior.

Dewey was one of a number of speakers at the 1909 National Negro Committee Conference, which included several presentations by W. E. B. DuBois and one by Ida Wells-Barnett. By the time of his 1909 address, Dewey was already a highly visible philosopher and writer. His participation in this conference was unusual for his contemporaries, even if it was primarily but an expression of support for the mission of the group and gathering. Scholars have raised criticisms of Dewey's thoughts on race, such as when he called primarily for the solidarity of disadvantaged people, without appreciation for unique problems for African Americans.[1]

Among the presentations at the conference, the misguided claim of hereditary conditioning had already been thoroughly debunked through scientific argument. In his address, beyond offering a show of support, Dewey built on the points already made at the conference about the mistakes of prejudiced beliefs about heredity. He then recalled John Stuart Mill's famous argument about women and education. In *The Subjection of Women*, Mill explained that when we draw only from male talent, we fail to gain from the widest pool of talent we can draw on as a society.[2] The same was true in Dewey's day because of the problems of racial discrimination and privilege.

The ground has already been so well covered in the matter of this scientific discussion, that I shall detain you but a moment or two; in fact I should not have appeared at all, were it not that it gave me the opportunity to express my sympathy with the purpose of this gathering and to give myself that privilege, I venture to detain you for these very few moments. One point that has been made on the scientific side, might perhaps be emphasized, namely with reference to the doctrine of heredity.

It was for a long time the assumption—an assumption because there was no evidence or consideration of evidence—that acquired characteristics of heredity, in other words capacities which the individual acquired through his home life and training, modified the stock that was handed down. Now the whole tendency of biological science at the present time is to make it reasonably certain that the characteristics which the individual acquired are not transmissible, or if they are transmissible, then in such a small degree as to be comparatively and relatively negligible. At first sight this taken by itself may seem to be a disappointing and discouraging doctrine, that what one individual attains by his own effort and training, does not modify the level from which the next generation then starts. But we have put over against that this other point that has been made with reference to social heredity, and the fact that there is a great difference between mental culture from the standpoint of the individual and mental culture from the standpoint of society.

This doctrine that acquired characteristics are not transmitted becomes a very encouraging doctrine because it means, so far as individuals are concerned, that they have a full, fair and free social opportunity. Each generation biologically commences over again very much on the level of the individuals of the past generation, or a few generations gone by. In other words, there is no "inferior race," and the members of a race so-called should each have the same opportunities of social environment and personality as those of a more favored race. Those individuals start practically to-day, where the members of the more favored race start again as individuals, and if they have more drawbacks to advance, they lie upon the side of their surrounding opportunities, the opportunities in education, not merely of school education but of that education which comes from vocation, from work responsibilities, from industrial and social responsibilities, and so on. It is therefore the responsibility of society as a whole, conceived from a strictly scientific standpoint leaving out all sentimental and all moral considerations—it is the business of society as a whole to-day, to see to it that the environment is provided which will utilize all of the individual capital that is being born into it.

For if these race differences are, as has been pointed out, comparatively slight, individual differences are very great. All points of skill are represented in every race, from the inferior individual to the superior individual, and a society that does not furnish the environment and education and the opportunity of all kinds which will bring out and make effective the superior ability wherever it is born, is not merely doing an injustice to that particular race and to those particular individuals, but it is doing an injustice to itself for it is depriving itself of just that much of social capital.

NOTES

First published in *Proceedings of the National Negro Conference, 1909* (New York: National Negro Conference Headquarters, n.d.), pp. 71–73, reprint, in MW.4.156–58.

1. Donald F. Koch and Bill E. Lawson, *Pragmatism and the Problem of Race* (Bloomington: Indiana University Press, 2004).
2. John Stuart Mill, *'On Liberty' and 'The Subjection of Women,'* edited by Alan Ryan (New York: Penguin Classics, 1869/2006).

3

A Symposium on Woman's Suffrage

(1911)

EDITOR'S INTRODUCTION

As in Dewey's 1909 "Address to National Negro Conference," here he once again draws on John Stuart Mill's writings on *The Subjection of Women*. Dewey's contributions to a "Symposium on Woman's Suffrage" appeared in 1911, nine years before the Nineteenth Amendment to the U.S. Constitution prohibited states from sex-based voting restrictions. Dewey saw women's suffrage as a clear necessity according to democratic values.

The debates about women's suffrage were settled long ago for the United States, yet there are a few radical conservatives who hold the view that women's suffrage was a terrible mistake. John Derbyshire, a contributor to the *National Review*, made such arguments in his 2009 book, *We Are Doomed: Reclaiming Conservative Pessimism*, endorsed by prominent figures including George Will, who called Derbyshire's book the answer to the need for "intelligent" and "sprightly conservatism." In chapter 5, Derbyshire makes what he calls "The Case Against Female Suffrage," which amounts to the claim that men are the real conservatives, nine-tenths of the time, and that "feminization is going to mean socialization." Referring to his experience living in communist China in the years just after Mao, he found that "if you wanted to hear a total-credulity, utterly unreflective parroting of the Party line, a woman was always your best bet."[1] Derbyshire hits many of the same notes that were played in Dewey's day, considering women emotional and thus less rational. His claims about women's inclinations toward equality and socialism resonate with Nietszchean themes that criticize the presumably weaker sex or group, demanding equality and wanting to control the strong because of their own weaker nature. In addition, Derbyshire implies that people who do not vote according to conservative values are illegitimate voters, a line that repeats themes used historically to argue against suffrage for nonwhite people. These themes continue today, such as when a Mississippi state senator railed against fellow Republican U.S. senator Thad Cochran for winning the 2014 Republican primary by courting black voters.[2]

Women's suffrage is not in jeopardy in today's United States, but women's issues remain important and call for democratic equality and justice. Women's testimony in relation to accusations of sexual misconduct or assault are often dismissed, blamed on the victim, or go entirely unheard, as we see in relation even to hearings about U.S. Supreme Court nominees today. In addition, conservatives continue to call into question the legitimacy of some voters' status when they may not share in conservative values. Dewey's short statements here remain relevant and worth revisiting, especially for the consideration of the condition of women in the United States and around the world.

By George Foster Peabody, Prof. Vida D. Scudder, Alexander Harvey, Robert Herrick, Annie Nathan Meyer, Prof. John Dewey, Edith Wynne Matthison, Elbert Hubbard, Hamilton Holt, Charlotte Perkins Gilman, Theodore Schroeder, Upton Sinclair.

The contributors to this symposium were asked the following four questions:

1. What in your opinion is the most powerful argument (a) For, or (b) Against woman's suffrage?
2. Are you in favor (a) Of a property, or (b) Of an educational qualification?
3. Are you in favor of militant methods?
4. Should a woman's moral standing affect her right to vote?

[Dewey's replies:]

1. The strongest argument for democracy is identical with the urgency of the social forces that have compelled the partial steps already taken throughout the Western world for democracy. It is my belief that woman's political enfranchisement is necessary not only to complete the democratic movement, but that till so completed many present evils which superficial observers attribute to democracy instead of to the inadequate character of our democracy, will persist.

2. It is too early to discuss limitations of the suffrage. What the future may ultimately bring forth no one can say. At present, a property qualification would be—either for men or women—a most reactionary move. The propertied classes will protect themselves pretty well under any conditions, and no political scheme yet devised will prevent their exercising a very large indirect influence upon government, through their economic power. Hence it is the masses—the poor—that most need the protection of the ballot. If by an educational qualification is meant a certain degree of literacy, it is a piece of academic foolishness to suppose that that ability to read or write is an adequate test of social and political intelligence.

3. Experience has not shown militant methods to be necessary in this country. If they are not necessary they are unwise. I do not presume to judge of English conditions, but it is the familiar habit of English political life to make no changes except under great pressure. This being the case, the women certainly needed some way of demonstrating that they were in earnest.

4. There is enough of a double standard of morality now. When a man's "moral standing affects" his right to vote, it should also affect a woman's—not till then.

NOTES

First published in *International* 3 (1911): 93–94, reprint, in MW.6.153–154.

1. John Derbyshire, "The Case Against Female Suffrage," in "Sex: Surplus to Requirements," chapter 5 of *We Are Doomed: Reclaiming Conservative Pessimism* (New York: Crown Forum, 2009), 87–88.
2. Janet Hook, "Cochran's Outreach Effort to Black Voters Draws Criticism, Cheers," *Wall Street Journal*, June 25, 2014, https://www.wsj.com/articles/cochrans-outreach-effort-to-black-voters-draws-criticism-cheers-1403727654.

4

The Challenge of Democracy to Education

—

(1937)

EDITOR'S INTRODUCTION

This essay addresses the fact that while democratic societies require education for the people to be self-governing, not just any kind of education will do. There are traditional forms of instruction that simply convey information, facts, and some basic skills. Dewey points out that these are not the same as understanding, learning how to bring intelligence to bear in making use of facts learned for the sake of social progress. The lesson we can draw today concerns the problem of narrow yet intensive testing in American public schools, which focuses on standardized tests as a central concern and as a driver of the curriculum, putting the cart before the horse.

Dewey recognizes the value of learning skills, such as in vocational education. While skills are important for everyone, understanding and intelligence are equally important in the labor of the wider public. Knowing the branches of government and the list of rights and procedures of the machinery of Washington, D.C., is not the same as knowing how to engage intelligently in social action or, more fundamentally, how to understand the entrenched or new challenges a community faces.

Today, we often find a strong separation between our technical and our liberal arts curricula, with little overlap of the two. Among the signs Dewey saw as positive was the development of social studies curricula, yet today such coursework is mostly neglected in favor of basic skills in our public schools. Policy makers, community leaders, school administrators, parents, and teachers all should read Dewey's essay with an eye to reorienting our public school curricula to the task of developing understanding and active intelligence for the sake of democratic engagement.

We are celebrating the one-hundredth anniversary of the beginning of the work of Horace Mann as Secretary of the Board of Education of Massachusetts, the beginning of that truly apostolic work to which he devoted his life. To him we owe the public school system of today more than to any other one person.

Anyone who has read anything of Horace Mann knows that he is a sort of patron saint of progressive education not only because of his ideas (very advanced for his day) about the way children should be treated, not only because he advocated a personal and humane atmosphere in the school in the relation of children and teachers, but because, above all, he was the prophet of the idea of the absolute necessity of free public education for the existence and preservation of a democratic way of life; or, as he said in the phraseology of his time, "republican institutions of self-government."

In an eloquent speech which he made after he had held his office some years, he insisted that while he believed thoroughly in the capacity of men and women for self-government, yet he also knew that it was only a capacity, not a complete inborn gift, and that public education for all was the only means by which the capacity should be made a reality.

"Education," he said, "is our only political safety; outside of this ark is the deluge." And again, he said: "The Common School is the greatest discovery ever made by man. Other social organizations are curative and remedial. This is preventive and an antidote."

So far as the institution for which he labored is concerned—namely, a public school system supported by public taxation and open to all children, training schools for teachers, and so on—the dream of Horace Mann, although not completely realized, has in the passage of a hundred years been realized to a surprising degree. But the problem for the solution of which Horace Mann labored is still with us. We have now in a very large measure the institution which he strove to bring into being. But we still have with us, and perhaps in an even more urgent and difficult way, the problem of how this institution is to be made to serve the needs of democratic society, of the democratic way of life. We certainly cannot rest on our accomplishments with respect to the school as the means of political democratic security.

Horace Mann asked in one of his public addresses whether the children in our schools are being educated in reference to themselves and their private interests only, or with regard to the great social duties and prerogatives that await them in adult life. We may well ask the same question today.

To my mind, the greatest mistake that we can make about democracy is to conceive of it as something fixed, fixed in idea and fixed in its outward manifestation.

The very idea of democracy, the meaning of democracy, must be continually explored afresh; it has to be constantly discovered, and rediscovered, remade and reorganized; while the political and economic and social institutions in which it is embodied have to be remade and reorganized to meet the changes that are going on in the development of new needs on the part of human beings and new resources for satisfying these needs.

No form of life does or can stand still; it either goes forward or it goes backward, and the end of the backward road is death. Democracy as a form of life cannot stand still. It, too, if it is to live, must go forward to meet the changes that are here and that are coming. If it does not go forward, if it tries to stand still, it is already starting on the backward road that leads to extinction.

In the fact that democracy in order to live must change and move, we have, I think, the challenge that democracy offers to education. One hundred years ago in the simpler conditions of life, when the social group was the neighborhood or the small community, before most of the inventions that have transformed modern society had come into existence—or, at least, before they had made any great impress on modes of living—it was not altogether unreasonable to advance the idea that individuals are born with a kind of democratic aspiration; and that given this innate disposition and tendency, schooling would enable them to meet the duties and responsibilities of life in a democratic society. In the comprehensive conditions of today, such an idea is fallacious. Only as the coming generation learns in the schools to understand the social forces that are at work, the directions and the cross-directions in which they are moving, the consequences that they are producing, the consequences that they might produce if they were understood and managed with intelligence—only as the schools provide this understanding, have we any assurance that they are meeting the challenge which is put to them by democracy.

Are our schools accomplishing these things? In what measure are they failing to accomplish them? For unless they are accomplishing them, the ark is not an ark of safety in a deluge. It is being carried by the deluge of outside forces, varying, shifting, turning aimlessly with every current in the tides of modern life. Just as democracy in order to live must move and move forward, so schools in a democracy cannot stand still, cannot be satisfied and complacent with what has been accomplished, but must be willing to undertake whatever reorganization of studies, of methods of teaching, of administration, including that larger organization which concerns the relation of pupils and teachers to each other, and to the life of the community. Failing in this, the schools cannot give democracy the intelligent direction of its forces which it needs to continue in existence.

Only as the schools provide an understanding of the movement and direction of social forces and an understanding of social needs and of the resources that may be used to satisfy them, will they meet the challenge of democracy. I use the word "understanding" rather than knowledge because, unfortunately, knowledge to so many people means "information." Information is knowledge about things, and there is no guarantee in any amount of "knowledge about things" that understanding—the spring of intelligent action—will follow from it. Knowledge about things is static. There is no guarantee in any amount of information, even if skillfully conveyed, that an intelligent attitude of mind will be formed. Indeed, whatever attitude it may form is very largely left as a matter of chance, and mostly of the conditions, circumstances, contacts, intercourses and pressures that are brought to bear on the individual outside the school.

I do not mean that we can have understanding without knowledge, without information; but I do mean that there is no guarantee, as I have just said, that the acquisition and accumulation of knowledge will create the attitudes that generate intelligent action.

I remember that years ago when I was in China I was told that the first elections held there were very honest. Before the next elections, Bryce's *American Commonwealth* was translated into Chinese. China got information about how bosses and machines, Tammany Hall and other institutions of the kind worked. This knowledge developed an attitude in some politicians, but not one that was intelligent or socially helpful.

The distinction between knowledge, information, and understanding is not a complicated or philosophical matter. An individual may know all about the structure of an automobile, may be able to name all the parts of the machine and tell what they are there for. But he does not understand the machine unless he knows how it works and how to work it; and, if it doesn't work right, what to do in order to make it work right. You can carry that simple illustration through any field that you please.

Understanding has to be in terms of how things work and how to do things. Understanding, by its very nature, is related to action; just as information, by its very nature, is isolated from action or connected with it only here and there by accident.

We have heard a great deal in recent years about the isolation of the school from life and about methods of overcoming or reducing that isolation. The point that I am emphasizing is that the isolation of the school is the isolation of knowledge from action. For social life, whatever else it is, is always a composite of activities that are going on and that are producing consequences.

I would ask, then, how far are studies, methods, and administration of our schools connecting knowledge, information, and skills with the way things are done socially and how they may be done. For only in this connection of knowledge and social action can education generate the understanding of present social forces, movements, problems, and needs that is necessary for the continued existence of democracy.

Consider, for example, two of the more modern tendencies in education which seem to support the idea that the isolation of knowledge from social action is breaking down. The first of these is the increasingly important place held by the social studies in the American school.

It certainly seems as if the social studies have a more intimate relation with social life than a great many of the other subjects that are taught in the school, and that accordingly their increasing introduction into the curriculum, the increasing emphasis upon them ought to be a means by which the school system meets the challenge of democracy.

But the crucial question is the extent to which the material of the social studies, whether economics or politics or history or sociology, whatever it may be, is taught simply as information about present society or is taught in connection with things that are done, that need to be done, and how to do them. If the first tendency prevails, I can readily imagine that the introduction of more and more social studies into the curriculum will simply put one more load onto a curriculum that is already overburdened, and that the supposed end for which they were introduced—the development of a more intelligent citizenship in all the ranges of citizenship (the complex ranges that now exist, including political but including also much more) will be missed.

I may illustrate the point by reference to that subject which is supposed to train particularly for political citizenship—the study of civics. There is, I think, considerable danger that this phase of social study will get submerged in a great flood of miscellaneous social study. When the subject was first introduced, I think there was a good deal of evidence of faith in the truly miraculous and magical power of information. If the students would only learn their federal and state Constitutions, the names and duties of all the officers and all the rest of the anatomy of the government, they would be prepared to be good citizens. And many of them—many of us, I fear—having learned these facts went out into adult life and became the easy prey of skillful politicians and political machines; the victims of political misrepresentation, say, on the part of the newspapers we happened to read.

There was a modicum of knowledge or information acquired in the school, but it wasn't connected; and I fear isn't today much connected with how government is actually run, with how parties are formed and managed, what machines are, what gives machines and political bosses their power. In fact, it might be dangerous in some cities if pupils in the schools were given not merely a formal and anatomical knowledge about the structure of the government but also acquired an understanding of how the government of their own community is run through giving special favors and through dealings with industrial powers. But without so rudimentary a preparation for intelligent voting or for intelligent legislation, how could we say that we were preparing for any kind of democratic self-government?

In a lecture entitled *The Retreat from Reason*,[1] Lancelot Hogben says: "As soon as you ask yourself what would have to be done to increase, diminish, or maintain at some fixed level the population of a community, you discover that you need to know a host of different things which would not occur to you if you set to yourself the more general question, how do populations grow."

The question of population is certainly an important question of social welfare. But the principle involved may be applied to the entire field of politics. If the classes in our schools asked, "What would have to be done to give us genuine democratic government in our states, local communities, and nation?" I think it is certainly true that a great many things had to be looked into and a great deal more knowledge obtained than is acquired as long as we simply take our democratic government as a fact and don't ask either how it is actively run or how it might be run.

Science as an area of the curriculum, although not so recent a development as the social studies, is also fairly recent. The natural sciences had to struggle to find any toe-hold in the school system. They had to find a place there against the very great resistance offered by the old classical, mathematical, and literary curriculum.

Certainly in modern life the natural sciences have a much closer connection with actual life and actual human relations than a great many of the studies that have come down from earlier times. It is not too much to say that science, through its applications in invention and technologies, is the greatest force in modern society for producing social changes and shaping human relations. It is no exaggeration to say that it has revolutionized the conditions on which human beings have associated for the last one hundred and fifty years, and that with the transition from the machine age to the power age, still greater social changes are in store because of science.

Again in this matter of the isolation of school material from life versus that connection with it which would give the kind of understanding of social forces that alone will prepare students to take an intelligent part in the maintenance and growing development of democracy, I ask: "How far is science taught in relation to its social consequences, actual and possible, if the resources which science puts at human disposal were utilized for general democratic social welfare?" I know that very great improvements are being made, but I am afraid that science is still taught very largely as a separate and isolated subject and that there are still those, including many scientists themselves, who would think that that wonderful thing "pure" science would be contaminated if it were brought into connection with social practice. And yet without this connection, students are certainly getting very little intelligent understanding of the forces that are now making human society and that might remake it.

I don't know that I am particularly enthusiastic about the question of choosing between communism and fascism. I am afraid that too much attention to that subject will give people the impression that sooner or later we have got to make such a choice. As far as I can see, the hope of maintaining democracy lies in using the enormous resources that science has put in our hands to inaugurate not merely an age of material plenty and material security, but also of cultural equality of opportunity—the opportunity of every individual to develop to his full capacity.

Unless our schools take science in its relation to the understanding of those forces which are now shaping society and, still more, how the resources of the organized intelligence that is science might be used in organized social action, the outlook for democracy is insecure. The resources of organized intelligence are working in present society, but working under political and economic conditions that are not favorable to the maintenance of democracy. If for a single generation psychology and physical science were related systematically and organically to understanding not merely how society is going, but how it might be intelligently directed, then I should have no fear about the future of democracy.

I may be thought to have omitted the fact that, after all, the schools spend a good deal of time not only with acquisition of knowledge but also with acquisition of skills. In a competitive and acquisitive society, I don't know that we need to be surprised that so much emphasis is placed upon acquisition either of information or of skills in the schools. It may be said, however, that the movement in the direction of vocational education of some form or other (including professional) is the most marked feature of education in, let us say, the last forty years, and that it, more than any other one thing, gives such unity of direction as exists.

This emphasis upon education for vocations or professions, like the increasing emphasis on the social studies and sciences, may also seem to be a contradiction of the idea that our schools are isolated from contemporary life.

But the question is: With what phases and aspects of social life has the whole vocational movement been most closely connected? Today it is most obviously intended to be an aid in preparing young people to get jobs and so earn a livelihood. It may prepare them quite effectively on the technical side and yet leave graduates with very little understanding of the place of those industries or professions in the social life of the present, and of what these vocations and professions may do to keep democracy a living, growing thing.

It seems to me to be a somewhat sad commentary on our educational system that there have to be separate schools that are called "labor schools" to prepare leaders in the struggle of labor in modern society, and that these few separate schools have a very great struggle to keep going. Wouldn't it seem as if in a really democratic system of education, in a really democratic society, that the history of labor, the significance of labor, the possibilities of labor, would be an important, integral part of the whole education scheme? Or, turning to another aspect of the matter, how shall we account for the fact that, with some notable exceptions, the medical profession is heartily opposed to the socialization of medicine and to making public health a common public asset? How are we to explain the fact that to such a large extent the lawyers who have had a professional and supposedly a competent professional education seem to be the advocates of the most reactionary political and social issues of the community at any given time?

These questions are at least worth asking, even if we can't find the answer. They seem to indicate that to a very considerable extent the movement in the direction of industrial, vocational, technical, and professional education has not come to grips either with the understanding of what the social forces and needs of the present are or of how things might be done to insure an ever-growing democratic life.

Hogben, in the lecture already referred to, says: "The training of the statesman and the man of letters gives him no prevision of the technical forces that are shaping the society in which he lives. The education of the scientist and the technician leaves him indifferent to the social consequences of his own action." Those are strong statements. They indicate that there is a very great split in our educational system. The people who are active in the direction of public affairs lack prevision because they have no understanding of the scientific technological forces that are actually shaping society. The education of the average scientist and the average technician, on the other hand, is such that he is left indifferent to the social consequences of his own activities. Hence, it is nobody's business to take stock of the resources of knowledge now available for social betterment. The question I am raising is whether it isn't the educator's business to see that the education given by schools be such that those who go out from them can take stock of the knowledge that is available for social betterment.

Part of the discredit of representative government in Europe today has come because of the feeling that politicians are able to talk glibly and write elegantly and argue forcibly; but that when it comes to the crises and necessities of action, they are not competent. It might be worthwhile to sacrifice a little of the purity of pure knowledge, to contaminate it here and there with relation to action, if we could save our country from a reaction against politics and politicians who can talk and argue, but who do not know how to act competently with reference to the social problems that have to be dealt with.

Education must have a tendency, if it is education, to form attitudes. The tendency to form attitudes which will express themselves in intelligent social action is something very different from indoctrination, just as taking intelligent aim is very different from firing BB shot in the air at random with the kind of vague, pious hope that somehow or other a bird may fly into some of the shot.

There is an intermediary between aimless education and the education of inculcation and indoctrination. The alternative is the kind of education that connects the materials and methods by which knowledge is acquired with a sense of how things are done and of how they might be done; not by impregnating the individual with some final philosophy, whether it comes from Karl Marx or from Mussolini or Hitler or anybody else, but by enabling him to so understand existing conditions that an attitude of intelligent action will follow from social understanding.

I don't know just what democracy means in detail in the whole range of concrete relations of human life—political, economic, cultural, domestic—at the present time. I make this humiliating confession the more readily because I suspect that nobody else knows what it means in full concrete detail. But I am sure, however, that this problem is the one that most demands the serious attention of educators at the present time.

What does democracy really mean? What would be its consequences in the complex life of the present? If we can answer those questions, then our next question will be: What direction shall we give to the work of the school so that the richness and fullness of the democratic way of life in all its scope may be promoted? The cooperative study of these questions is to my mind the present outstanding task of progressive education.

NOTES

First published in *Progressive Education* 14 (February 1937): 79–85, from a transcript of an address on November 13, 1936, at the Eastern States Regional Conference of the Progressive Education Association in New York City, reprint, in LW.11.181–91.

1. [Dewey's note:] Hogben, Lancelot, *The Retreat from Reason*. Watts, London, 1936.

5

America in the World

(1918)

EDITOR'S INTRODUCTION

In 2005, Thomas Friedman popularized the idea that today the world is flat, arguing that we are seeing a leveling of the playing field because of worldwide growth in education and industrial development. In 1918, the language of a "flat world" meant something quite different. It referred to the idea that the world is large and that the various nations spread across it could often be quite isolated. Dewey explains in "America in the World" that the United States had existed in relative isolation for so long because of its distance, especially from Europe.

In 1918, America's role and experience in the First World War were cause for reflection. Having existed in relative isolation, the United States was the prime locus for an idea, for the American experiment. The cultures of Europe had not seen a multicultural nation quite like the United States, and so the country's involvement in the war was a moment when the world would come to learn the results of the American experiment.

In this essay, Dewey proclaims America's success. The reader today might reasonably challenge his conclusion, given the conditions of African Americans in the South at the time and the struggle for women to get the vote. Despite some overstatement, Dewey was right to call attention to the American spirit of multiculturalism in the United States, which was exceptional and an acknowledged ideal worth spreading. In the context of writing about America's place in the world, therefore, Dewey contributes some rich thoughts here about how to understand some of the virtues of the American spirit.

Values that Dewey champions here bear repeating, furthermore, given the nationalism that has grown today and given present pushes for isolationism and the demonization of immigrants that have become more visible since the 2016 presidential election. The period referred to as Pax Americana, in which America has been called the world's policeman for the sake of peace,[1] has eroded as well, with the rise of conflicts involving Russia in which the United States is less involved than it might once have been.

There seems to be a little irony in the fact that upon Washington's Birthday the topic most apt for discussion is connected with the participation of America in a world war. Instead of a little strip of territory sparsely populated, able to maintain its own with the great nations of the world chiefly because of the advantage of remoteness, we are now a continental state, able to confer with the nations of the world on equal terms. While once there was enough to do in conquering a wilderness, we have now come to the end of the pioneer period, and have a margin of energy to draw upon.

The change has, of course, been brought about by that same development of industry and commerce which has annihilated distance, drawn all peoples into closer relations, and made the affairs and interests of one nation the concern of all, for weal or for woe. The fact that the interdependence which the new industry and the new methods of transportation and intercommunication have brought about should first reveal itself in strains and alignments for conflict does not alter the essential fact that the world for the first time now finds itself a round world, politically and economically as well as astronomically. That nations from every continent on the globe are engaged in the war is the outer sign of the new world struggling to be delivered.

It is a commonplace that whatever else the war means, it signifies for our own country the end of its period of isolation. Whether for better or for worse, America is no longer a people unto itself. America is now in the world. Unless this change of position is to mean that we are to be affected by the jealousies, the intrigues, and hostilities which have marked other nations longer in the world, we must see to it that those other nations accept and are influenced by the American idea rather than ourselves by the European idea. Of late we have been afflicted with national bashfulness, with a shy self-consciousness as to noting even that there is an American idea, lest we be guilty of spread-eagleism. We have assumed a self-depreciatory, almost apologetic, attitude towards the rest of the world. But unless our contribution to the present world struggle is to be confined to military and economic force, it must be that we have an idea to contribute, an idea to be taken into account in the world reconstruction after the war. What are the important aspects of this idea?

Politically, federation; *e pluribus unum*, where the unity does not destroy the many, but maintains each constituent factor in full vigor. It is not accident that the conceptions of a world federation, a concert of nations, a supreme tribunal, a league of nations to enforce peace, are peculiarly American contributions. They are conceptions which spring directly out of our own experience, which we have already worked out and tested on a smaller scale in our own political life. Leaders of other nations may regard them as iridescent dreams; we know better, for we have actually tried them.

One of the greatest problems which is troubling the Old World is that of the rights of nationalities which are included within larger political units—the Poles, the Irish, the Bohemians, the Jugo-Slavs, the Jews. Here, too, the American contribution is radical. We have solved the problem by a complete separation of nationality from citizenship. Not only have we separated the church from the state, but we have separated language, cultural traditions, all that is called race, from the state—that is, from problems of political organization and power. To us language, literature, creed, group ways, national culture, are social rather than political, human rather than national, interests. Let this idea fly abroad; it bears healing in its wings.

Federation, and release of cultural interests from political dictation and control, are the two great positive achievements of America. From them spring the other qualities which give distinction and inspiration to the American idea. We are truly interracial and international in our own internal constitution. The very peoples and races who are taught in the Old World that they have an instinctive and ineradicable antipathy to one another live here side by side, in comity, often in hearty amity. We have become a peace-loving nation both because there are no strong Powers close to our borders and because the diversified elements of our people have meant hope, opportunity, release of virile powers from subjection to dread, for use in companionship and unconstrained rivalries. Our uncoerced life has been at liberty to direct itself into channels of toleration, a general spirit of live and let live. Since our minds have not been constantly impressed with the idea that the growth of another power means the decay of our own, we have been emancipated to enjoy sharing in the struggles which exist wherever there is life, and to take its incidental defeats in good humor.

In working out to realization the ideas of federation and of the liberation of human interests from political domination we have been, as it were, a laboratory set aside from the rest of the world in which to make, for its benefit, a great social experiment. The war, the removal of the curtain of isolation, means that this period of experimentation is over. We are now called to declare to all the world the nature and fruits of this experiment, to declare it not by words or books, but by exhibiting the two primary conditions under which the world may achieve the happiness of a peace which is not the mere absence of war, but which is fruit-bearing concord. That we should have lost something of our spirit of boasting about our material greatness is a fine thing. But we need to recover something of the militant faith of our forefathers that America is a great idea, and add to it an ardent faith in our capacity to lead the world to see what this idea means as a model for its own future well-being.

NOTES

First published in *Nation* 106 (1918): 287, reprint, in MW.11.71–73.

1. Eric Weiner, "Should American Be the World's Policeman?," NPR, February 20, 2008, https://www.npr.org/2008/02/20/19180589/should-america-be-the-worlds-policeman.

6

Our National Dilemma

(1920)

EDITOR'S INTRODUCTION

At the close of the First World War, as Dewey noted in the previous selection, the United States of America could no longer remain isolationist. The value of isolationism was the fact that as a nation, the United States would not get entangled in others' disputes and wars. Upon the conclusion of the Great War, however, with isolation no longer an option, the United States was stuck needing to form alliances and partnerships, and with nations that were practicing troubling forms of imperialism. Britain and France, for example, were said to be governed by democratic values, yet they exploited people undemocratically around the world, from Africa to India to East Asia. In this prescient essay, Dewey advocated for cautious minimalism in U.S. partnerships abroad to avoid complicity in injustice.

Nothing is easier to say than that the period of our national isolation is past. Nothing is simpler to proclaim than that we are now called upon to assume the burden of sharing in the conduct of world affairs. Large words about these things make a double appeal. Our inherent idealism responds—and so does our vanity and our love of power. The two responses so intermingle, so cover each other, that the wonder is that the appeal has not been irresistible. Why has it failed? Under what conditions may it succeed?

Quite probably it is fortunate for us that nationalistic ambitions and imperialistic aggressions were so undisguisedly powerful in the peace negotiations. We owe monuments to Clemenceau, Sonnino and Balfour.[1] Probably in our excited idealism nothing less flagrant than the exhibition they gave could have averted our becoming innocent and ignorant accomplices in the old world game of diplomacy. As it was, the contrast between prior professions and actual deeds was so obvious as to evoke revulsion.

That the revulsion should have found most articulate expression in narrowly nationalistic inhibitions and repudiations of foreign responsibilities may be unfortunate; but it was, possibly, in its after effects better than nothing. The terms in which Republican Senators articulated American selfishness in response to European selfishness would not of themselves have commanded the assent of the American people.[2] There was a deeper instinct and emotion behind the rejection. Doubtless it was associated with our historic policy of no foreign entanglements. But it is desirable to clarify the emotion expressed in this attitude. What in addition to national egoism lies back of the instinct against being mixed up in the affairs of foreign nations?

The answer seems clear. We have a preference for democracy in politics. Our attachment is doubtless halting, and subject to deflections and corruptions, to say nothing of being not adequately enlightened. But it is genuine. Responsible government and publicity are our ideal, and upon the whole the ideal fares as well as most ideals in a rude and imperfect world. But, putting it roundly, democracy has never had even a look-in with respect to conducting the foreign affairs of peoples, and this is true even of nations that are democratic in their management of domestic affairs. By virtue of our geographical position and the fullness of our empire within, rather than by any moral virtue, we have maintained a state of relative innocence through abstention. We have had no foreign policy save to have none, barring the sacred Monroe Doctrine. We dwelt pleasantly enough in our Garden of Eden. During the war, we thought we could easily extend its blessings to the entire world. But the undisguised scramble after the armistice days reminded us of the Fall of Man, and we hurried back into our Paradise, though remaining on the lookout for remunerative investments in the outer world of sin and misery.

Yet it is true that a policy of isolation and non-participation is impossible. When we have invested enough in European countries they will be as near to us as Mexico now is. We may have the same tender interest in maintaining the stability of established powers, that democratic France has shown for the old autocratic regime of Russia. The war itself is sufficient demonstration that aloofness and neutrality have gone by the board; their day is over. We cannot longer piously inscribe the Open Door on parchments impressed with our national seal, and then complacently retire to such a distance that we can identify words with facts. But the most significant thing is not that our period of isolation is done with so that we must henceforth have foreign policies, League of Nations or no League. It is that henceforth our internal policies, our problems of domestic politics, are entangled with foreign questions and invaded by foreign issues.

It is not for us to choose whether we shall remain isolated. Who would have believed a few years ago that universal military service could be injected as a vital question into American politics? The problems of taxation that will come up in connection with our national debt will remind us that we cannot keep domestic politics pure and unspotted from the international world. We shall be fortunate if issues of bonuses and pensions do not become important partisan questions. The intimate connection of labor problems with immigration is another reminder. Pro-Irish, pro-British, or Jewish questions suggest another side of our entanglement.

Economic reactionaries have succeeded in creating a Bolshevist issue among us, the most contentedly middle class nation on earth. They are trying to "sell" this issue to the American people by wholesale advertising through news and editorial columns. Sixteen per cent of Americans raise the issue of one hundred percent Americanism in behalf of policies that judged by all sane American history are anti-American. Yes, wherever we turn we find plenty of reminders that the angel with a flaming sword forbids our return into the Garden of innocence and isolation.

The net effect, however, is a dilemma, a dilemma so serious that for the present there is no visible way out. We must guard ourselves against the idealizations with which we customarily protect ourselves from seeing the realities of an unpleasant situation. The dilemma is that while our day of isolation is over, international affairs are still conducted upon a basis and by methods that were instituted before democracy was heard of as a political fact. Hence we engage in foreign policies only at the risk of harming even such imperfect internal democracy as we have already achieved.

There is no use in blinking the non-democratic foreign policy of the democratic nations, of France and Great Britain. The Versailles Conference was not an untoward exceptional incident. It was a revelation of the standing realities. To recognize this fact is the sole guarantee that as we surrender our innocence we may yet be able to retain our integrity.

For example, as I write, a copy of the *New Republic* comes to hand with a discussion from a contributor and in an editorial of a naval alliance between Great Britain and the United States. A residence in the Far East makes one aware of the possibilities of such an alliance; it makes one almost ready to cheer for it on any terms. A Chinese owned newspaper in Shanghai carries at the top of its front page a standing slogan: "British-American cooperation in China is the A B C of safety and progress for China." And most Americans and British add a hearty amen.

And yet, and yet—an alliance, but an alliance for what? Just an alliance, without any definition or discussion of ends and methods which will make democratic control a reality and not a name? All treaties relating to the Far East are designed, if we trust their makers, to maintain the peace of the Orient, the territorial integrity of China and the Open Door. The additional expense of engrossing upon them that they are designed to promote the welfare of humanity would be slight. Now the main fact about British policy in China, in fact in Asia, is that it is conducted with one eye upon India, or rather with both eyes upon India and an occasional look elsewhere.

Is there as a matter of fact any use in discussing a naval alliance with Great Britain if we have not faced what our relation, say, to Britain's Indian policy is to be? Suppose that an economic blockade of India should become as desirable as that of Russia seemed lately to be;— are we to be accomplices in that also? The reverberation of our surrender of the Philippines upon all problems of the Far East, from Korea to India, will be great. What would be the effect of a formal alliance upon our Philippine policy? Would it not inevitably strengthen the propaganda that we retain them, lest their surrender "endanger the peace of the Far East"—as the phrase always goes?

The case is not even as if we had any guarantee that we are going to have democratic control of our own foreign policies when we enter upon them. And I am speaking generally, not of the special instance just mentioned. Congress must indeed share in the opening of war and the Senate in its concluding. But it is an elementary fact that we have not developed a technique of popular control. How was the Russian adventure of Great Britain finally halted? Partly, of course, by the common sense of diplomats who concluded it wouldn't pay. But from the popular side not by an effective check such as we take for granted in domestic affairs, but by fear of mutinies abroad and strikes at home. Would we be better off?

It is easier to state the dilemma that isolation is impossible and participation perilous than to state any solution. But meantime we should certainly tread warily. We should avoid all general commitments, and confine ourselves to the irreducible minimum, and that most specifically stated. "Meantime," until what? Until the labor parties of European democracies, or some other liberal organization, supervise and direct the foreign policies of those nations with jealous regard for democratic principles, and until we have ourselves attained not merely greater knowledge of foreign and international politics but have developed the sure means of popular control. Diplomacy is still the home of the exclusiveness, the privacy, the unchecked love of power and prestige, and one may say the stupidity, characteristic of every oligarchy. Democracy has not touched it. Beware of contamination through contact. That, I think, is the sound instinct, behind our aversion to foreign entanglements.

We are not holier than other nations, but there is an obligation upon us not to engage too much or too readily with them until there is assurance that we shall not make themselves and ourselves worse, rather than better, by what is called sharing the common burdens of the world, whether it be through the means of a League of Nations or some special alliance.

NOTES

First published in *New Republic* 22 (1920): 117–18, reprint, in MW.12.4–8.

1. [Editor's note: Georges Clémenceau was a French politician and leader during the First World War. He was known as Father Victory and as the Tiger ("Père Victoire" and "le Tigre"), inspiring French troops. He also led France's efforts in the Paris Peace Conference, which established a reparations commission to guide Germany's obligations to France and other nations. Baron Sidney Costantino Sonnino was Italy's minister of foreign affairs, and Lord Arthur James Balfour was Britain's foreign secretary. Both participated in the Paris Peace Conference with Clémenceau.]
2. [Editor's note: President Woodrow Wilson, a Democrat, needed a two-thirds majority of the Senate to ratify the Treaty of Versailles, which ended World War I. That meant that he needed to support from Republican senators who presented some resistance in the name of American interests.]

7

Pragmatic America

(1922)

EDITOR'S INTRODUCTION

In 1922, Bertrand Russell and John Dewey were among the most well-known living philosophers. Russell was known as a critic of American philosophical pragmatism, though he held Dewey in high esteem, devoting a chapter of his *History of Western Philosophy* to Dewey. Russell noted Dewey's profound influence in many areas and called him a man of "highest character."[1] Nevertheless, Russell associates the philosophical tradition of pragmatism with crass commercialism, prompting Dewey's humorous and biting response in this essay.

In the passage that motivated Dewey's 1922 essay in the *New Republic*, Russell repeats a critical refrain he and others raise against philosophical pragmatism. As an American tradition that cares about the "cash value" of ideas, pragmatism was often associated with American commercialism. To Dewey, the idea of truth or knowledge as profitable in his eyes was not about corruption but about journalism and education. Journalism was in fact a key spark in Dewey's inspiration to think about the value of ideas.[2] Russell promoted the idea of seeking truth for its own sake, without explaining why trivial truths are any less worthwhile than learning from Plato, if both involve truth.

In "Pragmatic America," Dewey assumes some familiarity on the reader's part with the philosophical movement so popular at the time, pragmatism. Charles Sanders Peirce and William James played central roles in germinating the pragmatist tradition, for which Dewey became one of the most famous proponents. As Dewey explains, pragmatism "presents consequences as a test and a responsibility of the life of reason." Pragmatism says that the meaning of our ideas is found in the conceivable consequences that the ideas yield for life.

In this essay, Dewey explains that pragmatism, when seen in the roots of everyday life, is an attitude or a faith, a belief that knowledge concerns matters that have a bearing on life. The pragmatic faith, he clarifies, sees the world as in the making, yet as influenced by what has been made so far. Dewey turns the tables on Russell, arguing that some of the crasser aspects of American commercialism are less inherent in commerce than products of the cultural conditions handed down from the made world of Europe. At the same time, Dewey acknowledges poignantly that neither William James nor Charles Peirce understood pragmatism to have anything to do with commercialism. The pragmatist's faith, instead, concerned the belief that the meaning of ideas is found in their relation to real life and practice, a view as important to the English philosopher Francis Bacon as it was to James, Peirce, or Dewey.

The American spirit Dewey draws on in this essay connects with the identity of pioneer life, the idea that the country was in the making. Europe was the "made" world, the world of feudalism, counter to democracy. Dewey warns that we must neither accept the problems of the "made" world of Europe nor hastily accept new concepts invented simply to fight the old world. Instead, we must depend upon the experimental methods of democratic intelligence. And in that respect, Dewey gives as good as he gets here, noting that Europe's feudalistic tendencies are impediments to the democratic respect for all, whether in pursuit of truth or in love of neighbor.

In a recent number of the *Freeman* Bertrand Russell writes: "The two qualities which I consider superlatively important are love of truth and love of our neighbour. I find love of truth in America obscured by commercialism of which pragmatism is the philosophical expression; and love of our neighbour kept in fetters by Puritan morality." The statement comes to us with double importance. For it is obviously dictated by Mr. Russell's own love of truth and love for us as his neighbor. Police records and newspaper columns do not seem to indicate that Puritanism is effective in fettering our love for our neighbor's wife however much it restricts our love for him. If pragmatism is the intellectual reflection of commercialism, pragmatists seem to be assured of a speedy victory of their philosophy in England and the continent of Europe; for there are rumors, apparently authentic, that commercialism exists in strength in these outlying parts of the world. But such matters may be passed over, especially as

Mr. Russell tells us that he is aware that the evils he finds in us are not unknown in the rest of the world, and that he urges their potency among us because we are more complacent, more boastful of our "idealism," less possessed of a critical minority than is the old world.

Mr. Russell is probably not entirely alone in the world in regarding love of truth and of neighbor as the two supreme human excellences. In the United States there are those who agree, at least in profession. The fact that the belief had some currency before he voiced it makes it the more important to consider the state of these virtues, and the power of their enemies among us. One otherwise attractive line of discussion is closed to us. We cannot cite evidence that we compare favorably with the rest of humanity in love of truth, and possibly a little more than favorably in respect to love of neighbors. For such a method turns against us. It is just another sample of our obdurate complacency, of the rationalizing idealization with which we obscure our critical perception of the truth.

The suggestion that pragmatism is the intellectual equivalent of commercialism need not, however, be taken too seriously. It is of that order of interpretation which would say that English neo-realism is a reflection of the aristocratic snobbery of the English; the tendency of French thought to dualism an expression of an alleged Gallic disposition to keep a mistress in addition to a wife; and the idealism of Germany a manifestation of an ability to elevate beer and sausage into a higher synthesis with the spiritual values of Beethoven and Wagner. Nor does the figure of William James exist in exact correspondence with a glorification of commercialism. The man who wrote that "callousness to abstract justice is the sinister feature of U.S. civilization," that this callousness is a "symptom of the moral flabbiness born of the exclusive worship of the bitch-goddess SUCCESS," and that this worship "together with the squalid cash interpretation put upon the word success is our national disease" was not consciously nor unconsciously engaged in an intellectual formulation of the spirit he abhorred. Nor was Charles Peirce conspicuous for conformity to commercial standards. Emotional irritation coexists in our humanity with the consideration that love of truth is a superlative good, and it is capable upon occasion of blinding that love.

Nevertheless, there is something instructive about our spiritual estate in the fact that pragmatism was born upon American soil, and that pragmatism presents consequences as a test and a responsibility of the life of reason. Historically the fact is testimony to "Anglo-Saxon" kinship; it is testimony to spiritual kinship with Bacon, who wrote that "truth and utility are the very same thing, and works themselves are of greater value as pledges of truth than as contributing to the comforts of life"; who taught that the end and the test of science and philosophy are their fruits for the relief and betterment of the estate of humanity;

while also holding that converting science and philosophy to immediate fruitage for lucre and reputation is their curse. American pragmatism is testimony that the tradition of Bacon carried on in divers ways by Hobbes, Locke and Hume has taken root here.

Yet there is special significance in the fact that this tradition was first revived and then made central by Peirce and James in the United States. Anyone who wishes to take a census of our spiritual estate (along with the censorship implied in a census) will assuredly find the pragmatic spirit important. It is a commonplace, however, that strength and weakness, excellence and defect, go together, because they are the two sides of the same thing. If, therefore, love of truth is to express itself in a discriminating way, it must be willing to attach itself to our sense that consequences are the test and the token of responsibility in the operation of intelligence until its significance is extracted. It is not in the first instance a question of the truth of this feeling. The disposition may be, if you please, as obnoxious to ultimate philosophic truth as it is repellent to certain temperaments. But first we have to find out what it means, what it means for both good and bad. Love of truth is manifest in desire to understand rather than in hurry to praise and blame.

A conviction that consequences in human welfare are a test of the worth of beliefs and thoughts has some obvious beneficial aspects. It makes for a fusion of the two superlatively important qualities, love of truth and love of neighbor. It discourages dogmatism and its child, intolerance. It arouses and heartens an experimental spirit which wants to know how systems and theories work before giving complete adhesion. It militates against too sweeping and easy generalizations, even against those which would indict a nation. Compelling attention to details, to particulars, it safeguards one from seclusion in universals; one is obliged, as William James was always saying, to get down from noble aloofness into the muddy stream of concrete things. It fosters a sense of the worth of communication of what is known. This takes effect not only in education, but in a belief that we do not fully know the meaning of anything till it has been imparted, shared, made common property. I well remember the remark of an unschooled American pioneer, who said of a certain matter that some day it would not only be found out, but it would be known. He was ignorant of books, but he declared the profound philosophy that nothing is really known till it operates in the common life.

Any such attitude is clearly a faith, not a demonstration. It too can be demonstrated only in its works, its fruits. Therefore it is not a facile thing. It commits us to a supremely difficult task. Perhaps the task is too hard for human nature. The faith may demonstrate its own falsity by failure. We may be arrested on the plane of commercial "success"; we may be diverted to search for consequences easier to achieve, and may noisily acclaim superficial and even disastrous "works" and fruits as proof of genuine success instead of evidence of failure. We not only may do so, but we actually are doing so. If the course of history be run, if our present estate be final, no honest soul can claim that success exceeds failure. Perhaps this will always remain the case. Humanity is not conspicuous for having made a successful job of life anywhere. But an honest soul will also admit that the failure is not due to inherent defects in the faith, but to the fact that its demands are too high for human power; that mankind is not up to making good the requirements of the faith, or at least that that part of a common humanity which inhabits these United States is not up to it, and that the experiment must be passed on to another place and time.

Yet the gloomiest view reminds us of another phase of the pragmatic faith. Undoubtedly in expressing his sense of a world still open, a world still in the making, William James reported, perhaps with some superfluous accretions of romanticism to his native idiom, a characteristic feature of the American scene. Be the evils what they may, the experiment is not yet played out. The United States are not yet made; they are not a finished fact to be categorically assessed. Mr. James' assertion that the world is still making does not import a facile faith. He knew well that the world has also its madness, and that what is done and over with fearfully complicates the task of making the future that human better we should like it to be.

A discriminating spiritual census of the United States will, therefore, ask about the already made things which we inherit and which mix with our creative making to arrest, divert and pervert it. After all we inherit from a Europe which was, compared with our scene, a made affair. Every day our cities are eloquent of the past fruits of a feudal Europe. His power far exceeds mine who can tell just how much of our present ill is due to the commercialism which is of our making and how much is due to deposit of an ancient feudalism. Commerce itself, let us dare to say it, is a noble thing. It is intercourse, exchange, communication, distribution, sharing of what is otherwise secluded and private. Commercialism like all isms is evil. That we have not as yet released commerce from bondage to private interests is proof of the solidity and tenacity of our European heritage. Commerce in knowledge, in intelligence, is still a side-issue, precarious, spasmodic, corrupt. Pragmatic faith walks in chains, not erect.

One other heritage of things already made still has to be reckoned with, reckoned with in social practice as well as in formulation. These United States were born when the pragmatic and experimental faith of the English tradition was in eclipse. Bacon did not exaggerate the control of nature to be obtained from study of nature. But he enormously underestimated that inertia of social forces which would resist free application of the new power to the relief and betterment of the human estate, and which would effect a private monopolization of the fruits of the new power of knowledge. Those who were called liberals lost their faith in experimental method. They were seduced into desiring a creed as absolute, as final, as eternal as that wielded by their opponents. The dogma of natural rights of the individual was the product. The pioneer, agrarian American scene was a congenial home for the new dogma. We tied ourselves down to political and legal practices and institutions radically hostile to our native disposition and endeavor. Legalism, along with feudalized commercialism, wedded to form modern commercialism, is the anti-pragmatic "made" which hinders and perverts our pragmatic makings. It is incarnate in constitutions and courts. The resulting situation is not one which calls for complacency. But the beginning of improvement is to place responsibility where it belongs.

Our noisy and nauseating "idealism" is an expression of the emotions which would cover and disguise a mixed situation. There is a genuine idealism of faith in the future, in experiment directed by intelligence, in the communication of knowledge, in the rights of the common man to a common share in the fruits of the spirit. This spirit when it works does not need to talk. But its workings are paralyzed here, arrested there, and more or less corrupted everywhere by a feudalized commercialism and a legalism which we cover up with eloquent speeches because we do not honestly confront them. Discrimination is the first fruit of love of truth and of love of neighbor. Till we discriminate we shall oscillate between wholesale revulsion and the sloppy idealism of popular emotion.

NOTES

First published in *New Republic* 30 (1922): 185–87, reprint, in MW.13.306–11.

1. Bertrand Russell, *History of Western Philosophy* (1946; London: Routledge, 1996), 730.
2. In an essay, I have argued that at moments such as those, Dewey appeared to have a possible influence on William James, though the general sense people have is of influence flowing in the opposite direction. See Eric Thomas Weber, "James, Dewey, and Democracy," *William James Studies* 4 (2009): 90–110, http://william jamesstudies.org/4.1/weber.pdf. In that paper, I quote key passages from the letter in question from Dewey to James.

8

The Basic Values and Loyalties of Democracy

(1941)

EDITOR'S INTRODUCTION

The American Federation of Teachers, founded in 1916, organized a periodical called *American Teacher*, which still runs today. Dewey contributed this essay in 1941, when the United States was fighting totalitarian states abroad. In that context, Dewey believed it to be vital to highlight the moral values and loyalties that democracy requires yet the United States was not embodying.

Dewey argues that dedication to truthful communication is a first, vital loyalty in democracy, as the darkness of falsehood and propaganda hinders the potential for democratic intelligence. Never has his insight been more important than today, when strange claims about "alternative facts" and a "post-truth world" have led to unprecedented levels of distrust in news media, leaders, and science.[1] Democracy implies belief in the potential of all individuals, and free and truthful communication fosters its development. These values may seem simple, yet there was at the time strong opposition to freedom of speech and press in the Soviet Union. The United States allied with the Soviet Union that year, and as Dewey explains, Americans who proclaimed democratic values nonetheless supported their ally's suppression of speech and of the press.

Dewey notes the shallowness of stating values in words but not in deeds. Denouncing the injustices in Germany, Italy, and the Soviet Union is empty when at home racial intolerance and anti-Semitism rage on. Dewey concludes with a call to return to the values of the French Revolution, a movement that was a great inspiration for Americans. In the United States, the third value is so often ignored in the motto "Liberty, Equality, Fraternity." Fraternity is the neglected moral value that is "the essence of cooperation." Dewey's call remains meaningful and much needed today in a country bitterly divided, polarized, and suffering from racially motivated attacks, anti-Semitism and anti-Muslim sentiment, and mass murder.

Values and loyalties go together, for if you want to know what a man's values are do not ask him. One is rarely aware, with any high degree of perception, what are the values that govern one's conduct. Observe a person's conduct over a period long enough to note the direction in which his activities tend and you will be able to tell where his loyalties lie, and knowing them, you will know the ends which stir and guide his actions: that is to say, the things that are values in actuality, not just in name. And if I begin with emphasizing the importance of observing the direction taken by behavior over a period of time rather than judging by words, it is because at no time in history have words meant as little as they do today.

One of the worst corruptions that totalitarianism has engendered is its complete violation of integrity of language. There is some truth in the saying, "at the border line, it is not easy to tell where education stops and propaganda begins." But the propaganda of the Soviet Union, Italy, Germany and Japan is easily identified by the fact that in every important matter the words used have to be read in reverse. They are selected and weighed with no reference to anything but their effect upon others. Criteria for judging slight deviations from fact are in the possession of every reasonably mature person, for his experience enables him to judge of probabilities. But complete inversions of truth are astonishingly confusing. They produce a state of daze that endures long enough to enable its creators to accomplish their will while darkness still prevails.

In short, a primary, perhaps *the* primary, loyalty of democracy at the present time is to communication. It cannot be denied that our American democracy has often made more in words of the liberties of free speech, free publication and free assembly than in action. But that the spirit of democracy is, nevertheless, alive and active is proved by the fact that publicity is a well established habit. It gives the opportunity for many silly and many false things to be uttered. But experience has confirmed the faith that silly things are of so many different kinds that they cancel each other over a period of time, and that falsities come out in the wash of experience as dirt comes out in soap and water.

The freedom which is the essence of democracy is above all the freedom to develop intelligence; intelligence consisting of judgment as to what facts are relevant to action and how they are relevant to things to be done, and a corresponding alertness in the quest for such facts. To what extent we are actually democratic will in the end be decided by the degree to which the existing totalitarian menace awakens us to deeper loyalty to intelligence, pure and undefiled, and to the intrinsic connection between it and free communication: the method of conference, consultation, discussion, in which there takes place purification and pooling of the net results of the experiences of multitudes of people. It is said that "talk" is cheap. But the hundreds and hundreds of thousands of persons who have been tortured, who have died, who are rotting in concentration camps, prove that talk may also be tragically costly, and that democracy to endure must hold it immensely precious.

It has been discouraging to American democrats to see how shallow has been loyalty to this value in those fellow Americans who, while professing democracy, have still defended suppression of liberty of speech, press and creed in the Soviet Union. One would have supposed that any American would by this time have enough of the democratic spirit in his very blood so that he would need nothing more than suppression to enable him to judge the policy of a country, no matter what one supposes it can say for itself on other matters. We are warned that we must feed and nourish this particular loyalty with much more energy and deliberate persistence than we have done in the past—beginning in the family and the school.

Since I cannot discuss all the loyalties that define the values of the democratic way of life, I confine myself to those which are emphasized by contrast with contemporary totalitarianism. In theory, democracy has always professed belief in the potentialities of every human being, and all the need for providing conditions that will enable these potentialities to come to realization. We shall miss the second most important lesson the present state of the world has to teach us if we fail to see and to feel intensely that this belief must now be greatly extended and deepened. It is a faith which becomes sentimental when it is not put systematically into practice every day in all the relationships of living. There are phrases, sanctioned by religion, regarding the sacredness of personality. But glib reciting of the verbal creed is no protection against snobbishness, intolerance and taking advantage of others when opportunity offers. Our anti-democratic heritage of Negro slavery has left us with habits of intolerance toward the colored race— habits which belie profession of democratic loyalty. The very tenets of religion have been employed to foster anti-semitism. There are still many, too many, persons who feel free to cultivate and express racial prejudices as if they were within their personal rights, not recognizing how the attitude of intolerance infects, perhaps fatally as the example of Germany so surely proves, the basic humanities without which democracy is but a name.

For it is humanity and the human spirit that are at stake, and not just what is sometimes called the "individual," since the latter is a value in potential humanity and not as something separate and atomic. The attempt to identify democracy with economic individualism as the essence of free action has done harm to the reality of democracy and is capable of doing even greater injury than it has already done.

So I close by saying that the third loyalty which measures democracy is the will to transform passive toleration into active cooperation. The "fraternity" which was the third member of the democratic trinity of the France of the Revolution has never been practiced on a wide scale. Nationalism, expressed in our country in such phrases as "America First," is one of the strongest factors in producing existing totalitarianism, just as a promise of doing away with it has caused some misguided persons to be sympathetic with Naziism. Fraternity is the will to work together; it is the essence of cooperation. As I have said, it has never been widely practiced, and this failure is a large factor in producing the present state of the world. We may hope that it, not the equality produced by totalitarian suppression, will constitute the "wave of the future."

NOTES

First published in *American Teacher* 25 (May 1941): 8–9, reprint, in LW.14.275–78.

1. See Gleb Tsipursky, "Towards a Post-Lies Future: Fighting 'Alternative Facts' and 'Post-Truth' Politics," *The Humanist* 77, no. 2 (March/April 2017): 12–15; Christopher Coons, "Scientists Can't Be Silent," *Science* 357, no. 6350 (August 4, 2017): 431.

9
Creative Democracy—
The Task Before Us

(1939)

EDITOR'S INTRODUCTION

This essay rates among Dewey's most elegant, accessible, and powerful, alongside "Democracy Is Radical." Horace Kallen read the essay on Dewey's behalf at a dinner in honor of the author's eightieth birthday in New York City in October 1939. It was a challenging year for democracy worldwide, as well as in the United States. In February, 20,000 people had attended a Nazi rally at Madison Square Garden in New York City advertised in the name of "Pro-Americanism."[1] Then, in September, Germany invaded Poland, sparking a series of declarations of war that launched World War II.

Dewey explains that he had turned eighty years old and that in his lifetime, countless major events in U.S. history had occurred. To illustrate, consider that he was born in 1859, just a few years before the American Civil War. During his lifetime, the United States engaged in numerous conflicts, including the Spanish American War, wars with Native American tribes and Mexico, World War I, and the start of World War II.

Dewey lived through the end of the Civil War and Reconstruction, though he was quite young at the time and lived in the North. Major scientific advances were achieved in his lifetime, including, most notably, the publication of Darwin's theories in *On the Origin of Species*, which was released the year Dewey was born. In the early twentieth century, he called for and saw progress for the women's suffrage movement, and he was an early member of the National Association for the Advancement of Colored People. He also lived through the Great Depression and was an advocate for using democratic means to pursue progress for all Americans. He rejected the undemocratic behavior of contemporary societies abroad, such as the fascists and communists.

Dewey noted that the United States was for a long time a frontier society, inspired by the ingenuity and creative problem solving necessary for that kind of world. In 1939, "the new frontier is moral," he said, "not physical." That condition still obtains today, and Dewey's essay should therefore speak to us as well, insofar as we can never fully realize democracy, the powerful and hopeful aims and conditions that he called for in this provocative and inspiring essay. Here again, he demonstrates his sense that democracy is an ideal and that ideal is a way of life rather than a mechanism of governance. In this essay, he argues that "merely legal guarantees of the civil liberties of free belief, free expression, free assembly are of little avail if in daily life freedom of communication, the give and take of ideas, facts, experiences, is choked by mutual suspicion, by abuse, by fear and hatred." One does not achieve real democracy just by holding elections, nor by any particular decree or set of rights. Democracy, Dewey argues, takes a set of attitudes that include respect for one's fellows across differences of race, creed, gender, and beliefs. Democracy requires, he explains, a faith in human potential, given that the right conditions are supplied. Those conditions include an openness to experience as the locus of authority rather than deferring to some authority outside of or beyond experience. In the current age of disheartening governmental spying on citizens, of public officials' charges of distrust in news media—accusations of "fake news"—of growing bigotry and hatred, the American public needs to heed Dewey's call as much as ever before.

Under present circumstances I cannot hope to conceal the fact that I have managed to exist eighty years. Mention of the fact may suggest to you a more important fact—namely, that events of the utmost significance for the destiny of this country have taken place during the past four-fifths of a century, a period that covers more than half of its national life in its present form.

For obvious reasons I shall not attempt a summary of even the more important of these events. I refer here to them because of their bearing upon the issue to which this country committed itself when the nation took shape—the creation of democracy, an issue which is now as urgent as it was a hundred and fifty years ago when the most experienced and wisest men of the country gathered to take stock of conditions and to create the political structure of a self-governing society.

For the net import of the changes that have taken place in these later years is that ways of life and institutions which were once the natural, almost the inevitable, product of fortunate conditions have now to be won by conscious and resolute effort. Not all the country was in a pioneer state eighty years ago. But it was still, save perhaps in a few large cities, so close to the pioneer stage of American life that the traditions of the pioneer, indeed of the frontier, were active agencies in forming the thoughts and shaping the beliefs of those who were born into its life. In imagination at least the country was still having an open frontier, one of unused and unappropriated resources. It was a country of physical opportunity and invitation. Even so, there was more than a marvelous conjunction of physical circumstances involved in bringing to birth this new nation. There was in existence a group of men who were capable of readapting older institutions and ideas to meet the situations provided by new physical conditions—a group of men extraordinarily gifted in political inventiveness.

At the present time, the frontier is moral, not physical. The period of free lands that seemed boundless in extent has vanished. Unused resources are now human rather than material. They are found in the waste of grown men and women who are without the chance to work, and in the young men and young women who find doors closed where there was once opportunity. The crisis that one hundred and fifty years ago called out social and political inventiveness is with us in a form which puts a heavier demand on human creativeness.

At all events this is what I mean when I say that we now have to re-create by deliberate and determined endeavor the kind of democracy which in its origin one hundred and fifty years ago was largely the product of a fortunate combination of men and circumstances. We have lived for a long time upon the heritage that came to us from the happy conjunction of men and events in an earlier day. The present state of the world is more than a reminder that we have now to put forth every energy of our own to prove worthy of our heritage. It is a challenge to do for the critical and complex conditions of today what the men of an earlier day did for simpler conditions.

If I emphasize that the task can be accomplished only by inventive effort and creative activity, it is in part because the depth of the present crisis is due in considerable part to the fact that for a long period we acted as if our democracy were something that perpetuated itself automatically; as if our ancestors had succeeded in setting up a machine that solved the problem of perpetual motion in politics. We acted as if democracy were something that took place mainly at

Washington and Albany—or some other state capital—under the impetus of what happened when men and women went to the polls once a year or so—which is a somewhat extreme way of saying that we have had the habit of thinking of democracy as a kind of political mechanism that will work as long as citizens were reasonably faithful in performing political duties.

Of late years we have heard more and more frequently that this is not enough; that democracy is a way of life. This saying gets down to hard pan. But I am not sure that something of the externality of the old idea does not cling to the new and better statement. In any case we can escape from this external way of thinking only as we realize in thought and act that democracy is a personal way of individual life; that it signifies the possession and continual use of certain attitudes, forming personal character and determining desire and purpose in all the relations of life. Instead of thinking of our own dispositions and habits as accommodated to certain institutions we have to learn to think of the latter as expressions, projections and extensions of habitually dominant personal attitudes.

Democracy as a personal, an individual, way of life involves nothing fundamentally new. But when applied it puts a new practical meaning in old ideas. Put into effect it signifies that powerful present enemies of democracy can be successfully met only by the creation of personal attitudes in individual human beings; that we must get over our tendency to think that its defense can be found in any external means whatever, whether military or civil, if they are separated from individual attitudes so deep-seated as to constitute personal character.

Democracy is a way of life controlled by a working faith in the possibilities of human nature. Belief in the Common Man is a familiar article in the democratic creed. That belief is without basis and significance save as it means faith in the potentialities of human nature as that nature is exhibited in every human being irrespective of race, color, sex, birth and family, of material or cultural wealth. This faith may be enacted in statutes, but it is only on paper unless it is put in force in the attitudes which human beings display to one another in all the incidents and relations of daily life. To denounce Naziism for intolerance, cruelty and stimulation of hatred amounts to fostering insincerity if, in our personal relations to other persons, if, in our daily walk and conversation, we are moved by racial, color or other class prejudice; indeed, by anything save a generous belief in their possibilities as human beings, a belief which brings with it the need for providing conditions which will enable these capacities to reach fulfilment. The democratic faith in human equality is belief that every human being, independent of the quantity or range of his personal endowment, has the right to equal opportunity with every other person for development of whatever gifts he has. The democratic belief in the principle of leadership is a generous one. It is universal. It is belief in the capacity of every person to lead his own life free from coercion and imposition by others provided right conditions are supplied.

Democracy is a way of personal life controlled not merely by faith in human nature in general but by faith in the capacity of human beings for intelligent judgment and action if proper conditions are furnished. I have been accused more than once and from opposed quarters of an undue, a utopian, faith in the possibilities of intelligence and in education as a correlate of intelligence. At all events, I did not invent this faith. I acquired it from my surroundings as far as those surroundings were animated by the democratic spirit. For what is the faith of democracy in the role of consultation, of conference, of persuasion, of discussion, in formation of public opinion, which in the long run is self-corrective, except faith in the capacity of the intelligence of the common man to respond with common-sense to the free play of facts and ideas which are secured by effective guarantees of free inquiry, free assembly and free communication? I am willing to leave to upholders of totalitarian states of the right and the left the view that faith in the capacities of intelligence is utopian. For the faith is so deeply embedded in the methods which are intrinsic to democracy that when a professed democrat denies the faith he convicts himself of treachery to his profession.

When I think of the conditions under which men and women are living in many foreign countries today, fear of espionage, with danger hanging over the meeting of friends for friendly conversation in private gatherings, I am inclined to believe that the heart and final guarantee of democracy is in free gatherings of neighbors on the street corner to discuss back and forth what is read in uncensored news of the day, and in gatherings of friends in the living rooms of houses and apartments to converse freely with one another. Intolerance, abuse, calling of names because of differences of opinion about religion or politics or business, as well as because of differences of race, color, wealth or degree of culture are treason to the democratic way of life. For everything which bars freedom and fullness of communication sets up barriers that divide human beings into sets and cliques, into antagonistic sects and factions, and thereby undermines the democratic way of life. Merely legal guarantees of the civil liberties of free belief, free expression, free assembly are of little avail if in daily life freedom of communication, the give and take of ideas, facts, experiences, is choked by mutual suspicion, by abuse, by fear and hatred. These things destroy the essential condition of the democratic way of living even more effectually than open coercion which—as the example of totalitarian states proves—is effective only when it succeeds in breeding hate, suspicion, intolerance in the minds of individual human beings.

Finally, given the two conditions just mentioned, democracy as a way of life is controlled by personal faith in personal day-by-day working together with others. Democracy is the belief that even when needs and ends or consequences are different for each individual, the habit of amicable cooperation—which may include, as in sport, rivalry and competition—is itself a priceless addition to life. To take as far as possible every conflict which arises—and they are bound to arise—out of the atmosphere and medium of force, of violence as a means of settlement into that of discussion and of intelligence is to treat those who disagree—even profoundly—with us as those from whom we may learn, and in so far, as friends. A genuinely democratic faith in peace is faith in the possibility of conducting disputes, controversies and conflicts as cooperative undertakings in which both parties learn by giving the other a chance to express itself, instead of having one party conquer by forceful suppression of the other—a suppression which is none the less one of violence when it takes place by psychological means of ridicule, abuse, intimidation, instead of by overt imprisonment or in concentration camps. To cooperate by giving differences a chance to show themselves because of the belief that the expression of difference is not only a right of the other persons but is a means of enriching one's own life-experience, is inherent in the democratic personal way of life.

If what has been said is charged with being a set of moral commonplaces, my only reply is that that is just the point in saying them. For to get rid of the habit of thinking of democracy as something institutional and external and to acquire the habit of treating it as a way of personal life is to realize that democracy is a moral ideal and so far as it becomes a fact is a moral fact. It is to realize that democracy is a reality only as it is indeed a commonplace of living.

Since my adult years have been given to the pursuit of philosophy, I shall ask your indulgence if in concluding I state briefly the democratic faith in the formal terms of a philosophic position. So stated, democracy is belief in the ability of human experience to generate the aims and methods by which further experience will grow in ordered richness. Every other form of moral and social faith rests upon the idea that experience must be subjected at some point or other to some form of external control; to some "authority" alleged to exist outside the processes of experience. Democracy is the faith that the process of experience is more important than any special result attained, so that special results achieved are of ultimate value only as they are used to enrich and order the ongoing process. Since the process of experience is capable of being educative, faith in democracy is all one with faith in experience and education. All ends and values that are cut off from the ongoing process become arrests, fixations. They strive to fixate what has been gained instead of using it to open the road and point the way to new and better experiences.

If one asks what is meant by experience in this connection my reply is that it is that free interaction of individual human beings with surrounding conditions, especially the human surroundings, which develops and satisfies need and desire by increasing knowledge of things as they are. Knowledge of conditions as they are is the only solid ground for communication and sharing; all other communication means the subjection of some persons to the personal opinion of other persons. Need and desire—out of which grow purpose and direction of energy—go beyond what exists, and hence beyond knowledge, beyond science. They continually open the way into the unexplored and unattained future.

Democracy as compared with other ways of life is the sole way of living which believes wholeheartedly in the process of experience as end and as means; as that which is capable of generating the science which is the sole dependable authority for the direction of further experience and which releases emotions, needs and desires so as to call into being the things that have not existed in the past. For every way of life that fails in its democracy limits the contacts, the exchanges, the communications, the interactions by which experience is steadied while it is also enlarged and enriched. The task of this release and enrichment is one that has to be carried on day by day. Since it is one that can have no end till experience itself comes to an end, the task of democracy is forever that of creation of a freer and more humane experience in which all share and to which all contribute.

NOTES

First published in *John Dewey and the Promise of America*, Progressive Education Booklet No. 14 (Columbus, OH: American Education Press, 1939), 12–17, from an address read by Horace M. Kallen at the dinner in honor of Dewey's eightieth birthday in New York City on October 20, 1939, reprint, in LW.14.224–231. Kallen read the piece because Dewey was ill.

1. Ryan Bort, "When Nazis Took Over Madison Square Garden," *Rolling Stone*, February 19, 2019, https://www.rollingstone.com/politics/politics-news/madison-square-garden-nazis-796197/.

PART II
Politics and Power

10

Politics and Culture

(1932)

EDITOR'S INTRODUCTION

In "Politics and Culture," Dewey wrestles with the longstanding tradition of understanding culture as a matter only for elites, as in "high culture," and on that conception's tension with democratic ideals. He challenges the limitation of seeing aesthetic development in terms of "high culture." Culture is a broader concept, though economic conditions can prevent people from real opportunities to engage ideas and beauty. Deep poverty and human struggle also accustom people to ugliness and harshness, which further illustrates the economic challenge underlying the democratic ideal of enabling all citizens to participate in appreciating and contributing to democratic culture.

Dewey published "Politics and Culture" a few years after the start of the Great Depression. When he refers to material and economic needs in this essay, therefore, he genuinely means the basic necessities of life. Some of Dewey's proposals in this essay might sound idealistic to readers, yet there are examples that have been achieved since that time. The U.S. Department of Agriculture's National School Lunch Program was established in 1946, fourteen years after this essay was published. In education, people cannot take part in aesthetic development when they go hungry. Insights like Dewey's here motivated programs like the provision of free and reduced-price lunches for public school students.

Another concern arises in this essay, which has become an even greater problem today. Dewey argues that too many of the great minds and energies in the United States have gone into industry and profit making when they could be put to the development of democratic culture and the expansion of access to it for all. Today, the term "social entrepreneur" refers to the kind of alternate route that Dewey might have had in mind, except it is tinged with individualism. He was all for industry's development and success in the provision of people's needs, but he believed that focus on pecuniary profit to the exclusion of attention to culture and democratic ideals was a terrible mistake.

This essay continues to speak to readers today on several themes of public importance. One is the value of appreciating everyone's participation in culture. Another concerns economic impediments to such participation. The growth of machine power can enable the liberation of people's time, enhancing laborers' productive power to give them more time to enjoy and participate in culture. Instead, however, it can also be said only to increase the resources of concentrated capital, yielding little benefit to average workers. For illustration, workers' productivity and corresponding hourly compensation rose together from 1948 through 1973, but since that year, compensation has only grown by 8.9 percent while productivity has risen by 143 percent, according to a 2015 report from the Economic Policy Institute.[1]

If I should try to go into the underlying philosophy that is implied in this problem, I would be raising one of the most difficult and disputed questions. I refer to the problem of the relationship between conditions, environment, and one's mental and aesthetic development. There are those who hold that politics is an external matter, and that ideas are capable of free development irrespective of outer environment. And similarly there are those who claim that it is also putting the cart before the horse to attempt any kind of political reform or modification of the economic system before having changed man's beliefs, man's desires and aspirations. They hold, in general, that if only you change people's faiths, their hopes, beliefs and desires, that social changes will then take care of themselves. Social changes in themselves they regard as external, as not really affecting the makeup of people's minds, thoughts, currents of feeling—what for short I call culture. The opposing view holds that the mind, thought and mental activity which we call culture is essentially, for the mass of the people, so conditioned by the social environment in which they live that it results in merely a futile appeal to something that does not exist when cultural development is separated from the environmental.

However, I am not going to discuss that problem in general, but rather to take up a specific and limited question.

It is obvious that there are two tests or measures which we can apply to any social system. One of them is the physical and material.

What does the given system do to and with people's lives with respect to ease, comfort, maintenance of a secure and decent standard of living? It does not need any argument at the present time to say that our existing social system does not stand up very well under the application of this particular test. The other measure is the relation of the social system to the development and maintenance of what I shall for the moment call culture.

One of the phases of culture is free, easy, ready effective distribution of knowledge and ideas. By this free circulation of knowledge and ideas, I mean something more than the mere absence of censors, mere absence of deliberate suppression of new ideas, and of forms of knowledge that are not in consonance with the beliefs of a particular group that has political control. Of course those barriers are very important. But there is something more included in free circulation of ideas than simply the absence of legal restrictions on their circulation. There are restrictions that are more insidious, more intangible, and in many ways, more effective. People may be shut out from free access to ideas simply because of preoccupation of their time and energy. So taken up are they with other things that they do not have intellectual strength, and energy and time left to give any time to "ideas."

There may be lack of free circulation simply because of class barriers, and because a limited minority group holds a virtual monopoly of whole ranges of ideas and of knowledge. Communication, in other words, is not something which takes place automatically merely by the removal of legal barriers of censorship and suppression. It requires a common background of common experiences and of common desires to bring about this free distribution of knowledge.

In all existing societies the members speak in more or less different languages. Everybody in the United States might conceivably speak what grammatically would be classified as the English language and yet there would be different languages spoken. A trained technician speaks a different language from the ordinary layman; the ecclesiastic, church-going citizen speaks a different language from those who have a different moral or religious tradition and background.

There is food for thought in this matter of the variety of languages spoken among people that are outwardly using the same tongue, since they form barriers to free circulation of ideas and knowledge of all kinds. One might perhaps point to literary criticism. The function of literature is to use a language which potentially is capable of being understood, and of being conveyed to great masses. Perhaps, starting from this point of view, we could draw conclusions as to some of the troubles and difficulties from which literature suffers in this country at the present time.

Another aspect of culture is the enjoyment of poetry, literature, drama, music, the arts in general: enlarged capacity for the enjoyment of natural beauties and such things as gardens, the furniture of our houses, the utensils that we use. We lose a great deal by identifying culture in its aesthetic phase only with the arts to which we prefix the word "fine." Aesthetic enjoyment is superficial when it is not based upon and is not drawn out of the environment. A multiplicity of smaller things are needed to peace and enjoyment constantly in the daily contacts of life. The third aspect of culture is the active side of the two forms which I have just mentioned. Genuine culture stimulates the creative powers of imagination, of mind and of thought. It includes not merely free access to things of mind and taste already in existence, but a positive production of them, so that the waters of knowledge and of ideas are kept really fresh and vital.

I have made this sketchy survey of the chief element of culture in order to raise a question: How does our own civilization, how does American life, our social system, stand the test of the application of this measure of value. Do we not come out here as badly as, perhaps even worse, than we do under the more direct physical and material tests?

That is a question upon which you get very supreme difference of opinion. There are those who seem professionally committed to glorify everything in this country; to shout that it is the most wonderful country, the most wonderful system, that ever existed anywhere. And there are others who think that pretty much everything is down or going down in this country.

I think no one can deny that in certain ways we have in this country provided the external means of a very general development of culture. We have our school systems from the kindergarten up to the university. We have our free libraries, our museums, books, periodicals and so on. There is a machinery for a very general wide circulation and distribution of knowledge. On the other hand, I suppose no one would claim that we take full advantage of this machinery, or that our schools fully realize all their possibilities. They are potential assets rather than actualized resources.

Most people will agree, in their honest moments, that we sacrifice quality to quantity, we tend to be satisfied when we have provided the physical plan and the administrative means, assuming that things are going to work themselves, irrespective of the human minds behind them. In the higher forms of culture, of science and art we have as yet not reached the level of some countries in Europe, even of countries that have few of our external facilities.

One answer to this criticism is that Americans have been too occupied making a conquest of new territory, bringing it under subjection to man, to have time to devote to higher things, and that we shall make culture when we shall be finished with the physical, material side of life.

Another reason given by some, is that culture, by its very nature, in its higher forms, is limited to a minority group, so that higher culture and aristocracy are practically inseparable things. It is asserted that the attempt to bring culture to everybody means a dilution, an attenuation to such a point that it loses everything that makes it most distinctive.

Historically there is a great deal to be said for this view. As a rule, small groups of people belonging to the ruling leisure class have been the patrons of the arts. This is true from the time of ancient Greece well into the eighteenth century—as the dedication even of the writings of the greater authors in English literature testify. The literary people were accustomed to look to some nobleman for patronage and recognition. This was the only way of securing themselves a livelihood.

In the days of the Czar, music, drama, and the novel in Russia represented the highest level of achievement of any country in Europe, in spite of the political backwardness of the country. This fact suggests the argument of those that democratic culture, in approaching universality, attains a level much lower than the high-water marks of aristocratic cultures of the past.

Now, I want to make an abrupt deviation to a consideration of the economic phase of the social order in respect to the development of culture along the three lines of which I have spoken. I wish to raise the question whether the limitations to widely distributed culture, are really due to limitations in human nature itself, limitations which weaken and dilute it in exact proportion as it spreads, so that the intensity of culture is in inverse ratio to the number of people that share it.

First, is it not possible that the commercialism of our economic system is a greater restricting force than the inherent mental or psychological deficiencies on the part of the mass of the population?

Adverse opinions as to the possibility of a general democratic culture are also based on the low standards, intellectually and aesthetically, of the radio, the movie and the popular theatre. Is there not a possibility that the standards of these things are low (I think we all agree that they are much lower than they ought to be) ultimately because of economic causes? Those in control of the existing system, those, that is, who are in control of the marketing of these products, find that the shortest and easiest way to get the money that they are after is to maintain low standards. It may be said in reply that they could not make money out of them unless they gave the people what they wanted, so that the fact that they can make money by giving a low order of product, intellectually and aesthetically, is none the less a proof of the incapacity of the mass to appreciate what is good. The argument, I think, is like that of the newspapers to the effect that they give the people what they want. First they created an appetite for certain kinds of things, and after they have led people to want those things, then they give it to them on the ground that they are merely handing out to people the things they want. It is not the populace that finally makes the demand but the source of supply which fixes its level. The pecuniary motivation that controls so much of art has to be taken into account. We should hardly get the kind of thing on the level that exists were it not for the pecuniary profit involved.

I have never been a great believer in what some people call "pure" science, meaning by that science with no human application. But there are a good many different kinds of application.

There is the application of physiology to the improvement of health and the removal of disease. There is the application of physics to making money. There is the application of chemistry in the production of poison gases and high explosives for use in war. Is the cause, then, of the comparative backwardness of the United States in the sciences, the mere fact of interest in practical application? Or is it the existence of an economic regime which places emphasis upon application for the sake of pecuniary profit? Is it not due to the deflection that is given intellectual activity by the enormous premium that our economic system puts not just on the application of science, but on dominance by commercial and pecuniary ends? Often, literary people criticize American culture and society without any reference to the underlying economic system. And hence to my mind they deal with effects rather than causes.

I want to discriminate definitely between application in general and application of the narrower commercial and money-making type. Just why a scientific man would the less be concerned with scientific discoveries because they can be put to human use in raising the level of human life, I have never been able to see. There are some people in whom the mere motive of research is so strong that they do not need to think of anything else. But many of these would not lose interest in truth and in discovery if they were also aware of beneficial applications of their discoveries.

I have never heard that Pasteur's researches, the beginning of the revolution of modern medicine, were any the less strictly scientific in character because

Pasteur was also moved by consideration of human suffering which might be relieved by the execution of his scientific researches.

One more illustration: I do not see how any very high popular artistic standard can exist where a great many of the people are living in slums. Such persons cannot get artistic culture simply by going to free concerts or the Metropolitan Museum to look at pictures, or the public library to read books, as long as their immediate surroundings, or what they come into direct contact with, unconsciously habituates them to ugly, sordid things. A small number of people may come through with genuine aesthetic appreciation even under these circumstances. Even those who have, economically speaking, the most opportunities for higher culture, become insensitive to the ugliness that exists in our human environment. Architectural critics point out, for example, that there are slums on Park Avenue as well as in other quarters of the city. The packing box architecture, produced for the sake of profit, has its advantage over that of tenement houses, but it is hardly of a type to raise the aesthetic and artistic standards.

When there has been a high popular degree of aesthetic appreciation, as by the free men in Athens, it was because the entire environment acted upon the senses so as to render them appreciative of symmetry and beauty, acutely aware of any deviation from the best type of aesthetic achievement.

We pride ourselves, and with some good reason, on a free universal system of education. But, leaving out even all question of quality, our accomplishment is rather elementary from the standpoint of the population that it reaches. Of course, there are a great many more colleges now than there existed forty years ago. But still over half the school population leaves school at twelve, fourteen, fifteen years of age.

When we consider the complexity of modern life, the extent to which it depends upon the application of scientific knowledge, and then consider how much the average young person of fourteen or fifteen can carry away from school at that age, we can see how the mentality is limited, if it has no further opportunities. We are still very far from having realized the ideal of a universal education even from the quantitative point of view. While the question of the qualitative values raises altogether too large a point to go into here.

Are, then, criticisms which are made as to the possibility of a genuine democratic culture rightly directed when they are centered upon the supposed inherent incapacity of a large part of the population? The problem is not a settled one. It is conceivable that the best possible economic system would still leave a very considerable part of the population remaining on a low intellectual and artistic level because of intrinsic incapacity. I say it is possible. But I also say that while it is conceivable, we simply do not know; there is no more evidence for that view than there is for the contrary, and for a very simple reason. No systematic effort has ever been made as yet to find out what the real capacities of human nature in the mass are. The idea that in spite of our public school system, the intelligence quotient of a large part of the population ranges low, has no force as evidence on this point. Before it could have any weight as positive evidence, we should have to know all of the conditions out of schools as well as in schools, the social, economic, political, indirect influences of all kinds that played on those persons who do not show up well in tests.

Some old Greek philosophers held that it is necessary that there should be a large class, intellectually undeveloped, in order to support the few, and to give that minority the leisure that would enable them to have a free intellectual and highly developed life. Perhaps they were right, under the limited conditions of production in the ancient world. With the modern machine and modern inventiveness, with present command of raw material and technical skill, the reason for separation between culture of an aristocratic few and the absence of culture of the great mass, no longer holds.

There is the type of literary critic who is very much troubled about the machine and what the machine is doing to people who think that the machine is inherently brutalizing. They think it is a sign of hard, unaesthetic type of mind if one does not join them in their condemnation of the machine.

Well, I agree with those who hold that what has brutalized us is not the machine, but the owners of the machine who for money profit speed up the machine, work people too many hours, and under unhealthful conditions, and shut them out from all the intelligent phases of industry, such as management.

It is quite obvious, on reflection, that the machine might be a great liberator not merely of the human hand and muscle, but of the human mind, giving increase of time, of leisure, removing unnecessary expenditure of energy on mere physical labor, so that opportunity for cultural development would be increased.

One conclusion seems so obvious that nobody except the stoniest defender of the present economic order could question it. We never have tried the experiment of producing a widespread culture throughout the whole of society. Culture instead, has been the private possession of a small number of individuals. In order to try the experiment we shall have to modify the economic system so as to provide a secure basis for the free operation of mind, imagination and emotion. We shall have to remove all of the barriers that now prevent the free circulation of knowledge and ideas. We shall have to change the motivation of human energy so that it will not be diverted and deflected into channels of getting power over others to anything like the present extent.

The greatest part of mental ability, acuteness of thought, ingenuity, etc., in this country has gone into business. Some of it has gone into industry, but more of it into the business of manipulating the needs of others so that pecuniary profit can be made out of them. Many phases of cultural depression are the heavy shadows cast by economic depression and oppression. Our original democratic ideas must apply culturally as well as politically, and this end cannot be accomplished without economic transformation.

There is no question, not even that of bread and clothing, more important than this question of the possibility of executing our democratic ideals directly in the cultural life of the country.

NOTES

First published in *Modern Thinker* 1 (May 1932): 168–74, 238, reprint, in LW.6.40–48.

1. Lawrence Mishel, Elise Gould, and Josh Bivens, "Figure 2: Workers Produced Much More, but Typical Workers' Pay Lagged Far Behind," in "Wage Stagnation in Nine Charts," Economic Policy Institute, January 6, 2015, https://www.epi.org/publication/charting-wage-stagnation/.

11

Intelligence and Power

(1934)

EDITOR'S INTRODUCTION

In 1934, the Great Depression was a continuing challenge for the United States and for much of the world. In efforts to address the pains it caused, disagreements so often hinged on the idea that what really determines policy and public effort is power, such as in struggles over class interests. Dewey did not deny the power of people's interests and of interest groups. At the same time, he was deeply concerned with a phenomenon which accompanied skepticism about the power of anything other than the fight for class interests and influence. In "Intelligence and Power," Dewey argues vigorously for seeing the potential for intelligence to play a role in power and politics. He admitted that intelligence does not have its own power, but it becomes powerful when applied to the resolution of human needs.

Today, we can see the continuing relevance of Dewey's point in this essay when we apply it to issues like education spending or innovation in educational efforts. On one side, conservatives typically fight to minimize expenditures on public education, one motivation for which is economic interests. On the other side, many liberals have opposed experiments with schooling, such as policies permitting the creation of charter schools. To the former, we can say that intelligent efforts to do the most for the sake of educational success are hindered or altogether untested in the name of diminishing the public expense involved. To the latter, the private interests of teachers' unions and others opposed to experimentation have in some cases prevented the methods of intelligence from trying new ways to enable impoverished students to succeed in school.

A final point is worth noting. We are used to hearing the phrase, derived from Francis Bacon, that says that "knowledge is power,"[1] and one might wonder what the force of Dewey's use of "intelligence" would be. There is a big difference between these concepts for Dewey. Intelligence refers to processes, methods, and capacities for inquiring and learning, which are altogether different and vastly more important and useful than simply knowing a set of facts. The difference is most simply conveyed in the analogy of giving someone a fish versus teaching them to fish. The latter is a vastly greater gift. In the analogy, giving someone knowledge is clearly of lesser value than teaching him or her the methods of intelligence, by which knowledge and judgment are pursued, developed, and refined.

Those who contend that intelligence is capable of exercising a significant role in social affairs and that it would be well if it had a much larger influence in directing social affairs can readily be made to appear ridiculous. From the standpoint of past human history it not only appears but is ridiculous. It takes little acquaintance with the past to realize what the forces have been that have determined social institutions, arrangements and changes. There has been oligarchical despotic power, political, ecclesiastic and economic, sometimes exercised openly, more often by all sorts of indirect and subtle means. Habit, custom and tradition have had a weight in comparison with which that of intelligence is feeble. Custom and tradition have originated in all sorts of ways, many of them accidental. But, once established, they have had weight independent of the conditions of their origin and have reinforced the power of vested interests. At critical times, widespread illusions, generated by intense emotions, have played a role in comparison with which the influence of intelligence is negligible.

What critics overlook is that there would be no point in urging the potential claims of intelligence unless the latter had been submerged in such ways as have been indicated. The net outcome of the domination of the methods of institutional force, custom and illusion does not encourage one to look with great hope upon dependence on new combinations among them for future progress. The situation is such that it is calculated to make one look around, even if from sheer desperation, for some other method, however desperate. And under such circumstances, it also seems as if the effort to stimulate resort to the method of intelligence might present itself as at least one desperate recourse, if not the only one that remains untried. In view of the influence of collective illusion in the past, some case might be made out for the contention that even if it be an illusion, exaltation of intelligence and experimental method is worth a trial. Illusion for illusion, this particular one may be better than those upon which humanity has usually depended.[2]

The success of this method in obtaining control over physical forces and conditions has been offered as evidence that the case for trying it in social matters is not altogether desperate nor yet illusory. This reference has also been misunderstood by critics. For it is not held that the particular techniques of the physical sciences are to be literally copied—though of course they are to be utilized wherever applicable—nor that experimentation in the laboratory sense can be carried out on any large scale in social affairs. It is held that the attitude of mind exemplified in the conquest of nature by the experimental sciences, and the method involved in it, may and should be carried into social affairs. And the force of the contention depends on the consideration already mentioned: What are the alternatives? Dogmatism, reinforced by the weight of unquestioned custom and tradition, the disguised or open play of class interests, dependence upon brute force and violence.

It is stated, however, that a fundamental difference in the two cases of physical and social intelligence is ignored. "The physical sciences, it is said, gained their freedom when they overcame the traditionalism based on ignorance, but the traditionalism which the social sciences face is based upon the economic interest of the dominant social classes who are trying to maintain their special privileges in society" (Niebuhr). Of course it is. But it is a naïve view of history that supposes that dominant class interests were not the chief force that maintained the tradition against which the new method and conclusions in physical science had to make their way. Nor is it supposed for a moment that the new scientific method would have won its way in a comparatively few centuries—not that it has completely conquered even yet in the physical field—unless it had found a lodgment in other social interests than the dominant ones and been backed by the constantly growing influence of other interests.

Here we come to the nub of the matter. Intelligence has no power *per se*. In so far as the older rationalists assumed that it had, they were wrong. Hume was nearer the truth, although guilty of exaggeration on the other side, when he said "reason is and always must be the slave of passion"—or interest. But dominant interest is never the exclusive interest that exists—not when there is a struggle taking place. The real problem is whether there are strong interests now active which can best succeed by adopting the method of experimental intelligence into their struggles, or whether they too should rely upon the use of methods that have brought the world to its present estate, only using them the other way around.

Intelligence becomes a *power* only when it is brought into the operation of other forces than itself. But power is a blanket term and covers a multitude of different things. Everything that is done is done by some form of power—that is a truism. But violence and war are powers, finance is a power, newspapers, publicity agents and propaganda are powers, churches and the beliefs they have inculcated are powers, as well as a multitude of other things. Persuasion and conference are also powers, although it is easy to overestimate the degree of their power in the existing economic and international system. In short, we have not said anything so long as we have merely said power. What first is needed is discrimination, knowledge of the distribution of power.

Intelligence becomes a power only as it is integrated into some system of wants, of effective demands. The doctrine that has prevailed in the past regarding the nature of intelligence is itself a reflex its separation from action. It has been conceived something complete in itself, action following after and upon it as a merely external expression of it. If I held that notion of intelligence I should more than agree with the critics who doubt that intelligence has any particular role in bringing about needed social change. For the notion is simply one aspect of the divorce of theory and practice that has obtained throughout most of the history of mankind. The peculiar significance of the method of the physical sciences is that they broke through this idea that had for so long hypnotized mankind, demonstrating that action is a necessary part of intelligence—namely, action that changes conditions that previously existed.

Hence the first effect of acceptance of the idea that the operation of control of social forces has something to learn from the experimental method of the physical sciences is a radical alteration in the prevailing conception of social knowledge. The current assumption is that knowledge comes first and then action may—or may not—proceed from it. Critics who have attacked the idea that intelligence has an important role to play have based their attack upon acceptance of this idea; they have criticized me on the basis of attributing to me the very idea that I have been concerned to overthrow. Thus on the basis of a passage in which I denied that any amount of fact-finding apart from action aiming at control of social processes—in other words, a planned economy—could ever build up social knowledge and understanding, Mr. Niebuhr imputes to me middle-class prejudices in ignoring the role of class interest and conflict in social affairs! He imputes to me a great exaggeration of the potentialities of education in spite of the fact that I have spent a good deal of energy in urging that no genuine education is possible without active participation in actual conditions, and have pointed out that economic interests are the chief cause why this change in education is retarded and deflected.

The question at issue is not a personal one, however, and it is not worth notice on personal grounds. Just because dominant economic interests are the chief cause for non-use of the method of intelligence to control social change, opponents of the method play into the hands of these interests when they discourage the potentialities of this method. In my judgment they perpetuate the present confusion, and they strengthen the forces that will introduce evil consequences into the result of any change, however revolutionary it may be, brought about by means into which the method of intelligence has not entered. "Education" even in its widest sense cannot do everything. But what is accomplished without education, again in its broadest sense, will be badly done and much of it will have to be done over. The crucial problem is how intelligence may gain increasing power through incorporation with wants and interests that are actually operating. The very fact that intelligence in the past has operated for narrow ends and in behalf of class interests is a reason for putting a high estimate upon its possible role in social control, not a reason for disparaging it.

NOTES

First published in *New Republic* 78 (April 25, 1934): 306–7, reprint, in LW.9.108–112.

1. "Knowledge itself is power," Bacon writes in Francis Bacon, *Meditationes Sacrae* (London: Excusum Impensis Humfredi Hooper, 1597).
2. [Dewey's note:] "The truest visions of religion are illusions which may be partially realized by being resolutely believed. For what religion believes to be true is not wholly true but ought to be true; and may become true if its truth is not doubted." Reinhold Niebuhr, "Moral Man and Immoral Society."

12

Force, Violence, and the Law

(1916)

EDITOR'S INTRODUCTION

In 1916, World War I was in its third year, and the United States had not yet entered it. There was much debate in the United States about whether to join the war, with pacifists challenging action on the grounds that force is wrong. In "Force, Violence, and the Law," Dewey offered a middle road for thinking about the nature of force and hence how to consider the issues at stake in debates about the use of force. He was highly critical of the identification of all force with violence since he believed that nothing can get done without force. In fact, he wished the pacifists would recognize the need for force in advocating for their own position, especially since he hoped that violent force would only be used as a last resort, after all other more efficient and less destructive forms of force had been genuinely tried.

In challenging the pacifists for misunderstanding the need for force in any pursuit, Dewey also highlights the importance of recognizing various forms of force that are least wasteful, both materially and morally. The United States joined the war in 1917. This essay represents an example of the great public philosopher's contribution to debate about truly pressing concerns.

What is force, and what are we going to do with it? This, I am inclined to think, is the acute question of social philosophy in a world like that of to-day. A generation which has beheld the most stupendous manifestation of force in all history is not going to be content unless it has found some answer to the question this exhibition has stirred into being. Having witnessed the spectacle of continuous wholesale bombing, can we henceforth reprimand the sporadic and private bombing of the anarchist without putting our tongues in our cheeks? Or shall we say that he is right in principle, but wrong just in that his exercise of force is casual and personal, not collective and organized? We are to "prepare." How are we to decide whether this willingness to resort to the threat of force is a pledge of the final loyalty to ideals, or an evidence of growing contempt for the precious fruits of human labor, the only things which stand between us and the brutes? Is force the highest kind of laborious industry or is it the negation of industry?

We cannot ask this about war without being led to extend our questioning. Once we have uttered the question, everything in civilization throws it back at us. From the barracks it is but a step to the police court and the jail. Behind the prison rises the smoke of the factory, and from the factory roads lead to the counting-house and the bank. Is our civic life other than a disguised struggle of brute forces? Are the policeman and the jailer the true guardians and representatives of the social order? Is our industrial life other than a continued combat to sift the strong and the weak, a war where only external arms and armor are changed? Is the state itself anything but organized force? In the seventeenth century political theorists talked frankly in terms of force and power. We have invented a more polite terminology. Much is now said of the common will and consciousness; the state figures as a moral personality, or at least as a juridical one. Hasn't our thinking lost in clearness and definiteness as our language has become more sentimentally courteous?

Yet common sense still clings to a *via media* between the Tolstoian, to whom all force is violence and all violence evil, and that glorification of force which is so easy when war arouses turbulent emotion, and so persistent (in disguised forms) whenever competition rules industry. I should be glad to make the voice of common sense more articulate. As an initial aid, I would call to mind the fact that force figures in different roles. Sometimes it is energy; sometimes it is coercion or constraint; sometimes it is violence. Energy is power used with a eulogistic meaning; it is power of doing work, harnessed to accomplishment of ends. But it is force none the less—brute force if you please, and rationalized only by its results. Exactly the same force running wild is called violence. The objection to violence is not that it involves the use of force, but that it is a waste of force; that it uses force idly or destructively. And what is called law may always, I suggest, be looked at as describing a method for employing force economically, efficiently, so as to get results with the least waste.

No matter what idealists and optimists say, the energy of the world, the number of forces at disposal, is plural, not unified. There are different centres of force and they go their ways independently. They come into conflict; they clash. Energy which would otherwise be used in effecting something is then used up in friction; it goes to waste. Two men maybe equally engaged about their respective businesses, and their businesses may be equally reputable and important, and yet there may be no harmony in their expenditures of energy. They are driving opposite ways on the road and their vehicles collide. The subsequent waste in quarreling is as certain as the immediate waste in a smash-up. The rule that each shall turn to the right is a plan for organizing otherwise independent and potentially conflicting energies into a scheme which avoids waste, a scheme allowing a maximum utilization of energy. Such, if I mistake not, is the true purport of all law.

Either I am mistaken, or those persons who are clamoring for the "substitution of law for force" have their language, at least, badly mixed. And a continuous use of mixed language is likely to produce a harmful mixture in ideas. Force is the only thing in the world which effects anything, and literally to substitute law for force would be as intelligent as to try to run an engine on the mathematical formula which states its most efficient running. Doubtless those who use the phrase have their hearts in the right place; they mean some method of regulating the expenditure of force which will avoid the wastes incident to present methods. But too often the phrase is bound up with intellectual confusion. There is a genuine emotional animosity to the very idea of force. The "philosophy of force" is alluded to scornfully or indignantly—which is somewhat as if an engineer should speak deprecatingly of the science of energy.

At various times of my life I have, with other wearied souls, assisted at discussions between those who were Tolstoians and—well, those who weren't. In reply to the agitated protests of the former against war and the police and penal measures, I have listened to the time-honored queries about what you should do when the criminal attacked your friend or child. I have rarely heard it stated that since one cannot even walk the street without using force, the only question which persons can discuss with one another concerns the most effective use of force in gaining ends in specific situations. If one's end is the saving of one's soul immaculate, or maintaining a certain emotion unimpaired, doubtless force should be used to inhibit natural muscular reactions. If the end is something else, a hearty fisticuff may be the means of realizing it. What is intolerable is that men should condemn or eulogize force at large, irrespective of its use as a means of getting results. To be interested in ends and to have contempt for the means which alone secure them is the last stage of intellectual demoralization.

It is hostility to force as force, to force intrinsically, which has rendered the peace movement so largely an anti-movement, with all the weaknesses which appertain to everything that is primarily anti-anything. Unable to conceive the task of organizing the existing forces so they may achieve their greatest efficiency, pacifists have had little recourse save to decry evil emotions and evil-minded men as the causes of war. Belief that war springs from the emotions of hate, pugnacity and greed rather than from the objective causes which call these emotions into play reduces the peace movement to the futile plane of hortatory preaching. The avarice of munition-makers, the love of some newspapers for exciting news, and the depravity of the anonymous human heart doubtless play a part in the generation of war. But they take a hand in bringing on war only because there are specific defects in the organization of the energies of men in society which give them occasion and stimulation.

If law or rule is simply a device for securing such a distribution of forces as keeps them from conflicting with one another, the discovery of a new social arrangement is the first step in substituting law for war. The ordinary pacifist's method is like trying to avoid conflict in the use of the road by telling men to love one another, instead of by instituting a rule of the road. Until pacifism puts its faith in constructive, inventive intelligence instead of in appeal to emotions and in exhortation, the disparate unorganized forces of the world will continue to develop outbreaks of violence.

The principle cuts, however, two ways. I know of no word more often deprived of meaning and reduced to a mere emotional counter than the word "end," of which I have made free use. Men appeal to ends to justify their resort to force when they mean by ends only footless desires. An end is something which concerns results rather than aspirations. We justify the use of force in the name of justice when dealing with criminals in our infantilely barbaric penal methods. But unless its use is actually an effective and economical means of securing specific results, we are using violence to relieve our immediate impulses and to save ourselves the labor of thought and construction. So men justify war in behalf of words which would be empty were they not charged with emotional force—words like honor, liberty, civilization, divine purpose and destiny—forgetting that a war, like anything else, has specific concrete results on earth. Unless war can be shown to be the most economical method of securing the results which are desirable with a minimum of the undesirable results, it marks waste and loss: it must be adjudged a violence, not a use of force. The terms honor, liberty, future of civilization, justice, become sentimental fantasies of the same order as the catchwords of the professional pacifist. Their emotional force may keep men going, but they throw no light on the goal nor on the way traveled.

I would not wish to cast doubt on anything which aims to perceive facts and to act in their light. The conception of an international league to enforce peace, an international police force, has about it a flavor of reality. Nevertheless force is efficient socially not when imposed upon a scene from without, but when it is an organization of the forces *in* the scene. We do not enjoy common interests and amicable intercourse in this country because our fathers instituted a United States and armed it with executive force. The formation of the United States took place because of the community of interests and the amicable intercourse already existent. Doubtless its formation facilitated and accelerated the various forces which it concentrated, but no amount of force possessed by it could have imposed commerce, travel, unity of tradition and outlook upon the thirteen states. It was their union, their organization. And no league to enforce peace will fare prosperously save as it is the natural accompaniment of a constructive adjustment of the concrete interests which are already at work. Not merely the glorification of either war or peace for their own sakes, but equally the glorification of diplomacy, prestige, national standing and power and international tribunals at large, tends to keep men's thoughts engaged with emotional abstractions, and turns them away from the perception of the particular forces which have to be related. The passage of force under law occurs only when all the cards are on the table, when the objective facts which bring conflicts in their train are acknowledged, and when intelligence is used to devise mechanisms which will afford to the forces at work all the satisfaction that conditions permit.

NOTE

First published in *New Republic* 5 (1916): 295–297, reprint, in MW.10.211–16.

13

Why I Am Not a Communist

(1934)

EDITOR'S INTRODUCTION

In 1934, the *Modern Monthly* published a symposium on the subject of communism. The British philosopher Bertrand Russell and the American philosopher John Dewey both contributed short articles each explaining why they were not communists. Their contributions and others were soon after collected in a short book and pamphlet, *The Meaning of Marx*, edited by Sidney Hook, a philosopher and Marxist from New York University.[1]

Both Dewey and Russell rejected the Marxist idea of "dialectical materialism," a view that thought that matter, not mind, guided human history and that history accordingly proceeded in ways causally necessitated by the forces of matter and through a dialectical struggle between opposing forces. Neither Russell nor Dewey believed in the inevitability of progress, nor that all depends solely on matter.[2]

As advocates for democracy and against authoritarianism, Dewey and Russell both opposed the views proclaimed by official communist movements and governments, which said that a dictatorial stage on the road to true communism was necessary and thereby justified. Communist dictatorships on the Left, no less than fascist regimes on the Right, were antithetical to the democratic understanding of justice, of public inquiry and intelligence, of freedom of the press, and of other civil liberties.

At the end of the essay, Dewey concedes that his opposition centers on the official "Communism," which he referred to with a capital "c," as understood and pursued in his day, something entirely different from the "small-c" communism, which was simply the idea of shared ownership of the means of production, something which could be said to be exemplified at times and in some communities.³

Dewey believed that changes were needed in the United States, but only when pursued through democratic means, never by authoritarian and violently suppressive rule.

Having had the opportunity to see the contribution of Mr. Bertrand Russell, I have doubts as to whether I can say much that he has not already said. But I begin by emphasizing the fact that I write with reference to being a Communist in the Western world, especially here and now in the United States, and a Communist after the pattern set in the U.S.S.R.

1. *Such* Communism rests upon an almost entire neglect of the specific historical backgrounds and traditions which have operated to shape the patterns of thought and action in America. The autocratic background of the Russian Church and State, the fact that every progressive movement in Russia had its origin in some foreign source and has been imposed from above upon the Russian people, explain much about the form Communism has taken in that country. It is therefore nothing short of fantastic to transfer the ideology of Russian Communism to a country which is so profoundly different in its economic, political, and cultural history. Were this fact acknowledged by Communists and reflected in their daily activities and general program, were it admitted that many of the practical and theoretical features of Russian Communism (like belief in the plenary and verbal inspiration of Marx, the implicit or explicit domination of the Communist party in every field of culture, the ruthless extermination of minority opinion in its own ranks, the verbal glorification of the mass and the actual cult of the infallibility of leadership) are due to local causes, the character of Communism in other countries might undergo a radical change. But it is extremely unlikely that this will take place. For official Communism has made the practical traits of the dictatorship *of* the proletariat and *over* the proletariat, the suppression of the civil liberties of all nonproletarian elements as well as of dissenting proletarian minorities, integral parts of the standard Communist faith and dogma. It has imposed and not argued the theory of dialectic materialism (which in the U.S.S.R. itself has to undergo frequent restatement in accordance with the exigencies of party factional controversy) upon all its followers. Its cultural philosophy, which has

many commendable features, is vitiated by the absurd attempt to make a single and uniform entity out of the "proletariat."

2. Particularly unacceptable to me in the ideology of official Communism is its monistic and one-way philosophy of history. This is akin to the point made above. The thesis that all societies must exhibit a uniform, even if uneven, social development from primitive communism to slavery, from slavery to feudalism, from feudalism to capitalism, and from capitalism to socialism, and that the transition from capitalism to socialism must be achieved by the same way in all countries, can be accepted only by those who are either ignorant of history or who are so steeped in dogma that they cannot look at a fact without changing it to suit their special purposes. From this monistic philosophy of history, there follows a uniform political practice and a uniform theory of revolutionary strategy and tactics. But where differences in historic background, national psychology, religious profession and practice are taken into account—and they must be considered in every scientific theory—there will be corresponding differences in political methods, differences that may extend to general policies as well as to the strategy of their execution. For example, so far as the historic experience of America is concerned, two things among many others are overlooked by official Communists whose philosophy has been projected on the basis of special European conditions. We in the United States have no background of a dominant and overshadowing feudalism. Our troubles flow from the oppressive exercise of power by financial over-lords and from the failure to introduce new forms of *democratic* control in industry and government consonant with the shift from individual to corporate economy. It is a possibility overlooked by official Communists that important social changes in the direction of democratization of industry may be accomplished by groups working *with* the working-class although, strictly speaking, not *of* them. The other point ignored by the Communists is our deeply-rooted belief in the importance of individuality, a belief that is almost absent in the Oriental world from which Russia has drawn so much. Not to see that this attitude, so engrained in our habitual ways of thought and action, demands a very different set of policies and methods from those embodied in official Communism, verges to my mind on political insanity.

3. While I recognize the existence of class-conflicts as one of the fundamental facts of social life to-day, I am profoundly skeptical of class war as *the* means by which such conflicts can be eliminated and genuine social advance made. And yet this is a basic point in Communist theory and is more and more identified with the meaning of dialectic materialism as applied to the social process. Historically speaking, it may have been necessary for Russia in order to achieve peace for her war-weary soldiers, and land for her hungry peasants, to convert

incipient class-war into open civil war culminating in the so-called dictatorship of the proletariat. But nonetheless Fascism in Germany and Italy cannot be understood except with reference to the lesson those countries learned from the U.S.S.R. How Communism can continue to advocate the kind of economic change it desires by means of civil war, armed insurrection and iron dictatorship in face of what has happened in Italy and Germany I cannot at all understand. Reliable observers have contended that the communist ideology of dictatorship and violence together with the belief that the communist party was the foreign arm of a foreign power constituted one of the factors which aided the growth of Fascism in Germany. I am firmly convinced that imminent civil war, or even the overt threat of such a war, in any western nation, will bring Fascism with its terrible engines of repression to power. Communism, then, with its doctrine of the necessity of the forcible overthrow of the state by armed insurrection, with its doctrine of the dictatorship of the proletariat, with its threats to exclude all other classes from civil rights, to smash their political parties, and to deprive them of the rights of freedom of speech, press and assembly—which Communists *now* claim for themselves under capitalism—Communism is itself, an unwitting, but nonetheless, powerful factor in bringing about Fascism. As an unalterable opponent of Fascism in every form, I cannot be a Communist.

4. It is not irrelevant to add that one of the reasons I am not a Communist is that the emotional tone and methods of discussion and dispute which seem to accompany Communism at present are extremely repugnant to me. Fair-play, elementary honesty in the representation of facts and especially of the opinions of others, are something more than "bourgeois virtues." They are traits that have been won only after long struggle. They are not deep-seated in human nature even now—witness the methods that brought Hitlerism to power. The systematic, persistent and seemingly intentional disregard of these things by Communist spokesmen in speech and press, the hysteria of their denunciations, their attempts at character assassination of their opponents, their misrepresentation of the views of the "liberals" to whom they also appeal for aid in their defense campaigns, their policy of "rule or ruin" in their so-called united front activities, their apparent conviction that what they take to be the end justifies the use of *any* means if only those means promise to be successful—all these, in my judgment, are fatal to the very end which official Communists profess to have at heart. And if I read the temper of the American people aright, especially so in this country.

5. A revolution effected solely or chiefly by violence can in a modernized society like our own result only in chaos. Not only would civilization be destroyed but the things necessary for bare life. There are some, I am sure, now holding

and preaching Communism who would be the first to react against it, if in this country Communism were much more than a weak protest or an avocation of literary men. Few communists are really aware of the far-reaching implications of the doctrine that civil war is the *only* method by which revolutionary economic and political changes can be brought about. A comparatively simple social structure, such as that which Russia had, may be able to recover from the effects of violent, internal disturbance. And Russia, it must be remembered, had the weakest middle class of any major nation. Were a large scale revolution to break out in highly industrialized America, where the middle class is stronger, more militant and better prepared than anywhere else in the world, it would either be abortive, drowned in a blood bath, or if it were victorious, would win only a Pyrrhic victory. The two sides would destroy the country and each other. For this reason, too, I am not a Communist.

I have been considering the position, as I understand it, of the orthodox and official Communism. I cannot blind myself, however, to the perceptible difference between communism with a small *c*, and Communism, official Communism, spelt with a capital letter.

NOTES

First published in *Modern Monthly* 8 (April 1934): 135–37, reprint, in LW.9.91–96.

1. Sidney Hook, ed., *The Meaning of Marx: A Symposium* (New York: Farrar & Rinehart, 1934). Hook had been Dewey's student and studied Marx early on in his career. He later became strongly anticommunist and President Reagan awarded him a Presidential Medal of Freedom. See Associated Press, "13 Are Named Winners of Medal of Freedom," *New York Times*, April 9, 1985, https://www.nytimes.com/1985/04/09/us/13-are-named-winners-of-medal-of-freedom.html.
2. For Dewey scholars, it is worth noting that he would say that minds depend upon matter, but are not wholly reducible to it. In other words, mind and matter are two aspects of experience, just as an ocean wave is more than merely water yet could not behave as it does except in relation to matter.
3. A village in Spain has come to be known as a very successful example. See Dan Hancox, *The Village Against the World* (New York: Verso, 2014).

14
Dualism and the Split Atom

(1945)

EDITOR'S INTRODUCTION

A central value in all of Dewey's work is the optimal direction of human intelligence and powers to security, personal growth, and social well-being. In 1945, humanity's destructive powers were enormously enlarged, but that only made Dewey's task more important. Dewey rejects the traditional split between the human side and the physical and scientific side of life. He argues that such thinking is a source of grave inhumanity. It is wrong, he claims, to argue that science and technological development were the problem at issue in the development and use of the atomic bomb. Implicit in that mistaken belief is an anti-intellectual outlook that pits science against morality, much as people in recent years have fought against the teaching of evolutionary biology, claiming it to be a threat to young people's moral development.

Dewey also responds to those who believe democracy to be the problem, thinking that the only solution to save humanity from itself was to submit to external authority. Dewey saw such views as belief that "an evil can be improved by intensifying it." He showed the parallel nature of the problems inherent in the atomic bomb and in the forces aligned against democracy, namely, in the threat they both posed to the masses of people.

SCIENCE AND MORALS IN THE ATOMIC AGE

There is an immediate issue and a longtime problem presented by the splitting of the atom and the production of the atomic bomb. The former naturally engrosses public attention and public discussion. For it concerns the bearing of the discovery and the invention in question upon the urgent problem of the security of the peoples of the earth, including most emphatically our own. The urgency is increased because the bomb appeared as an agency of destruction toward the close of the greatest scene of human destruction the world has ever seen. The irony of the situation is that an instrumentality which was developed as a means of security during war presents itself in the cold light of the day after as the greatest threat to security that human imagination can encompass.

The long-term problem concerns the position and the use, actual and potential, of physical science and the technologies of industrial production in present and future human life if it is to be genuinely humane. The particular development of science and technology is new. But it is only a consummation of the scientific and industrial developments of the past. The particular culmination is indeed novel, so novel as to seem sensationally unprecedented. But there is nothing new or unprecedented in the scientific and industrial achievements which have led up to it. And what is more serious—there is nothing new or unprecedented in the kind of problem that is presented to mankind: the problem of systematic use of the resources of physical science and the industry based upon it for human security and well-being, instead of for insecurity and destruction. The advent of the atomic bomb dramatizes and highlights issues that have been in active process for generations. Science and industrial technology are themselves too new to have made their way into the more basic conditions of our civilization. They have been superimposed as external strata upon institutions and habits so old as to be established beyond the reach of easy fundamental transformation.

In short, the splitting of the atom as a scientific discovery and production of the atomic bomb as a technological development bring into central focus events that for a long time have been working in piecemeal and scattered fashion. These events have been going on since the scientific revolution of the seventeenth century and the industrial revolution of the eighteenth and nineteenth. In bringing them to a head, the later development as a summation of what had preceded, forces upon our observation tendencies that we had not previously seen—and to some extent had not wanted to see. No intelligent person can henceforth fail to note that the physical science and the industrial technology of our time are out of gear with the heritage of moral values and aims by which we belatedly profess to live.[1]

It is customary to give the name of "cultural lag" to the discrepancy in question. It is that, of course. But merely calling it a *lag* tends to conceal from view the fateful fact that it brings with it a deep tragic split between what is distinctively human on one side and the science and technology we label merely material on the other side. As long as the split exists, science and technology will too often operate in inhuman ways. Voices that learned their speech in an earlier age are accordingly clamorously putting the entire blame for present evils upon the side of science and technology. They say, these things operate inherently on a material and non-moral plane, and that the uses and enjoyments they have brought to mankind have seduced men from proper care for higher "spiritual" things. The materialistic has thus, they say, been allowed to trespass upon a realm where it has no rights. The remedy is to keep physical science and industrial technology in a strict subjection to what representatives of this group *call* "moral," irrespective of the immense changes that are taking place in all the conditions of human life.

One may, or rather must, agree that something is seriously out of joint. But we may and must radically disagree with the creed as to how integration of life is to be achieved. On one hand, the scientific and industrial revolutions are not the kind of revolutions that go backward. It is idle to suppose that exhortations, addressed chiefly to the emotions, will create subjection to abstract moral principles. The impotency of this method is evident; it has lost the support of the traditions, customs, and institutions which once gave it whatever efficacy it possessed. The loss has come about, moreover, through the practical impact of just the scientific and industrial developments which are deplored. The inefficacy of this method is so obvious that added vigor has been given, on the other hand, to those who urge that our only salvation is in a return to obedient acceptance of externally imposed authority; to one that is said to have a monopoly of the higher moral and "spiritual" truths upon which the ordered life of mankind is dependent; to one that has before our very eyes proved itself ineffective.

The claims of the latter group raise a question of fundamental importance: How far do the confusions and conflicts from which we suffer arise from the perpetuation, under changed conditions, of just the doctrines to which we are urged to return? *For one of the main tenets of the latter was precisely that there is a split in the very nature of things, and hence not to be overcome, between what is "material" and what is moral and ideal—that which is euphemistically and emotionally called "spiritual." And the practical consequences of this division are a large part of just the evils that now need to be overcome.*[2]

If the split in question were merely a matter of something labelled philosophy, it would be too remote and anemic to be of consequence. But theoretical formulation of this division originated as an intellectual expression and attempted justification of established institutional conditions. When the work of the world was done by those who, if not slaves or serfs, were politically disfranchised and who were economically dispossessed and disprivileged, who were morally abject, their menial status was inevitably reflected in the idea that the things and processes with which they were occupied were inherently base. Since the industrial arts were matters of custom, acquired by manual apprenticeship on the part of those who practiced them, "reason" and true science were taken to be the manifestation of faculties possessed only by a superior group.

Industrial arts, or technologies are today the product of inventions made possible only by scientific insight which has been acquired through command of highly intellectualized (or "rational") procedures—a fact dramatically demonstrated in the atomic bomb. But it is still true that the great mass of workers are shut out, because of defective education and economic disadvantage, from sharing in the knowledge on which their work is based. The idea that this subjection would be improved or remedied by still more systematic subjection to external authority is the idea that an evil can be improved by intensifying it. And it is still true that in spite of the abolition of slavery and serfdom by means of political emancipation, the workers of the world have little share in control of the work they perform. Actual institutional conditions are still such as to give color and practical support to the philosophy of separation between matter and mind (even though practical dealings with "matter" are the expression of intelligent understanding), between nature and man, between science and morals. Meantime, the actual conditions that are supposedly justified by this philosophy are the source of the main problems and dangers of our time.

What has all this to do with the atomic bomb? The same conditions that render it a threat to human security and well-being are the kind of thing which, before the bomb was dreamed of, threatened the security of masses of people. The very things that occasion fear that the atomic bomb will add power to the forces of destruction are the kind of things that have created those divisions of classes, groups, races, sects, which in turn create recourse to force as the agency for settling differences and conflicts. The way out is not to return to subjection to the alleged authority of representatives of the dogmas and institutions which embody and perpetuate the divisions from which we suffer. It is to carry forward the application of our best scientific procedures and results so that they will operate within, not just outside of and against, the moral values and concerns of humanity. It is the business of modern man to use every effort to see to it that the immense technological resources now at our command are not limited in use to aims which are degraded in advance as merely material or utilitarian in some low sense, but are systematically employed in behalf of human—that is, common and widespread—security and well-being.

And, underlying and overtopping all, is the fact that if the atomic splitting by science and its technological application in the bomb fail to teach us that we live in a world of change so that our ways of organization of human interrelationships must also change, the case is well-nigh hopeless.

NOTES

First published in *New Leader* 28 (November 22, 1945): 1, 4, reprint, in LW.15.199–204.
1. [Editor's note: Emphasized in boldface in the original.]
2. [Editor's note: Emphasized in italics as in the original.]

15

Is There Hope for Politics?

(1931)

EDITOR'S INTRODUCTION

In 1931, Dewey wrote about the need for a new political party in several essays. In "Is There Hope for Politics," we get one of his briefer presentations of his ideas. He argues that at the time people really felt that the two political parties ultimately were powered by the same forces. So, realistically, people were apathetic and felt no hope for politics because differences in name were no real differences at all.

Today, America feels more polarized than at any time since the Civil War.[1] To appreciate Dewey's point for our day, consider some examples. When the Democrats worked to draft the bill which became the Affordable Care Act, there were critics who believed that the United States should adopt a single-payer model. Those critics argued that the Democrats and the Republicans both amounted to the same thing: a defense of the status quo for big business in medicine. The claim was that the ACA only further entrenched insurance companies, said to be part of the problem. Some disaffected Americans believed that there was no great difference between Republicans and Democrats.

For further examples, consider the advocate for smaller government who often feels that both parties want to spend more, but on different things, or the politically moderate or independent voter who has come to feel less and less represented as the parties have grown further from the middle. Responding to this apathy, Dewey argued that a third party could unify the disaffected citizens and enable them to reject the troubling uniformities of both parties, which perpetuate the country's problems. Consider for today that in a 2013 Gallup poll, nearly 42 percent of Americans declined to claim a party affiliation.[2]

Dewey's most ambitious proposal calls for democratizing economies. He offers examples about effective monopolies like railways and utilities. Many of the suggestions he offers have in fact come to pass in the United States since his day or have been partly established.

The most marked trait of our recent political life is the growing disregard of politics. The disregard is shown in apathy, cynicism, and contempt. Indifference is proved by the difficulty that is experienced in getting voters to the polls. One out of two possible voters exercises the right of franchise. Even the last presidential election, which drew upon the outside interests of religion and personal tastes in drink, did not increase the ratio very much. There is no other country in which anything like so much money is spent in political campaigns, and there is none in which citizens are so apathetic about taking part in an election. To this indifference is added cynical contempt. There is apathy because the potential electorate feels that nothing in especial is gained by voting; nothing happens of public significance in consequence of approval of one party rather than another. But joined to this feeling is one of positive disrespect for politicians which reacts to create the belief that politics itself is an unworthy and low affair. "Politician" has always conveyed a sense of depreciation in this country. In latter years the feeling has deepened into a conviction that they are chiefly occupied with promoting their own private interests. Holding down the job is the main thing, and the public is thought lucky when the job is not also made the source of personal profits outside the official scope of the job. Politics is assumed to be so much of a racket that it is extremely difficult to arouse public indignation even when corruption comes to light. "What did you expect, anyway?" is the comment, voiced or silent, of multitudes of citizens.

The rapid growth of competing interests is one great cause of apathy. Interest in government has declined from the same causes which have brought about decline of interest in the church. There are too many other interesting things to do and to enjoy. When men gather together there is likely to be one conversation about the affairs of government to a hundred about automobiles and trips. Politics may appear on the first page and on the editorial page of newspapers, but the sport pages occupy more space, and the average reader turns to these pages with an eagerness which contrasts with the languid way in which he reads the political news and skips the editorials. At election time political speeches get the attention of thousands or millions on the radio; but dance music and Amos 'n Andy continue the year around. I should venture to say that there is more conversation in the homes of the nation about the fortunes of Amos 'n Andy than there is on any one political theme. And all this ignores the preoccupation of men and women with their own business and domestic affairs, which are more complicated and more absorbing than ever before.

By the side of the fact that competing interests are more numerous and more attractive than in previous times stands the fact that real governmental affairs are more technical than they used to be. They are problems for the expert, and experts are few. The raiser of sheep pays attention to the wool schedule in the tariff bill, and the manufacturer of dyes to the chemical schedule. But the tariff as a whole is so complex and its impact on the average citizen is effected in such roundabout ways that he gives up the whole matter in despair. This fact is symbolic of about every issue and problem that concerns the governments of the nation, of states, and of municipalities. Even the cities have grown so big and their public interests so multifarious and complicated that the average citizen does not know how to take an intelligent interest in them even if he wants to. The situation makes the opportunity for special interests to have their way, since they know what they want and how to get it, and the result only increases the distrust and disgust of private citizens with the whole business of politics.

And then there is the whole inescapable affair of prohibition. About that topic there is plenty of conversation wherever men and women gather together. It is both a political and a non-political matter. It is non-political in that it primarily concerns personal tastes and moral principles. It is non-political in the party sense, since up to the present both parties have either officially dodged it, or have given the prohibitory amendment and the Volstead Act their nominal indorsement. It is in politics because it demands action on the part of legislators and administrators. It is getting more and more in politics as it becomes not only a theme of eternal discussion, but also raises the question of whether a candidate is wet or dry.

The net effect is to obscure and deflect *general* political interest. The question of prohibition lies across all other issues and covers them from view. It does not line itself definitely and emphatically with any consistent set of principles and policies on other matters. The Democratic party in the South is dry; in the North and West, where it is concentrated in big cities and industrial centres, it tends to be wet. The Republican party on the whole is dry in the West and wet in the East. If there were a movement in the insurgent elements of the two parties, say in the Senate and the House, to unite in a declaration of common positive principles and in appeal to the public for support of them irrespective of party affiliations, the movement would be faced by the differences of opinion among the progressives on the subject of prohibition. And these differences would probably check organized union in behalf of progressive principles. There are those whose political history is distinctly conservative and reactionary who arrogate to themselves the title of liberals on the ground of opposition to interference by the government with personal taste in food and drink. These would identify liberalism with the political policies of old-fashioned "individualism" and thus use their "liberalism" to support and extend the *laissez-faire* policy of allowing big business to go its own way, unregulated by law and administration. Those who have been most active in promoting liberal principles in that loose sense attached to the word "progressive" are largely dry in *personnelle*. Prohibition thus cuts across definitely political issues so that there is little hope of interest in it arousing a wider and more intelligent interest in political life in general. In fact, I think it makes in the other direction.

Is there any hope in politics? Is there any hope *for* politics as a serious concern of the masses who are not interested in governmental jobs? These questions are not academic. Much less are they arbitrary and forced. They are, for example, definitely connected with the decline of democracy and the growing despair of its efficiency. For the theory of political democracy was predicated upon the assumption that with the widening of the franchise there would also go a wholesome widening and deepening of watchfulness, concern, and activity in the points and places where government in any of its aspects touches the life of the people. The contrary has largely been the case. The more extensive the influence of government, the more indirect and concealed do its ramifications become. That individual to whom I have made frequent reference, the average citizen, gives up the problem, much as he gives up the prospect of understanding the theory of Einstein about the universe in which also he lives. And as in the case of Einstein, attention to ideas and principles gets transferred into an exaggerated and irrelevant interest in personalities. Even were the level of intelligence of the general population as low as those assume who talk glibly about morons, boobs, and persons with eleven-year-old mentality, that level might work effectively enough when conditions are fairly simple. But now even superior minds are distracted and appalled by the intricacy and extent of the problems which confront society.

Is there hope to be had from the formation of a new party? The question is pertinent. A very considerable part of the apathy to which I have alluded is due to the feeling that there is no important difference between the two old parties and that accordingly a vote for one or the other signifies little. Shrewd observers tell us that a large part of the half of the electorate that does still vote is voting against something or somebody rather than from positive belief and expectation. Ten years ago the assertion of the basic similarity of the two major parties was a novelty. To-day it is almost a platitude, an accepted commonplace.

Acceptance of the idea will be found in the most unexpected places, including partisans who vote the regular ticket from force of inertial habit. In spite of the stable hold of the Republican party on the national government, independence has grown to a point where it is the despair of old-line politicians. I cite three facts in evidence. One is the insurgency of individuals nominally committed to a party. Effective opposition to the policies of Harding, Coolidge, and Hoover has come largely from within the Republican party. The most important measures of the latter two Presidents have been shot to pieces from within the party; opposite policies have been kept from the statute-book only by presidential veto. The second fact is the election of Democratic governors in states in which the other party triumphs in national elections. The third consideration is the kind of treatment now given by the large newspapers, both in news and editorial columns, to political matters. Partisanship has not disappeared, but desire to hold the reading constituencies has compelled an impartiality not found twenty years ago.

Growing independence, hastened undoubtedly in many places (though not everywhere) by the enfranchisement of women, does not, however, guarantee either the development of a new interest in politics, or the development of a new party. There are many and long steps to be taken before the disgust of scattered and unorganized persons will be crystallized. The situation does, however, indicate that with success in the creation of a new party is bound up such success as may be achieved in renewal of trust in political action and in renewal of hope of something significant coming out of political life. To put the matter baldly and briefly, indifference to politics is the product of unbelief in the sincerity of the old parties. Nothing is hoped from them because it is felt that they are both the servants of the same dominant railway, banking, and corporate industrial forces. Disgust with politics, cynical acquiescence in corruption, is due to the fact that this covert, this unavowed, alliance of government in cities, states, and the nation with "big business" is known to be the chief cause of graft and loot in politics. There was a general resentment directed against corrupt politicians in the nineties and early years of the present century. The indignation which was aroused led to a series of political house-cleanings, more or less successful for the movement. Now there is wide-spread recognition of the fact that the guilty politicians are not the ultimately guilty parties. The political racket is a symptom of an underlying economic racket. Seeing no way to deal with the latter, it seems a saving of time and energy not to get too excited about the former.

This situation, however, does not make it any easier to bring a new party to birth. Indeed, it indicates the difficulty in the way of it. The radiations and ramifications of the economic régime under which we live are so subtle and wide that they create a feeling of general helplessness and timidity about the possibility of any significant change. The open flouting by Mencken and his followers of the idea of any real improvement in public and social affairs finds a feebler echo in the minds of "tired liberals." They would like to do something, but they do not know how to go to work nor where to begin. The whole situation is out of hand.

I am not content, however, to stop without pointing out that the revival of intelligent hope for and from political life is identical with the cause of creating a new political party. There are certain practical conclusions which follow from this unity. One is the fundamental character of the principles upon which a new party must be built. It must start from the fact that all vital political questions of the day have an economic origin, and have their impact where men live, industrially and financially, in the shop, home, and office. The principles and policies of new political thought and interest must not be afraid to borrow and to develop many measures which have been stigmatized as socialistic and which have been allowed, in their political bearing, to become too much a monopoly of a practically ineffective socialistic party. It is not enough to make the masses aware of the extent to which government has become an instrument of economic privilege, and to urge abolition of this control exercised by a small class in behalf of their own advantage. Negations and oppositions sometimes arouse temporary sentiment of great immediate force. But they are transient in themselves and in their effects.

I shall not try to write a platform which will fulfil the condition of basing political action upon industrial, commercial, and financial realities, instead of upon sham issues long dead historically. But certain matters may be pointed out to illustrate and give body to the idea. Modern business is carried on by money and especially credit. Those who control the giving and withholding of credit govern the country, whoever controls government in name. The government must resume in fact control of credit. Private, unregulated ownership of natural resources in land, which signifies mines, oil, timber, and water-power—which means, also, to-day, electrical power—must yield to drastic taxation of the land values created by the community and necessary to the healthy development of the community. Operations which tend to be become natural monopolies, like railway transportation, public utilities, means of communication, must come under a governmental regulation so complete as not to be distinguished from public ownership. It must be realized that civil rights, liberty of speech, assembly, publication, are not merely individual rights, but are essential to the welfare, the healthy growth, of society. Such points as these at least illustrate the nature of the principles upon which alone a new party can be built, while they demonstrate the fundamental and radical character of the political thinking which must be done.

The situation also discloses a fact important for the tactics to be pursued. They must be long-time, and at first primarily educational, tactics. I should have little faith in what a new party could accomplish if it came into power in 1932 or 1936. Past third-party movements have been ineffectual because they aimed too much at immediate success, and because these had done little preliminary work in thought, study, and the preparation of men able to carry new ideas into effect in legislation and administration. My statements may suggest to some persons a continuation of the tactics which rendered liberalism ineffectual in the fact. By "educational activities" may be understood a cloistered withdrawal from the scene of action, an idea that "appeal to reason" is enough. But such procedure is not education; it is at best a preparation for education, and is likely to be something much more futile. There is no education when ideas and knowledge are not translated into emotion, interest, and volition. There must be constant accompanying organization and direction of organized action into practical work. "Ideas" must be linked to the practical situation, however hurly-burly that is.

The thing which gives me least fear and discouragement is the statement, no matter how often it is reiterated, that such a movement can appeal only to a minority, and at the outset a comparatively small minority. In the first place, there is already political discontent and unrest among the masses. These need direction and organization, but there is something there to direct and to organize. Apathy is in large measure due to the fact that nothing fundamental, nothing sufficiently radical in the way of principles, has been offered. And in the second place, every movement of any account in the history has been the work of minorities. I do not agree with the statements which are freely propagated in the interest of reactionary policies about the low mentality of the masses. The adult is more apt to learn than youth. But the courage and conviction which instruct them must first proceed from the few. The question of whether there is hope in and for politics is finally a question whether there is a minority having the requisite courage, conviction, and readiness for sacrificial work.

NOTES

First published in *Scribner's* 89 (May 1931): 483–87, reprint, in LW.6.182–190.
1. Jocelyn Kiley, "In Polarized Era, Fewer Americans Hold a Mix of Conservative and Liberal Views," Pew Research Center, October 23, 2017, http://www.pewresearch.org/fact-tank/2017/10/23/in-polarized-era-fewer-americans-hold-a-mix-of-conservative-and-liberal-views/.
2. Jeffrey M. Jones, "Record-High 42% of Americans Identify as Independents," Gallup Politics, January 8, 2014, http://www.gallup.com/poll/166763/record-high-americans-identify-independents.aspx.

16

A Liberal Speaks Out for Liberalism

(1936)

EDITOR'S INTRODUCTION

In 1936, Dewey recognized the need for people to see the common roots of two branches of the liberal tradition, namely humanitarian and laissez-faire liberalism. Differences over how to end the Great Depression were polarizing the American people, with one group believing in the power of government action to pursue liberal ends and the other holding only unimpeded enterprise as the path out of economic depression.

The apparent dichotomy of outlooks is really more a matter of disagreeing siblings from the same family of beliefs. These two threads both grew out of the liberal tradition, with the humanitarian side motivated by Wesleyan Protestant Christians, who emphasized the norm that one ought to love one's neighbor as oneself. The laissez-faire side of liberalism prized liberty and individuality but was inspired by the potential for emerging industries to empower all.

The common thread important to both approaches to liberalism, Dewey argued, is the importance of seeking solutions cooperatively rather than through violence and imposition. Violent imposition of one side had its example in communism and the other in fascism. Today we use these terms loosely as labels for dismissing ideas different from our own, yet in Dewey's day these political orientations and their use of force for pursuing their stated aims were real and troubling.

The enduring message in Dewey's essay is that voluntary cooperation is vital for the security and legacy of the democratic development of individuality and liberty. He believes that the hard-line laissez-faire branch of liberalism has run its course and encountered many difficulties, and the radical critiques of humanitarian liberalism have had some merit, inasmuch as it has left much to be desired with respect to the quality of life of the masses. At the same time, he rejects the belief that radical change can only be achieved by means of violence. He calls the strain of nonviolent liberalism, which believes in the potential for free, cooperative social action to improve the lives of the masses of people, "democratic liberalism."

Liberalism as a conscious and aggressive movement arose in Great Britain as two different streams flowed into one. One of these streams was the humanitarian and philanthropic zeal that became so active late in the eighteenth century and that in various forms is still a mighty current. It was expressed in the feeling that man is his brother's keeper and that the world is full of suffering and evil that are caused by failure to recognize this fact. In consequence of the failure, political and social institutions are horribly and tragically harsh and cruel in their effect upon the mass of men, women and children.

This humanitarian movement itself represents the conflux of many separate streams. There was, for example, the tremendous influence exerted by Rousseau, the real author of the doctrine of the forgotten man and the forgotten masses. His influence was quite as great in literature as in politics. It helped create the novel of the common man in England in the eighteenth century, a literary influence that found such vivid expression in the nineteenth century in the novels of Dickens.

Independent of Rousseau, but reinforced by his influence, there was a reaction against the importance attached by most eighteenth-century thought to "reason." Reason, it was felt if not argued, is a prerogative of a select few. The mass of men are influenced by feeling and instinct, and the hope of the world lies in giving free play to the instinct of sympathy, rather than to logic and reason.

This new attitude found expression in the deification of the "man of sentiment" so characteristic of one period of English thought. The interest in the "noble savage" is another expression of the same attitude. Aside from the fact that he was supposed, in a wholly illusory way, to be independent and free from the constraints of convention and custom, he was idealized as the creature of instinct and emotion.

Another influence that finally joined in to form the humanitarian current was the religious. In England it was stimulated by the Wesleyan movement, with its peculiar appeal to the "lower" and neglected classes. But it affected the established church as well. Ardent, aggressive missionary zeal for saving the souls of men, especially those of the humble and poor, ran over into efforts to improve their condition by abolishing harsh and cruel inequalities.

The movement, instigated by religion, was active in attack upon slavery, upon the abuses of prison life, upon brutal and mechanical methods of administering charity, and, through the factory laws, upon the inhuman conditions of labor of women and children in mines and factories. In every one of these movements evangelical zeal was the motive force.

The other great stream that entered into the formation of liberalism sprang from the stimulus to manufacturing and trade that came from the application of steam to industry. The great intellectual leader of this movement was Adam Smith. His theories found practical reinforcement in the endeavor of manufacturers and traders to get free from the immense number of laws and customs that restricted the freedom of movement of laborers, that subjected the market price to prices legally fixed and that hampered freedom of exchange especially with foreign markets.

This mass of restrictions, that tended to strangle at birth the new infant industry, held over from agrarian feudalism and was kept in force by the influence of landed interests. Because the restrictive and oppressive conditions were embodied in law and because law was the voice of government in control of human action, government was taken to be the great enemy of liberty; interference with human industry engaged in satisfaction of human needs was taken to be the chief cause why progress was retarded and why a reign of harmony of interests and peace did not exist.

Freedom of production would, it was held, lead to the maximum stimulation of human effort and automatically direct abilities into the channels in which, in bringing most reward to the individual, they would also be most serviceable to society. Freedom of exchange would create an interdependence that would automatically create harmony of interests. The negative side of the doctrine, its opposition to governmental action in production and trade, came to full flower in the principle of laissez-faire: hands off on the part of government and the maximum of free activity on the part of producer and trader in the advancement of his own interests.

This historical summary is more than historical. It is indispensable to any understanding of liberalism as a social and political movement. For, while the two streams came together, they never coalesced.

Although the humanitarian movement expressed itself most actively in personal and voluntary effort, it was far from averse to employing governmental agencies to achieve its reforms. Most of them, in fact, like abolition of the slave trade, prison reform, removal of abuses attending the labor of women and children, could not be effected without some intervention on the part of government.

The whole movement toward what is known as social legislation with its slogan of social justice derives from this source and involves more and more appeal to governmental action. Hence there was from the beginning an inner split in liberalism. Any attempt to define liberalism in terms of one or the other of its two strains will be vehemently denied by those attached to the other strain.

Historically, the split was embodied in the person of one of the chief representatives of nineteenth-century liberalism, Jeremy Bentham. Whether he was aware of it or not, his leading principle, that of the greatest happiness of the greatest number, was derived from the philanthropic and humanitarian movement. But when it came to the realization of this goal, he ranked himself, with some exceptions, such as public health and public education, with laissez-faire liberalism.

He was strong for political action to reform abuses of judicial procedure, of law-making and methods of electing law-makers, but he regarded the abuses to be corrected as the product of the failure of government in the past to confine itself to its proper sphere. When the abuses of governmental action by government were once removed, he believed that the free play of individual initiative and effort would furnish the sure road to progress and to producing the greatest happiness of the greatest number.

As I have indicated, the inner breach in liberalism has never been healed. On the Continent, so-called liberal parties have been almost universally the political representatives of big industry, banking and commerce. In Great Britain, true to the spirit of tradition and compromise so strong in English affairs, liberalism has been a mixture of the two strains, leaning now in one direction and now in another.

In the United States liberalism has been identified largely with the idea of the use of governmental agencies to remedy evils from which the less-fortunate classes suffer. It was "forward-looking" in the Progressive movement; it lies, nominally at least, behind Square Deals and New Deals. It has favored employer-liability acts, laws regulating hours and conditions of labor, antisweatshop legislation, supplementation of private charity by public relief and public works, generous appropriations for public schools, graded higher taxation of larger incomes and of inheritances; in general, when there has been a conflict between labor and employers it has sided with labor.

Its philosophy has rarely been clear cut. But so far as it has had a philosophy it has been that government should regularly intervene to help equalize conditions between the wealthy and the poor, between the overprivileged and the underprivileged. For this reason liberals of the other, or laissez-faire, school have always attacked it as pink socialism, as disguised radicalism; while at the present time the favorite charge is that it is instigated, of all places in the world, from Moscow.

As a matter of fact, up to this time in this country political liberalism has never attempted to change the fundamental conditions of the economic system or to do more than ameliorate the estate in which the mass of human beings live. For this reason liberalism at present is under more violent attack from radicals than from conservatives. In the mouth of radicals liberalism is a term of hissing and reproach.

In spite of the extreme clash, both schools of liberalism profess devotion to the same ultimate ideal and goal. The slogan of both schools is the utmost possible liberty of the individual. The difference between them concerns the province in which liberty and individuality are most important and the means by which they are to be realized.

One has only to read any outgiving of the adherents of laissez-faire liberalism to see that it is the liberty of the entrepreneur in business undertakings which they prize and which they come close to identifying with the heart of all liberty.

To the spokesmen of the Liberty League and to ex-President Hoover in his doctrine of rugged individualism, any governmental action that interferes with this particular kind of liberty is an attack upon liberty itself. The ruggedness, independence, initiative and vigor of individuals upon which they set chief store is that of the individuals who have come to the top in the existing economic system of finance capitalism. They are exposed to the charge of identifying the meaning of liberty and of rugged individualism with the maintenance of the system under which they have prospered.

The charge is given force by the fact that they have for the most part supported the system of protective tariffs, against which original simon-pure laissez-faire liberals directed some of their most violent attacks. The author of the phrase "rugged individualism" used the government to come to the aid of industry when it was in straits by means of the Reconstruction Finance Corporation, and, as far as I know, the opponents of governmental intervention made no protest at this flagrant case of governmental interference with the free course of private industry.

The most vocal spokesmen for this special form of liberty have never attacked land monopoly and if they think at all about Henry George, they think of him as one of the subversive and dangerous radicals. They have themselves built up financial and industrial systems so concentrated as to be semi-monopolies or monopolies proper.

Liberals of the other school are those who point to things like those just mentioned and who assert that the system of industry for private profit without regard to social consequences has had in fact a most unfavorable effect upon the real liberty of the mass of individuals.

Their conception of what I called the province of liberty and individuality is broader and more generous than is that of those who come forward as the self-appointed champions of liberty. They think that liberty is something that affects every aspect and phase of human life, liberty of thought, of expression, of cultural opportunity, and that it is not to be had, even in the economic sphere, without a degree of security that is denied to millions by the present economic system.

They point out that industry, banking and commerce have reached a point where there is no such thing as merely private initiative and enterprise. For the consequences of private business enterprise affect so many persons and in such deep and enduring ways that all business is affected with a public interest. Since the consequences of business are social, society must itself look after, by means of increased organized control, the industrial and financial causes of these consequences.

There is, accordingly, no doubt in my own mind that laissez-faire liberalism is played out, largely because of the fruits of its own policies. Any system that cannot provide elementary security for millions has no claim to the title of being organized in behalf of liberty and the development of individuals. Any person and any movement whose interest in these ends is genuine and not a cover for personal advantage and power must put primary emphasis in thought and action upon the means of their attainment.

At present those means lie in the direction of increased social control and increased collectivism of effort. Humane liberalism in order to save itself must cease to deal with symptoms and go to the causes of which inequalities and oppressions are but the symptoms. In order to endure under present conditions, liberalism must become radical in the sense that, instead of using social power to ameliorate the evil consequences of the existing system, it shall use social power to change the system.

Radicalism in the minds of many, however, both among its professed adherents and its bitter enemies, is identified with a particular method of changing the system. To them, it means the change of the present system by violent overthrow. Radicalism of this sort is opposed to liberalism and liberalism is opposed to it. For liberalism both by its history and by its own nature is committed to democratic methods of effecting social change.

The idea of forcing men to be free is an old idea, but by nature it is opposed to freedom. Freedom is not something that can be handed to men as a gift from outside, whether by old-fashioned dynastic benevolent despotisms or by newfashioned dictatorships, whether of the proletarian or of the Fascist order. It is something which can be had only as individuals participate in winning it, and this fact, rather than some particular political mechanism, is the essence of democratic liberalism.

The denial of the democratic method of achieving social control is in part the product of sheer impatience and romantic longing for a short-cut which if it were taken would defeat its own end. It is in part the fruit of the Russian revolution, oblivious of the fact that Russia never had any democratic tradition in its whole history and was accustomed to dictatorial rule in a way that is foreign to the spirit of every Western country. In part, it is the product of the capture of the machinery of democratic legislation and administration by the dominant economic power, known for short as plutocracy or "the interests."

Discontent with democracy as it operates under conditions of exploitation by special interests has justification. But the notion that the remedy is violence and a civil war between classes is a counsel of despair.

If the method of violence and civil war be adopted the end will be either fascism, open and undisguised, or the common ruin of both parties to the struggle. The democratic method of social change is slow; it labors under many and serious handicaps imposed by the undemocratic character of what passes for democracy. But it is the method of liberalism, with its belief that liberty is the means as well as the goal and that only through the development of individuals in their voluntary cooperation with one another can the development of individuality be made secure and enduring.

NOTE

First published in *New York Times Magazine*, February 23, 1936, 3, 24 reprint, in LW.11.282–289.

17

Future of Liberalism

(1935)

EDITOR'S INTRODUCTION

In this short essay, Dewey engaged the noted writer and journalist Walter Lippmann on the topic of freedom, but he also aimed his words at the various activists and movements longing for change in the thick of the Great Depression. When Lippmann wrote about freedom, he committed an error that many people still commit today. The idea that freedom means only the lack of government imposition or interference is missing something crucial, Dewey noted. This idea, often found in laissez-faire libertarian outlooks, would say that a child abandoned in the woods and left to die is free. This is absurd.

Freedom is not merely the absence of government imposition. It is broader than that. Young people must develop and grow into free citizens, not only free from restrictions but also enabled to be free to act and execute their plans in life. Dewey's essay in this case is not about young people, though he has a great deal to say about them in other works. Nevertheless, they help us see his point. Freedom from governmental restrictions on walking for people who are bedridden is meaningless. What will promote their freedom is nourishment and healing.

Dewey ends this short essay with a word to those who advocate for change from laissez-faire forms of freedom to some alternative end or arrangement. The most radical advocates were dissatisfied with incremental change and believed that Dewey's civility and appeal to seeking change through intelligent means, such as communication, argument, and political advocacy, were too gradual or too slow. Dewey reassures the reader that just because he discourages violence, it does not mean that he opposes radical change. Instead, he is concerned about how change is to be brought about. Dewey believed that you could not achieve democratic ends by undemocratic means, a lesson he often repeated. Violent force is the abandonment of intelligent democratic methods. So he urged the advocates for change to seek their radical ends but through democratic means.

I should like to make the general principles of liberal social philosophy a little more concrete by application to existing issues. The first of the applications concerns the changing content of liberty. I read, for example, Walter Lippmann's *The Method of Freedom* with the hope of getting light on the present theme. But I found instead two things that reflect its traditional limitation. In the first place, the kind of freedom discussed is that which is restricted to the question of governmental intervention. In the second place, even this is discussed exclusively with reference to the freedom of individuals in the conduct of business enterprise. The special conclusion reached upon the first point involves rejection of laissez-faire individualism. So far there *is* modification of one form of traditional liberalism. But the policy advanced, that of the governmental intervention to redress the imbalances brought about by freedom of business entrepreneurs is not connected with any idea of extending the scope of freedom and expanding its meaning. The action recommended is rather thought of as a restriction of liberty in behalf of greater social security. No reference is made to the regimentation and lack of freedom now suffered by the great mass of workers. Nothing is said about the larger phases of liberty that have to do with freedom of the many to participate in the culture that is now possessed by society but not distributed. It may be said that the latter point is outside the scope of his particular discussion. But the former point is not outside; it belongs in any discussion of freedom that is limited to the economic phase. Moreover, it appears when a socially planned economy is adversely considered. But as far as workers are concerned the only thing taken up is security, and that not as a prerequisite of freedom, as a necessary condition of social stability. If this is as far as liberalism can go, I fear it is bankrupt and doomed.

The other point of contact which concrete contemporary movements wish to set up, concerns the emphasis upon intelligence in action as well as in thought as the method of social change. In view of the, at present, vogue of reliance upon the use of massed force to effect social change, a liberal is bound to emphasize the crucial importance of the means and methods by which change is brought about. Every absolute dogmatism, whether upheld in the name of Karl Marx or of Mussolini, separates means from ends. It is not a question of the advisability or the morality of making the separation. The point is that it cannot be done. The kind of means used, determines the kind of consequences actually reached—the ends in the only sense in which "ends" do not signify abstractions. At the present juncture, probably the most significant thing the theory of social liberalism can do, is to insist upon this point. You may set up ends that are intrinsically desirable, but what you actually get will depend upon the means you use to attain them. The most important thing about the means employed for attainment is the ratio of intelligence to force that characterizes them. Sheer violence signifies force used with the minimum of intelligence.

Preaching the use of violence as distinct from that of intelligent action in the use of forces that have a minimum of brute force about them, means just that much failure to bring intelligence to bear, and in so far compromises the consequences that follow. When intelligence and force are set up as opposed methods, the reactionary is likely, under present conditions, to have a monopoly of force if not of intelligence. In any case, reliance upon mere massed force accomplishes results such that the ends originally in view have to be achieved over again, bit by bit by the use of intelligence.

Sheer force or violence is always to be dreaded and as far as may be averted as an eventuality, not something to be cultivated and urged as a necessary means and method. Liberalism is not opposed to intelligent radicalism in policy and action. It is opposed to that unintelligent radicalism that suicidally would make sheer force and war, the main factor in effecting revolutionary social changes. If anybody thinks that the method of intelligence is so easy as to be a sign of weakness of positive conviction and of lack of courage, my reply is: Let him try the use of it. It is dependence upon violence as the way out that shows desire for short cuts and easy methods. The foes of intelligence in action are stronger than the foes of sheer force, and every appeal to the latter strengthens the enemies of social change. It strengthens without and within: in those who do not want social change to take place and in those whose hearts, if not minds, are set on social change.

NOTE

First published in *People's Lobby Bulletin* 4 (February 1935): 1–2, reprint, in LW. 11.258–261.

PART III
Education

18

What Is a School For?

(1923)

EDITOR'S INTRODUCTION

Henry S. Pritchett and Robert A. Franks, president and treasurer, respectively, of the Carnegie Foundation for the Advancement of Teaching published an annual report in 1922, which included a section titled "What Is a School For?" The *New York Times* published a symposium on the topic on two successive Sundays, March 11 and 18, 1923.

The first two responders were Alfred E. Stearns, principal of Exeter Academy, and Dr. Charles W. Eliot, a forty-year president at Harvard. Stearns said that some educators, himself included, "have for years protested against the ever-increasing tendency to load our public school curricula with purely practical and utilitarian subjects and to make these schools an experimental laboratory for the testing of almost every new fad and frill that the human mind can conceive." Eliot wrote that "what some people call frills or fads in schools and family life, like music and drawing, are really of fundamental importance."

Dewey's contribution came on the second Sunday, taking the majority of a page in the *Times*, along with a far shorter response by Frank P. Graves, commissioner of the New York State Department of Education.[1] Graves essentially defends existing practices and priorities without saying much about the purposes of education. He does note, however, that what some call "fads" and "frills" in education, others reasonably see as valuable and essential. At the same time, Graves rejects the idea of trying to cover too many subjects in an already loaded curriculum.

It is undeniable that the *Times* chose to emphasize Dewey's contribution, affording it far more room on the page. In addition, the paper called him "foremost among educators in the country." Dewey challenges nostalgia for the old ways, arguing that there was at the time no evidence of the superiority of traditional school over progressive schools. He explains that broadened curricula that connect with students' interests have proven beneficial. With the critics of expansive education, he agrees about the need to avoid waste, but with the innovators, he believes that more money can be spent wisely and efficiently.

Today, there are persistent threats to so-called frills fields like art and music, replaced by uniform education and standardized testing in narrow and traditional subjects. Dewey calls for educating the whole person and criticized uniformity in school curricula. He would lament today's ubiquitous high-stakes testing. In characteristic fashion, Dewey notes the extent to which different sides in the debate about schools' purpose contribute something important and right.

What is a school for? It is significant that Mr. Stearns comes nearest to approving of the position of the Carnegie report. It is significant because it suggests the difference in "what for" between a private and a public school. The former may exist for some special training, intellectual or otherwise. The public school must exist to serve the purposes of the community as a whole, to develop good citizens in the most comprehensive sense of that term.

Hence the general answer to the question of what public schools should teach is easy. They should teach those subjects which are found to be, first, necessary, and, secondly, highly useful in serving this purpose of developing good citizenship, industrial and political, for leisure as well as for work, good members of the family and the neighborhood as well as of the political state and the workshop and farm.

The difficulty lies in making this general answer specific; in finding out just what topics are necessary and what are so highly useful that they should, if possible, be introduced. The question cannot be answered in the a priori way in which the report answers it. It is a matter of experience, and experiencing cannot avoid some experimenting and some waste and blunders. The experience that is required in order to answer the question is still in the process of making. The older experience upon which President Pritchett and Dr. Stearns rely gives little help, because it had nothing to do with the problem of fitting all the youth of the community for proper membership in the community. It was a class education for special class purposes.

If we bear these facts in mind, the positions of the practical educators, Strayer, McAndrew, Tigert, Ettinger, and the causes of their difference in opinion to Pritchett and Stearns are clear. The former are facing the problem of the actual situation. They are engaged in the working out of the studies and methods which will serve the new democratic aim of public school education. The two sides are talking different languages, for they have different aims in mind. A person who is not actually engaged in the process of readapting education to fit the new conditions and purposes thinks of education as something old and finished, something which has been going on for a long time, and which has well established principles. Change looks to him like a departure from sanity and order, and its results like waste and confusion. To others education is something new, almost contemporary, for which there are few guiding precedents, and where principles are still being slowly and often painfully worked out.

The same situation explains what some call the enrichment of the curriculum and others call fads and frills. It is a question of the breadth and range of the social purposes of the schools.

President Eliot has a generous view of the capacities of human beings and of social life, and so he stands for a curriculum full enough to realize these capacities. Others regard the work of the school as more special, and, so to say, private and personal want; they want a much narrower curriculum. To talk about thoroughness and discipline is to beg the question until we have decided what the purpose is. There is, however, a good deal of nonsense talked about the effectiveness of the older kind of schools. Any one who will recall the tastes and habits of the majority of the pupils who were his schoolmates will admit, I am sure, that the narrowness of the course of study did not secure complete attention and constant application. My own school days were considerably before the days of enriching the curriculum, the days of the good old three Rs. A large part of the pupils enriched their curriculum on the side by reading dime novels inserted behind their textbooks. There is no objective evidence whatsoever that the pupils then mastered spelling, writing, arithmetic a bit better than they do now, when there are more studies. There is considerable evidence that the broadening of the course of study has supplied motives for better mastering of these subjects. About the increase of skill and ease in reading and broadening of tastes in reading there can be no doubt.

Any one who reads between the lines will see also what a great impetus has been given to the study of the human mind, and the methods of influencing and developing the mind by the widening out of education. A narrow curriculum can be taught and was taught mainly on the basis of routine, of following precedents—ways of instruction as restricted as were the subjects taught.

Teachers to be successful nowadays have to be informed about individual capacities, abilities, and weaknesses and their out-of-school environment in order that they may adapt teaching to these varying conditions. It is quite likely that in the future a movement will succeed, not to narrow studies, but to trim off excrescences, eliminate superfluities and organize, or, as James Harvey Robinson says, re-synthesize, studies into a more solid and coherent whole. But this change will be dependent upon what has been learned during the recent expansive process.

We are not spending enough on education. But we are not always getting the worth of our money. As I write I have received an analysis of our national budget showing that 85 per cent. of our Federal expenses is due directly and indirectly to consequences of past wars and preparation for possible future wars. Two per cent. of national funds go to research and what may broadly be called educational expenditures. At least we probably get more for our money in the latter case than in the former. But we should check up on the educational side. And administrators of the public schools have been at work on this question for some time. The last meeting of the Department of Superintendence at Cleveland devoted detailed attention to ways and means of doing just this thing. It is a problem, however, of spending our money wisely and efficiently, not of spending less money.

NOTES

First published in the *New York Times*, March 18, 1923, reprint, in MW.15.189–193.
1. Frank P. Graves, "Fads and Frills Have Found No Strong Support in the Schools," *New York Times*, March 18, 1923.

19

Dewey Outlines Utopian Schools

(1933)

EDITOR'S INTRODUCTION

Dewey's presentation before a conference at Columbia University's Teachers College in 1933 was one of his more creative essays. It was published in the *New York Times* a few days later, three years after his retirement from Columbia University. In this piece, he considers what Utopian schools would look like and what people in a Utopian society would say about schools and education in response to the conventional questions asked in his day. They were questions that people continue to ask today.

Dewey's device here, of asking the people of Utopia questions about education, enables him to reveal assumptions implicit in the typical questions we ask about schools, which the people of his vision of Utopia do not accept. Among them is the refrain that education is primarily a means to economic ends, which are then means to the endless accumulation of things. This feature of the economic liberalism of his day is no less relevant today, with respect to the forces we now typically call "neoliberalism," a totalizing belief in markets and a valuing of individual economic gain over all other considerations.

While the aim today of making our schools the best that they can be is laudable, Dewey would worry about high-stakes testing and the standardization of curricula that we have seen in recent years. His essay speaks also to those people today who wish to emphasize vocational education without education of the whole person. In addition, it addresses those who presently are attacking higher education in the United States, seeking to cut liberal arts education and to place all emphasis on short-term employment-related data, with no concern of the broader educational needs of a free people.[1]

Dewey's essay about education in Utopia offers us a statement of ideals, which could very well be taken up as guiding values for the future of education today.

⁂

The most Utopian thing in Utopia is that there are no schools at all. Education is carried on without anything of the nature of schools, or, if this idea is so extreme that we cannot conceive of it as educational at all, then we may say nothing of the sort at present we know as schools. Children, however, are gathered together in association with older and more mature people who direct their activity.

The assembly places all have large grounds, gardens, orchards, greenhouses, and none of the buildings in which children and older people gather will hold much more than 200 people, this having been found to be about the limits of close, intimate personal acquaintance on the part of people who associate together.

And inside these buildings, which are all of them of the nature of our present open-air schools in their physical structure, there are none of the things we usually associate with our present schools. Of course, there are no mechanical rows of screwed-down desks. There is rather something like a well-furnished home of today, only with a much greater variety of equipment and no messy accumulations of all sorts of miscellaneous furniture; more open spaces than our homes have today.

Then there are the workshops, with their apparatus for carrying on activities with all kinds of material—wood, iron, textiles. There are historic museums and scientific laboratories, and books everywhere as well as a central library.

The adults who are most actively concerned with the young have, of course, to meet a certain requirement, and the first thing that struck me as a visitor to Utopia was that they must all be married persons and, except in exceptional cases, must have had children of their own.[2] Unmarried, younger persons occupy places of assistance and serve a kind of initiatory apprenticeship. Moreover, older children, since there are no arbitrary divisions into classes, take part in directing the activities of those still younger.

The activity of these older children may be used to illustrate the method by which those whom we would call teachers are selected. It is almost a method of self-selection. For instance, the children aged say from about 13 to 18 who are especially fond of younger children are given the opportunity to consort with them. They work with the younger children under observation, and then it soon becomes evident who among them have the taste, interest and the kind of skill which is needed for effective dealing with the young.

As their interest in the young develops, their own further education centres more and more about the study of processes of growth and development, and so there is a very similar process of natural selection by which parents are taken out of the narrower contact with their own children in the homes and are brought forward in the educational nurture of larger numbers of children.

The work of these educational groups is carried on much as painters were trained in, say, Italy, when painting was at its height. The adult leaders, through their previous experience and by the manner of their selection, combine special knowledge of children with special gifts in certain directions.

They associate themselves with the young in carrying on some line of action. Just as in these older studios younger people were apprentices who observed the elders and took part along with them in doing at first some of the simpler things and then, as they got more experience, engaged directly in the more complex forms of activity, so in these directed activities in these centres the older people are first engaged in carrying on some work in which they themselves are competent, whether painting or music or scientific inquiry, observation of nature or industrial cooperation in some line. Then the younger children, watching them, listening to them, begin taking part in the simpler forms of the action—a minor part, until as they develop they accept more and more responsibility for cooperating.

Naturally I inquired what were the purposes, or, as we say now, the objectives, of the activities carried on in these centres. At first nothing puzzled me more than the fact that my inquiry after objectives was not at all understood, for the whole concept of the school, of teachers and pupils and lessons, had so completely disappeared that when I asked after the special objectives of the activity of these centres, my Utopian friends thought I was asking why children should live at all, and therefore they did not take my questions seriously.

After I made them understand what I meant, my question was dismissed with the remark that since children were alive and growing, "of course, we, as the Utopians, try to make their lives worth while to them; of course, we try to see that they really do grow, that they really develop." But as for having any objective beyond the process of a developing life, the idea still seemed to them quite silly. The notion that there was some special end which the young should try to attain was completely foreign to their thoughts.

By observation, however, I was led to the conclusion that what we would regard as the fundamental purposes were thoroughly ingrained in the working of the activities themselves. In our language it might be said to be the discovery of the aptitudes, the tastes, the abilities and the weaknesses of each boy and girl, and then to develop their positive capacities into attitudes and to arrange and reinforce the positive powers so as not to cover up the weak points but to offset them.

I inquired, having a background of our own schools in mind, how with their methods they ever made sure that the children and youth really learned anything, how they mastered the subject matter, geography and arithmetic and history, and how they ever were sure that they really learned to read and write and figure. Here, too, at first I came upon a blank wall. For they asked, in return to my question, whether in the period from which I came for a visit to Utopia it was possible for a boy or girl who was normal physiologically to grow up without learning the things which he or she needed to learn—because it was evident to them that it was not possible for any one except a congenital idiot to be born and to grow up without learning.

When they discovered, however, that I was serious, they asked whether it was true that in our day we had to have schools and teachers and examinations to make sure that babies learned to walk and to talk.

It was during these conversations that I learned to appreciate how completely the whole concept of acquiring and storing away things had been displaced by the concept of creating attitudes by shaping desires and developing the needs that are significant in the process of living.

The Utopians believed that the pattern which exists in economic society in our time affected the general habits of thought; that because personal acquisition and private possession were such dominant ideals in all fields, even if unconsciously so, they had taken possession of the minds of educators to the extent that the idea of personal acquisition and possession controlled the whole educational system.

They pointed not merely to the use in our schools of the competitive methods of appeal to rivalry and the use of rewards and punishments, of set examinations and the system of promotion, but they also said that all these things were merely incidental expressions of the acquisitive system of society and the kind of measure and test of achievement and success which had to prevail in an acquisitive type of society.

So it was that we had come to regard all study as simply a method of acquiring something, even if only useless or remote facts, and thought of learning and scholarship as the private possession of the resulting acquisition. And the social change which had taken place with the abolition of an acquisitive economic society had, in their judgment, made possible the transformation of the centre of emphasis from learning (in our sense) to the creation of attitudes.

They said that the great educational liberation came about when the concept of external attainments was thrown away and when they started to find out what each individual person had in him from the very beginning, and then devoted themselves to finding out the conditions of the environment and the kinds of activity in which the positive capacities of each young person could operate most effectually.

In setting creation, productivity, over against acquiring, they said that there was no genuine production without enjoyment. They imagined that the ethics of education in the older period had been that enjoyment in education always had to be something deferred; that the motto of the schools, at least, was that man never is, but always is to be, blest; while the only education that really could discover and elicit power was one which brought these powers for immediate use and enjoyment.

Naturally, I inquired what attitudes they regarded as most important to create, since the formation of attitudes had taken the place with the young of the acquisition of information. They had some difficulty in ranking attitudes in any order of importance, because they were so occupied with an all-around development of the capacities of the young. But, through observation, I should say that they ranked the attitude which would give a sense of positive power as at least as basic and primary as the others, if not more so.

This attitude which resulted in a sense of positive power involved, of course, elimination of fear, of embarrassment, of constraint, of self-consciousness; eliminated the conditions which created the feeling of failure and incapacity. Possibly it included the development of a confidence, of readiness to tackle difficulties, of actual eagerness to seek problems instead of dreading them and running away from them. It included a rather ardent faith in human capacity. It included a faith in the capacity of the environment to support worthwhile activities, provided the environment was approached and dealt with in the right way.

NOTES

First published in *New York Times*, April 23, 1933, Education section, from an address on April 21, 1933, to the Conference on the Educational Status of the Four- and Five-Year-Old Child at Teachers College, Columbia University, reprint, in LW.9.136–141.

1. I emphasize here the fact that the employment data are most often involved in short-term trends, for people generally consider matters like starting salaries in evaluating the consequences of different fields of study, when midcareer median

salaries are a much more important indicator of economic impact. The point here is not to agree with the unique emphasis on economic consequences in education but to show that even when economic impact is considered, critics fail to recognize that those who study philosophy earn considerably greater salaries at midcareer than many people who engage in what are considered more "practical" areas of study. Even making this point, however, sadly plays into the narrow salary-driven perspective at issue. See PayScale.com; and "Degrees That Pay You Back: Salary Increase by Major," *Wall Street Journal*, 2015, http://online.wsj.com/public/resources/documents/info-Degrees_that_Pay_you_Back-sort.html.

2. [Editor's note: Today this passage may sound surprising. Consider that in Dewey's day, roughly 80 percent of teachers were women. In addition, they were typically allowed neither to marry nor to have children. One way to interpret Dewey here would be to read this passage as advocacy for women's liberty as employees in the schools. The tone of it today sounds like a requirement for quality teaching, in his effort to make a point about a perfectly reasonable way to be as an adult and a teacher. The qualification of marriage and parenthood for teachers might have seemed reasonable to him, as people who intimately understand the needs of young people. At the same time, it is important to note the discrimination against women and mothers at the time. In West Virginia, for example, the Upshur County Board of Education in 1940 drafted an explicit policy not to employ "any married woman who has had a child of her own or a child in her custody whose age is less than the minimum school age." The policy listed "pregnancy" as the first condition which "shall constitute just and legal reason for the dismissal of any woman teacher." See Robert J. O'Brien, "Persecution and Acceptance: The Strange History of Discrimination Against Married Women Teachers in West Virginia," *West Virginia History* 56 (1997): 56–75.]

20

Industrial Education—
A Wrong Kind

(1915)

EDITOR'S INTRODUCTION

In 1913 and 1915, Indiana passed school laws laying out the state's plan for instruction and compulsory education. The parents and guardians of all young people between the ages of seven and fourteen were required to enroll those children in public, private, or parochial schools. At the age of fourteen, a young person could seek permission to accept employment and be released from further school requirements. All people between fourteen and sixteen who were not employed were expected to complete two more years of schooling.

Indiana's "School Laws" also specified a set of definitions to guide students' vocational education. As Dewey notes in this essay, the law says that "vocational education shall mean *any* education the controlling purpose of which is to fit for profitable employment." Item two on the list of relevant definitions in the law explains that " 'Industrial Education' shall mean that form of vocational education which fits for the trades, crafts and wage-earning pursuits, including the occupation of girls and women carried on in stores, workshops, and establishments."[1] Additional forms of education alongside "industrial education" included "agricultural education" and "domestic science," an earlier version of what was later referred to as "home economics."

The main problem Dewey sees in the legislation at the time was the early tracking it would generate. Once a young person was placed in a certain industry, the school system was inflexible for him or her. Young people might realize that they are better suited for a career different from what they were prematurely placed into at a young age. Dewey writes, "One of the chief evils of the present state of affairs is the accidental and unintelligent way in which workers, especially of the youthful age, find their jobs."

Today we rarely track young people in the way that the Indiana laws allowed. Experimentation and searching are considered common now, both in kindergarten through twelfth grade and in higher education. The value of exploration and breadth in education have been on the decline in the last thirty-five years with the what can be called the "standards-based movement," however.[2] Dewey was an advocate for general education and also for liberty in education. Without them, people have little opportunity to explore their options in life and to develop as individuals over the course of their education. Consistent with his generally empirical orientation and pragmatist philosophy, he argues that people had crafted problematic laws on the basis of theory not properly rooted in an understanding of contemporary conditions and problems. Taking such an approach creates problems and in a context in which the law could be "nowhere more useless or more harmful than in matters of education."

In education, as in so many other things, we have the advantages as well as the disadvantages of our decentralized system. Experimentation is stimulated and wholesome emulation aroused. Many states have not waited for Federal aid to initiate undertakings in industrial education. Since each such action affords a precedent likely to influence subsequent legislation, its provisions are of more than local import and should receive close scrutiny. In 1913 the state of Indiana passed a law for the promotion of vocational education, quite comprehensive in that it applies to agricultural and domestic training as well as to industry in its narrower sense. Its main administrative features are well considered, and fit it, in a general way, for imitation by states considering action. The interests of vocational education are entrusted to the State Board which has charge of other school interests, with provision for needed additional agencies. The fiscal measures are sensible, providing that each locality provide buildings, equipment, etc., out of local tax funds, while the state will meet two-thirds of the special expense for instruction.

Unfortunately, the distinctively educational provisions do not equally well fit the law to serve as a model. The bodies which have been most active in pushing industrial education in this country have a pronounced fear lest funds and other agencies furnished for it be diverted to the purposes of general education. This fear, which has some justification, seems to have dictated the measures of the Indiana law. The fear works to put a fence around industrial education, to mark it off as sharply as possible from other school activities and interests. Everything must proclaim and emphasize the distinctively industrial aim. However laudable this purpose, it does harm to the real cause of industrial education when it leads to distrust of existing school authorities, teachers and facilities, and when it operates to exclude the concrete facts of the local situation from exercising due influence upon the measures taken. To shape a law on the basis of fear rather than with regard to actual conditions is to act upon theoretical rather than upon practical considerations.

The Indiana system contains features which can hardly be explained except on the supposition that they have been dictated by the fears of theorists. And these features have been still further emphasized by the official interpretation of the law by the State Board of Education. The law very properly makes provision for part-time and evening classes—in other words, for "continuation" schools. But it provides for state aid only if the instruction in them "deals with the subject matter of the day employment," or is complementary to such employment. In line with this requirement the official statement says, "It is important to provide a means whereby the workers who have got into 'blind alley' jobs may be able to fit themselves for more skilled occupations, but a school having this aim cannot be state-aided." It also rules that training which aims at fitting workers for more remunerative or more skilled trades than those in which they are actually employed cannot be aided by the state funds. The classes "must give instruction which will actually add to the stock-in-trade of a wage-earner who has already entered upon the skilled calling he expects to follow as his life work." But even this statement is too mild. The intention of the law seems to aim at keeping as the life work of a wage-earner that upon which he has actually entered, even if he might himself wish a change. For the statement goes on, "A practical farmer would not be eligible to enter a class in plumbing or a plumber to a class in market gardening in a state-aided vocational evening class."

So far as the regular or whole-time schools are concerned, official construction appears to go further than the law itself. The law reads that "vocational education shall mean *any* education the controlling purpose of which is to fit for profitable employment." But the Board takes the liberty of making the rule laid down for part-time and evening schools apply as far as possible to the regular vocational schools as well. For it defines vocational education as "that form of education whose controlling purpose is to fit for useful and efficient service in the shop, home and on the farm, given *only* to persons who have already indicated their intention to enter such employment, or who are already engaged therein, and who wish to increase their efficiency in their *chosen* occupation." And in order to make quite sure that existing high schools do not receive state aid by adding courses for future wage-earners to the courses they already have, it rules that if an existing school adds a vocational department, it must have a separate head or director, a separate course of study, group of teachers and pupils. This effort at complete segregation is partially mitigated by provision that a portion of the "related academic work" may be taught by regular teachers in case they "have the vocational point of view."

Now all this appears to be theory run mad. I call it theory because it is so obviously due to fear that "general" education will make use of a plea of vocational education in order to grab state funds, while practical considerations would lead to a plan that positively meets the most pressing needs, and would then develop administrative control to prevent abuse of funds. I call it bad theory because in a state like Indiana—in almost any state except those having a large number of great industrial centres—the plan automatically works against much of anything being accomplished, while it makes the little which can be done work in the wrong direction. One of the chief evils of the present state of affairs is the accidental and unintelligent way in which workers, especially of the youthful age, find their jobs. What then shall we say of a law which says that state-aided instruction is forbidden except in these accidentally selected jobs? What shall we say of a measure which is expressly construed to forbid aid to "schools giving general industrial or prevocational courses designed to enable students to test or determine their vocational aims, or to lay a necessary or helpful basis for future vocational work"? (I insert the quotation marks to assure the reader that the *reductio ad absurdum* is not of my own making.) Add the fact that the youth for whom the law is mainly intended cannot, for the most part, possibly be engaged in very skilled callings; that they are mostly engaged in running odd jobs or "operating" machines that require little but automatic feeding, and the law which requires their instruction to be confined to what they are already doing certainly has little to do with the practical needs of the case. The attention given to eliminating "general education" might, in the case of those engaged in monotonous, routine occupation, well be changed to an insistence that such workers, in the interests of their own industrial efficiency and the economic well-being of the state, have a more considerable general education.

Yet these features are of comparatively slight import compared with the inherent impracticability of the law. Four or five states in the Union have a sufficiently large number of big industrial centres so that they could make some use of a system like that provided by the Indiana law. It seems to have been drawn on the basis of conditions found in New York, Chicago, Philadelphia, Pittsburgh, and so forth. In cities like these there are large groups of workers from which a constituency could be drawn for trade schools of the type to which the Indiana system is restricted—though it should be noted that even in Philadelphia the regular trade schools are not especially popular, since pupils who can afford the time prefer a less limited sort of training. In states where such cities abound, provision should be made for increasing the skill of wage-earners in the occupations in which they are already engaged, such provision being only one factor in a more comprehensive scheme. In Indiana it may be doubted whether there is more than one city in the state where much use can possibly be made of the law. Outside of perhaps Indianapolis, the industrial population in a given city is not large enough, nor sufficiently distributed in permanently marked-off occupations, to create a demand for either regular or continuation schools of a narrow trade type in which the pupils shall be instructed only in the trade upon which they have already entered. Gary, for instance, is one of the largest industrial centres in Indiana. It happens also to be a town which is already famous throughout the country for the breadth and excellence of its school work in pre-vocational and vocational training. It would be interesting to know what use, if any, this city has been able to make of the Indiana law. My guess would be, none, or next to none. If the guess is anywhere near correct, it would be impossible to put in stronger relief the essentially theoretical character of the law.

These remarks are negative in kind, but they point a positive moral. They indicate that a state should adopt a law only after a careful survey of its own actual local conditions and needs. Previous to framing the law, both the industrial and the educational situation in each of the larger towns should be studied. It is "dollars to doughnuts" that if the leading school men of Indiana had been systematically consulted before the existing law was framed, and if what they were actually doing and what they would like to do and could do with greater facilities had been investigated, the result would have been a law which would almost immediately have been taken advantage of by ten or a dozen of the larger cities. The money and two or three years' time spent by an expert commission in making such a survey would save itself a score of times over.

The other chief lesson is that the statute should contain only broad and flexible provisions, and that the State Board of Education should be entrusted with large discretionary powers in its execution. Our American law already recognizes the existence of these powers in the authorities in charge of public health and public education. We have just seen in New York State an educational commissioner overrule in effect, if not in name, a court decision as well as the action of a local board, while from his decision there is no appeal. When the tendency of the day is to commit wider and wider activities to administrative commissions in all modes of public utility, it is no time to attempt to limit, by means of minute provisions of statute law, the duties of such bodies in educational matters. By all accounts, the thing in the Indiana law which has worked best is its provision for agricultural education. With respect to this, there was no organization of theorists to influence the law, and more freedom was allowed. Its provision for county agents in agriculture is one which might well be imitated by other states in providing for industrial education. At the present time nothing would be more useful than a body of experts who should be engaged in the continuous investigation of both local schools and industries, and who should influence public opinion, make suggestions and institute experiments. The American habit of passing minute laws and then leaving their administration to look out for itself is nowhere more useless or more harmful than in matters of education.

NOTES

First published in *New Republic* 2 (1915): 71–73, reprint, in MW.8.118–123.

1. See Chas. A. Greathouse, *Indiana School Laws: Enacted by the General Assemblies of 1913 and 1915* (Fort Wayne, IN: Fort Wayne Printing Co., Contractors for State Printing and Binding, 1916), 73.
2. Jenny Froehle, "What the Standards-Based Movement Got Wrong," *Education Week,* November 28, 2017, https://www.edweek.org/ew/articles/2017/11/29/what-the-standards-based-movement-got-wrong.html.

21

Why Have Progressive Schools?

(1933)

EDITOR'S INTRODUCTION

"Why Have Progressive Schools?" appeared in *Current History*, a periodical founded in 1914 by the *New York Times*. The publication's longer format permitted Dewey space to begin with some history of education in the United States. Changing times and environments led to changes in schooling, and in the scope of that history, progressive education arose as a set of experiments. Traditional schooling in contrast built on memorization of material as well as harsh disciplinary practices intended to produce obedience to authority. Dewey argued that if nothing else, the advances that progressive schools had achieved and that had been taken up in traditional schools suffice to show the value of the former's experiments. At bottom, progressive schools built on the best insights from psychology and the scientific study of education for forming a new curriculum and set of methods for the education of young people, rooted in individual interest and growth.

Today, public schools in nineteen states still make use of corporal punishment, a harsh form of disciplinary action that empirical studies have shown to be associated with detrimental long-term outcomes.[1] Dewey's essay still speaks to people who in a number of ways resist experimentation in schooling and who make use of outmoded and poorly supported educational curricula and disciplinary methods.

One of the commonest charges brought against the progressive schools and schoolmasters who advocate modern methods is that they express the aims of their kind of education in vague and general terms. What they say sounds well, but what does it mean?

What is any education for? Let the reader try to answer this question. He will evolve a generalized formula much like those of the specialists. However definite his own picture of what he means may be, the words he uses will be capable of as many interpretations as he has listeners. This is as true of the statements of the aims of old-fashioned education as of those of the most advanced schools. Some of the shortest and simplest answers are: A preparation for life; to learn to live; to give the child what he needs, or will need, to know; to develop good citizens; to develop well-rounded, happy, efficient individuals. Can the reader point to any one of these and say with confidence, "This belongs to the new," or, "This rules out the new"? No, not of these, nor of any other definitions of the purpose of education. He cannot because the differences of opinion about what education should be lie, not in the purpose of education, but in personal views about people and society.

The purpose of education has always been to every one, in essence, the same—to give the young the things they need in order to develop in an orderly, sequential way into members of society. This was the purpose of the education given to a little aboriginal in the Australian bush before the coming of the white man. It was the purpose of the education of youth in the golden age of Athens. It is the purpose of education today, whether this education goes on in a one-room school in the mountains of Tennessee or in the most advanced progressive school in a radical community. But to develop into a member of society in the Australian bush had nothing in common with developing into a member of society in ancient Greece, and still less with what is needed today. Any education is, in its forms and methods, an outgrowth of the needs of the society in which it exists.

No one is surprised that the educational methods in Soviet Russia are different from those here. That other methods will develop in a Hitlerized Germany is easy to understand. Yet even within two such rigid and controlled societies as these two countries are at present striving for, there is and will be experimentation, discussion and difference of opinion among teachers as to the best methods of developing members of those societies. There will be satisfied parents and dissatisfied parents. There will be happy children who like the schools and adjust to them easily, and children who do not adjust and whose difficulties are blamed on the schools.

The Australian aboriginal, the Athenian, the Soviet citizen, the Hitlerite had, or have, societies that can be defined in definite terms; the aims of which, whatever we think of them, can be recognized by any one. Accept these aims and there will be comparatively little difference of opinion about the kind of education that should be given youth in any one of the societies. In our American democracy aims have, until recently, been stated in terms of the individual, not in those of the society he is to be educated for.

In the early days of education in this country all that seemed to be necessary for the attainment of the ideals of democracy was to give every child an equal start in life by furnishing him with certain fundamentals of learning, then turn him loose and let him do the rest.

The little red school houses of the country were started with a curriculum that did just this and no more. Higher schools of learning were not thought of as general educational institutions, but as strictly professional schools where ministers, lawyers, doctors and teachers learned the technical facts they needed for the pursuit of their vocations. This system of education worked, not because it was an inspired program for assuring the workings of the ideals of democracy, but because life was simple and the country offered almost unlimited opportunity for the individual. Life centred in the home. There, or in a neighborhood shop where his father worked, the child saw the industries of the country being carried on—baking, canning, dressmaking, farming, carpentry, blacksmithing, printing, wheelwrighting and so on. There, by taking part in the daily life, he learned habits of industry and perseverance and imbibed his ethical and moral standards. The small homogeneous community life of the early days enabled him to learn civics at first hand, through seeing and hearing about the running of his own town. There were space, air, fields and trees everywhere accessible, so that his play needed no specialized facilities and supervision. The only opportunities that this sharing in the life of the home and the village did not offer were for "book learning"—the Three Rs. The child went to school to learn to read, write and figure. His life outside school gave him the rest of the training he needed.

Then life began to change. The things once made at home were now made in factories and the child knew nothing of them. The inventions and discoveries in science brought railroads, the telegraph and telephone, gas and electricity, farm machinery—a host of things about which one could not really know without far more training than was given by mere practice in using the finished product. Industrialization brought the big city, with its slums and palaces, its lack of play space, its sharp distinction between city and country. Finally it brought the automobile, the movies and the radio, with their enormous influence in taking the family out of the home and making even the little child much more part of the great world than had ever been dreamed of in the past.

These changes did not happen all at once. If they had, perhaps it would have been necessary to scrap the simple curriculum of the first schools and begin afresh with one that recognized all these new and tremendously different factors at once. Instead, what happened was that gradually, as one new need was felt, a new subject was added to the course of study. The simple device of teaching reading, writing and arithmetic through the medium of the new subject did not occur to any one. Even literature and reading, and penmanship and writing, became four separate subjects. The great increase in leisure and in the well-to-do classes made its contribution, too, to the number of subjects taught. Parents began to demand that schools teach some of the things that would enrich the use of leisure, some of the things that it would be nice to have children know, as well as the things that were necessary to enable the child to get along in the world. Thus art, music, dancing, French, and so on, were introduced into the schools. The growth of wealth and leisure also enormously increased the number of pupils in the schools of higher learning. Gradually the academy or preparatory school and the colleges ceased to be merely places for technical training and became places where one might go to go on being educated more or less regardless of what specific thing one was being educated for. And these schools, too, added more subjects to their curricula as the number of students and their demands increased.

Just as subjects were added one by one to the once-sufficient Three Rs, so the methods that had been adequate for the three continued and were used unchanged. When the child's educational life, in the larger sense, was lived at home, what he needed was practice and drill in the Three Rs, so that he could take them home and use them. So the new subjects were taught by drill, whether the home he would take them to offered any opportunities for their use or not. If these methods were not as successful with the new subjects, the fault lay not in the method but in the fact that because these subjects were new they were frills, lacking in the inherent disciplinary value of the old fundamentals.

The science of individual psychology began to develop after the enrichment of the curriculum was well on its way, so that the two developments went on in parallel lines touching almost not at all. The discoveries of the former about the way people learn, about individual differences and the interrelation of effort and interest, were unknown to schoolmasters, or were thought of as too newfangled for consideration. It was a little as if no one had been willing to put radios on the market because it was obviously an absurd idea that sound can be transmitted for vast distances through mountains and brick walls without special means like wires. And although these psychological discoveries are many of them as well established today as the facts of the radio, they are still temperamentally abhorrent to a great many schoolmasters and parents. A great many others are willing to admit them when stated in general terms, but feel the strongest emotional reluctance to giving children the benefit of them by applying them to teaching methods. In brief, these three discoveries may be stated as follows:

1. The human mind does not learn in a vacuum; the facts presented for learning, to be grasped, must have some relation to the previous experience of the individual or to his present needs; learning proceeds from the concrete to the general, not from the general to the particular.

2. Every individual is a little different from every other individual, not alone in his general capacity and character; the differences extend to rather minute abilities and characteristics, and no amount of discipline will eradicate them. The obvious conclusion of this is that uniform methods cannot possibly produce uniform results in education, that the more we wish to come to making every one alike the more varied and individualized must the methods be.

3. Individual effort is impossible without individual interest. There can be no such thing as a subject which in and by itself will furnish training for every mind. If work is not in itself interesting to the individual or does not have associations or by-products which make its doing interesting, the individual cannot put his best efforts into it. However hard he may work at it, the effort does not go into the accomplishment of the work, but is largely dissipated in a moral and emotional struggle to keep the attention where it is not held.

The progressive education movement is the outgrowth of the realization by educators of the fact that our highly complex, rapid, crowded civilization demands and has been met by changes in school subjects and practice; that to make these changes effective something more is needed than simply the addition of one subject after another. The new subjects should be introduced with some relation to each other and the ways in which they operate and integrate in the world outside of school. It is also the outgrowth of the desire to put into practice in the classroom what the new science of psychology has discovered about individual learning and individual differences.

The kinds of schools, together with the methods used in them, which have developed from the desire to adjust the curriculum to society and to use the new psychology to increase the pupil's learning are numerous, almost as numerous as the schools themselves. When an individual or a group tries to adjust the curriculum to society, it immediately becomes necessary to formulate a conception of what that society is. What are its strengths that should be stressed in the schools, what its weaknesses that children should understand?

Is it a good thing to bring up the young with desires and habits that try to preserve everything just as it is today, or should they be able to meet change, to weigh the values and find good in the new? How much of the background and development of our civilization do children need to be able to understand what is in the world today? How much do they need to become cultivated individuals, able to enjoy leisure and carry on worth-while traditions? The answers to these and many other questions and the skill used in translating them into practice will determine the kind of school. Both these factors will differ according to the temperament, beliefs, background and experience of the individuals who answer them. This to the writer does not seem to be an indictment of progressive schools.

In a world changing as rapidly as ours, in a democracy with so short a history to draw on for choice of the best ways to succeed, expression of differences of opinions by different kinds of schools is a wholesome sign. In developing anything new, it is a good plan to have different methods working side by side, to experiment, to compare. This kind of difference has nothing whatever to do with whether a particular school is a good school or a bad school, with whether children learn what they are taught and are happy and successful at school and at home. Nor does this mean that all progressive schools just by the fact of being labeled "progressive" are good schools. It simply means that progressive education has not one formula, is not a fixed and finished thing about which it is legitimate and safe to make generalizations. It is as ridiculous to say that all progressive schools are good, as it is to say that the principles of progressive education are bad and unworkable because one school is poor, or because one child does not succeed in one school.

We are used to the faults of traditional schools, so used to them that when any difficulty arises we tend to lay the blame on the child or the home he comes from. There are, however, good teachers and bad teachers in traditional schools, and no curriculum, no matter how old, how cut and dried, how uniform it is, can possibly give a higher quality of output than the quality of the teacher who is using it. Probably nine-tenths of the violent criticism of progressive schools as progressive, that is so popular, would melt away like Summer snows if we would look at traditional schools as we look at modern schools, or if we expected only the same amount from them. A progressive school to escape damnation has to be practically perfect, has to give each child just what his particular parents think he should have, has to succeed with every child, if he is a genius or just average, if he is nervously unstable, if he changes schools every year, however queer or unadjusted at home he may be. A traditional school is not expected to make good unless the child fits in, conforms and raises no problems. Two instances of the kind of criticism that is commonly leveled at a progressive school and practically never at an old-fashioned school are the matters of learning to read and of discipline.

Some children are backward about learning to read. They either have great difficulty learning or are so slow about it that their parents begin to think they never will. When this happens in an old-fashioned school the child either gets "left back," and has to repeat the work of the first or second grade, or the school tells the mother that she will have to teach the child to read at home if he is to go on with his class. And without any special fuss every one assumes that there is something the matter with the child. When this happens in a progressive school the chances are that parents and friends immediately assume that it is the school's fault, that the school does not even bother to teach reading, or at least does not think it important enough to "make" the child learn; the child would of course be reading fluently long ago were it not for the school's lax methods. We know today that certain children have reading difficulties, due sometimes to eye peculiarities, sometimes to left-handedness, sometimes to other more obscure causes. The only way to tell why one child does not learn to read is often a rather elaborate examination into all these possibilities. Experience has shown that if the child is mentally normal he will learn to read anyway by the time he is ten or so, and that in after life it is impossible to tell these late readers from the children who teach themselves when they are three.

In the matter of discipline the progressive school is even more subject to attack. If a child misbehaves in an old-fashioned school, he is naughty and his parents meekly undertake to see that he stops giving trouble. If he misbehaves in a modern school, the school is spoiling him, it has no standards of conduct, it sets no store by those sterling qualities obedience and orderliness. It is probably true that a progressive school seems disorderly to visitors who cannot imagine a school except as a place where rows of silent children sit quietly at desks until told to do something by a teacher. But modern education does not aim at this kind of order. Its aim is the kind of order that exists in a roomful of people, each one of whom is working at a common task. There will be talking, consulting, moving about in such a group whether the workers are adults or children. The standard for order and discipline of a group is not how silent is the room, or how few and uniform the kinds of tools and materials that are being used, but the quality and amount of work done by the individuals and the group. A different technique is required of the teacher in such a room from that required by a teacher in a room where each pupil sits at a screwed down desk and studies the same part of the same lesson from the same textbook at the same time. There are progressive teachers who have not mastered the technique. There are good teachers and poor teachers in progressive schools just as there are in traditional schools. But there is absolutely no scientific objective evidence to support the view that behavior problems are relatively more common in progressive schools than in traditional schools, or that the former are less successful in straightening out those that do arise than the latter.

Another common criticism of progressive education is that individual development and the training of special abilities or talents are stressed at the expense of learning social adjustment, good manners, how to get along with adults—that all progressive schools have a highly individualistic philosophy. If we confine ourselves to the philosophy, just the opposite seems to be the truth. It is the modern schools that have formulated their aims in definite social terms. It is they that are trying to work out some method of achieving harmony between the democratic belief in the liberty of the individual and his responsibility for the welfare of the group. A group of conservatives are already attacking them because they have expressed the belief that the schools have a responsibility to educate so that recurrence of present economic conditions will be impossible.

Individualism run riot is laid at the doors of modern schools, probably because it is these schools that first adopted teaching methods based on the new knowledge of individual psychology and on the recent findings about the growth of young bodies. To many the mere fact that children are free to move about, to seek help from others, to undertake pieces of work in small groups is taken as evidence that the aim of the methods must be to develop individualists, to let the children do as they please. These methods were, in fact, introduced because we know that physical freedom is necessary to growing bodies and because psychological investigations have proved that learning is better and faster when the learner understands his problem as a whole and does his work under his own motive power rather than under minute, piecemeal dictation from a boss.

Many others who grow up under the stern old adage, "Spare the rod and spoil the child," cannot bear, apparently, to believe that any more pleasant or congenial method of learning can possibly be good for the young. They cherish many vestiges of the old idea that children are little limbs of Satan and that the only way to bend them to the uses of civilization is force and long training in doing things just because they are told to do them, regardless of whether or not the work is of any immediate use or interest. Without this training, they claim, one will never be able to see a difficult or dull job through to completion in later life. The strong moralistic bias that colors these views seems to make it impossible for their holders to see that in giving meaning, in his own daily life, to the work a child does, there is actually a gain in the disciplinary value of the work, rather than a loss. There is gain because the work is immediately valuable and satisfactory to the child. Therefore his best effort goes into it and his critical powers and initiative are exercised and developed. Moral and intellectual powers increase in vigor when the force of the worker's spontaneous interest and desire to accomplish something are behind them. This is as true of children as of adults. It is these powers that the progressive schools seek to release. If they sometimes fail, if they sometimes make mistakes, it must be remembered that their techniques are still being developed, that they are new. We should remember, too, that the time-honored and hoary techniques of the traditional school do not always succeed in teaching every pupil to extract square roots fluently, or to be able to push every difficult and wearisome task through to a triumphant conclusion. How much shirking and bluffing goes on in old-fashioned schools?

It is also frequently said that progressive methods may work with young children, but that when the high school is reached these schools are forced to give up their methods and go back to the old so that their pupils can pass college entrance examinations. It is true that college entrance examinations require the accumulation of such a vast number of specific facts that a great deal of drill and cramming is necessary if a pupil is to know enough answers to pass. This does not mean, however, that as children grow older the only way they can learn is by drill and cramming, or that progressive methods applied at the high-school age fail to educate. It simply means that to get into college a young person has to spend a great deal of time memorizing details so that he can answer a great many detailed questions.

Some colleges have for a number of years made exceptions in entrance requirements for the graduates of a few progressive schools. Reports are that these pupils have been able to carry on college work with records as good as, if not better than, pupils from conventional high schools. At present nearly twenty progressive schools have completed arrangements with almost all the accredited colleges and universities to begin, in 1936, admitting their graduates on other bases than the passing of the regular entrance examinations. The school will furnish a recommendation to the effect that the graduate has the necessary intelligence to do college work, has serious interests and purposes, and has demonstrated ability to work in one or more fields in which the college gives instruction. It will also furnish a careful record of the student's school life, including his records in the school examinations and his scores in various kinds of diagnostic tests. This will allow these schools to develop the curricula and teaching methods they believe best suited to the education of their students while they are in school, instead of forcing them to train for one special event in the child's future. After a reasonable number of pupils, whose high-school studies were carried on under this system, have graduated from college we shall have an authoritative answer as to whether progressive methods can be used in high schools with pupils who are going to college. If the plan works it will probably do more to reconcile the public to the fact that change and experimentation are needed in education than any other one thing.

Meantime, change and experimentation will go on anyway because life outside the school is changing, because scientific knowledge of the nature of growth is developing, and because parents want things for their children that they did not obtain when they went to school. The real measure of the success of the progressive schools is the modifications that finally take place in conservative schools because of the experimental pioneering. Judged by that standard alone, the progressive movement is making good.

I have emphasized the movement rather than schools as schools. For by the nature of the case, the various progressive schools differ widely from one another, more widely than traditional schools that have only to adhere to well-recognized standards. But also by the nature of the case, the progressive schools have something in common. They all aim at greater attention to distinctively individual needs and characteristics. Hence they are pervaded by a great degree of freedom of action and discussion. Secondly, they all utilize the outgoing activities of students to a much larger degree than does the traditional school. In other countries, especially in Latin countries, their popular name is "schools of action." Thirdly, they aim at an unwonted amount of cooperation of pupils with one another and of pupils with teachers. The latter function as fellow-workers in the activities that are going on rather than as rulers set on high. This fact determines the distinctive character of discipline in progressive schools. It is meant to be self-discipline as far as is possible, gained through sharing in work and play in which all have a common interest.

Within the limits of these three principles, there remain great possibilities of variation. But in spite of differences, their like elements sum up in the conviction that every worth-while education is a direct enrichment of the life of the young and not merely a more or less repellent preparation for the duties of adult life. They all believe that life is growth, that growth, while it involves meeting and overcoming obstacles, and hence has hard and trying spots, is essentially something to be enjoyed now. That learning is not necessarily a disagreeable process is the discovery, or re-discovery, of modern progressive education.

NOTES

First published in *Current History* 38 (July 1933): 441–48, reprint, in LW.9.147–158.

1. Elizabeth Thompson Gershoff, "Corporal Punishment by Parents and Associated Child Behaviors and Experiences: A Meta-Analytic and Theoretical Review," *Psychological Bulletin* 128, no. 4 (2002): 539–79. See also Gershoff et al., "The Strength of the Causal Evidence Against Physical Punishment of Children and Its Implications for Parents, Psychologists, and Policymakers," *American Psychologist* 73, no. 5 (2018): 626–38.

22

Can Education Share in Social Reconstruction?

(1934)

EDITOR'S INTRODUCTION

In the midst of the Great Depression, Dewey firmly believed in the potential of democratizing economies and capitalism. In 1934, when he published "Can Education Share in Social Reconstruction," Wisconsin was the first state to have enacted an unemployment insurance law, which six other states emulated in 1935. Nearly all of the economic controls and safety nets for people that we have today were yet to have been created. "Democratizing" an economy might sound radical today, as the United States has become highly polarized. When it comes to debates about Social Security, however, public officials primarily engage in disagreements about the best ways to fund it.

When this essay was published, great numbers of people were unemployed, experiencing tremendous economic instability, and lacking assistance and protections that we provide today. In this context, Dewey addresses the ideas and ideals driving a harsh economic form of "rugged individualism," which calls for social reconstruction.

Dewey was a great believer in public education, but he notes that schools and teachers are only part of the process of social reconstruction. They can play a role in bringing democracy and social control to economics and to capitalism, yet teachers are influenced by economic considerations as well. Courageous teachers can aid in reconstruction, but their efforts must be accompanied in the wider culture by a movement for change, he explains. In this essay, we can clearly see Dewey acting as a cultural critic, contributing to intellectual and moral leadership through publicly engaged and accessible philosophical writing.

That upon the whole the schools have been educating for something called the status quo can hardly be doubted by observing persons. The fallacy in this attempt should be equally evident. There is no *status quo*—except in the literal sense in which Andy explained the phrase to Amos: a name for the "mess we are in." It is not difficult, however, to define that which is called the "*status quo*"; the difficulty is that the movement of actual events has little connection with the name by which it is called.

For the alleged *status quo* is summed up in the phrase "rugged individualism." The assumption is—or was—that we are living in a free economic society in which every individual has an equal chance to exercise his initiative and his other abilities, and that the legal and political order is designed and calculated to further this equal liberty on the part of all individuals. No grosser myth ever received general currency. Economic freedom has been either non-existent or precarious for large masses of the population. Because of its absence and its tenuousness for the majority, political and cultural freedom has been sapped; the legally constituted order has supported the ideal of *beati possidentes*.[1]

There is no need here to review the historic change from a simple agrarian order, in which the idea of equal opportunity contained a large measure of truth, to a complex industrial order with highly concentrated economic and political control. The point is that the earlier idea and theory persisted after it had lost all relevance to actual facts, and was then used to justify and strengthen the very situation that had undermined it in practice. What then is the real status quo? Is it the condition of free individuality postulated by the ruling theoretical philosophy, or is it the increasing encroachment of the power of a privileged minority, a power exercised over the liberties of the mass without corresponding responsibility?

It would not be difficult to make out a case for a positive and sweeping answer in favor of the latter alternative. Let me quote, as far as schools are concerned, from Roger Baldwin.[2] "On the whole, it may be said without question that the public schools have been handed over to the keeping of the militant defenders of the *status quo*—the Daughters of the American Revolution, the American Legion, the Fundamentalists, the Ku Klux Klan, and the War Department.

Look at the twelve year record! Compulsory patriotic rites and flag saluting by law in most states; compulsory reading of the Protestant Bible in eighteen states, contrary to the provision for the separation of church and state; compulsory teaching of the Constitution by prescribed routine; making a crime of the teaching of evolution in three states; special oaths of loyalty not required of other public servants in ten states; loyalty oaths required of students as a condition of graduation in many cities; history textbooks revised under pressure to conform to prejudice; restriction or ban on teachers' unions affiliated with the labor movement; laws protecting tenure beaten or emasculated; compulsory military training in both high schools and colleges, with inevitable pressure on students and teachers by the military mind." To these forms of outward and overt pressure may be added—as indeed Mr. Baldwin does add—more powerful, because more subtle and unformulated, pressures that act constantly upon teachers and students.

It might seem then that, judged by the present situation, limitation upon the efforts of teachers to promote a new social order—in which the ideal of freedom and equality of individuals will be a fact and not a fiction—tremendously outweighs the element of possibility of their doing so. Such is not the case, however, great as are the immediate odds against effort to realize the possibility. The reason is that the actual status quo is in a state of flux; there is no status quo, if by that term is meant something stable and constant. The last forty years have seen in every industrialized society all over the world a steady movement in the direction of social control of economic forces. Pressure for this control of capital—or if you please for its "regimentation"—is exercised both through political agencies and voluntary organizations. Laissez faire has been dying of strangulation. Mr. Hoover, who gave currency to the phrase "rugged individualism" while President, acted repeatedly and often on a fairly large scale for governmental intervention and regulation of economic forces. The list of interferences with genuine educational freedom that has been cited is itself a sign of an effort, and often a conscious one, to stem a tide that is running in the opposite direction— that is, toward a collectivism that is hostile to the idea of unrestricted action on the part of those individuals who are possessed of economic and political power because of control of capital.

I hope the bearing of these remarks upon the theme of the limitations and the possibilities of educational effort for establishing a new social order is fairly evident. Teachers and administrators often say they must "conform to conditions" rather than do what they would personally prefer to do. The proposition might be sound if conditions were fixed or even reasonably stable. But they are not. They are highly unstable; social conditions are running in different, often opposed directions. Because of this fact the educator in respect to the relation of educational work to present and future society is constantly compelled to make a choice. With what phase and direction of social forces will he throw in his energies? The chief evil is that the choice is so often made unconsciously by accommodation to the exigencies of immediate pressure and of estimate of probability of success in carrying out egoistic ambitions.

I do not think, accordingly, that the schools can in any literal sense be the builders of a new social order. But the schools will surely, as a matter of fact and not of ideal, share in the building of the social order of the future according as they ally themselves with this or that movement of existing social forces. This fact is inevitable. The schools of America have furthered the present social drift and chaos by their emphasis upon an economic form of success which is intrinsically pecuniary and egoistic. They will of necessity, and again not as a matter of theory, take an active part in determining the social order—or disorder—of the future, according as teachers and administrators align themselves with the older so-called "individualistic" ideals—which in fact are fatal to individuality for the many—or with the newer forces making for social control of economic forces. The plea that teachers must passively accommodate themselves to existing conditions is but one way—and a cowardly way—of making a choice in favor of the old and the chaotic.

If the teacher's choice is to throw himself in with the forces and conditions that are making for change in the direction of social control of capitalism—economic and political—there will hardly be a moment of the day when he will not have the opportunity to make his choice good in action. If the choice is conscious and intelligent, he will find that it affects the details of school administration and discipline, of methods of teaching, of selection and emphasis in subject-matter. The educator is, even now, I repeat, making this choice, but too often is making it blindly and unintelligently. If he or she is genuinely committed to alliance with present forces that tend to develop a social order which will, through collective control and ownership, make possible a genuine and needed "rugged individualism" (in the sense of individuality) for all members of the community, the teacher will, moreover, not be content with generalities about the desired future order. The task is to translate the desired ideal over into the conduct of the detail of the school in administration, instruction, and subject-matter. Here, it seems to me, is the great present need and responsibility of those who think the schools should consciously be partners in the construction of a changed society. The challenge to teachers must be issued and in clear tones. But the challenge is merely a beginning. What does it mean in the particulars of work in the school and on the playground? An answer to this question and not more general commitment to social theory and slogans is the pressing demand.

In spite of the lethargy and timidity of all too many teachers, I believe there are enough teachers who will respond to the great task of making schools active and militant participants in creation of a new social order, provided they are shown not merely the general end in view but also the means of its accomplishment. Dr. Kandel,[3] at the close of a somewhat scornful article as to the part of the schools in this task of social reconstruction, says of society in general: "It would welcome help from any direction to correct the existing abuses and make it true to itself; beyond that it would not permit the schools to go. If the teaching body, whose duty it is to define and interpret society's culture and ideal to the oncoming generation, undertook this much it would still be faced with a formidable task; it may lay the basis for a new social order, but society and not the teaching body will determine its particulars."

There are, in this statement, many words and phrases that I am tempted to underscore: correction of abuses; the duty of the teacher; the basis for a new social order; leaving particulars to society. But I content myself with asking what more can any educator, however "radical," want? Abuses cannot be corrected by merely negative means; they can be eliminated only by substitution of just and humane conditions. Laying the basis, intellectual and moral, for a new social order is a sufficiently novel and inspiring ideal to arouse a new spirit in the teaching profession and to give direction to radically changed effort. Those who hold such an ideal are false to what they profess in words when they line up with reactionaries by ridicule of those who would make the profession a reality. That task may well be left to educational fascists.

NOTES

First published in *Social Frontier* 1 (October 1934): 11–12, reprint, in LW.9.205–210.

1. [Editor's clarification: This phrase means essentially "blessed are those who possess."]
2. [Editor's note: Roger Baldwin cofounded the American Civil Liberties Union (ACLU).]
3. [Editor's note: Dr. Isaac Leon Kandel earned his Ph.D. at Teachers College, Columbia University, where he served as an instructor, associate professor, and then professor of education. He was a scholar of the history of education, especially of secondary education, comparative education, and educational theory.]

23

Nationalizing Education

(1916)

EDITOR'S INTRODUCTION

In July of 1916, Dewey delivered this address at the annual conference of the National Education Association. World War I had begun two years earlier, though the United States officially joined the war the year after Dewey's presentation. The Great War was cause for reflection on nationalism, especially on the uniqueness of the United States from the nations of Europe. In this essay, Dewey highlights one of the key elements of the American spirit, namely, its democracy, which, he argues, is evident in the push for equal opportunity and in the rejection of racism and classism.

The defining feature of Americans is their internationalism, Dewey claims. Today, some minority groups are referred to in a compound way, as African American or Latin American, but Dewey emphasizes that all Americans are compound in origin. That is our special national character. There is no preexisting "American" to which peculiar other characteristics are added. Thus, the impulse to reject immigrants today would represent a kind of treason to American democratic ideals for Dewey.

Although Dewey believed in some potential benefit of increased guidance in education offered centrally, he was no advocate for uniformity, nor for assimilation of differences. He appreciated the value of helping states in need of support. He also saw the nations of Europe as culturally uniform while the United States was a great amalgamation. Among the richer elements of Dewey's point here was that all citizens brought different cultural backgrounds whose strengths and values contribute to the whole that is the American nation. Appreciation for the unique contributions that all people and cultures have to offer in the country was called for in the American spirit of democracy. Ultimately, he believed that teachers were the crucial guides to achieving harmony in union between different people. Nationalized education for Dewey was not about some cumbersome bureaucracy but rather about the education of citizens in the attitudes of respect for differences and of cooperation and learning from all for the sake of democratic flourishing.

In recent years, the movement for nationalizing standards has grown and the "Common Core" curriculum has spread despite devastating critiques about its lack of grounding in educational research evidence as well as the threat it poses to democracy.[1] When Dewey wrote about nationalizing education, he believed in recognizing that Americans are inherently a diverse group, not that they should be rendered more uniform. In his own day, Dewey was a strong critic of standardization as well as top-down dictation in education. As such, readers must not identify Dewey's intentions in this important essay with the movement we have now of high-stakes standardized testing, which Dewey would have rejected as the exact opposite of what is ideal, a point he makes clear in his 1933 speech published in the *New York Times*, "Dewey Outlines Utopian Schools" (chapter 19 of this volume).[2]

The words nation and national have two quite different meanings. We cannot profitably discuss the nationalizing of education unless we are clear as to the difference between the two. For one meaning indicates something desirable, something to be cultivated by education, while the other stands for something to be avoided as an evil plague. The idea which has given the movement toward nationality which has been such a feature of the last century its social vitality is the consciousness of a community of history and purpose larger than that of the family, the parish, the sect and the province. The upbuilding of national states has substituted a unity of feeling and aim, a freedom of intercourse, over wide areas for earlier local isolations, suspicions, jealousies and hatreds. It has forced men out of narrow sectionalisms into membership in a larger social unit, and created loyalty to a state which subordinates petty and selfish interests.

One cannot say this, however, without being at once reminded that nationalism has had another side. With the possible exception of our own country the national states of the modern world have been built up through conflict. The development of a sense of unity within a charmed area has been accompanied by dislike, by hostility, to all without. Skilful politicians and other self-seekers have always known how to play cleverly upon patriotism, and upon ignorance of other peoples, to identify nationalism with latent hatred of other nations. Without exaggeration, the present world war may be said to be the outcome of this aspect of nationalism, and to present it in its naked unloveliness.

In the past, our geographical isolation has largely protected us from the harsh, selfish and exclusive aspect of nationalism. The absence of pressure from without, the absence of active and urgent rivalry and hostility of powerful neighbors, has perhaps played a part in the failure to develop an adequate unity of sentiment and idea for the country as a whole. Individualism of a go-as-you-please type has had too full swing. We have an inherited jealousy of any strong national governing agencies, and we have been inclined to let things drift rather than to think out a central, controlling policy. But the effect of the war has been to make us aware that the days of geographical isolation are at an end, and also to make us conscious that we are lacking in an integrated social sense and policy for our country as a whole, irrespective of classes and sections.

We are now faced by the difficulty of developing the good aspect of nationalism without its evil side; of developing a nationalism which is the friend and not the foe of internationalism. Since this is a matter of ideas, of emotions, of intellectual and moral disposition and outlook, it depends for its accomplishment upon educational agencies, not upon outward machinery. Among these educational agencies, the public school takes first rank. When sometime in the remote future the tale is summed up and the public as distinct from the private and merely personal achievement of the common school is recorded, the question which will have to be answered is, What has the American public school done toward subordinating a local, provincial, sectarian and partisan spirit of mind to aims and interests which are common to all the men and women of the country—to what extent has it taught men to think and feel in ideas broad enough to be inclusive of the purposes and happiness of all sections and classes? For unless the agencies which form the mind and morals of the community can prevent the operation of those forces which are always making for a division of interests, class and sectional ideas and feelings will become dominant, and our democracy will fall to pieces.

Unfortunately at the present time one result of the excitement which the war has produced is that many influential and well-meaning persons attempt to foster the growth of an inclusive nationalism by appeal to our fears, our suspicions, our jealousies and our latent hatreds. They would make the measure of our national preparedness our readiness to meet other nations in destructive war rather than our fitness to cooperate with them in the constructive tasks of peace. They are so disturbed by what has been revealed of internal division, of lack of complete national integration, that they have lost faith in the slow policies of education. They would kindle a sense of our dependence upon one another by making us afraid of peoples outside of our border; they would bring about unity within by laying stress upon our separateness from others. The situation makes it all the more necessary that those concerned with education should withstand popular clamor for a nationalism based upon hysterical excitedness or mechanical drill, or a combination of the two. We must ask what a real nationalism, a real Americanism, is like. For unless we know our own character and purpose we are not likely to be intelligent in our selection of the means to further them.

I want to mention only two elements in the nationalism which our education should cultivate. The first is that the American nation is itself complex and compound. Strictly speaking it is interracial and international in its make-up. It is composed of a multitude of peoples speaking different tongues, inheriting diverse traditions, cherishing varying ideals of life. This fact is basic to *our* nationalism as distinct from that of other peoples. Our national motto, "One from Many," cuts deep and extends far. It denotes a fact which doubtless adds to the difficulty of getting a genuine unity. But it also immensely enriches the possibilities of the result to be attained. No matter how loudly any one proclaims his Americanism, if he assumes that any one racial strain, any one component culture, no matter how early settled it was in our territory, or how effective it has proved in its own land, is to furnish a pattern to which all other strains and cultures are to conform, he is a traitor to an American nationalism. Our unity cannot be a homogeneous thing like that of the separate states of Europe from which our population is drawn; it must be a unity created by drawing out and composing into a harmonious whole the best, the most characteristic which each contributing race and people has to offer.

I find that many who talk the loudest about the need of a supreme and unified Americanism of spirit really mean some special code or tradition to which they happen to be attached. They have some pet tradition which they would impose upon all. In thus measuring the scope of Americanism by some single element which enters into it they are themselves false to the spirit of America. Neither Englandism nor New-Englandism, neither Puritan nor Cavalier any more than Teuton or Slav, can do anything but furnish one note in a vast symphony.

The way to deal with hyphenism, in other words, is to welcome it, but to welcome it in the sense of extracting from each people its special good, so that it shall surrender into a common fund of wisdom and experience what it especially has to contribute. All of these surrenders and contributions taken together create the national spirit of America. The dangerous thing is for each factor to isolate itself, to try to live off its past, and then to attempt to impose itself upon other elements, or, at least, to keep itself intact and thus refuse to accept what other cultures have to offer, so as thereby to be transmuted into authentic Americanism.

In what is rightly objected to as hyphenism the hyphen has become something which separates one people from other peoples—and thereby prevents American nationalism. Such terms as Irish-American or Hebrew-American or German-American are false terms because they seem to assume something which is already in existence called America to which the other factor may be externally hitched on. The fact is the genuine American, the typical American, is himself a hyphenated character. This does not mean that he is part American, and that some foreign ingredient is then added. It means that, as I have said, he is international and interracial in his make-up. He is not American plus Pole or German. But the American is himself Pole-German-English-French-Spanish-Italian-Greek-Irish-Scandinavian-Bohemian-Jew-and so on. The point is to see to it that the hyphen connects instead of separates. And this means at least that our public schools shall teach each factor to respect every other, and shall take pains to enlighten all as to the great past contributions of every strain in our composite make-up. I wish our teaching of American history in the schools would take more account of the great waves of migration by which our land for over three centuries has been continuously built up, and made every pupil conscious of the rich breadth of our national make-up. When every pupil recognizes all the factors which have gone into our being, he will continue to prize and reverence that coming from his own past, but he will think of it as honored in being simply one factor in forming a whole, nobler and finer than itself.

In short, unless our education is nationalized in a way which recognizes that the peculiarity of our nationalism is its internationalism, we shall breed enmity and division in our frantic efforts to secure unity. The teachers of the country know this fact much better than do many of its politicians. While too often politicians have been fostering a vicious hyphenatedism and sectionalism as a bid for votes, teachers have been engaged in transmuting beliefs and feelings once divided and opposed into a new thing under the sun—a national spirit inclusive not exclusive, friendly not jealous. This they have done by the influence of personal contact, cooperative intercourse and sharing in common tasks and hopes. The teacher who has been an active agent in furthering the common struggle of native born, African, Jew, Italian and perhaps a score of other peoples to attain emancipation and enlightenment will never become a party to a conception of America as a nation which conceives of its history and its hopes as less broad than those of humanity—let politicians clamor for their own ends as they will.

The other point in the constitution of a genuine American nationalism to which I invite attention is that we have been occupied during the greater part of our history in subduing nature, not one another or other peoples. I once heard two foreign visitors coming from different countries discuss what had been impressed upon them as the chief trait of the American people. One said vigor, youthful and buoyant energy. The other said it was kindness, the disposition to live and let live, the absence of envy at the success of others. I like to think that while both of these ascribed traits have the same cause back of them, the latter statement goes deeper. Not that we have more virtue, native or acquired, than others, but that we have had more room, more opportunity. Consequently the same conditions which have put a premium upon active and hopeful energy have permitted the kindlier instincts of man to express themselves. The spaciousness of a continent not previously monopolized by man has stimulated vigor and has also diverted activity from the struggle against fellow-man into the struggle against nature. When men make their gains by fighting in common a wilderness, they have not the motive for mutual distrust which comes when they get ahead only by fighting one another. I recently heard a story which seems to me to have something typical about it. Some manufacturers were discussing the problem of labor; they were loud in their complaints. They were bitter against the exactions of unions, and full of tales of an inefficiency which seemed to them calculated. Then one of them said: "Oh, well, poor devils! They haven't much of a chance and have to do what they can to hold their own. If we were in their place, we should be just the same." And the others nodded assent and the conversation lapsed. I call this characteristic, for if there was not an ardent sympathy, there was at least a spirit of toleration and passive recognition.

But with respect to this point as well as with respect to our composite make-up, the situation is changing. We no longer have a large unoccupied continent. Pioneer days are past, and natural resources are possessed. There is danger that the same causes which have set the hand of man against his neighbor in other countries will have the same effect here. Instead of sharing in a common fight against nature, we are already starting to fight against one another, class against class, haves against have-nots. The change puts a definite responsibility upon the schools to sustain our true national spirit. The virtues of mutual esteem, of human forbearance and well-wishing which in our earlier days were the unconscious products of circumstances must now be the conscious fruit of an education which forms the deepest springs of character.

Teachers above all others have occasion to be distressed when the earlier idealism of welcome to the oppressed is treated as a weak sentimentalism, when sympathy for the unfortunate and those who have not had a fair chance is regarded as a weak indulgence fatal to efficiency. Our traditional disposition in these respects must now become a central motive in public education, not as a matter of condescension or patronizing, but as essential to the maintenance of a truly American spirit. All this puts a responsibility upon the schools which can be met only by widening the scope of educational facilities. The schools have now to make up to the disinherited masses by conscious instruction, by the development of personal power, skill, ability and initiative, for the loss of external opportunities consequent upon the passing of our pioneer days. Otherwise power is likely to pass more and more into the hands of the wealthy, and we shall end with this same alliance between intellectual and artistic culture and economic power due to riches which has been the curse of every civilization in the past, and which our fathers in their democratic idealism thought this nation was to put an end to.

Since the idea of the nation is equal opportunity for all, to nationalize education means to use the schools as a means for making this idea effective. There was a time when this could be done more or less well simply by providing schoolhouses, desks, blackboards and perhaps books. But that day has passed. Opportunities can be equalized only as the schools make it their active serious business to enable all alike to become masters of their own industrial fate. That growing movement which is called industrial or vocational education now hangs in the scales. If it is so constructed in practice as to produce merely more competent hands for subordinate clerical and shop positions, if its purpose is shaped to drill boys and girls into certain forms of automatic skill which will make them useful in carrying out the plans of others, it means that instead of nationalizing education in the spirit of our nation, we have given up the battle, and decided to refeudalize education.

I have said nothing about the point which my title most naturally suggests—changes in administrative methods which will put the resources of the whole nation at the disposition of the more backward and less fortunate portions, meaning by resources not only money but expert advice and guidance of every sort. I have no doubt that we shall move in the future away from a merely regional control of the public schools in the direction of a more central regulation. I say nothing about this phase of the matter at this time not only because it brings up technical questions, but because this side of the matter is but the body, the mechanism of a nationalized education. To nationalize American education is to use education to promote our national idea,—which is the idea of democracy. This is the soul, the spirit, of a nationalized education, and unless the administrative changes are executed so as to embody this soul, they will mean simply the development of red tape, a mechanical uniformity and a deadening supervision from above.

Just because the circumstances of the war have brought the idea of the nation and the national to the foreground of everyone's thoughts, the most important thing is to bear in mind that there are nations and nations, this kind of nationalism and that. Unless I am mistaken there are some now using the cry of an American nationalism, of an intensified national patriotism, to further ideas which characterize the European nations, especially those most active in the war, but which are treasonable to the ideal of our nation. Therefore, I have taken this part of your time to remind you of the fact that our nation and democracy are equivalent terms; that our democracy means amity and good will to all humanity (including those beyond our border) and equal opportunity for all within. Since as a nation we are composed of representatives of all nations who have come here to live in peace with one another and to escape the enmities and jealousies which characterize old-world nations, to nationalize our education means to make it an instrument in the active and constant suppression of the war spirit, and in the positive cultivation of sentiments of respect and friendship for all men and women wherever they live. Since our democracy means the substitution of equal opportunity for all for the old-world ideal of unequal opportunity for different classes and the limitation of the individual by the class to which he belongs, to nationalize our education is to make the public school an energetic and willing instrument in developing initiative, courage, power and personal ability in each individual. If we can get our education nationalized in spirit in these directions, the nationalizing of the administrative machinery will in the end take care of itself. So I appeal to teachers in the face of every hysterical wave of emotion, and of every subtle appeal of sinister class interest, to remember that they above all others are the consecrated servants of the democratic ideas in which alone this country is truly a distinctive nation—ideas of friendly and helpful intercourse between all and the equipment of every individual to serve the community by his own best powers in his own best way.

NOTES

First published in *Journal of Education* 84 (1916): 425–28. Republished in MW 10.202–211.

1. Diane Ravitch, "Does Evidence Matter?," *Education and Culture* 31, no. 1 (2015): 3–15; Nicholas Tampio, *Common Core: National Education Standards and the Threat to Democracy* (Baltimore, MD: Johns Hopkins University Press, 2018).
2. John Dewey, "Dewey Outlines Utopian Schools," *New York Times*, April 23, 1933, Education section, reprint, in LW.9.136–141 and here as chapter 19.

24

The Teacher and the Public

(1935)

EDITOR'S INTRODUCTION

"The Teacher and the Public" is among the most furious speeches that Dewey ever delivered. It was first a radio address he gave as part of the NBC series, "University of the Air."[1] In the piece, he used harsh and biting language, calling those capitalists who live off the labor of others "parasites." It is vital to understand the context of his remarks since the essay might otherwise seem out of character for the typically calm and coolheaded philosopher.

Recall that when Dewey wrote this piece in 1935, the country was in the throes of the Great Depression. In 1934, Congress passed the Securities and Exchange Act, which addressed a whole host of dishonest and unfair practices engaged in by the group of owners of capital who lived on interest and dividends paid by the labor of others. Also in 1934, Matthew Josephson helped to further popularize the term "robber barons," who were thought to be the worst of the capitalists exploiting laborers unethically, caring only for higher and higher profits.

In 1935, the unemployment rate in the United States had fallen from nearly 22 percent the year before to 20 percent, still a remarkably high level. Contrast that with a national unemployment rate of 3.9 percent in 2018. Later in the year that Dewey delivered this speech, Congress passed the Banking Act, the Emergency Relief Apportionment Act, the National Labor Relations Act, and the Social Security Act. Public sentiment was powerfully convinced of the need for protections of the people, of labor, against the terrible abuses of industrialists. Three years later, Congress passed the Fair Labor Standards Act, which established the first minimum wage at $0.25 per hour. At the time, $0.25 was worth roughly $4.28 in 2018 dollars.

In his address, Dewey argues that the production and consumption of material goods depends upon the production of intellectual and moral goods. The United States was suffering in part because it needed more and better education, which produces these latter goods. In the face of that greater need, the country was lowering teacher salaries, closing "multitudes of schools," increasing class sizes, and diminishing the quality of the education so desperately needed. Dewey challenges teachers to let go of their common tendency to think of themselves as separate from laborers, for they too are workers. He calls them to let their unity in labor inspire their instruction as well as their fight for change against the class resistant to creating protections for the people from economic instability and catastrophe. Ultimately, he advocates for the formation of teachers' unions, to fight for what teachers need to do their jobs as they should. Teachers are workers, and their work will fail and be undervalued unless they stand up together and with others to fight for education. Teachers' unions today are frequently criticized. Were he alive today, Dewey would likely defend the need for unions, but also call for conflict-resolution measures as well.

Who is a worker? Are teachers workers? Do workers have common ties to unite them? Should these ties be expressed in action? These are some of the questions I want to discuss with you for a few moments this evening.

Who is a worker? I answer this question by saying that all who engage in productive activity are workers. It is customary to speak of a certain class of criminals as "second-story workers." The appellation is obviously humorous, and so it is when we speak of one person "working" another to get something out of him. Not every form of activity, even if it brings in some return to the person engaged in it, is work. It is work only when it is productive of things that are of value to others, and of value not simply in a particular case but when that kind of activity, is generally of service. Those who live upon the work of others without rendering a return are parasites of one kind or another. The man who lives upon interest, dividends or rent is, so far as that includes what he does, a parasite. There is something intellectually and morally, as well as economically, topsy-turvy when honor, esteem and admiration go to a section of society because its members are relieved from the necessity of work. To believe otherwise is to believe that those who subtract from the real wealth of society instead of adding to it are the highest type. Everybody assents to this statement in theory, but in fact the attention given in this country to the rich just because they are rich, proves that we do not live up to our theoretical belief.

Are teachers workers? The basis for answering this question has been given. Are they engaged in productive activity? Are only those persons who turn out material products producers?

Physicians who maintain the health of the community are certainly producers of a fundamental social good. The business of the teacher is to produce a higher standard of intelligence in the community, and the object of the public school system is to make as large as possible the number of those who possess this intelligence. Skill, ability to act wisely and effectively in a great variety of occupations and situations, is a sign and a criterion of the degree of civilization that a society has reached. It is the business of teachers to help in producing the many kinds of skill needed in contemporary life. If teachers are up to their work, they also aid in production of character, and I hope I do not need to say anything about the social value of character.

Are teachers producers, workers? If intelligence, skill and character are social goods, the question answers itself. What is really important is to see how the production of material things depends finally upon production of intellectual and moral goods. I do not mean that material production depends upon these things in quantity alone, though that is true. The quality of material production depends also upon moral and intellectual production. What is equally true and finally even more important is that the distribution and consumption of material goods depends also upon the intellectual and moral level that prevails. I do not need to remind you that we have in this country all the means necessary for production of material goods in sufficient quantity, and also, in spite of the low grade often produced because of desire for profit, that we have all the resources, natural and technical, for production of sufficient quantities of good quality. Nevertheless, we all know without my telling you that millions have no work, no security and no opportunity either to produce or to enjoy what is produced. Ultimately, the state of affairs goes back to lack of sufficient production of intelligence, skill and character.

Why do I say these things which are, or should be, commonplace? I say them because of their bearing on the third question I raised. Do teachers as workers, as producers of one special kind of goods, have close and necessary ties with other workers, and if they do, how shall these ties be made effective in action?

Some of the facts that indicate the answer to these questions are found in the fact that schools and teachers, education generally, have been one of the chief sufferers from that vast industrial and economic dislocation we call the depression. Salary or wage cuts are almost universal; multitudes of schools have been closed. Classes have been enlarged, reducing the capacity of teachers to do their work. Kindergartens and classes for the handicapped have been lopped off. Studies that are indispensable for the production of the skill and intelligence that society needs have been eliminated. The number of the unemployed has been increased in consequence, and the mass consuming power necessary for recovery has been contracted. But along with these consequences, there has been a greater injury. The productive work that is the special business of teachers has been greatly impaired, and impaired at just the time when its products of intelligence, skill and character are most needed.

The cause is well known. It is in part the inability of large numbers to pay taxes, combined, however, with the desire of those able to pay taxes to escape what they regard as a burden. In other words, it is due to the depression on one side and on the other side to the control exercised by the small class that represents the more parasitical section of the community and nation, those who live upon rent, interest and dividends. If something striking, striking home, was necessary to demonstrate to teachers that they are workers in the same sense in which farmers, factory employees, clerks, engineers, etc., are workers, that demonstration has been provided. The same causes that have created the troubles of one group have created those of the other group. Teachers are in the same boat with manual, white collar workers, and farmers. Whatever affects the power of the latter to produce, affects the power of teachers to do their work. By the same token whatever measures will improve the security and opportunity of one, will do the same thing for the other. In both the causes that produce the trouble and the remedies that will better and prevent the recurrence, teachers are bound by necessity to workers in all fields.

Teachers have been slow to recognize this fact. They have felt that the character of their work gave them a special position, marked off from that of the persons who work with their hands. In spite of the fact that the great mass of their pupils come from those who work with their hands on farms, in shops and factories, they have maintained an aloof attitude toward the primary economic and political interests of the latter. I do not need to go into the causes of this attitude that has been so general. One phase of it, however, is definitely related to my main topic. I have said that the business of the teachers is to produce the goods of character, intelligence and skill. I have also said that our present situation shows and is proof of lack of these goods in our present society. Is not this fact a proof, it may be asked, of a widespread failure of teachers to accomplish their task?

The frank answer to this question is, Yes. But neither the question nor the answer gives the cause of the failure. The cause goes back to the excessive control of legislation and administration exercised by the small and powerful class that is economically privileged. Position, promotion, security of the tenure of teachers has depended largely upon conformity with the desires and plans of this class. Even now teachers who show independence of thought and willingness to have fair discussion of social and economic questions in school are being dismissed, and there is a movement, sponsored by men of wealth to label (bolsheviks, reds, and subversives) all those who wish to develop a higher standard of economic intelligence in the community.

This fact brings me to the answer of the last question asked. If teachers are workers who are bound in common ties with all other workers, what action do they need to take? The answer is short and inclusive. Ally themselves with their friends against their common foe, the privileged class, and in the alliance develop the character, skill and intelligence that are necessary to make a democratic social order a fact. I might have taken for my text the preamble of the constitution of the national American Federation of Teachers. A part of it reads as follows: "We believe that the teacher is one of the most highly productive of workers, and that the best interests of the schools and of the people demand an intimate contact and an effective cooperation between the teachers and the other workers of the community—upon whom the future of democracy must depend."

In union is strength, and without the strength of union and united effort, the state of servility, of undemocratic administration, adherence to tradition, and unresponsiveness to the needs of the community, that are also pointed out in the same document, will persist. And in the degree in which they continue, teachers will of necessity fail in the special kind of productive work that is entrusted to them.

NOTES

First published in *Vital Speeches of the Day* 1 (January 1935): 278–79, from a speech broadcast January 16, 1935, over radio station WEVD, New York City, as part of the NBC "University of the Air" series, reprint, in LW.11.158–62.

1. At the time of this writing, there is no known recording available of this address.

25

Democracy and Education in the World of Today

(1938)

EDITOR'S INTRODUCTION

In 1876, Dr. Felix Adler founded the New York Society for Ethical Culture.[1] The society published this essay in pamphlet form in 1938. According to the society, "Adler's lectures before the Society on Sundays were well known and attended, and were routinely reported on in *The New York Times*." Adler died in 1933, but the society continues to this day. It was recognized in 2010 by Mayor Michael Bloomberg, who proclaimed October 23 "New York Society for Ethical Culture Day" in the City of New York to recognize the society's efforts to "promote social justice and improve the lives of underserved New Yorkers."

For the sixtieth anniversary of the Ethical Culture schools, Dewey delivered the first annual Felix Adler Lecture at the Society's meeting house on October 24, 1938. He argues that not only does democracy depend on education for its functioning and flourishing but also democracy is a mode of education. He notes that the United States had made considerable progress pursuing Horace Mann's vision of universal education, or coming close. After serving in the Massachusetts state legislature, Mann was appointed the first secretary of the state's Board of Education in 1837. Mann was known as the "Father of the Common School Movement."[2]

While recognizing progress, Dewey is unafraid to point out where more was still needed. Long before the Civil Rights Movement, he notes a troubling hypocrisy. People felt comfortable and superior when criticizing the prejudice and disrespect for citizens that were rampant in Germany's and Italy's fascisms. At the same time, in America immigrants and black and Jewish citizens were terribly mistreated and often denied an education. The problems that Dewey recognized in his day continue today as we observe troubling findings about a "school-to-prison pipeline" that disproportionately affects poor and minority citizens.[3]

It is obvious that the relation between democracy and education is a reciprocal one, a mutual one, and vitally so. Democracy is itself an educational principle, an educational measure and policy. There is nothing novel in saying that even an election campaign has a greater value in educating the citizens of the country who take any part in it than it has in its immediate external results. Our campaigns are certainly not always as educational as they might be, but by and large they certainly do serve the purpose of making the citizens of the country aware of what is going on in society, what the problems are and the various measures and policies that are proposed to deal with the issues of the day.

Mussolini remarked that democracy was passé, done with, because people are tired of liberty. There is a certain truth in that remark, not about the democracy being done with, at least we hope not, but in the fact that human beings do get tired of liberty, of political liberty and of the responsibilities, the duties, the burden that the acceptance of political liberty involves. There is an educational principle and policy in a deeper sense than that which I have just mentioned in that it proposes in effect, if not in words, to every member of society just that question: do you want to be a free human being standing on your own feet, accepting the responsibilities, the duties that go with that position as an effective member of society?

The meaning of democracy, especially of political democracy which, of course, is far from covering the whole scope of democracy, as over against every aristocratic form of social control and political authority, was expressed by Abraham Lincoln when he said that no man was good enough or wise enough to govern others without their consent; that is, without some expression on their part of their own needs, their own desires and their own conception of how social affairs should go on and social problems be handled.

A woman told me once that she asked a very well known American statesman what he would do for the people of this country if he were God. He said, "Well, that is quite a question. I should look people over and decide what it was that they needed and then try and give it to them."

She said, "Well, you know, I expected that to be the answer that you would give. There are people that would ask other people what they wanted before they tried to give it to them."

That asking other people what they would like, what they need, what their ideas are, is an essential part of the democratic idea. We are so familiar with it as a matter of democratic political practice that perhaps we don't always think about it even when we exercise the privilege of giving an answer. That practice is an educational matter because it puts upon us as individual members of a democracy the responsibility of considering what it is that we as individuals want, what our needs and troubles are.

Dr. Felix Adler expressed very much the same idea. I am not quoting his words, but this was what he said, that "no matter how ignorant any person is there is one thing that he knows better than anybody else and that is where the shoes pinch on his own feet"; and because it is the individual that knows his own troubles, even if he is not literate or sophisticated in other respects, the idea of democracy as opposed to any conception of aristocracy is that every individual must be consulted in such a way, actively not passively, that he himself becomes a part of the process of authority, of the process of social control; that his needs and wants have a chance to be registered in a way where they count in determining social policy. Along with that goes, of course, the other feature which is necessary for the realization of democracy—mutual conference and mutual consultation and arriving ultimately at social control by pooling, by putting together all of these individual expressions of ideas and wants.

The ballot box and majority rule are external and very largely mechanical symbols and expressions of this. They are expedients, the best devices that at a certain time have been found, but beneath them there are the two ideas: first, the opportunity, the right and the duty of every individual to form some conviction and to express some conviction regarding his own place in the social order, and the relations of that social order to his own welfare; second, the fact that each individual counts as one and one only on an equality with others, so that the final social will comes about as the cooperative expression of the ideas of many people. And I think it is perhaps only recently that we are realizing that that idea is the essence of all sound education.

Even in the classroom we are beginning to learn that learning which develops intelligence and character does not come about when only the textbook and the teacher have a say; that every individual becomes educated only as he has an opportunity to contribute something from his own experience, no matter how meagre or slender that background of experience may be at a given time; and finally that enlightenment comes from the give and take, from the exchange of experiences and ideas.

The realization of that principle in the schoolroom, it seems to me, is an expression of the significance of democracy as the educational process without which individuals cannot come into the full possession of themselves nor make a contribution, if they have it in them to make, to the social well-being of others.

I said that democracy and education bear a reciprocal relation, for it is not merely that democracy is itself an educational principle, but that democracy cannot endure, much less develop, without education in that narrower sense in which we ordinarily think of it, the education that is given in the family, and especially as we think of it in the school. The school is the essential distributing agency for whatever values and purposes any social group cherishes. It is not the only means, but it is the first means, the primary means and the most deliberate means by which the values that any social group cherishes, the purposes that it wishes to realize, are distributed and brought home to the thought, the observation, judgment and choice of the individual.

What would a powerful dynamo in a big power-house amount to if there were no line of distribution leading into shops and factories to give power, leading into the home to give light? No matter what fine ideals or fine resources, the products of past experience, past human culture, exist somewhere at the centre, they become significant only as they are carried out, or are distributed. That is true of any society, not simply of a democratic society; but what is true of a democratic society is, of course, that its special values and its special purposes and aims must receive such distribution that they become part of the mind and the will of the members of society. So that the school in a democracy is contributing, if it is true to itself as an educational agency, to the democratic idea of making knowledge and understanding, in short the power of action, a part of the intrinsic intelligence and character of the individual.

I think we have one thing to learn from the anti-democratic states of Europe, and that is that we should take as seriously the preparation of the members of our society for the duties and responsibilities of democracy, as they take seriously the formation of the thoughts and minds and characters of their population for their aims and ideals.

This does not mean that we should imitate their universal propaganda, that we should prostitute the schools, the radio and the press to the inculcation of one single point of view and the suppression of everything else; it means that we should take seriously, energetically and vigorously the use of democratic schools and democratic methods in the schools; that we should educate the young and the youth of the country in freedom for participation in a free society. It may be that with the advantage of great distance from these troubled scenes in Europe we may learn something from the terrible tragedies that are occurring there, so as to take the idea of democracy more seriously, asking ourselves what it means, and taking steps to make our schools more completely the agents for preparation of free individuals for intelligent participation in a free society.

I don't need to tell these readers that our free public school system was founded, promoted, just about 100 years ago, because of the realization of men like Horace Mann and Henry Barnard[4] that citizens need to participate in what they called a republican form of government; that they need enlightenment which could come about only through a system of free education.

If you have read the writings of men of those times, you know how few schools existed, how poor they were, how short their terms were, how poorly most of the teachers were prepared, and, judging from what Horace Mann said, how general was the indifference of the average well-to-do citizen to the education of anybody except his own children.

You may recall the terrible indictment that he drew of the well-to-do classes because of their indifference to the education of the masses, and the vigor with which he pointed out that they were pursuing a dangerous course; that, no matter how much they educated their own children, if they left the masses ignorant they would be corrupted and that they themselves and their children would be the sufferers in the end. As he said, "We did not mean to exchange a single tyrant across the sea for a hydra-headed tyrant here at home"; yet that is what we will get unless we educate our citizens.

I refer to him particularly because to such a very large extent the ideas, the ideals which Horace Mann and the others held have been so largely realized. I think even Horace Mann could hardly have anticipated a finer, more magnificent school plan, school building and school equipment than we have in some parts of our country. On the side of the mechanical and the external, the things that these educational statesmen 100 years ago strove for have been to a considerable extent realized. I should have to qualify that. We know how poor many of the rural schools are, especially in backward states of the country, how poorly they are equipped, how short their school years are; but, in a certain sense, taking what has been done at the best, the immediate ideals of Horace Mann and the others have been realized. Yet the problem we have today of the relation of education and democracy is as acute and as serious a problem as the problem of providing school buildings, school equipment, school teachers and school monies was a hundred years ago.

If, as we all know, democracy is in a more or less precarious position throughout the world, and has even in our own country enemies of growing strength, we cannot take it for granted as something that is sure to endure. If this is the actual case, one reason for it is that we have been so complacent about the idea of democracy that we have more or less unconsciously assumed that the work of establishing a democracy was completed by the founding fathers or when the Civil War abolished slavery. We tend to think of it as something that has been established and that it remains for us simply to enjoy.

We have had, without formulating it, a conception of democracy as something static, as something that is like an inheritance that can be bequeathed, a kind of lump sum that we could live off and upon. The crisis that we are undergoing will turn out, I think, to be worthwhile if we learn through it that every generation has to accomplish democracy over again for itself; that its very nature, its essence, is something that cannot be handed on from one person or one generation to another, but has to be worked out in terms of needs, problems and conditions of the social life of which, as the years go by, we are a part, a social life that is changing with extreme rapidity from year to year.

I find myself resentful and really feeling sad when, in relation to present social, economic and political problems, people point simply backward as if somewhere in the past there were a model for what we should do today. I hope I yield to none in appreciation of the great American tradition, for tradition is something that is capable of being transmitted as an emotion and as an idea from generation to generation. We have a great and precious heritage from the past, but to be realized, to be translated from an idea and an emotion, this tradition has to be embodied by active effort in the social relations which we as human beings bear to each other under present conditions. It is because the conditions of life change, that the problem of maintaining a democracy becomes new, and the burden that is put upon the school, upon the educational system is not that of stating merely the ideas of the men who made this country, their hopes and their intentions, but of teaching what a democratic society means under existing conditions.

The other day I read a statement to the effect that more than half of the working people in shops and factories in this country today are working in industries that didn't even exist forty years ago. It would seem to mean that, as far as the working population is concerned, half of the old industries have gone into obsolescence and been replaced by new ones. The man who made that statement, a working scientist, pointed out that every worker in every industry today is doing what he is doing either directly or indirectly because of the progress that has been made in the last half century in the physical sciences. In other words, in the material world, in the world of production, of material commodities and material entities, the progress of knowledge, of science, has revolutionized activity (revolutionized is not too strong a word) in the last fifty years.

How can we under these circumstances think that we can live from an inheritance, noble and fine as it is, that was formed in earlier days—one might as well say pre-scientific and pre-industrial days—except as we deliberately translate that tradition and that inheritance into the terms of the realities of present society which means simply our relations to one another.

Horace Mann and other educators 100 years ago worked when the United States was essentially agricultural. The things with which we are most familiar that enter into the formation of a material part of our life didn't exist. Railways were just beginning, but all the other great inventions that we take for granted were hidden in the darkness of future time. Even then in those earlier days, Thomas Jefferson predicted evils that might come to man with the too-rapid development of manufacturing industries, because, as he saw it, the backbone of any democratic society was the farmer who owned and cultivated his own land. He saw the farmer as a man who could control his own economic destiny, a man who, therefore, could stand on his own feet and be really a free citizen of a free country. What he feared was what might happen when men lost the security of economic independence and became dependent upon others.

Even Alexander Hamilton, who belonged to the other school of thought, when speaking of judges, maintained that those who controlled a man's subsistence controlled his will. If that is true of judges on the bench it is certainly true to a considerable extent of all people; and now we have economic conditions, because of the rapid change in industry and in finance, where there are thousands and millions of people who have the minimum of control over the conditions of their own subsistence. That is a problem, of course, that will need public and private consideration, but it is a deeper problem than that; it is a problem of the future of democracy, of how political democracy can be made secure if there is economic insecurity and economic dependence of great sections of the population if not upon the direct will of others, at least upon the conditions under which the employing sections of society operate.

I mention this simply as one of the respects in which the relation of education and democracy assumes a very different form than it did in the time when these men supposed that "If we can only have schools enough, only have school buildings and good school equipment and prepared teachers, the necessary enlightenment to take care of republican institutions will follow almost as a matter of course."

The educational problem today is deeper, it is more acute, it is infinitely more difficult because it has to face all of the problems of the modern world. Recently we have been reading in some quarters about the necessity of coalition, whether in arms or not, at least some kind of a coalition of democratic nations, formed to oppose and resist the advance of Fascist, totalitarian, authoritarian states. I am not going to discuss that issue, but I do want to ask a few questions. What do we mean when we assume that we, in common with certain other nations, are really democratic, that we have already so accomplished the ends and purposes of democracy that all we have to do is to stand up and resist the encroachments of non-democratic states?

We are unfortunately familiar with the tragic racial intolerance of Germany and now of Italy. Are we entirely free from that racial intolerance, so that we can pride ourselves upon having achieved a complete democracy? Our treatment of the Negroes, anti-Semitism, the growing (at least I fear it is growing) serious opposition to the alien immigrant within our gates, is, I think, a sufficient answer to that question. Here, in relation to education, we have a problem; what are our schools doing to cultivate not merely passive toleration that will put up with people of different racial birth or different colored skin, but what are our schools doing positively and aggressively and constructively to cultivate understanding and goodwill which are essential to democratic society?

We object, and object very properly, to the constant stream of false propaganda that is put forth in the states for the suppression of all free inquiry and freedom, but again how do we stand in those respects? I know we have in many schools a wonderful school pledge where the children six years old and up probably arise and pledge allegiance to a flag and to what that stands for—one indivisible nation, justice and liberty. How far are we permitting a symbol to become a substitute for the reality? How far are our citizens, legislators and educators salving their conscience with the idea that genuine patriotism is being instilled in these children because they recite the words of that pledge? Do they know what allegiance and loyalty mean? What do they mean by an indivisible nation when we have a nation that is still more or less torn by factional strife and class division? Is that an indivisible nation and is the reciting of a verbal pledge any educational guarantee of the existence of an indivisible nation?

And so I might go on about liberty and justice. What are we doing to translate those great ideas of liberty and justice out of a formal ceremonial ritual into the realities of the understanding, the insight and the genuine loyalty of the boys and girls in our schools?

We say we object, and rightly so, to this exaggerated, one-sided nationalism inculcated under the name of devotion to country, but until our schools have themselves become clear upon what public spirit and good citizenship mean in all the relations of life, youth cannot meet the great responsibilities that rest upon them.

We deplore, also, and deplore rightly, the dependence of these authoritarian states in Europe upon the use of force. What are we doing to cultivate the idea of the supremacy of the method of intelligence, of understanding, the method of goodwill and of mutual sympathy over and above force? I know that in many respects our public schools have and deserve a good reputation for what they have done in breaking down class division, creating a feeling of greater humanity and of membership in a single family, but I do not believe that we have as yet done what can be done and what needs to be done in breaking down even the ordinary snobbishness and prejudices that divide people from each other, and that our schools have done what they can and should do in this respect.

And when it comes to this matter of force as a method of settling social issues, we have unfortunately only to look at our own scene, both domestic and international. In the present state of the world apparently a great and increasing number of people feel that the only way we can make ourselves secure is by increasing our army and navy and making our factories ready to manufacture munitions. In other words, somehow we too have a belief that force, physical and brute force, after all is the best final reliance.

With our fortunate position in the world I think that if we used our resources, including our financial resources, to build up among ourselves a genuine, true and effective democratic society, we would find that we have a surer, a more enduring and a more powerful defense of democratic institutions both within ourselves and with relation to the rest of the world than the surrender to the belief in force, violence and war can ever give. I know that our schools are doing a great deal to inculcate ideas of peace, but I sometimes wonder how far this goes beyond a certain sentimental attachment to a realization of what peace would actually mean in the world in the way of cooperation, goodwill and mutual understanding.

I have endeavored to call your attention first to the inherent, the vital and organic relation that there is between democracy and education from both sides, from the side of education, the schools, and from the side of the very meaning of democracy. I have simply tried to give a certain number of more or less random illustrations of what the problems of the schools are today with reference to preparing the youth of the country for active, intelligent participation in the building and the rebuilding and the eternal rebuilding—because, as I have said, it never can be done once for all—of a genuinely democratic society, and, I wish to close (as I began) with saying, that after all the cause of democracy is the moral cause of the dignity and the worth of the individual. Through mutual respect, mutual toleration, give and take, the pooling of experiences, it is ultimately the only method by which human beings can succeed in carrying on this experiment in which we are all engaged, whether we want to be or not, the greatest experiment of humanity—that of living together in ways in which the life of each of us is at once profitable in the deepest sense of the word, profitable to himself and helpful in the building up of the individuality of others.

NOTES

First published as a pamphlet by the Society for Ethical Culture, New York, 1938, 15 pp. Republished in LW.13.294–304.

1. "About," New York Society for Ethical Culture, https://ethical.nyc/about/.
2. See Thomas L. Good, ed., *21st Century Education: A Reference Book* (Thousand Oaks, CA: Sage, 2008), 267.
3. Mary Ellen Flannery, "The School-to-Prison Pipeline: Time to Shut It Down," *NEA Today*, January 5, 2015, http://neatoday.org/2015/01/05/school-prison-pipeline-time-shut/.
4. [Editor's note: As I said in the introduction to this essay, Horace Mann was known as the "Father of the Common Schools Movement." Henry Barnard was also an influential and noted educational reformer. Barnard was a member of the Connecticut House of Representatives and served four years as secretary of Connecticut's Board of Commissioners of Common Schools. In addition, for more than twenty years he edited the *American Journal of Education*.]

PART IV
Social Ethics and Economic Justice

26

Capitalistic or Public Socialism?

(1930)

EDITOR'S INTRODUCTION

In 1930, the Great Depression was spiraling. In the name of prosperity and thus of the supposed economic interests of individuals, politicians had put in place economic supports for corporations, such as in agriculture, while the masses lacked the safety nets that we have today. Responding to charges that public socialism is government control of the economy, Dewey argues in this essay that capitalistic socialism was protecting the interests of the few, not of the many. He claims that economic subsidies of corporations at the time were not truly serving the old ideal of individualism, which anyway was the dream of a bygone era. The masses of people desperately needed security and stability, but were neglected.

Dewey published a series of essays in the *New Republic* in 1929 and 1930, which he released later in 1930 as a book titled *Individualism, Old and New*. "Capitalistic or Public Socialism?" was the sixth chapter. The book addressed the old idea of individualism in America, which is the still familiar notion today that we associate historically with people like the farmer who reaps the rewards of his or her own hard work and investment. The "dominant party" he refers to at the time were Republicans, who were identified as the party of prosperity, and hence agriculture and select other businesses gained their support substantially. Today, the agricultural industry has dramatically shifted into the hands of fewer and fewer "megacorporations," further undermining the idea that corporate subsidies for farming have anything to do with individualism.[1]

Dewey claims that the dominant party was employing its own kind of socialism, by means of government action and investment in industries or by means of tax reductions. In Dewey's time, however, it was evident that the masses of people were suffering, not thriving, while the few grew exponentially in wealth. Already in 1930, Americans held strongly negative associations with the word "socialism," yet public economic intervention in the name of prosperity wasn't considered to be in violation of individualism. In this essay, Dewey powerfully argues that corporatization and aggregated wealth among the few was no advancement of individualism. Corporate, impersonal interests were the opposite of the promotion of well-being of individuals. Dewey called for forms of socialism that were sorely needed at a time when the elderly lacked the protections we have now, such as of Social Security.

In this essay, Dewey argues that some kind of socialism is coming and inevitable. Today, Americans tend not to think of Social Security, Medicare, and Medicaid as "socialism," because they are American, yet any calls for expanding such social provisions, like President Obama's Medicaid expansion, generally is met with the label of "socialism." Were Dewey alive today, he might suggest that relevant debates today are about matters of degree of socialism. When so many Americans lived on very little, in terribly unstable economic circumstances, Dewey called for a substantial tax increase on the wealthy. He notes here that for the wealthiest Americans, 80 percent or more of their earnings are not income, but gains on capital. He called for a substantial taxation of such wealth, not merely on income, long preceding the same call that Thomas Piketty champions in his 2013 book, *Capital in the Twenty-First Century*.[2]

It is reasonable to think that Dewey today might be an advocate for "democratic socialism," such as we find in candidates like Bernie Sanders, though scholars from a great variety of political points of view have learned from and built upon Dewey's philosophy. It is worth noting how many of the things Dewey called for here in fact came to pass, such as in the increase of the top marginal tax rate, which is the tax rate for those in the highest income bracket. In 1922, it was 58 percent and was reduced to 24 percent by 1929. With the crash into the Great Depression, it rose by 1932 to 63 percent and reached 94 percent by 1944, in the midst of World War II.[3] The income bracket to which such rates applied in 1944, of $200,000 or more, in would be equivalent to an income of $2,956,413 in 2019 dollars.[4] Today, the rate is 37 percent for individuals earning over $510,300 or over $612,350 for married couples.[5] So when Americans say that we cannot afford college for all or universal health care, surely Dewey would note that depends on where we are willing to set our tax rates.

A further point worth considering is the fact that in Dewey's day, the gap between the wealthy and the poor was far smaller than it is today.[6] Advocates for the Trump administration tout our low unemployment numbers, at 3.7 percent in 2019, yet 44 percent of all workers qualify as "low-wage," with median annual earnings of $18,000.[7] In addition, the proportion of Americans of working age who are either working or actively looking for work, technically referred to as the labor force participation rate, stands at only 63 percent,[8] a percentage that is likely considerably lower than it might be if wages were higher.

A final point worth considering as we look to Dewey's 1930 essay is that when he talks about corporations and capital aggregated among the few, he was critical of concentrated wealth inattentive to the needs of the masses. Today, a movement is growing to advance employee stock ownership plans (ESOPs),[9] which represent a kind of democratization of the economy consistent with a more democratic capitalism that Dewey would likely have cheered, so long as it was championed along with the good of all.

I once heard a distinguished lawyer say that the earlier American ideas about individual initiative and enterprise could be recovered by an amendment of a few lines to the federal Constitution. The amendment would prohibit all joint stock enterprises and permit only individual liability to have a legal status. He was, I think, the only unadulterated Jeffersonian Democrat I have ever met. He was also logical. He did not delude himself into supposing that the pioneer gospel of personal initiative, enterprise, energy and reward could be maintained in an era of aggregated corporate capital, of mass production and distribution, of impersonal ownership and of ownership divorced from management. Our political life, however, continues to ignore the change that has taken place except as circumstances force it to take account of it in sporadic matters.

The myth is still current that socialism desires to use political means in order to divide wealth equally among all individuals, and that it is consequently opposed to the development of trusts, mergers and consolidated business in general. It is regarded, in other words, as a kind of arithmetically fractionized individualism. This notion of socialism is of the sort that would naturally be entertained by those who cannot get away from the inherent conception of the individual as an isolated and independent unit. In reality, Karl Marx was the prophet of just this period of economic consolidation. If his ghost hovers above the American scene, it must find legitimate satisfaction in our fulfilment of his predictions.

In these predictions, however, Marx reasoned too much from psychological economic premises and depended too little upon technological causes—the application of science to steam, electricity and chemical processes. That is to say, he argued to an undue extent from an alleged constant appropriation by capitalists of all surplus values created by the workers—surplus being defined as anything above the minimum needed for their continued subsistence. He had no conception, moreover, of the capacity of expanding industry to develop new inventions so as to develop new wants, new forms of wealth, new occupations; nor did he imagine that the intellectual ability of the employing class would be equal to seeing the need for sustaining consuming power by high wages in order to keep up production and its profits. This explains why his prediction of a revolution in political control, caused by the general misery of the masses and resulting in the establishment of a socialistic society, has not been realized in this country. Nevertheless, the issue which he raised—the relation of the economic structure to political operations—is one that actively persists.

Indeed, it forms the only basis of present political questions. An intelligent and experienced observer of affairs at Washington has said that all political questions which he has heard discussed in Washington come back ultimately to problems connected with the distribution of income. Wealth, property and the processes of manufacturing and distribution—down to retail trade through the chain system—can hardly be socialized in outward effect without a political repercussion. It constitutes an ultimate issue which must be faced by new or existing political parties. There is still enough vitality in the older individualism to offer a very serious handicap to any party or program which calls itself by the name of Socialism. But in the long run, the realities of the situation will exercise control over the connotations which, for historical reasons, cling to a word. In view of this fact, the fortunes of a party called by a given name are insignificant.

In one important sense, the fundamental character of the economic question is not ignored in present politics. The dominant party has officially constituted itself the guardian of prosperity; it has gone further and offered itself as the author of prosperity. It has insinuated itself in that guise into the imagination of a sufficient number of citizens and voters so that it owes its continuing domination to its identification with prosperity. Our presidential elections are upon the whole determined by fear. Hundreds of thousands of citizens who vote independently or for Democratic candidates at local elections and in off-year congressional elections regularly vote the Republican ticket every four years. They do so because of a vague but influential dread lest a monkey-wrench be thrown into the economic and financial machine. The dread is as general among the workers as among small traders and storekeepers. It is basically the asset that keeps the dominant party in office. Our whole industrial scheme is so complex, so delicately interdependent in its varied parts, so responsive to a multitude of subtle influences, that it seems definitely better to the mass of voters to endure the ills they may already suffer rather than take the chance of disturbing industry. Even in the election of 1928, in spite of both the liquor and the Catholic issue,[10] this was, I believe, the determining factor.

Moreover, the fact that Hoover offered himself to the popular imagination as a man possessed of the engineer's rather than the politician's mind was a great force. Engineering has accomplished great things; its triumphs are everywhere in evidence. The miracles that it has wrought have given it the prestige of magical wonder-working. A people sick of politicians felt in some half-conscious way that the mind, experience and gifts of an engineer would bring healing and order into our political life. It is impossible to present statistics as to the exact force of the factors mentioned. Judgment on the two points, especially the latter, must remain a matter of opinion. But the identification of the Republican party with the maintenance of prosperity cannot be denied, and the desire for the engineer in politics is general enough to be at least symptomatic.

Prosperity is largely a state of mind, and belief in it is even more so. It follows that skepticism about its extent is of little importance when the mental tide runs with the idea. Although figures can be quoted to show how spotty it is, and how inequitably its economic conditions are distributed, they are all to no avail. What difference does it make that eleven thousand people, having each an annual income of over $100,000, appropriated in 1927 about one twenty-fifth of the net national income?[11] What good does it do to cite official figures showing that only 20 percent of the income of the favored eleven thousand came from salaries and from profits of the businesses they were personally engaged in, while the remaining 80 percent was derived from investments, speculative profits, rent, etc.? That the total earnings of eight million wage workers should be only four times the amount of what the income-tax returns frankly call the "unearned" income of the eleven thousand millionaires goes almost without notice. Moreover, income from investments in corporate aggregations increases at the expense of that coming from enterprises personally managed. For anyone to call attention to this discrepancy is considered an aspersion on our rugged individualism and an attempt to stir up class feeling. Meanwhile, the income-tax returns for 1928 show that in seven years the number of persons having an annual income of more than $1,000,000 has increased from sixty-seven to almost five hundred, twenty-four of whom had incomes of over $10,000,000 each.[12]

Nevertheless, the assumption of guardianship of prosperity by a political party means the assumption of responsibility, and in the long run the ruling economic-political combination will be held to account. The over-lords will have to do something to make good. This fact seems to me to be the centre of the future political situation. Discussion of the prospective political development in connection with corporate industry may at least start from the fact that the industries which used to be regarded as staple, as the foundations of sound economy, are depressed. The plight of agriculture, of the coal and textile industries, is well known. The era of great railway expansion has come to a close; the building trades have a fluctuating career. The counterpart of this fact is that the now flourishing industries are those connected with and derived from new technical developments. Without the rapid growth in the manufacture and sale of automobiles, radios, airplanes, etc.; without the rapid development of new uses for electricity and super-power, prosperity in the last few years would hardly have been even a state of mind. Economic stimulus has come largely from these new uses for capital and labor; surplus funds drawn from them have kept the stock market and other forms of business actively going. At the same time, these newer developments have accelerated the accumulation and concentration of super-fortunes.

These facts seem to suggest the issue of future politics. The fact of depression has already influenced political action in legislation and administration. What will happen when industries now new become in turn overcapitalized and consumption does not keep up in proportion to investment in them; when they, too, have an excess capacity of production? There are now, it is estimated, eight billions of surplus savings a year, and the amount is increasing. Where is this capital to find its outlet? Diversion into the stock market gives temporary relief, but the resulting inflation is a "cure" which creates a new disease. If it goes into the expansion of industrial plants, how long will it be before they, too, "overproduce"? The future seems to hold in store an extension of political control in the social interest. We already have the Interstate Commerce Commission, the Federal Reserve Board, and now the Farm Relief Board—a socialistic undertaking on a large scale sponsored by the party of individualism. The probabilities seem to favor the creation of more such boards in the future, in spite of all concomitant denunciations of bureaucracy and proclamations that individualism is the source of our national prosperity.

The tariff question, too, is undergoing a change. Now, it is the older industries which, being depressed, clamor for relief. The "infant" industries are those which are indifferent, and which, with their growing interest in export trade, are likely to become increasingly indifferent or hostile. The alignment of political parties has not indeed been affected so far by economic changes—beyond the formation of insurgent blocs within the old parties. But this fact only conceals from view the greater fact that, under cover of the old parties, legislation and administration have taken on new functions due to the impact of trade and finance. The most striking example, of course, is the effort to use governmental agencies and large public funds to put agriculture on a parity with other forms of industry. The case is the more significant because the farmers form the part of the population that has remained most faithful to the old individualistic philosophy, and because the movement is definitely directed to bringing them within the scope of collective and corporate action. The policy of using public works to alleviate unemployment in times of depression is another, if lesser, sign of the direction which political action is taking.

The question of whether and how far the newer industries will follow the cycle of the older and now depressed ones, becoming overcapitalized, overproductive in capacity and overcharged with carrying costs, is, of course, a speculative one. The negative side of the argument demands, however, considerable optimism. It is at least reasonably certain that if depression sets in with them, the process of public intervention and public control will be repeated. And in any case, nothing can permanently exclude political action with reference to old age and unemployment. The scandalous absence even of public inquiry and statistics is emphasized at present by the displacement of workers through technical developments, and by the lowering, because of speeded-up processes, of the age-limit at which workers can be profitably employed. Unemployment, on the scale at which it now "normally" exists—to say nothing of its extent during cyclic periods of depression—is a confession of the breakdown of unregulated individualistic industry conducted for private profit. Coal miners and even farmers may go unheeded, but not so the industrial city workers. One of the first signs of the reawakening of an aggressive labor movement will be the raising of the unemployment problem to a political issue. The outcome of this will be a further extension of public control.

Political prophecy is a risky affair and I would not venture into details. But large and basic economic currents cannot be ignored for any great length of time, and they are working in one direction. There are many indications that the reactionary tendencies which have controlled American politics are coming to a term. The inequitable distribution of income will bring to the fore the use of taxing power to effect redistribution by means of larger taxation of swollen income and by heavier death duties on large fortunes. The scandal of private appropriation of socially produced values in unused land cannot forever remain unconcealed. The situation in world production and commerce is giving "protection and free trade" totally new meanings. The connection of municipal mismanagement and corruption with special favors to big economic interests, and the connection of the alliance thus formed with crime, are becoming more generally recognized. Local labor bodies are getting more and more discontented with the policy of political abstention and with the farce of working through parties controlled by adverse interests. The movement is cumulative and includes convergence to a common head of many now isolated factors. When a focus is reached, economic issues will be openly and not merely covertly political. The problem of social control of industry and the use of governmental agencies for constructive social ends will become the avowed centre of political struggle.

A chapter is devoted to the political phase of the situation not because it is supposed the place of definitely political action in the resolution of the present split in life is fundamental.[13] But it is accessory. A certain amount of specific change in legislation and administration is required in order to supply the conditions under which other changes may take place in non-political ways.[14] Moreover, the psychological effect of law and political discussion is enormous. Political action provides large-scale models that react into the formation of ideas and ideals about all social matters. One sure way in which the individual who is politically lost, because of the loss of objects to which his loyalties can attach themselves, could recover a composed mind, would be by apprehension of the realities of industry and finance as they function in public and political life. Political apathy such as has marked our thought for many years past is due fundamentally to mental confusion arising from lack of consciousness of any vital connection between politics and daily affairs. The parties have been eager accomplices in maintaining the confusion and unreality. To know where things are going and why they are is to have the material out of which stable objects of purpose and loyalty may be formed. To perceive clearly the actual movement of events is to be on the road to intellectual clarity and order.

The chief value of political reference is that politics so well exemplify the existing social confusion and its causes. The various expressions of public control to which reference has been made have taken place sporadically and in response to the pressure of distressed groups so large that their voting power demanded attention. They have been improvised to meet special occasions. They have not been adopted as parts of any general social policy. Consequently their real import has not been considered; they have been treated as episodic exceptions. We live politically from hand to mouth. Corporate forces are strong enough to secure attention and action now and then, when some emergency forces them upon us, but acknowledgment of them does not inspire consecutive policy. On the other hand, the older individualism is still sufficiently ingrained to obtain allegiance in confused sentiment and in vocal utterance. It persists to such an extent that we can maintain the illusion that it regulates our political thought and behavior. In actuality, appeal to it serves to perpetuate the current disorganization in which financial and industrial power, corporately organized, can deflect economic consequences away from the advantage of the many to serve the privilege of the few.

I know of no recent event so politically interesting as President Hoover's calling of industrial conferences after the stock-market crash of 1929. It is indicative of many things, some of them actual, some of them dimly and ambiguously possible. It testifies to the disturbance created when the prospect of an industrial depression faces a party and administration that have assumed responsibility for prosperity through having claimed credit for it. It testifies to the import of the crowd psychology of suggestion and credulity in American life. Christian Science rules American thought in business affairs;[15] if we can be led to think that certain things do not exist, they perforce have not happened. These conferences also give evidence of our national habit of planlessness in social affairs, of locking the barn-door after the horse has been stolen. For nothing was done until after a crash which every economist—except those hopelessly committed to the doctrine of a "new economic era"—knew was certain to happen, however uncertain they may have been as to its time.

The more ambiguous meaning of these conferences is connected with future developments. It is clear that one of their functions was to add up columns of figures to imposing totals, with a view to their effect on the public imagination. Will there be more than a psychological and arithmetical outcome? A hopeful soul may take it as the beginning of a real application of the engineering mind to social life in its economic phase. He may persuade himself that it is the commencement of the acceptance of social responsibility on a large scale by American industrialists, financiers and politicians. He may envisage a permanent Economic Council finally growing out of the holding of a series of conferences, a council which shall take upon itself a planned coordination of industrial development. He may be optimistic enough to anticipate a time when representatives of labor will meet on equal terms, not for the sake of obtaining a pledge to abstain from efforts to obtain a rise of wages and from strikes, but as an integral factor in maintaining a planned regulation of the bases of national welfare.

The issue is still in the future and uncertain. What is not uncertain is that any such move would, if carried through, mark the acknowledged end of the old social and political epoch and its dominant philosophy. It would be in accord with the spirit of American life if the movement were undertaken by voluntary agreement and endeavor rather than by governmental coercion. There is that much enduring truth in our individualism. But the outcome would surely involve the introduction of social responsibility into our business system to such an extent that the doom of an exclusively pecuniary-profit industry would follow. A coordinating and directive council in which captains of industry and finance would meet with representatives of labor and public officials to plan the regulation of industrial activity would signify that we had entered constructively and voluntarily upon the road which Soviet Russia is traveling with so much attendant destruction and coercion. While, as I have already said, political action is not basic, concentration of attention upon real and vital issues such as attend the public control of industry and finance for the sake of social values would have vast intellectual and emotional reverberations. No phase of our culture would remain unaffected. Politics is a means, not an end. But thought of it as a means will lead to thought of the ends it should serve. It will induce consideration of the ways in which a worthy and rich life for all may be achieved. In so doing, it will restore directive aims and be a significant step forward in the recovery of a unified individuality.

I have tried to make a brief survey of the possibilities of the political situation in general, and not to make either a plea or a prophecy of special political alignments. But any kind of political regeneration within or without the present parties demands first of all a frank intellectual recognition of present tendencies. In a society so rapidly becoming corporate, there is need of associated thought to take account of the realities of the situation and to frame policies in the social interest. Only then can organized action in behalf of the social interest be made a reality. We are in for some kind of socialism, call it by whatever name we please, and no matter what it will be called when it is realized. Economic determinism is now a fact, not a theory. But there is a difference and a choice between a blind, chaotic and unplanned determinism, issuing from business conducted for pecuniary profit, and the determination of a socially planned and ordered development. It is the difference and the choice between a socialism that is public and one that is capitalistic.

NOTES

First published as "Capitalistic or Public Socialism? The Fourth Article in Professor Dewey's Series, 'Individualism, Old and New,'" *New Republic* 62 (March 5, 1930): 64–67, reprint, in LW.5.91.99.

1. See Farm Aid, "Letter to Congress: Stop Big Ag Mega-Mergers," November 12, 2018, https://www.farmaid.org/issues/corporate-power/letter-to-congress-stop-big-ag-mega-mergers/; and Emily Moon, "Big Ag Monopolies Have Stifled Small Farmers. 2020 Democrats Want to Break Them Up," *Pacific Standard*, July 31, 2019,

https://psmag.com/social-justice/big-ag-monopolies-have-stifled-small-farmers-2020-democrats-want-to-break-them-up.
2. Thomas Piketty, "A Global Tax on Capital," in *Capital in the Twenty-First Century* (2013; Cambridge, MA: Harvard University Press, 2014), 515–39.
3. Jeff Haden, "How Would You Feel About a 94% Tax Rate?" CBS News, December 7, 2011, https://www.cbsnews.com/news/how-would-you-feel-about-a-94-tax-rate/.
4. Bureau of Labor Statistics, "Consumer Price Index (CPI) Inflation Calculator," https://data.bls.gov/cgi-bin/cpicalc.pl?cost1=200000&year1=1944 01&year2=201911.
5. Brookings Institution, "Historical Highest Marginal Income Tax Rates," Tax Policy Center & Urban Institute, 2018, https://www.taxpolicycenter.org/statistics/historical-highest-marginal-income-tax-rates.
6. Pedro Nicolaci da Costa, "America's Humongous Wealth Gap Is Widening Further," *Forbes*, May 29, 2019, https://www.forbes.com/sites/pedrodacosta/2019/05/29/americas-humungous-wealth-gap-is-widening-further/.
7. Louis Uchitelle, "Unemployment Is Low, but That's Only Part of the Story," *New York Times*, July 11, 2019, https://www.nytimes.com/2019/07/11/business/low-unemployment-not-seeking-work.html; Martha Ross and Nicole Bateman, "Low-Wage Work Is More Pervasive Than You Think, and There Aren't Enough 'Good Jobs' to Go Around," *Brookings Blog*, November 21, 2019, https://www.brookings.edu/blog/the-avenue/2019/11/21/low-wage-work-is-more-pervasive-than-you-think-and-there-arent-enough-good-jobs-to-go-around/.
8. Bureau of Labor Statistics, "Labor Force Statistics from the Current Population Survey: Concepts and Definitions," https://www.bls.gov/cps/definitions.htm#lfpr; Bureau of Labor Statistics, "Graphics for Economic News Releases: Civilian Labor Force Participation Rate," https://www.bls.gov/charts/employment-situation/civilian-labor-force-participation-rate.htm.
9. Michael E. Murphy, "The ESOP at Thirty: A Democratic Perspective," *Willamette Law Review* 41 (2005): 655–61.
10. [Editor's note: Here Dewey is referring to prohibition with the reference to "liquor" and to anti-Catholic sentiment that factored into the 1928 presidential election, in which Alfred E. Smith was the Democratic candidate and a Catholic. See Kathleen P. Munley, "The 'Catholic Issue' in the Election of 1928 in Lackawanna County, Pennsylvania," *Records of the American Catholic Historical Society of Philadelphia* 108, no. 1/2 (Spring–Summer 1997): 51–73.]
11. [Editor's note: The Bureau of Labor Statistics' Consumer Price Index Inflation Calculator shows that $100,000 in 1927 would have the same buying power as $1,469,760 in 2019 dollars. https://data.bls.gov/cgi-bin/cpicalc.pl?cost1=100%2Co 00.00&year1=192701&year2=201911.]
12. [Editor's note: $1,000,000 in 1928 would have the buying power of $14,867,514 in 2019 dollars. $10,000,000 would translate to $148,675,144. https://data.bls.gov.]
13. [Editor's note: Here Dewey refers to this essay as a chapter in his overarching book, *Individualism, Old and New*, in which this essay was chapter 6.]
14. [Editor's note: It is worth noting here that legislation was enacted in 1974 establishing employee stock ownership plans (ESOPs), mentioned in my editor's introduction, as a

form of retirement plan. This is an example of political action that established conditions that can prompt democratization in the industrial and private spheres. See Ronald Ludwig, "Conversion of Existing Plans to Employee Stock Ownership Plans," *American University Law Review* 26, no. 3 (1977): 632–56.]

15. [Editor's note: Christian Science is the movement based on Mary Baker Glover's book, *Science and Health*, which argued that sickness is a belief only, an illusion, which can be corrected with prayer, also called faith healing. Mary Baker Glover, *Science and Health with Key to the Scriptures* (Boston: Christian Scientist Publishing Company, 1875).]

27

Does Human Nature Change?

(1938)

EDITOR'S INTRODUCTION

In 1922 Dewey published *Human Nature and Conduct*, one of his most influential works. Consistent with the inspiration that he drew from Darwin's revolutionary insights, he emphasizes the malleability of human conduct. In this later essay, Dewey addresses the obstacles to the reform of human conduct that are erected on the basis of claims about human nature. Calling some things "unnatural" is in very few instances justifiable. In most cases, people call reforms contrary to human nature simply because of the force of deeply entrenched habits of conduct that could in fact be conducted in other ways. "Does Human Nature Change?" is among the most successful examples of Dewey's efforts to write accessibly for audiences beyond the academy.

Today, Dewey's point is helpful for understanding the changes that have taken place with respect to gay marriage. Homosexuality has long been called "unnatural," yet in a generation the American people have made a remarkable shift in their habits of conduct with regard to it.

I have come to the conclusion that those who give different answers to the question I have asked in the title of this article are talking about different things. This statement in itself, however, is too easy a way out of the problem to be satisfactory. For there is a real problem, and so far as the question is a practical one instead of an academic one, I think the proper answer is that human nature *does* change.

By the practical side of the question, I mean the question whether or not important, almost fundamental, changes in the ways of human belief and action have taken place and are capable of still taking place. But to put this question in its proper perspective, we have first to recognize the sense in which human nature does not change. I do not think it can be shown that the innate needs of men have changed since man became man or that there is any evidence that they will change as long as man is on the earth.

By "needs" I mean the inherent demands that men make because of their constitution. Needs for food and drink and for moving about, for example, are so much a part of our being that we cannot imagine any condition under which they would cease to be. There are other things not so directly physical that seem to me equally engrained in human nature. I would mention as examples the need for some kind of companionship; the need for exhibiting energy, for bringing one's powers to bear upon surrounding conditions; the need for both cooperation with and emulation of one's fellows for mutual aid and combat alike; the need for some sort of aesthetic expression and satisfaction; the need to lead and to follow; etc.

Whether my particular examples are well chosen or not does not matter so much as does recognition of the fact that there are some tendencies so integral a part of human nature that the latter would not be human nature if they changed. These tendencies used to be called instincts. Psychologists are now more chary of using that word than they used to be. But the word by which the tendencies are called does not matter much in comparison to the fact that human nature has its own constitution.

Where we are likely to go wrong after the fact is recognized that there is something unchangeable in the structure of human nature is the inference we draw from it. We suppose that the manifestation of these needs is also unalterable. We suppose that the manifestations we have got used to are as natural and as unalterable as are the needs from which they spring.

The need for food is so imperative that we call the persons insane who persistently refuse to take nourishment. But what kinds of food are wanted and used are a matter of acquired habit influenced by both physical environment and social custom. To civilized people today, eating human flesh is an entirely unnatural thing. Yet there have been peoples to whom it seemed natural because it was socially authorized and even highly esteemed. There are well-accredited stories of persons needing support from others who have refused palatable and nourishing foods because they were not accustomed to them; the alien foods were so "unnatural" they preferred to starve rather than eat them.

Aristotle spoke for an entire social order as well as for himself when he said that slavery existed by nature. He would have regarded efforts to abolish slavery from society as an idle and utopian effort to change human nature where it was unchangeable. For according to him it was not simply the desire to be a master that was engrained in human nature. There were persons who were born with such an inherently slavish nature that it did violence to human nature to set them free.

The assertion that human nature cannot be changed is heard when social changes are urged as reforms and improvements of existing conditions. It is always heard when the proposed changes in institutions or conditions stand in sharp opposition to what exists. If the conservative were wiser, he would rest his objections in most cases, not upon the unchangeability of human nature, but upon the inertia of custom; upon the resistance that acquired habits offer to change after they are once acquired. It is hard to teach an old dog new tricks and it is harder yet to teach society to adopt customs which are contrary to those which have long prevailed. Conservatism of this type would be intelligent and it would compel those wanting change not only to moderate their pace, but also to ask how the changes they desire could be introduced with a minimum of shock and dislocation.

Nevertheless, there are few social changes that can be opposed on the ground that they are contrary to human nature itself. A proposal to have a society get along without food and drink is one of the few that are of this kind. Proposals to form communities in which there is no cohabitation have been made and the communities have endured for a time. But they are so nearly contrary to human nature that they have not endured long. These cases are almost the only ones in which social change can be opposed simply on the ground that human nature cannot be changed.

Take the institution of war, one of the oldest, most socially reputable of all human institutions. Efforts for stable peace are often opposed on the ground that man is by nature a fighting animal and that this phase of his nature is unalterable. The failure of peace movements in the past can be cited in support of this view. In fact, however, war is as much a social pattern as is the domestic slavery which the ancients thought to be an immutable fact.

I have already said that, in my opinion, combativeness is a constituent part of human nature. But I have also said that the manifestations of these native elements are subject to change because they are affected by custom and tradition.

War does not exist because man has combative instincts, but because social conditions and forces have led, almost forced, these "instincts" into this channel.

There are a large number of other channels in which the need for combat has been satisfied, and there are other channels not yet discovered or explored into which it could be led with equal satisfaction. There is war against disease, against poverty, against insecurity, against injustice, in which multitudes of persons have found full opportunity for the exercise of their combative tendencies.

The time may be far off when men will cease to fulfill their need for combat by destroying each other and when they will manifest it in common and combined efforts against the forces that are enemies of all men equally. But the difficulties in the way are found in the persistence of certain acquired social customs and not in the unchangeability of the demand for combat.

Pugnacity and fear are native elements of human nature. But so are pity and sympathy. We send nurses and physicians to the battlefield and provide hospital facilities as "naturally" as we change bayonets and discharge machine guns. In early times there was a close connection between pugnacity and fighting, for the latter was done largely with the fists. Pugnacity plays a small part in generating wars today. Citizens of one country do not hate those of another nation by instinct. When they attack or are attacked, they do not use their fists in close combat, but throw shells from a great distance at persons whom they have never seen. In modern wars, anger and hatred come after the war has started; they are effects of war, not the cause of it.

It is a tough job sustaining a modern war; all the emotional reactions have to be excited. Propaganda and atrocity stories are enlisted. Aside from such extreme measures there has to be definite organization, as we saw in the World War, to keep up the morale of even non-combatants. And morale is largely a matter of keeping emotions at a certain pitch; and unfortunately fear, hatred, suspicion, are among the emotions most easily aroused.

I shall not attempt to dogmatize about the causes of modern wars. But I do not think that anyone will deny that they are social rather than psychological, though psychological appeal is highly important in working up a people to the point where they want to fight and in keeping them at it. I do not think, moreover, that anyone will deny that economic conditions are powerful among the social causes of war. The main point, however, is that whatever the sociological causes, they are affairs of tradition, custom, and institutional organization, and these factors belong among the changeable manifestations of human nature, not among the unchangeable elements.

I have used the case of war as a typical instance of what is changeable and what is unchangeable in human nature, in their relation to schemes of social change. I have selected the case because it is an extremely difficult one in which to effect durable changes, not because it is an easy one. The point is that the obstacles in the way are put there by social forces which do change from time to time, not by fixed elements of human nature. This fact is also illustrated in the failures of pacifists to achieve their ends by appeal simply to sympathy and pity. For while, as I have said, the kindly emotions are also a fixed constituent of human nature, the channel they take is dependent upon social conditions.

There is always a great outburst of these kindly emotions in time of war. Fellow feeling and the desire to help those in need are intense during war, as they are at every period of great disaster that comes home to observation or imagination. But they are canalized in their expression; they are confined to those upon our side. They occur simultaneously with manifestation of rage and fear against the other side, if not always in the same person, at least in the community generally. Hence the ultimate failure of pacifist appeals to the kindly elements of native human nature when they are separated from intelligent consideration of the social and economic forces at work.

William James made a great contribution in the title of one of his essays, "The Moral Equivalent of War." The very title conveys the point I am making. Certain basic needs and emotions are permanent. But they are capable of finding expression in ways that are radically different from the ways in which they now currently operate.

An even more burning issue emerges when any fundamental change in economic institutions and relations is proposed. Proposals for such sweeping change are among the commonplaces of our time. On the other hand, the proposals are met by the statement that the changes are impossible because they involve an impossible change in human nature. To this statement, advocates of the desired changes are only too likely to reply that the present system or some phase of it is contrary to human nature. The argument pro and con then gets put on the wrong ground.

As a matter of fact, economic institutions and relations are among the manifestations of human nature that are most susceptible of change. History is living evidence of the scope of these changes. Aristotle, for example, held that paying interest is unnatural, and the Middle Ages reechoed the doctrine. All interest was usury, and it was only after economic conditions had so changed that payment of interest was a customary and in that sense a "natural" thing, that usury got its present meaning.

There have been times and places in which land was held in common and in which private ownership of land would have been regarded as the most monstrous of unnatural things. There have been other times and places when all wealth was possessed by an overlord and his subjects held wealth, if any, subject to his pleasure. The entire system of credit so fundamental in contemporary financial and industrial life is a modern invention. The invention of the joint stock company with limited liability of individuals has brought about a great change from earlier facts and conceptions of property. I think the need of owning something is one of the native elements of human nature. But it takes either ignorance or a very lively fancy to suppose that the system of ownership that exists in the United States in 1938, with all its complex relations and its interweaving with legal and political supports, is a necessary and unchangeable product of an inherent tendency to appropriate and possess.

Law is one of the most conservative of human institutions; yet through the cumulative effect of legislation and judicial decisions it changes, sometimes at a slow rate, sometimes rapidly. The changes in human relations that are brought about by changes in industrial and legal institutions then react to modify the ways in which human nature manifests itself, and this brings about still further changes in institutions, and so on indefinitely.

It is for these reasons that I say that those who hold that proposals for social change, even of rather a profound character, are impossible and utopian because of the fixity of human nature, confuse the resistance to change that comes from acquired habits with that which comes from original human nature. The savage, living in a primitive society, comes nearer to being a purely "natural" human being than does civilized man. Civilization itself is the product of altered human nature. But even the savage is bound by a mass of tribal customs and transmitted beliefs that modify his original nature, and it is these acquired habits that make it so difficult to transform him into a civilized human being.

The revolutionary radical, on the other hand, overlooks the force of engrained habits. He is right, in my opinion, about the indefinite plasticity of human nature. But he is wrong in thinking that patterns of desire, belief, and purpose do not have a force comparable to the momentum of physical objects once they are set in motion, and comparable to the inertia, the resistance to movement, possessed by these same objects when they are at rest. Habit, not original human nature, keeps things moving most of the time, about as they have moved in the past.

If human nature is unchangeable, then there is no such thing as education and all our efforts to educate are doomed to failure. For the very meaning of education is modification of native human nature in formation of those new ways of thinking, of feeling, of desiring, and of believing that are foreign to raw human nature. If the latter were unalterable, we might have training but not education. For training, as distinct from education, means simply the acquisition of certain skills. Native gifts can be trained to a point of higher efficiency without that development of new attitudes and dispositions which is the goal of education. But the result is mechanical. It is like supposing that while a musician may acquire by practice greater technical ability, he cannot rise from one plane of musical appreciation and creation to another.

The theory that human nature is unchangeable is thus the most depressing and pessimistic of all possible doctrines. If it were carried out logically, it would mean a doctrine of predestination from birth that would outdo the most rigid of theological doctrines. For according to it, persons are what they are at birth and nothing can be done about it, beyond the kind of training that an acrobat might give to the muscular system with which he is originally endowed. If a person is born with criminal tendencies, a criminal he will become and remain. If a person is born with an excessive amount of greed, he will become a person living by predatory activities at the expense of others; and so on. I do not doubt at all the existence of differences in natural endowment. But what I am questioning is the notion that they doom individuals to a fixed channel of expression. It is difficult indeed to make a silk purse out of a sow's ear. But the particular form which, say, a natural musical endowment will take depends upon the social influences to which he is subjected. Beethoven in a savage tribe would doubtless have been outstanding as a musician, but he would not have been the Beethoven who composed symphonies.

The existence of almost every conceivable kind of social institution at some time and place in the history of the world is evidence of the plasticity of human nature. This fact does not prove that all these different social systems are of equal value, materially, morally, and culturally. The slightest observation shows that such is not the case. But the fact in proving the changeability of human nature indicates the attitude that should be taken toward proposals for social changes. The question is primarily whether they, in special cases, are desirable or not. And the way to answer that question is to try to discover what their consequences would be if they were adopted. Then if the conclusion is that they are desirable, the further question is how they can be accomplished with a minimum of waste, destruction, and needless dislocation.

In finding the answer to this question, we have to take into account the force of existing traditions and customs; of the patterns of action and belief that already exist. We have to find out what forces already at work can be reinforced so that they move toward the desired change and how the conditions that oppose change can be gradually weakened. Such questions as these can be considered on the basis of fact and reason.

The assertion that a proposed change is impossible because of the fixed constitution of human nature diverts attention from the question of whether or not a change is desirable and from the other question of how it shall be brought about. It throws the question into the arena of blind emotion and brute force. In the end, it encourages those who think that great changes can be produced offhand and by the use of sheer violence.

When our sciences of human nature and human relations are anything like as developed as are our sciences of physical nature, their chief concern will be with the problem of how human nature is most effectively modified. The question will not be whether it is capable of change, but of how it is to be changed under given conditions. This problem is ultimately that of education in its widest sense. Consequently, whatever represses and distorts the processes of education that might bring about a change in human dispositions with the minimum of waste puts a premium upon the forces that bring society to a state of deadlock, and thereby encourages the use of violence as a means of social change.

NOTE

First published in *Rotarian* 52 (February 1938): 8–11, 58–59, reprint, in LW.13.286–294.

28

The Ethics of Animal Experimentation

—

(1926)

EDITOR'S INTRODUCTION

Ethical debates about the humane treatment of animals are even livelier today than they were in 1926, when Dewey published "The Ethics of Animal Experimentation." A growing movement started in the latter half of the twentieth century in which advocates have called for the better treatment of animals in general, especially criticizing the practices of factory farming but also addressing concerns about the treatment of animals in scientific research. Some activists have threatened the lives of scientists who experiment on animals.[1] Today, research ethics policies include significant steps in the oversight of the treatment of animals in research and experimentation on great apes is illegal in some countries.[2]

In Dewey's day, the movement to regulate farming practices concerning the ethical treatment of animals was not nearly as intense, but experimentation on animals was a topic of active debate. In this essay, Dewey challenges the critics of animal experimentation who have vastly more work to do on farming practices, he explains, and who were not considering the moral equation he offered for justifying the use of animals in saving and improving human lives.

Where experimentation aims to extend life or substantially to improve it, there is in Dewey's view reason to make use of animals, albeit while minimizing pain to them. In fact, researchers have an obligation, Dewey argues, to make use of animals in their experimentation, particularly given the difference in the depth of the suffering that humans can bear in contrast with animals like mice.

Today interesting research into the emotions of primates reinforces the policies that have rendered research on such animals among the most carefully directed for the sake of humane treatment.

It is worth noting that Dewey lost his son Morris to diphtheria in 1895 and his son Gordon to typhoid in 1904. The pain of losing one's child is an example of the deep suffering human beings endure in ways that most animals used in experimentation are held not to.[3]

Different moralists give different reasons as to why cruelty to animals is wrong. But about the fact of its immorality there is no question, and hence no need for argument. Whether the reason is some inherent right of the animal, or a reflex bad effect upon the character of the human being, or whatever it be, cruelty, the wanton and needless infliction of suffering upon any sentient creature, is unquestionably wrong. There is, however, no ethical justification for the assumption that experimentation upon animals, even when it involves some pain or entails, as is more common, death without pain,—since the animals are still under the influence of anaesthetics,—is a species of cruelty. Nor is there moral justification for the statement that the relations of scientific men to animals should be under any laws or restrictions save those general ones which regulate the behavior of all men so as to protect animals from cruelty. Neither of these propositions conveys, however, the full truth, for they are couched negatively, while the truth is positive. Stated positively, the moral principles relating to animal experimentation would read as follows:—

1. Scientific men are under definite obligation to experiment upon animals so far as that is the alternative to random and possibly harmful experimentation upon human beings, and so far as such experimentation is a means of saving human life and of increasing human vigor and efficiency.

2. The community at large is under definite obligations to see to it that physicians and scientific men are not needlessly hampered in carrying on the inquiries necessary for an adequate performance of their important social office of sustaining human life and vigor.

Let us consider these propositions separately.

I

When we speak of the moral right of competent persons to experiment upon animals in order to get the knowledge and the resources necessary to eliminate useless and harmful experimentation upon human beings and to take better care of their health, we understate the case. Such experimentation is more than a right; it is a duty. When men have devoted themselves to the promotion of human health and vigor, they are under an obligation, no less binding because tacit, to avail themselves of all the resources which will secure a more effective performance of their high office. This office is other than the mere lessening of the physical pain endured by human beings when ill. Important as this is, there is something much worse than physical pain, just as there are better things than physical pleasures.

The person who is ill not merely suffers pain but is rendered unfit to meet his ordinary social responsibilities; he is incapacitated for service to those about him, some of whom may be directly dependent upon him. Moreover, his removal from the sphere of social relations does not merely leave a blank where he was; it involves a wrench upon the sympathies and affections of others. The moral suffering thus caused is something that has no counterpart anywhere in the life of animals, whose joys and sufferings remain upon a physical plane. To cure disease, to prevent needless death, is thus a totally different matter, occupying an infinitely higher plane, from the mere palliation of physical pain. To cure disease and prevent death is to promote the fundamental conditions of social welfare; is to secure the conditions requisite to an effective performance of all social activities; is to preserve human affections from the frightful waste and drain occasioned by the needless suffering and death of others with whom one is bound up.

These things are so obvious that it almost seems necessary to apologize for mentioning them. But anyone who reads the literature or who hears the speeches directed against animal experimentation will recognize that the ethical basis of the agitation against it is due to ignoring these considerations. It is constantly assumed that the object of animal experimentation is a selfish willingness to inflict physical pain upon others simply to save physical pain to ourselves.

On the moral side, the whole question is argued as if it were merely a balancing of physical pain to human beings and to animals over against each other. If it were such a question, the majority would probably decide that the claims of human suffering take precedence over that of animals; but a minority would doubtless voice the opposite view, and the issue would be, so far, inconclusive.

But this is not the question. Instead of being the question of animal physical pain against human physical pain, it is the question of a certain amount of physical suffering to animals—reduced in extent to a minimum by the precautions of anaesthesia, asepsis, and skill—against the bonds and relations which hold people together in society, against the conditions of social vigor and vitality, against the deepest of shocks and interferences to human love and service.

No one who has faced this issue can be in doubt as to where the moral right and wrong lie. To prefer the claims of the physical sensations of animals to the prevention of death and the cure of disease—probably the greatest sources of poverty, distress, and inefficiency, and certainly the greatest sources of moral suffering—does not rise even to the level of sentimentalism.

It is accordingly the duty of scientific men to use animal experimentation as an instrument in the promotion of social well-being; and it is the duty of the general public to protect these men from attacks that hamper their work. It is the duty of the general public to sustain them in their endeavors. For physicians and scientific men, though having their individual failings and fallibilities like the rest of us, are in this matter acting as ministers and ambassadors of the public good.

II

This brings us to the second point: What is the duty of the community regarding legislation that imposes special restrictions upon the persons engaged in scientific experimentation with animals? That it is the duty of the State to pass general laws against cruelty to animals is a fact recognized by well-nigh all civilized States. But opponents of animal experimentation are not content with such general legislation; they demand what is in effect, if not legally, class legislation, putting scientific men under peculiar surveillance and limitation. Men in slaughterhouses, truck drivers, hostlers, cattle and horse owners, farmers and stable keepers, may be taken care of by general legislation; but educated men, devoted to scientific research, and physicians, devoted to the relief of suffering humanity, need some special supervision and regulation!

Unprejudiced people naturally inquire after the right and the wrong of this matter. Hearing accusations of wantonly cruel deeds—actuated by no higher motive than passing curiosity—brought against workers in laboratories and teachers in classrooms, at first they may be moved to believe that additional special legislation is required. Further thought leads, however, to a further question: If these charges of cruelty are justified, why are not those guilty of it brought up for trial in accordance with the laws already provided against cruelty to animals? Consideration of the fact that the remedies and punishments already provided are not resorted to by those so vehement in their charges against scientific workers leads the unprejudiced inquirer to a further conclusion.

Agitation for new laws is not so much intended to prevent specific instances of cruelty to animals as to subject scientific inquiry to hampering restrictions. The moral issue changes to this question: What ought to be the moral attitude of the public toward the proposal to put scientific inquiry under restrictive conditions? No one who really asks himself this question—without mixing it up with the other question of cruelty to animals that is taken care of by already existing laws—can, I imagine, be in doubt as to its answer. Nevertheless, one consideration should be emphasized. *Scientific inquiry has been the chief instrumentality in bringing man from barbarism to civilization, from darkness to light, while it has incurred, at every step, determined opposition from the powers of ignorance, misunderstanding, and jealousy.*

It is not so long ago, as years are reckoned, that a scientist in a physical or chemical laboratory was popularly regarded as a magician engaged in unlawful pursuits, or as in impious converse with evil spirits, about whom all sorts of detrimental stories were circulated and believed. Those days have gone; generally speaking, the value of free scientific inquiry as an instrumentality of social progress and enlightenment is acknowledged. At the same time, it is possible, by making irrelevant emotional appeals and obscuring the real issues, to galvanize into life something of the old spirit of misunderstanding, envy, and dread of science. The point at issue in the subjection of animal experimenters to special supervision and legislation is thus deeper than at first sight appears. In principle it involves the revival of that animosity to discovery and to the application to life of the fruits of discovery which, upon the whole, has been the chief foe of human progress. It behooves every thoughtful individual to be constantly on the alert against every revival of this spirit, in whatever guise it presents itself.

III

It would be agreeable to close with these positive statements of general principles; but it is hardly possible to avoid saying a few words regarding the ethics of the way in which the campaign against animal experimentation is often waged. Exaggerated statements, repetitions of allegations of cruelty which have never been proved or even examined, use of sporadic cases of cruelty to animals in Europe a generation or two ago as if they were typical of the practice in the United States today, refusal to accept the testimony of reputable scientific men regarding either their own procedure or the benefits that have accrued to humanity and to the brute kingdom itself from animal experimentation, uncharitable judgment varying from vague insinuation to downright aspersion—these things certainly have an ethical aspect which must be taken into account by unbiased men and women desirous that right and justice shall prevail.

It is also a fair requirement that some kind of perspective and proportion shall be maintained in moral judgments. Doubtless more suffering is inflicted upon animals in a single day in a single abattoir in some one city of our country than in a year, or years, in all the scientific and medical laboratories of all the United States. Do they come into court with clean hands who complacently, without protest and without effort to remedy or to alleviate existing evils, daily satisfy their own physical appetites at the cost of the death of animals after suffering, in order then to turn around and cry out against a relatively insignificant number of deaths occurring, after skilled precautions against suffering, in the cause of advancement of knowledge for the sake of the relief of humanity? Surely, until it is finally decided that the taking of animal life for human food is wrong, there is something morally unsound in any agitation which questions the right to take animal life in the interests of the life and health of men, women, and children, especially when infinitely more precautions are used to avoid animal suffering in the latter case than in the former.

NOTES

First published in *Atlantic Monthly* 138 (September 1926): 343–46, reprint, in LW.2.98–103.

1. Thomas G. Watkins, "Researchers to Animal-Rights Activists: We're Not Afraid," CNN, October 8, 2009, http://www.cnn.com/2009/CRIME/10/08/animal.rights.threats/index.html.
2. Today, there are bans on great ape research or severe restrictions on such research in a number of European countries, including the Netherlands, the United Kingdom, Sweden, Germany, and Austria, as well as in New Zealand. Pascal Gagneux, James J. Moore, and Ajit Varki, "The Ethics of Research on Great Apes," *Nature* 437 (September 2005), 27–29.

3. It is certainly fair to say that humans are not the only animals who grieve. Researchers are studying animal emotions and the more we learn, the better we can inform our policies and practices. See Mark Bekoff, "Grief in Animals: It's Arrogant to Think We're the Only Animlas Who Mourn," *Psychology Today*, October 29, 2009, https://www.psychologytoday.com/us/blog/animal-emotions/200910/grief-in-animals-its-arrogant-think-were-the-only-animals-who-mourn.

29

Ethics and International Relations

(1923)

EDITOR'S INTRODUCTION

In this essay, published five years after the end of World War I, Dewey takes a historical look at moral frameworks that have had influence in international affairs. The first and longest lasting among these was the natural law tradition, which was generally associated with Christianity. Dewey notes that the natural law tradition had left little result in law or policy at the international level, even though it bore so many ties to the values of Christians throughout Europe. Modern moral theories, both utilitarian—based on maximizing the happiness of the greatest number of people—and Hegelian or Hobbesian—based on the belief that moral authority resides in a supreme national sovereign—lacked coherence at the international level as grounds for ethics. Remember that in Dewey's day the world was not flat in the sense popularized by Thomas Friedman. Communications were not instantaneous, and distances were considerably more difficult to travel.

Among Dewey's central claims is that "one important factor in the present problem of ethics and international relations is found on the side of ethical beliefs themselves in their confused and contending divergencies." Showing the history of flaws in ethical bases at the international level, Dewey does offer one centerpiece on which ethics in international relations could be based: the outlawing of war. Dewey's proposal may seem utopian. Consider, however, that at one time it was permitted to resolve disputes through the use of duels. Outlawing duels might have sounded utopian at one point also. Dewey argues that until war is called illegal, international relations had no real potential for the development of a meaningful set of shared moral values.

Dewey and others contributed to the peace movement that inspired the Kellogg-Briand Pact of 1928, signed in Paris, which sought to avoid another World War. When we consider the matter today, wars are typically justified only on defensive grounds, complex and contested though they may be. Given that, in general, wars of aggression or conquest are considered illegitimate and unjust today.

The situation that exists among nations in their relations to one another is such that it tempts even those who ordinarily come far short of cynicism to say that there is no connection between ethics and international relations. The title is also a temptation to indulge in a drastic attack upon present international relations as inherently immoral. One might make out a case for the proposition that they are ruled by force, fraud and secret intrigue, and that whenever moral considerations come into conflict with national ambitions and nationalistic ideas they go by the board. Or, identifying the moral with that which ought to be, whether it is or not, one might appeal to some ideal of what ought to be and point out the discrepancies that are found between this ideal of what should be and what actually is. The latter method naturally terminates in exhortation, in appeal to the moral consciousness of mankind.

These considerations are not adduced in order to develop them, but to suggest the extraordinary confusion that is found in current moral ideas as they are reflected in the ethics of international relations. I do not intend, then, to discuss international relations from the moral point of view, but rather to discuss the uncertain estate, the almost chaotic condition, of moral conceptions and beliefs as that condition bears upon the international situation. Why is it that men's morals have so little effect in regulating the attitude of nations to one another? Even the most cynical would hesitate to declare that the habits, to say nothing of the ideals, of the average decent man and woman in their ordinary affairs were adequately embodied in the existing reign of hatred, suspicion, fear and secrecy in international politics. The truth seems to be rather that man's morals are paralyzed when it comes to international conduct; that they are swept away and rendered impotent by larger forces that go their own way irrespective of the morals that are employed in everyday matters.

The problems suggested by this state of affairs may be approached from two angles. We may ask what are the actual forces that have grown so powerful that they have escaped from moral control? What are the factors that prevent moral habits and ideas from operation? This opens a large and extremely complex field to be attacked only by cooperative efforts of historians, publicists, lawyers, and economists. There is open, however, a less pretentious method of approach. One may make the inquiry from the side of moral conceptions and doctrines, and ask whether they are intellectually competent to meet the needs of the situation. Some of the trouble may be due to the lack of coherent and generally accepted moral ideas; not of ideas in a vague and abstract sense but of ideas sufficiently concrete to be operative. This intellectual factor may not be in itself very large or powerful, and yet it may represent a factor that, although small in itself, is an indispensable condition of straightening out objective political and economic forces that are much more energetic and active.

In such an appraisal the historic conditions under which the laws applicable to international relations were formulated furnish a natural starting point. There can be no doubt that the intellectual work of Grotius and his successors had great practical influence.[1] It was not academic and professorial, nor was it conceived primarily in the interests of the claims and ambitions of some particular state. These men were genuinely international, and for a time they had great effect in appeasing international strife and moralizing actual international relations. These basic contributions all sprang from a common moral source. They all expressed the idea of laws of nature which are moral laws of universal validity. The conception of laws of nature that are the fundamental moral laws of all human conduct of every kind and at all times and places was not a new one. Roman moralists had worked out the idea in connection with Roman jurisprudence; it was familiar to every civilian and canonist, and indeed to every educated man.

The Catholic church had made the notion fundamental to its whole doctrine of secular ethics, that is of all obligations not springing from divine revelation. And even these obligations only expressed a higher and more ultimate nature of things not accessible to man's unaided reason. The Protestant moralists and theologians equally built upon the conception; at most they only put a greater emphasis upon an inner light in the conscience of individuals which revealed and acknowledged the laws of nature as the supreme standards of human behavior.

There was thus a principle and method of morals which was universally recognized throughout Christendom; there was also general agreement as to the contents of the code of obligations defined by the principle. The great achievement of Grotius and his followers consisted in studying existing international customs and in criticizing and organizing them by the help of the commonly accepted standard of laws of nature. More than one living authority in jurisprudence—like Pollock—has pointed out the service rendered by the conception of laws of nature in the development of various branches of law, private as well as public, and in equity practice.[2] They all agree that its use in formulating the rules governing international conduct was its first and most conspicuous service. Now I do not mean to intimate that without responsive factors in the actual political and economic situation the intellectual application of the concept of natural laws to international relations would have exercised the moderating and humane influence which followed upon the labors of the school of Grotius. But it is meant that the general unquestioning and pervasive acknowledgment of the law of nature as the supreme ethical standard enabled the moral sentiments and ideals of Christendom to be concentrated upon problems of international conduct, so that whatever moral ideas can accomplish in practical regulation of human behavior was effectually accomplished.

During the nineteenth century, the notion of natural law in morals fell largely into discredit and disuse outside the orthodox moralists of the Catholic church. Of recent years there has been an increasing recognition that in principle all that is meant by a law of nature is a moral law to be applied to the criticism and construction of positive law, legislative and judicial. It has been pointed out that either we must surrender the notion that moral principles have anything to do with positive laws, international and municipal, or else admit the idea of natural law in some shape or form. But there is a wide difference between admitting the general notion of moral laws over against custom and positive law, and imputing to the law of nature the character and content which was attributed to it by seventeenth century moralists. While Grotius asserted that the law of nature would still be binding even if there were no revelation and no God as supreme lawgiver and judge, yet in the popular mind and in his mind the idea still had a theological background and a religious force. The laws of nature still represented the purposes of God and his injunctions concerning the ways in which his purposes as governing the life of man were to be realized. The secular science as well as the secular morals of the period only substituted "secondary" causes and laws for the primary and direct action of God.

But as men's minds gradually got away from the habit of connecting secular things with theological and religious matters, primary or secondary, the enormous force of the religious associations and sanctions of the law of nature gradually ceased. And among Protestants at least, even among those in whom religious ideas retained their old force in morality, most men got out of the habit of associating the religious factor in morals with laws of nature and indeed, to a large extent, with law at all. Divine love and desire for man replaced the concept of divine commands, injunctions and prohibitions. Thus in international relations, as elsewhere, the notion of a definite and universal moral norm in the shape of laws of nature weakened and died out. Even when retained, as in some texts, it was in perfunctory deference to tradition rather than as a living intellectual force. But its decay has not been accompanied by the development of any other moral principle of equal generality and equally wide current acceptance. In its stead we have a multiplicity of moral doctrines, more or less opposed to one another, and none of them held with any great assurance except by a small band of ardent partisans.

Moreover, aside from the question of religious reinforcement, other factors have rendered the old concept of natural law uncongenial. It was always associated with the idea of reason as a force or faculty in things as well as a force and faculty in minds. The laws of nature signified that certain rational principles are actually embodied in the nature of man in his connection with the rest of nature. To obey the law of nature was all one with obeying the dictates of reason. And reason was thought of not just as a psychological possession of the individual mind but as the bond of unity in society. Even the physical laws of nature, since they were universal and "governed" particular empirical phenomena, were rational. Animals had laws of reason embodied in their structure and instincts which they followed without knowing them. The superiority of man is simply that he can be aware of the rational principles which physical things and animals unconsciously obey. It is not possible, I think, for any one today to estimate the power added to the concept of laws of nature by their implicit and unquestioned association with reason and with the common ends and interests that hold men together in society.

It is hardly necessary to note the various influences that undermined this association and, in undermining it, weakened also the working influence of moral ideas on custom and law. Even among those who might give a formal allegiance to similar ideas, if they were presented already formulated, the ideas have little vital power. Modern science has familiarized even the man in the street with a radically different notion about laws of nature. In writing these pages I have felt almost bound to use the term "law of nature" instead of the words "natural law," so different are the familiar connotations of the latter term. Natural law in the popular conception is physical rather than rational; it is associated with energies—heat, light, gravitation, electricity—not with rationality. And it would be difficult today to get even a serious hearing in most circles for the idea that reason is what holds men together in society. Economists, sociologists, historians, psychologists have worked together to displace this idea, to make it seem unreal and faded, even when they disagree radically among themselves as to just what is the nature of the social tie. When we ask what has taken the place of the old law of nature, of reason in nature and society, we are confronted with a scene of contention, confusion and uncertainty. Where is the moral idea capable of exercising the crystallizing, concentrating and directing force upon positive law and custom once exercised by the idea of laws of nature? Few of those who insist that it is necessary to revive the concept in order to have a basis of criticism and constructive effort would revive the idea in its older shape. And they are divided when asked what we should put in its place. This division among intellectuals would not be of any great importance were it not that it reflects division, confusion and uncertainty in the popular mind.

Of course there have been many attempts to fill the void created by the gradual disappearance from the practical scene of the idea of laws of nature, and some of the attempts have been successful in forming not only schools of thought but in exerting considerable practical influence upon affairs. From among these schools we may select the utilitarian and what for convenience may be called the Hegelian for special consideration. The utilitarian school cannot be charged with lack of definiteness and assurance of conviction. And no candid student of English legal, political and social reforms of the last century can assert that it lacked great practical influence. Ignoring technical details that are connected mainly with a psychology of feelings and pleasures and pains which has been largely outgrown by the advance of mental inquiry, we may say that the formula of the greatest good for the greatest number, every individual to count as one and only one in the enumeration, has been translated into the conviction that social welfare is the last and the legitimate moral standard. Regard for the general welfare is the proper source of all moral rules and moral obligations. Instead of considering antecedent ready-made laws, we should search social consequences to find principles of criticism of positive laws and current customs and of plans for legislation and new social arrangements.

Great as was the efficacy of this idea in domestic affairs, where shall we look to find traces of its influence upon international morality? Even admitting that it presents to us a sound view of the moral standard and the source of moral laws, has it been applied with any effectiveness to the conduct of international affairs? As a moral standard it puts upon an equal footing the happiness of citizens of foreign lands and of the home land. Where has this principle determined an important branch of international law? What has it done, I will not say to prevent war, but to mitigate its horrors? To most people, I suppose, the idea of its general application to international relations would seem as Utopian as the literal application of the teachings of Jesus. It is sometimes said that utilitarianism supplies us with a low and somewhat sordid moral principle. But in this respect, at least, it would seem to be too high, too far above and beyond present attainment.

More concretely, various attempts to show that war in particular and methods relying upon force and intrigue in general do not pay, may be said to represent examples of the attempt to apply the utilitarian theory in international affairs. The demonstration that war does not pay even the nations that win is probably sufficiently convincing to most persons since the Great War. But the demonstration and the conviction do not appear to have much practical influence. It is too rationalistic; it assumes in too exclusive a way that men are governed by considerations of advantage, of profit and loss. Not only critics of utilitarianism but a great utilitarian, John Stuart Mill, criticized the earlier Benthamite version, on the ground that it leaned too heavily on the material interests of man without enough regard for the motives that may, according to one's bias, be termed sentimental, ideal or spiritual. And it might almost be said that the very existence of war with its willingness to sacrifice life and property for a cause is proof of the soundness of the criticism. War is as stupid as you please but it does not persist because of wrong calculations of profit, even though wrong estimates of national advantage may sometimes play a part in the minds of statesmen in starting a war.

The reasons for the practical failure of utilitarianism in international morality can be found within the doctrine itself. It is a theory not only of the moral standard but also of the moral motive, namely, concern for the general happiness. Now the utilitarians themselves recognized that after consideration for the standard has shown what should be done, the question remains of linking up the moral end with the motives that will make it prevail in conduct. They listed the motives that may be relied upon: natural sympathy with others; education into social ways of looking at conduct; mutual advantage through industrial interdependence, division of labor and exchange; and the penal sanction—personal suffering when anti-social motives are given sway.

Now it is obvious that under existing conditions these motives have little chance to operate in international affairs. The extent of sympathy is conditioned in the concrete among the mass of persons by habitual contact and familiar association. It may work strongly where these conditions are found and be very weak when there are barriers of language, custom, and political affiliation. Sympathy with one's immediate fellows is easily turned into antipathy to the outsider and stranger. Education is limited also by range of contact and intercourse, and at present the forces that educate into nationalistic patriotism are powerful and those that educate into equal regard and esteem for aliens are weak. The economic motive works both ways. As already stated, war almost undoubtedly entails loss for a nation as a whole; the risk of loss through defeat is great. But there are also profiteers, those who stand to gain for themselves, and there is no guarantee that they will not occupy places of power and influence. Aside from profiteering, the existence of protective tariffs shows how far men are from believing that free exchange is of necessity a mutual advantage.

As for the legal penal sanction, that is manifestly totally lacking, since there is no common political superior that makes laws with penalties attached for violation. In short, all the conditions that made utilitarianism domestically and internally effective are either absent or much enfeebled in international relations. It will be understood that these remarks are no more an attack upon utilitarianism than they are a defense of it. They are made not for the sake of making any assessment of utilitarianism but because they throw light upon the present lack of a coherent body of moral ideas that may be efficaciously applied in international matters. The evidence is the more striking in the case of utilitarian moral beliefs, because although not universally accepted—in fact although bitterly attacked—they were none the less effective within a nation.

The type of moral doctrine that for convenience in having a single name was called Hegelian is in fact much wider than any one school of philosophy. It goes back in its cruder form to Machiavelli and Hobbes. Both of these writers were attacked in their own day and ever since that day as immoralists rather than moralists. But nevertheless they represent a distinct type of moral ideas. Their underlying principle, when we eliminate idiosyncrasies of personality and surroundings, is that institutions having authority, especially that institution we call the state, are a necessary precondition of the morality of individuals. Hence, the social organization has a privileged, indeed, a unique moral position. Being the condition without which morality in the concrete is impossible, it is also above morals in the ordinary sense, in the sense in which private persons and voluntary communities are required to be moral. The idea came into later German philosophy not from Machiavelli and Hobbes direct but by a revival of Greek (especially Aristotelian) political ethics interpreted by the teaching of Spinoza. The latter, living in a period of almost universal war, external and civil, with all its attendant insecurity of existence, immensely deepened the teaching of Hobbes. He taught expressly that the authority of the state is a necessary precondition of stability of social and personal life and of any wide-spread freedom and rationality of life. Even the most rational of beings cannot put his rationality into effect and achieve freedom except as he has the external support as well as the positive assistance of others. Without political power most men will be governed by their passions, and the wisest of men will be constantly at the mercy of his environment and of appetite and passion.

The political condition of Germany, internal and external, after the Napoleonic wars created a situation favorable to the revival of these ideas. It also furnished a situation in which these ideas were important intellectual weapons in regenerating and unifying the separate and particularistic states of Germany under the hegemony of Prussia. These ideas, first taught in the universities, were so congenial to the needs of political Germany that they soon bore practical fruit. If they were not active forces in bringing about the centralization of previously scattered political authority they at least formulated the end and gave it intellectual justification.

It is not necessary to spend much time showing that this type of ethical thought, a type which insisted upon certainty, unity and stability of institutions, as utilitarians insisted upon the spread of general personal happiness, did not and could not favorably affect international morality. Its whole tendency was toward an intellectual glorification of the national state. Struggle between states was a necessary incident of history; more than this, it operated to strengthen and consolidate the authority of institutions. Success in war was objective evidence of a superior social organization, and hence of superior morality. If a single peaceful international order is ever attainable it is only by means of a *Pax Romana*;[3] some one state must become so powerful as to be able to enforce its will upon all other communities.

I do not mean to intimate that these two types of moral doctrine exhaust the ethical conceptions that have developed in the void left by the subsidence of the theory of natural law. There are others of considerable importance. But the career of the two selected types may serve to illustrate our main thesis: one important factor in the present problem of ethics and international relations is found on the side of ethical beliefs themselves in their confused and contending divergencies. The trouble does not reside wholly on the practical side. It is not my intent to propose any set of moral beliefs which might in my opinion remedy this state of affairs. I content myself with pointing out that since we are still in a very early period of anything which may be called the modern world there is no ground for despair as to the future. Every condition of life as it moves toward coherent organization develops its own ethos, its own standards and codes. In spite of the wide extent and internal complexity of the present situation, so much greater than anything in previous history, there is sufficient ground for believing that we are working toward a more coherent condition of life, and that a unified moral code will grow up when social relations are better adjusted. It is trite to say that we live in a time of immense transitions; we do not sufficiently note that ethical confusion always attends such epochs.

But future expectations give little comfort and stay in the present. It seems to me that there is one measure that would at least concentrate and direct moral sentiments and moral desires and emotions, which are certainly still widespread amid our intellectual confusion and uncertainty. *Law* has always served the purpose of condensing and defining the moral wishes and expectations of the community. No matter how much it is behind the highest moral aspirations of the developed members of the community, law has precipitated average moral sentiment in a way that has rendered it more effective than it would otherwise be. It has canalized moral emotions so that they may flow to a purpose. Changing the metaphor, it has given them positive leverage.

Now it seems to me that there is one legal change which, were it made, would effect an enormous change in clarifying the present situation and would give the development of sound ideas and valid practises a great impetus. I refer to the movement, originally launched in this country by Mr. Levinson, a successful lawyer of Chicago, for the outlawry of war. Under present international law war is legal. There is indeed no such thing as illegal war, except the kind of war that appears to most persons the most justifiable from the moral standpoint—internal wars of liberation. War is not only legal; it is the *most* authorized method of settling disputes between nations that are intense. Resort to organized force is the *ultima ratio* of states. This fact constitutes by far the greatest gap that exists in any realm of life between moral sentiment and authorized practise. With respect to all lesser disputes there are regular methods of settlement which are alone legal. There are laws, courts and procedures for settling them. I am not hopeful that causes of dispute between nations will cease any more than causes of disputes between individuals. But we no longer permit individuals to settle disputes by waging private war; even in cases when honor is impugned the duel is outlawed.

I do not see how anybody who faces the situation can do otherwise than be convinced that the legality of war constitutes the greatest anomaly that now anywhere exists in morals.

As long as it persists, moral sentiment is in a self-contradictory position; there is a double standard of moral ideas introducing an almost hopeless conflict, till a person has no choice except between belligerent loyalty to his own community and a non-resistant pacifism which comes close to moral passivism. The outlawing of war as a method of settling national disputes under any circumstances, with the attendant institution of courts having complete jurisdiction in disputes that might lead to war, operating under a carefully thought out code, would put an end to this fatal moral dualism.

Community of moral feeling exists even among those of diverse intellectual moral beliefs. The outlawing of war provides a common centre for the expression of this community of moral emotion and desire. International law against war would produce the same condensing, precipitating, crystallizing effect for morals with respect to international relations that law has supplied everywhere else in its historic development. It is the logical completion of the historic development of courts as the instrumentalities for settling disputes, and until it is reached the influence of moral sentiment is split and scattered.

The argument is not that wars would necessarily cease. Laws have not prevented other crimes; it may be that war though a crime would still be resorted to. But the person who believes that law which should brand war for what it is instead of permitting it as legal would have no effect, has a peculiar view of history and human nature. There is an old saying that what the sovereign permits he commands. It is not needful to take this saying literally to recognize that the existing legal sanction of war inevitably confers upon it a moral sanction which in the end encourages war. What law authorizes is a powerful influence in determining moral ideas and aspirations in the mass of men. But above all what is asserted is that until war is outlawed by conjoint international action there is no opportunity for existing moral sentiments to function effectively in international relations, and next to no hope for the speedy development of a coherent and widely accepted body of moral ideas which will be effective in determining international relations. The first move in improving international morality is to outlaw war. Till this move is taken I do not see much chance that any other improvement in international relations will win general assent or be practicable in execution.

NOTES

First published in *Foreign Affairs* 1 (1923): 85–95, reprint, in MW.15.53–65.

1. [Editor's note: Hugo Grotius was a jurist in the Dutch Republic known for his natural law outlook, which served as a basis for early international law.]
2. [Editor's note: Sir Frederick Pollock was an English jurist known for his *History of English Law Before the Time of Edward I*. See Frederick Pollock and Frederic William Maitland, *History of English Law before the Time of Edward I*, 2 vols. (1895; New York: Cambridge University Press, 1968). Pollock's legal scholarship focused on identifying common principles underlying insights which could be drawn from specific cases.]
3. [Editor's note: *Pax Romana* refers to the relative peace that lasted for nearly two hundred years as a result of the reign of the Roman Empire and its consequent stability in the first and second centuries AD.]

30
Dewey Describes Child's New World

(1932)

EDITOR'S INTRODUCTION

In 1931, the Century Company published a report on President Hoover's "White House Conference on Child Health and Protection" held the previous year. The president had called for a study of "the present status of the health and well-being of the children of the United States and its possessions; to report what is being done; to recommend what ought to be done and how to do it."[1]

In 1932, the *New York Times* published a series of remarks on the conference and its report, one of which notably was by Mrs. Franklin D. Roosevelt. Dewey's essay was the first in the series. Dewey was not only influential in responding to the conference report, but he also had inspired its authors before the report's publication. In a passage by the "Committee on the School Child," the authors cite Dewey as an inspiration, writing that as "John Dewey has said, 'What the best and wisest parent wants for his own child, that must the community want for all of its children.'"[2]

Dewey was both a philosopher of education and a moral leader. In this essay, he argues that care for the child's conditions represents "the most fundamental philosophy of social order and progress which can be formulated." His review of the changing conditions for children in the United States is sweeping, yet offers for his time many areas in which intelligent direction and action could make a difference. He extols and champions the descriptions and prescriptions set forth in the conference's report, arguing that "the question is no longer whether resources are at hand for an indefinitely better nurture of children than existed at any previous time in the history of the world, but whether society is ready to acknowledge its responsibility for the extensive use of the resources it possesses."

Today, many states have been accused of underfunding their public schools. We do ensure that children generally have access to medical care, but, before his time, Dewey noted the crucial importance of something that largely goes undertreated, namely, mental illness.[3] It is of growing concern today, but there is still a long way to go. And Dewey was definitely right that concern should begin with young people. Dewey's overall message remains relevant and deeply important.[4] Americans are far from assuring that all children have opportunities and the conditions that the best and wisest parents would want for their own.

Explicit acknowledgment of the importance for society of the physical, intellectual and moral development of every child born into the world seems to come late in human history.

But the delay is not due to absence of affection and sympathy in former days. The present recognition springs from two great causes. One is the existence of social relations so complex, so intertwined, that the family alone cannot secure to children all the conditions that are required to insure their best growth. The other cause is the development of knowledge which has put in the hands of society scientific resources which did not formerly exist.

A treatise on sociology would be required to state the social changes which in the last century have affected the life of the child, and these words are not a sociological treatise.

But it is matter of common knowledge that the walls which formerly surrounded the individual family have broken down. Mothers as well as fathers are in industry. American life has changed from rural to urban. The family home with its environing land for free play and work has disappeared for millions of children. The city apartment and tenement, with no outlet save the congested and perilous streets, has taken its place.

The industries of the household and the neighborhood, open to view, offering opportunity for instruction and for gradual sharing in intimate responsibilities, have well nigh disappeared.

The substitute is the factory with its machinery and mechanical operations. The systems of apprenticeship by which the young were once prepared for adult duties have gone.

The home and household are no longer the centres of recreation and amusement. They are found outside, on the street, in the movie house, the automobile.

At the same time that the social horizon has immensely widened, so that the future citizen will find himself living in a wide world, affected by complex and remote conditions, the homes of most children are less able than ever before to prepare for any worthy citizenship on even a narrow scale.

It is not the children of the poor alone who suffer from these changed conditions, but those of the well-to-do as well. For opportunities for natural participation in the activities of an intimate group are vanishing. Everywhere we look, the older means for securing the well-being of children are relaxing.

On the other hand, the development of medicine and hygiene have made us aware that many evils once regarded as inevitable are within human control. It has been discovered that, with present knowledge, a high death rate among infants is wholly unnecessary. Contagion and infection can be enormously reduced, and in principle at least eliminated. Various devices have made it possible to secure practical immunity against such a scourge as diphtheria. Although the mortality of mothers at child birth has been on the increase, the need and the possibility of prenatal care of mothers is becoming generally acknowledged.

On the physical side, the question is no longer whether resources are at hand for an indefinitely better nurture of children than existed at any previous time in the history of the world, but whether society is ready to acknowledge its responsibility for the extensive use of the resources it possesses.

The sphere of preventive and remedial care has been extended to include unfortunate children—the crippled, blind, deaf, subnormal. In these matters, as in proper medical care of illness, hundreds of thousands of families are in no condition, whether from ignorance or from economic incapacity, to give the attention which is needed.

Closely bordering on these cases are those of children who are orphans, or who are deserted by one or more parents. When left to unorganized individual care, these children largely drift into lives of little social usefulness or into positive crime. When systematically cared for, experience has already demonstrated that the great majority, even with apparently bad heredity, become self-respecting and useful members of the community.

While scientific knowledge and methods in psychology and psychiatry are relatively not as advanced as the physical and biological, there has already taken place an intellectual revolution. We know almost infinitely more than we formerly did about the processes of mental development and the conditions which are favorable and unfavorable than did our grandparents. Those who deal with mental instability in adult life are convinced that in a large number of instances the causes are found in emotional and social maladjustments of childhood. In matters of moral and intellectual health the principle that prevention is better than cure applies in an intense degree.

With the increase in mental disorders characteristic of our civilization, the duty of society to check and reduce the great number of sufferers is clear. When one recalls that the number of beds in institutions for the mentally ill is equal to those for all other forms of disease, and that society has to provide this care, merely selfish economic reasons dictate the unremitting use in childhood of all available scientific resources.

This then is the situation. There is a junction of a new social necessity and a new ability, due to knowledge and skill. It is this situation which makes the problem of childhood an urgent one and which inspires the remarkable cooperative efforts recorded in the proceedings of the White House Conference.

It is the simplest and most familiar of all facts that all who have matured to adult life die. The fact is familiar, but its full import is often overlooked. Civilization is not transmitted by physical means, but by care, nurture and education. It would die out in two short generations if it were not renewed by the newly born. The kind of training the latter receive determines the future of society itself. There have been simple and relatively static civilizations in which family and friends sufficed to insure that reproduction of the culture of the community which would maintain its continued existence. The fact that every civilized country has found it necessary to adopt systems of public education proves that we are no longer living in that period.

But what is characteristic of our own day is the recognition that mere schooling is not enough to achieve the renewal of civilization. Prospective parents must be educated. The mother must have adequate prenatal, natal and post-natal care. If the future citizen is to contribute to the advancement of society, instead of being a drag upon it, his health must be looked to by all possible measures of prevention, including regular examinations by competent persons. The sources of infection must be guarded against. There must be a proper environment, including not merely protection against foul air, milk and water, bad and inadequate food, but through supply of the positive conditions of a proper home and facilities for recreation. The body is maimed by accident and weakened by lack of nourishment and by illness. But it is also such a delicate mechanism that it is warped, and sanity of mind and body injured, whenever the home and neighborhood environment is defective.

It is impossible to separate care of the body from other means of nurture. The brain and nervous system are part of the body, but they develop properly only when an adequate mental and moral education is secured.

It is hardly necessary to say today that such an education includes more than mere absence of illiteracy, more than mere book learning. It is a social as well as individual necessity that each child be prepared to do his part in the industrial organization of society. He must be so educated that he can contribute through his work to serving others and to making secure his own happiness in his work.

The resources of scientific knowledge must be used to discover his strong and weak points, uncover his tastes and talents, and insure both him and society against the unhappiness and the loss that come from the square peg in the round hole. When there were but few callings, and those few were simple, organized attention to development for the selection of the right calling and for proficiency in it were not necessary. Today they are necessary.

And so one might go through the whole circle of relationships and responsibilities incumbent upon the future citizen and show the necessity of that systematic development which only organized social action can secure. Unless the family and civic life, from the local community to the Federal State and the community of nations, are to disintegrate and be wracked by disorder and war, there must be the devoted and unremitting devotion of society to serve the needs of the young who are component members of future adult society.

The problem is an extraordinarily difficult one, the hardest in many respects that the world has ever faced. But we have at command, as has been stated, new resources of knowledge and skill. If the problem is once recognized as a general social responsibility, these new energies will not be dissipated and directed to lesser and technical ends, but will be directed to meeting the need.

Fortunately, there is a strong sentimental reservoir which can be drawn upon. Affection for children is one of the strongest traits of human nature. And in our country, as perhaps never before in the world, there is the widespread desire on the part of parents that their children shall have better and fairer opportunities in the world than they themselves ever had, and not merely economic opportunities but as well those for a richer and fuller share in all the things that make life lovely, significant, worth while.

The reservoir of energy with which to meet the problem is, however, much more than that of affection of parents for children. There is involved the entire concern of thoughtful persons for the future well-being of society itself. Personal affection is reinforced by all patriotic and humane considerations.

The Children's Charter adopted by the White House Conference touches every side of the life of the child that affects the welfare of society itself. In recognizing "the rights of the child as the first rights of citizenship," it adopts the most fundamental philosophy of social order and progress which can be formulated. As far as the citizens of the nation carry out in action the philosophy which the charter sets forth we may face the future with confidence.

NOTES

First published in *New York Times*, April 10, 1932, sec. 3, reprint, in LW.6.137–142.

1. See Dewey, *The Collected Works: Later Works*, vol. 6, ed. Jo Ann Boydston (Carbondale: Southern Illinois University Press, 1985), 519.
2. White House Conference on Child Health and Protection, *Preliminary Committee Reports of the White House Conference on Child Health and Protection* (New York: The Century Company, 1930), 200.
3. The Editors, "The Neglect of Mental Illness Exact a Huge Toll, Human and Economic," *Scientific American*, March 1, 2012, https://www.scientificamerican.com/article/a-neglect-of-mental-illness/.
4. Valerie Strauss, "This Is What Inadequate Funding at a Public School Looks and Feels Like," *Washington Post*, February 9, 2018, https://www.washingtonpost.com/news/answer-sheet/wp/2018/02/09/this-is-what-inadequate-funding-at-a-public-school-looks-and-feels-like-as-told-by-an-entire-faculty/.

31

The Collapse of a Romance

(1932)

EDITOR'S INTRODUCTION

In the Great Depression, the United States reached the apex of unemployment in 1932 and 1933 at around 25 percent. Dewey wrote often for the public at the time, demonstrating the important role that philosophers can play as critics of culture. For as culture involves people's use of language, their beliefs, and their practices, philosophers' examination and analysis of these aspects of public life can contribute to intellectual and moral leadership.

In the years before the Great Depression, the U.S. economy was booming, and the mainstream rhetoric in the country enjoyed a vigorous optimism about private industry and its capitalist economy. In "The Collapse of a Romance," Dewey reveals the danger in the nation's expansionist and industrial spirit, which rests on a romantic ideology about business and rugged individualism. Included in the romance was an overzealous belief in the rational economic actor and the invisible hand. Dewey makes plain that the problem for Americans was not simply a lack of confidence: the romance of business masks the fact that business is fundamentally a trade on insecurity. He calls for intelligent planning for business and economics and for many mechanisms that Americans have put in place since his time, such as Social Security.

In times of economic expansion, people feel comfortable in their success, unworried about the truth or falsity of their beliefs. Critics of unbridled capitalism are considered naysayers or communists simply for questioning blind faith in markets and private interests. That kind of hubris supports an anti-intellectual orientation, which leaves the people to suffer from whatever crisis comes from economic collapse.

In the wake of the Great Recession of 2007 and 2008, Dewey's warnings and insights resound. When he wrote this piece, the romance of traditional economic theories of business and exchange had collapsed, and they have done so again, in smaller ways. Today, we have unemployment insurance, Social Security, and other safety nets as a result of the acceptance, prompted by the Great Depression, of the need for economic security measures for the people. Nevertheless, many Americans are struggling economically today, and threats to and attacks on social safety nets are a constant danger.[1]

Carlyle, who was a romantic, called political economy the dismal science. And it is true that the roseate hopes of the earlier economists had well nigh disappeared by his day. Ricardo had indicated that there was not enough land to go around and Malthus that there were altogether too many people.[2] Natural laws seemed to doom many to live on the edge of the subsistence line. In the United States, however, for fairly obvious reasons the earlier glow revived and business was ordained as the great romantic adventure.

Although the rebirth of glamor was dependent upon local American conditions, there was a genuinely romantic factor in economic theory; we did not create the romanticism, we only gave it the chance to flourish. Strange as it sounds, the economic man was himself a hero of romance. Of course another branch of the romantic tradition did not consider him as such; he figures there as withdrawing from the realm of romance into the counting room, there to engage in a prosaic grubbing into musty ledgers. But different romanticists rarely understand one another, and while the earlier tradition tended to prevail in the books, the new romantic spirit took possession of the scene of action.

The new hero of romance did not seek justification for himself in theory; the adventure was its own justification. But if he had turned to economic theory he would have found written warrant. For, in that theory, wants and desires were glorified power; at their magic touch the world was to be transformed; they were, when unshackled from legal artifice and political despotism, the sure source of prosperity and continual progress; the earthly savior of mankind. Wants stirred man to energy, rendered him creative, moved him to thrift and produced the embellishment of the world, urged him to exchange and so made man, apart from his will, the mutual servant of his fellows. The romance of business did not stop there. Economic man had another asset beside his desires; he had an unfailing intelligence which showed him just how to direct the energy, thrift, exchange, by which in satisfying his wants he made the world over. To the eye of the romantic who lived in the genteel literary tradition, this ascription of self-sufficient rationality seemed the negation of romance. How could adventure be cool, calculating, concerned with debtor and creditor accounts, and still be romantic?

But it was just at this point that the new romanticism of business so cleverly came in. Human imagination had never before conceived anything so fantastic as the idea that every individual is actuated in all his desires by an insight into just what is good for him, and that he is equipped with the sure foresight which will enable him to calculate ahead and get just what he is after. Nor did the imaginative flight pause with this conclusion. All the work of the world, from the most ordinary to the most extraordinary, is presided over by this omnipresent deity of calculating reason, who through his uniform presence in each separate individual is summed up by integral calculus into a virtually omniscient mind. Through its beneficent and overruling power, self-interest becomes a social lubricant instead of a cause of friction, and the zeal of each one to get ahead of everybody else promotes the general welfare. If there are those who seem to be left out of its distribution, there is always the assurance that the ways of Providence are proverbially mysterious.

It is characteristic of romance, of the glamorous and imaginative projection of excited emotion, to remain outside the sphere of argument. One is either inside the romance or outside it. It is true and is the standard of truth, if you are inside; it is silly or insane, if you are outside. Thus, when one says that the present world crisis is merely the consequence of the general acceptance of the particular romance which has gone by the name of business, one speaks from the outside. It is commonly assumed that the explanation of the economic crisis must be itself economic. So it must—if one stays inside the business dream. Since it is part of the dream that cool, far-sighted intelligence controls the operation of the energies and instruments by which desires are satisfied, one within the dream must seek for a rational explanation. From outside the romance, that fact itself gives the key to the explanation; we cannot call gambling an exercise of cool and calm rationality without sooner or later tripping up.

The dictionary defines gambling as staking money on some fortuitous event. Since business is in the condition it is, since it has brought about a state of universal insecurity, it is fairly evident that the bets have gone wrong. But more fundamental still is the fact to which the present insecurity testifies. As the function of intelligent control is to achieve order, stability, security, the whole theory of the relation between business and calculating intelligence is evidently sheer fiction. Business postulates insecurity and uncertainty. It thrives on it and increasingly creates it, in order that more business may be done.

If the existing insecurity were localized in one country or restricted to one class, some explanation of it might be found or invented which would be consistent with a definition of the economic process as a rationally guided process of satisfying wants. There would also then be some sense in blaming financiers and industrial leaders for their stupidity in bringing us to this pass. But since the essence of the whole thing is the romance of adventuring on the sea of uncertainty, one might as well subject Don Quixote to criticism on the basis of reason. Because wagering on uncertainty is the heart of the whole process, the banker, as insecure as the debtor, has ceased to function; the manufacturer is as doubtful of a market for his goods as the worker is of a market for his labor and the farmer for his products. That "securities" are now so largely insecurities is typical of the whole affair.

The present scene is only an exhibition of what is inherent in business all the time, but it now happens on such a scale that the uncertainty always characteristic of it has become too overt to be ignored. The only thing abnormal about it is that the normal insecurity has got out of hand to the extent that it cannot be concealed from general recognition. In other words, the essentially romantic nature of the idea that business is a rational way of expending energy for the satisfaction of human wants becomes apparent to those who have eyes to see. There are various "rational" explanations of the present breakdown. Each has its measure of truth, but all they explain is some aspect of the irrationality, the trading on uncertainty, which is business itself.

It is interesting to note the ways in which a recognition of the identity of business with betting on an uncertain event all but explicitly comes through. We hear every day and many times a day that everything would be all right if we only had "confidence." Undoubtedly. But confidence in what or in whom? The industrialist would be pleased if the banker had enough confidence to lend him money; the banker would be pleased if someone else had sufficient confidence to buy his frozen assets at a good price; the farmer would love to have confidence that if he plants a lot of grain and cotton he will get a good price next summer; the laborer would like to have confidence that he is going to get a job, and the depositor that he is going to get his money from the bank when he wants it. Meantime, the appeal to confidence sounds like a confidence game. Can anyone imagine anything more humorous—if it were not terribly tragic—than the appeal to put confidence in a situation of complete insecurity? Again we are constantly told that the whole basis of modern business is credit. What does that signify when credit tends automatically toward inflation and the only way to deflate is to withhold credit, except that the whole business of business is to trade on insecurity, concealing the insecurity as long as possible by an ingenious pyramiding of it?

The psychology and morale of business are based on trading in insecurity. They are criticized by serious moralists as if the animating spirit were that of acquisition. These accusations do not reach the mark. Business is a game which cannot be carried on without acquisition, any more than poker can be played without chips. But it is the excitement of the game which counts; acquisition is important because it enables the game to go on at a more furious pitch. We hunt the dollar, but hunting is hunting, not dollars. It is said that love of power over others is the dominant thing. But if you have a game which cannot be played except when power over others is a condition of success, love of power grows up as a secondary and derived fact, not as an original and animating force. I see no reason to believe that the majority of important and "successful" business men are sadistic, and love the cruelty arising from power over others for its own sake. I can see how zest for the game may cause even cruelty to take on a romantic visage and render it tolerable in contemplation.

In saying that business is intrinsically a gamble in uncertainties, it is not said that manufacture or transportation of goods is a gamble. They are technological operations, based on physical knowledge of physical materials and energies. The locomotive runs on coal and steam, not on psychical acts of "confidence." But for this reason production and distribution of goods are not themselves business. In business they become instruments of a game in which trumps are possession of capital as a temporary insurance against insecurity. But the game has such a wide reach that there comes a time when the insecurity of the masses spells insecurity for the one holding trumps. The essence of business, as distinct from the techniques of production and distribution, is of course profits. But why profits? Anyone can give the answer. There must be profits in order to induce persons to "take the risks"; it is only fair that those who assume the risks should get paid for doing it. Since there is no explanation of profits which does not come down to this fact, what other evidence is needed of the intrinsic connection of business with insecurity?

Living is attended with risks; there will always be an element of uncertainty in it. One cannot object to business for taking account of this fact. But anyone whom the crisis has awakened from a romantic dream will object to any procedure which systematically sets out to glorify the process of trading in insecurity on the ground that this is the road to profits. We should at least get rid of the vast load of nonsense which now adds to our depression if we were coolly to take business for just what it is, i.e., the pursuit of profit, and cease glorifying it for what it is not. Personally, I believe there would be a great rise in the so-called native I.Q. of the average American if we would get rid of this one source of mental confusion and paralysis. But what is more objectionable is the piling up of insecurity. There is enough risk in living anyway without deliberately increasing it. Take money, for example. We are told that it is a medium of exchange. Well, if it were, it would of course add to the security of existence. As a matter of fact, it is something else. It is a medium for *controlling* exchange. Hence the concentrated possession of money is a means of intensifying insecurity. The ability to control exchange is the ability to stop it, to tax it, to deflect it. To create a risk and then make a profit by assuming it, is a good rule—for those who control money.

The breakdown in which we are living is the breakdown of the particular romance known as business. It is the revelation that the elated excitement of the romantic adventure has to be paid for with an equal depression. If one knew where the glamor of imagination would next find its outlet, one could predict the future. But the reason why no one has had any success in foretelling the great turns of history is precisely because they come from the imagination and its enthusiasms and not from logic and reason. I do not think the next voyage of imagination is immediately imminent. There is one stage of the present romance not yet exhausted. We are now being captured by the romance of introduction of planning into business. What could be more romantic than the idea of retaining business, which is the process of placing wagers on uncertainties for the sake of profit, and at the same time introducing stability and security into it? So that last act of the present drama will presumably be undertaken before the imagination takes its flight to a new field.

NOTES

First published in *New Republic* 70 (27 April 1932): 292–94, reprint, in LW.6.69–75.

1. Dylan Matthews, "The War on the Poor," *Vox*, November 22, 2016, https://www.vox.com/policy-and-politics/2016/11/22/13641654/paul-ryan-trump-poverty-safety-net.
2. [Editor's note: Thomas Carlyle (1795–1881) was a romantic author who was one of the "most powerful and widely-read figures in the Victorian intellectual landscape." See John Morrow, *Thomas Carlyle* (London: Continuum, 2006), ix. David Ricardo (1772–1823) and Thomas Malthus (1766–1834) were among the most influential British political economists, along with Adam Smith.]

32

The Economic Situation: A Challenge to Education

—

(1932)

EDITOR'S INTRODUCTION

On February 22, 1932, Dewey addressed the general session of the Department of Supervisors and Teachers of Home Economics at a meeting of the National Education Association in Washington, DC. The presentation was published that June in the *Journal of Home Economics*, a periodical that was founded in 1909 and ran through 1993.[1] The association is still around today, but in 1994 it changed its name to the American Association of Family and Consumer Sciences.

In his address, Dewey argues that teachers must see themselves not as tools for the perpetuation of the status quo but as agents in the effort to improve public conditions. Teachers need to unite, become better informed about the economic crises of their day, and fight for the intellectual freedom to educate young people. Curricula should center on real, existing conditions rather than on the fictions advanced by powerful interests.

Today, the pressure of high-stakes testing and concentration on narrow, basic skills frustrates the crucial aim of nurturing young critical thinkers. Dewey's call for teachers to empower their students to be scientific and intellectual about their culture and social conditions offers vital insights for today's readers, teachers, and policy makers. Both Republicans and Democrats have focused intensely upon test scores and their modest improvement, to the neglect or exclusion of key democratic aims for education.

Since the present economic collapse is a challenge to every institution in our present civilization, it surely is also a challenge to our schools. This fact is so evident that it is useless to dwell upon it. The important thing is to know how the schools might and should meet this challenge. But, when statesmen falter, industrial chieftains are bewildered, and economists hesitate to express a judgment regarding either causes or remedies, those of us who approach the matter from the educational side may well be at a loss. I am so far from knowing what the schools can actually do to prevent the recurrence of a similar breakdown in the future that I shall have to confine myself to one aspect of the problem. I believe that if we, in common with others, can honestly and courageously face the situation, our combined wisdom, if it holds the problem steadily in view over a long time, can accomplish what overwhelms the mind of any one individual.

In the first place, let me say that the words I have just used, "honest and courageous facing of the elements in the problem," suggest the main thing of which I wish to speak. It takes a good deal of courage for educators to face the situation, and it requires an unusual amount of mental energy to be honest in fact and not merely in intention. One of the functions of education is to equip individuals to see the moral defects of existing social arrangements and to take an active concern in bettering conditions. Our schools have failed notably and lamentably in that regard. We are depressed just now, and trouble makes persons more willing to think and certainly more willing to criticize and to listen to criticism. But foresight and prevention are better than afterthought and cure, socially as well as medically. The atmosphere in our period of seeming economic prosperity tended to suppress serious thought on fundamental social matters and to encourage a complacent emotional acquiescence in and laudation of things as they are, or were.

One illustration will indicate what I mean. I heard a debate the other evening on military preparedness. A speaker, who held that this preparedness tended to provoke war, cited the fact that Holland held Java, perhaps the richest colonial possession in the world, and yet was free from all danger of attack although having no army and navy to speak of. He said that during most of the nineteenth century the United States with negligible military forces was secure, and that only after adoption of an imperialistic policy, which had made us feared and disliked, did the cry for a big army and navy arise. I am not concerned here to consider the justice of these remarks, although to me personally they seem sound. My point concerns the reception they received. General Fries, speaking for military preparedness, said that if the speaker and others like him thought so highly of Holland while he criticized the United States, why didn't they go to

Holland to live and leave the country they thought so poorly of. There was great applause from a certain part of the audience, and members of so-called patriotic societies rose to their feet to lead the cheering.

The episode in itself is trivial or even childish. But as an illustration it has tremendous significance. It is typical of an attitude which has too nearly dominated teachers, and increasingly so, ever since the outbreak of the World War at least. It is "unpatriotic" to point out or even to admit that there are any weak spots in our institutions and habits and to suggest that there are matters in which we might learn from other countries. There has been a heavy pall of "hush-hush" imposed upon teachers, and the easy way for them, the way of inertia, has been to become "yes" men and women.

I do not know how it is today, but only a few years ago the names of some of the leaders of thought in this country were on the black books of departments in Washington as dangerous characters, potentially seditious because they had indulged in criticism of our tendencies in industry and were not afraid to put their fingers on sore spots like suppression of free speech. The branch of the War Department which is responsible for military training in colleges in one of its published statements for use in stimulating military spirit in the colleges called Jane Addams, whom most Americans call the best beloved woman in America, the recent recipient of the Nobel prize, the "most dangerous woman in America."

Again, such an instance, taken by itself, seems silly to the point of childishness. Miss Addams has obviously come to no harm. But for the few who by temperament and fortunate circumstances can rise above such attacks there are scores and scores who are induced to keep quiet, to gloss over social ills, and to accustom students to believe that all is for the best in this best of all possible countries. The representatives of large economic interests have been especially sensitive to anything approaching criticism of the existing economic régime and have pretty well succeeded in attaching to critics of it the epithet of "red" or "Bolshevist"; so much so that the publicity agent of the power interests is on public record as advising that all teachers who discuss public ownership favorably should be branded Bolshevists.

Now, when such a spirit prevails through the schools, it is impossible that education should accomplish its social function. For the primary social duty of education is not to perpetuate the existing social order—economic, legal, and political—but to contribute to its betterment. This work is constructive and positive, but it cannot be effected by indiscriminate laudation of the *status quo* any more than a physician can better the health of a patient by carefully averting attention from everything which ails the latter. And the doing of the work depends on the courage and energy of teachers.

The result is that the great majority of the students in our schools go forth unprepared to meet the realities of the world in which they live. They have been filled with highly idealized pictures of the actual state of things, idealizations created in part by omission of any reference to ills and unsolved problems, partly by excessive glorification of whatever good things exist. Then the graduates find themselves in a very different kind of a world. The split between their generous beliefs and liberal hopes and what they get into is often tragic; for the sensitive and thoughtful it requires a painful readjustment to find the gap which exists between what they had been taught to believe and things as they are. But even if they succumb without a struggle and accommodate themselves to the *status quo* in the hope of getting ahead individually, they are not qualified to cope with the causes which produce such catastrophes as our present economic breakdown. They are rather positively disqualified. Consequently, we all stand aghast and impotent, while some resort to measures of desperation like pumping oxygen into a sinking patient.

This actual incapacitation, much worse than mere failure to prepare, comes from the fact that the policy of concealment and laudation which is so strongly encouraged by the ruling economic elements gives students the impression that they live in a static world where pretty much everything has been fixed and settled and where all that is necessary is for individuals to take personal advantage of what is provided for them. I remember the experience of those of us who almost fifty years ago went to take graduate work in Johns Hopkins University. The previous schooling of most, if not all of us, had been conducted as if the book of knowledge had already been written full to the last page and that all we as students had to do was to absorb something from its finished pages. But there we found ourselves breathing a new atmosphere. Everywhere was the feeling that what was known was little in comparison with what remains to be found out and that it was possible for us to contribute; that we could and should transform ourselves from mere absorbing sponges of what was already known into active creators of new knowledge.

In this instance, the sudden change was salutary and inspiring. For the readjustment was only intellectual. But the change from the fixed and finished world of an idealized social *status quo* to the moving, dynamic, changing world of actual existence demands a practical readjustment which most persons fail to make because they are not equipped to meet it. In reading lately Merriam's book on *The Making of Citizens*, I was much struck by the testimony of this scholar of politics. He says,

> ... the state must make its case not once and for all, but continuously for each new generation and each new period.... Plans of civic training that do not

reckon with the social background of political power are defective.... The appearances of power are deceiving.... Facing the stern lines of authority with its steel and stone, and looking perhaps into haughty faces equally steely and stony, it is difficult to realize the poverty of power.

He speaks also of the "false front of omnipotence and unassailability."

Dr. Merriam is speaking of political institutions and power. If their fixity is so illusory, what shall we say of the stability of other social forms and arrangements, the everyday and secular affairs of men in industry, business, and finance, affected by almost every new scientific invention and changing with every change in the desires and plans of human beings? Over against this scene of constant change we have our schools, of which it is not too much to say that they engage in eulogistic contemplation of the false front of an unassailable stability.

The point which I am making may seem remote from the question of just what education can do about such things as the present economic depression. But it is my conviction that it cannot do anything important until there is a change in that underlying intangible thing which we call atmosphere and spirit. The change from acquiescent complacency to honest critical intelligence, from the fiction of a static and finished political and industrial society to the reality of a constantly shifting, altering, unstable society will not of itself enable those who go forth from our schools to forestall and prevent such crises as the present nor to cope with them when they come. But I believe that the detailed ideas and plans, which are indispensable if these results are to be brought about, cannot get a hearing, much less be adopted, unless there is a prior change in the prevailing tone and spirit of educational undertakings.

Accordingly, I shall make no apology for speaking of another general consideration that at first sight is also remote from the immediate emergency. Critics of American life have said a great deal of late about the standardization of opinion and regimentation of belief in American life. There is, I think, a much more deliberate attempt to produce this uniformity than there used to be. But it is my observation, growing out of an experience covering a good many years, that among cultivated people there were never as many truly free minds as there are now. I do not recall a time when one met so many persons mentally alert, forming their conclusions after informed inquiry and not on the basis of prejudice. There are, I feel, many more persons than there used to be emancipated from stereotyped ideas; fewer who are content to give utterance to what they regard as wise ideas or sayings merely because they have become stale with time. In my opinion, this country has never seen a time when so many persons took delight in ideas and in finding out things.

But, on the other hand, I cannot remember a time when collective thinking—the ideas that are organic to large numbers—was so stupid, so incredibly incompetent as it is today. It is a common remark that we have a surprising absence of effective leadership in this crisis, domestic and international, economic and political. Now leadership, like a bargain, has two sides. There can be leadership as there can be following only when human beings think together about a common theme with a shared purpose to a common result. Leadership is absent because this power of collective thinking in connection with solidarity of emotion and desire is lacking today. We have in its stead attempts to whip up a seeming unity of idea and sentiment by means of catch-words, slogans, and advertising devices. Few persons, however, are fooled by them except possibly those engaged in promulgating them.

Now this contrast between the alert state of the minds of cultivated individuals and the dead and impotent condition of collective thought is so paradoxical that it, too, issues a challenge to education. Why does this contrast exist? How did it come about?

One thing seems quite certain. Traditions form our collective beliefs; they are the intellectual cement of a society. Certain traditions in religion, morals, economics, and politics are still nominally held by the mass of adults, men and women. They are taught in schools. But the actual movements of social life are contrary to these traditions. They contradict and undermine them. We believe one thing in words and, to a considerable extent, in sentiment. We believe another thing in our deeds. The split prevents the older traditions from giving us real guidance, while they retain enough hold on people's minds so that they are not replaced by other collective ideas.

For example, our tradition in economics and industry is that of rugged individualism. We are taught to believe that all start equal in the economic race without any external handicaps being imposed on any persons and that reward and victory go to those of superior personal energy, ability, industry, and thrift, while, barring the exceptional cases of physical disease and accident, those who fall behind do so because of individual defects. We are taught that in this equal struggle between individuals all the great virtues of initiative, self-respect, self-help, standing on one's own feet, moral independence, and the rest are acquired.

Now these things may have been true once. They are not true now. Industry is mainly collective and corporate today, and economic opportunities are dependent upon collective conditions, as the condition of hundreds of unemployed men and women, graduates of colleges and technical schools, testifies at this moment. The concentrated control of finance and business is the basic and conditioning fact of industry today. But recognition of the fact goes contrary to our cherished tradition of equality of opportunity and of advancement solely through individual merit. The public clings for the most part to the nominal acceptance of the tradition, and the schools are forced to cling to it still more closely. Under these circumstances, it is practically impossible that there should be effective collective thinking regarding our economic situation in general and the depression in particular. Thinking could become effective only by being relevant to realities; in order to be related to the realities of the situation it would have to recognize that collective conditions call for collective control by the public in its own interest.

I think that teachers who led students to observe this state of things would find themselves called opprobrious names, and would be lucky if nothing worse happened to them. But unless and until we permit or rather encourage the schools to abandon the following of traditions—that is of collective ideas—which have no relation to existing social realities, our thinking in matters of the greatest public concern, including peace and war as well as industrial prosperity and depression, will continue to be thoroughly stupid and our leaders will be such only in the sense in which the blind lead the blind.

Since the schools are subject to pressure exercised by powerful forces outside the school, the challenge issuing from the present economic situation cannot be said to be primarily directed to educators. There is one aspect, however, of the challenge which comes home directly to teachers. They have been too passive, too submissive, to the dictation of these outside powers. It is our part to maintain the intellectual independence of the educative process and to strive for the right to present the defects as well as the excellencies of the existing economic order, even if by so doing some interests are offended. It is our duty as well as our right to show present society as dynamic, undergoing continuous change. To accomplish these things is the least we can do in faithfulness to the work of education itself. If we can make clear that otherwise we are failing in the operation of education, we shall also at least prepare the type of mind that can deal more effectively with economic conditions and crises than they are dealt with at present. This may not seem a very high ideal at which to aim compared with ambitious schemes which might be proposed. But those who realize the difficulties which stand in the way of securing for teachers the right to a critical and realistic consideration of existing economic realities will not despise the suggestion that the schools be emancipated from the clutches of those economic interests with their allied military and political auxiliaries which have done so much to bring the world to its present pass.

A group of educators, speaking from the standpoint of history, has recently put forth a manifesto in which they say that textbooks used in our schools still reflect more or less "the distortions of war-time propaganda" and fail to reveal that "millions of citizens in all nations were moved again and again to acts of supreme idealism and unselfishness by propaganda of interested groups controlling national interests."

Those would be naïve who assumed that the principle here stated is confined to war and the story of wars. It operates constantly in peace time and with reference to economic matters; and until schools escape its influence through a declaration of independence by teachers, it will prevent the schools' meeting the challenge made by economic crises. The first challenge, accordingly, is to teachers to unite to inform themselves more adequately about economic and social realities and then to combine to impress upon public opinion the right and duty of intellectual freedom to deal with these realities in their teaching.

NOTES

First published in *Journal of Home Economics* 24 (June 1932): 495–501, reprint, in LW.6.123–131.

1. The Institute of Museum and Library Services funded the complete digitization of the journal, every issue of which is now online, hosted by Cornell University: http://hearth.library.cornell.edu/h/hearth/browse/title/4732504.html.

33
The Jobless—A Job for All of Us

(1931)

EDITOR'S INTRODUCTION

The League for Industrial Democracy was founded in 1921, and Dewey was elected to serve as its vice president in 1930. He was again elected vice president and then president in 1935 and 1939, respectively. The organization published a short-lived periodical called *Unemployed*. In 1931, the journal published Dewey's essay, titled "The Jobless—a Job for All of Us." He addresses people concerned about the deep and troubling economic conditions of the Great Depression and the need for solidarity as a country.

Dewey argues that charity and public action after the fact are understandable reactions to unpredictable problems. Unemployment, however, is a chronic problem. Therefore, he claims, to react only to great crises of unemployment with measures after the fact, be they private or public, neglects the cause of the problem—a troubled economic system. Dewey argues that the task of helping the jobless is a publicly important matter for which the people must think ahead and act regularly, not occasionally or optionally through charity alone.

Dewey claims that no one could speak against some of the views he expresses in the essay, but it is important to remember that his context involved the start of the Great Depression. Today political polarization has yielded some divisive figures of various stripes who might well disagree with him. The United States has recently had politicians calling for decreasing or not extending the duration of benefits from unemployment insurance, but the very existence of such policies and programs is attributable to advocates like Dewey and to the dire conditions that the country endured at the time. The year after Dewey wrote this essay, the state of Wisconsin passed the first unemployment insurance laws, followed by six states, leading ultimately to the Social Security Act of 1935.[1]

※

It is no longer necessary to convince sensible persons that lack of employment is not a sign of laziness, shiftlessness or unreliable character. There is probably no one at the present time who does not have the knowledge of persons out of work who are industrious, faithful and competent; persons who want work above all else and yet cannot get it.

It is adding insult to injury to hold these persons, thousands, millions, of them, responsible for their inability to work. They are victims of the economic system. They are victims just as a man who suffers a physical accident when a railway train is thrown off the track is a victim. Something goes wrong in the running of our industrial train, and uncounted numbers suffer.

There is not a civilized country which does not recognize in some way its responsibility for those who cannot support themselves and those who are dependent upon their labors. Poor houses, poor relief, organized charity are indirect acknowledgments of social responsibility. Every humane person takes shame to himself and to the society in which he lives when he hears that one of his fellow creatures has starved to death. The right to life is the fundamental right which society has to secure to its members. When murder is rife and life is generally insecure, we know that the social system is at fault, not the men who are murdered. The right to life is invaded when men and women desirous of doing an honest day's work find themselves thrown out and left stranded. The social responsibility is the same as when because of general social lawlessness these men are directly and physically attacked.

Although public charity is a recognition of social responsibility it is a belated recognition. It comes after the catastrophe. Prevention is always better than cure, and charity is rarely even a cure. It is at best a temporary stopgap. And when the suffering and the catastrophe are constantly recurring, the recourse to charity, as an afterthought, is criminal. If a railway system had a continuous succession of derailments in which many persons were injured, every one would recognize the absence of competence and of foresight in the system itself.

Unemployment is not only recurrent but chronic. There exists all the time what is known as "normal" unemployment. Our industrial system is speeded up beyond its power to stand the wracking that comes from its own movement.

Such a crisis as the present calls attention in a dramatic, even a sensational, way to something that exists all the time, but which under ordinary circumstances most men are too blind to observe. At such a time as the present, private committees raise large funds, private organizations open soup kitchens, and make provision for bread lines. Legislatures make special appropriations out of public funds raised by taxation. These are tacit and half-hearted recognitions of social responsibility, which are forced upon us by the stress of tragic circumstance.

They are necessary, and in the midst of an emergency, no one can say a word against such methods. Common humanity demands them. But they touch symptoms and effects, not causes. I said that civilized peoples show indirect recognition of social responsibility for unemployment. But I ought to have said that as long as this recognition operates only after the evil has shown itself and millions are suffering from no fault of their own (except too great patience with a bad system), the nations are only half-civilized.

Social responsibility, through charity, for unemployment is a back-handed, clumsy, inhuman, way of admitting society's responsibility for furnishing men and women security through steady employment at a living wage. The industrial system which cannot do this thing has written its own indictment and predicted its own down-fall. That men should starve because there is no bread in time of famine is a tragedy. But that men should lack bread because there is too much wheat, because farmers cannot sell although they have a superabundance and others cannot buy because they have no work and nothing to buy with, is no tragedy of nature's making. It is man's doing, and men, especially the men who manage and men who support the present economic system, are responsible.

To split hairs about over-production and under-consumption is like two men quarrelling when scales do not balance, one man saying it is because one pan is too heavy and the other man insisting the other is too light. The fact is the whole thing is out of balance.

When the present crisis is over in its outward sensational features, when things have returned to a comparatively more comfortable state called "normalcy," will they forget? Will they even complacently congratulate themselves upon the generosity with which society relieved distress? Or will they locate the causes of the distress of unemployment and modify the social system? If they do the former, the time of depression will recur sooner or later with renewed violence until the social system is changed by force. The alternative is such a recognition of society's responsibility for the evil as will by planned foresight and deliberate choice change the economic and financial structure of society itself.

Only a change in the system will ensure the right of every person to work and enable every one to live in security.

NOTES

First published in *Unemployed*, February 1931, 3–4, reprint, in LW.6.153–156.

1. Office of Congressional and Intergovernmental Affairs, "Unemployment Insurance 75th Anniversary: History of Unemployment Insurance in the United States," U.S. Department of Labor, Washington, DC, 2010, http://www.dol.gov/ocia/pdf/75th-Anniversary-Summary-FINAL.pdf.

PART V
Science and Society

34

The Influence of Darwinism on Philosophy

(1909)

EDITOR'S INTRODUCTION

Popular Science Monthly was founded in 1872 and still circulates today as *Popular Science* or *PopSci*. Its aim is "to disseminate scientific knowledge to the educated layman." In a 1909 issue, Dewey published "The Influence of Darwinism on Philosophy" on the scientist's profound influence on American philosophy.

Dewey attends especially to a crucial shift in modern times from ways of thinking that originated in ancient philosophy. Plato believed that our world is not the ultimate realm of reality. He thought that what is unchanging and permanent is most real, true, and good. So ideal forms, like the perfect form of Justice, Truth, or Beauty, for example, are what are supremely real. The world of experience, to Plato, was a realm of imperfect imitation of the forms. In addition, the world is constantly in flux, changing. This way of thinking permeated all areas of philosophy for over two thousand years. In connection with Plato, Dewey refers to the "Schoolmen" of what is known as the "Scholastic" tradition, which depended especially on Aristotle's teaching. Aristotle did not share all of Plato's beliefs, yet the scholastics, following Aristotle and Plato, had yet to appreciate the changing nature of animals over time and looked to Aristotle's teachings on the nature of causes, as the idea of a "final"—in the sense of traced back or "first"—cause complemented their religious beliefs.

For Dewey, the insight that animals adapt to their environments and that they use and improve tools for the sake of survival helped to shape his understanding of human nature and of the way ideas, beliefs, and communication work. Concepts, habits, and communication are some of the tools that human beings have used to address our environmental and social challenges. Understood in that way, we see why some ideas that may have been useful at one time can become outmoded, such as in narrow understandings of marriage that have been recently challenged.

Darwin's understanding of how species "originate" implies that they change, with new species coming into being. Before Darwin, the biological sciences were dominated by the idea referred to as the Great Chain of Being.[1] That outlook saw species as unchanging and ranked hierarchically. Darwin's revolutionary insights offered empirical evidence that refuted that long held viewpoint, which had been used to differentiate not only between people and animals but also between different races of human beings. Some figures, like Asa Gray, sought to reconcile Darwin's insights with design in a way that harkened back to Aristotle's and the Scholastics' understanding of causes considered secondary versus "first causes." Dewey refers to this as the "installment plan," critiquing the idea that the divinity could not design intended beings at once but needed to roll out their development over time.

It is helpful to note in reading this essay that Darwin's wife, Emma, was a firm religious believer who insisted that her husband remain open to divine inspiration despite his skepticism. She was supportive nonetheless of his research and writing. Dewey mentions in passing Darwin's "female relatives," who were among the religious voices with whom Darwin interacted.

Dewey's Darwinian approach to seeing ideas as tools helps us to understand cultural change, given that concepts like marriage can need updating. Darwin also helped to undermine one of the justifications for racist beliefs about different kinds of human beings, an important step in rendering democracy more inclusive.

"The Influence of Darwinism on Philosophy" is one of Dewey's most important essays in many ways, including, for example, the fact that he is best known for his book *Democracy and Education* and that work was fundamentally rooted in his evolutionary understanding of biology. For educational practice according to Dewey is best designed with an eye to understanding the nature of organisms, their communal lives, and their methods for growth and adaptation to new challenges and opportunities in their varied environments. Standardization and uniformity therefore are clearly opposed to the processes that enable new and innovative ideas and practices to emerge through the variation and adaptation of individuals' and communities' powers. In addition, his recognition of the value of differences, biological and social, is directly influential on his understanding of the nature and value of democracy.

I

That the publication of the *Origin of Species* marked an epoch in the development of the natural sciences is well known to the layman. That the combination of the very words origin and species embodied an intellectual revolt and introduced a new intellectual temper is easily overlooked by the expert. The conceptions that had reigned in the philosophy of nature and knowledge for two thousand years, the conceptions that had become the familiar furniture of the mind, rested on the assumption of the superiority of the fixed and final; they rested upon treating change and origin as signs of defect and unreality. In laying hands upon the sacred ark of absolute permanency, in treating the forms that had been regarded as types of fixity and perfection as originating and passing away, the *Origin of Species* introduced a mode of thinking that in the end was bound to transform the logic of knowledge, and hence the treatment of morals, politics and religion.

No wonder then that the publication of Darwin's book, a half-century ago, precipitated a crisis. The true nature of the controversy is easily concealed from us, however, by the theological clamor that attended it. The vivid and popular features of the anti-Darwinian row tended to leave the impression that the issue was between science on one side and theology on the other. Such was not the case—the issue lay primarily within science itself, as Darwin himself early recognized. The theological outcry he discounted from the start, hardly noticing it save as it bore upon the "feelings of his female relatives." But for two decades before final publication he contemplated the possibility of being put down by his scientific peers as a fool or as crazy; and he set, as the measure of his success, the degree in which he should affect three men of science: Lyell in geology, Hooker in botany and Huxley in zoology.

Religious considerations lent fervor to the controversy, but they did not provoke it. Intellectually, religious emotions are not creative but conservative. They attach themselves readily to the current view of the world and consecrate it. They steep and dye intellectual fabrics in the seething vat of emotions; they do not form their warp and woof. There is not, I think, an instance of any large idea about the world being independently generated by religion. Although the ideas that rose up like armed men against Darwinism owed their intensity to religious associations, their origin and meaning are to be sought in science and philosophy, not in religion.

II

Few words in our language foreshorten intellectual history as much as does the word species. The Greeks, in initiating the intellectual life of Europe, were impressed by characteristic traits of the life of plants and animals; so impressed indeed that they made these traits the key to defining nature and to explaining mind and society. And truly life is so wonderful that a seemingly successful reading of its mystery might well lead men to believe that the key to the secrets of heaven and earth was in their hands. The Greek rendering of this mystery, the Greek formulation of the aim and standard of knowledge, was in the course of time embodied in the word species, and it controlled philosophy for two thousand years. To understand the intellectual face-about expressed in the phrase "Origin of Species," we must, then, understand the long dominant idea against which it is a protest.

Consider how men were impressed by the facts of life. Their eyes fell upon certain things slight in bulk, and frail in structure. To every appearance, these perceived things were inert and passive. Suddenly, under certain circumstances, these things—henceforth known as seeds or eggs or germs—begin to change, to change rapidly in size, form and qualities. Rapid and extensive changes occur, however, in many things—as when wood is touched by fire. But the changes in the living thing are orderly; they are cumulative; they tend constantly in one direction; they do not, like other changes, destroy or consume, or pass fruitless into wandering flux; they realize and fulfil. Each successive stage, no matter how unlike its predecessor, preserves its net effect and also prepares the way for a fuller activity on the part of its successor. In living beings, changes do not happen as they seem to happen elsewhere, any which way; the earlier changes are regulated in view of later results. This progressive organization does not cease till there is achieved a true final term, a $\tau\varepsilon\lambda\acute{o}\varsigma$, a completed, perfected end. This final form exercises in turn a plenitude of functions, not the least noteworthy of which is production of germs like those from which it took its own origin, germs capable of the same cycle of self-fulfilling activity.

But the whole miraculous tale is not yet told. The same drama is enacted to the same destiny in countless myriads of individuals so sundered in time, so severed in space, that they have no opportunity for mutual consultation and no means of interaction. As an old writer quaintly said, "things of the same kind go through the same formalities"—celebrate, as it were, the same ceremonial rites.

This formal activity which operates throughout a series of changes and holds them to a single course; which subordinates their aimless flux to its own perfect manifestation; which, leaping the boundaries of space and time, keeps individuals distant in space and remote in time to a uniform type of structure and function: this principle seemed to give insight into the very nature of reality itself. To it Aristotle gave the name, εἶδος. This term the scholastics translated as *species*.

The force of this term was deepened by its application to everything in the universe that observes order in flux and manifests constancy through change. From the casual drift of daily weather, through the uneven recurrence of seasons and unequal return of seed time and harvest, up to the majestic sweep of the heavens—the image of eternity in time—and from this to the unchanging pure and contemplative intelligence beyond nature lies one unbroken fulfilment of ends. Nature, as a whole, is a progressive realization of purpose strictly comparable to the realization of purpose in any single plant or animal.

The conception of εἶδος, species, a fixed form and final cause, was the central principle of knowledge as well as of nature. Upon it rested the logic of science. Change as change is mere flux and lapse; it insults intelligence. Genuinely to know is to grasp a permanent end that realizes itself through changes, holding them thereby within the metes and bounds of fixed truth. Completely to know is to relate all special forms to their one single end and good: pure contemplative intelligence. Since, however, the scene of nature which directly confronts us is in change, nature as directly and practically experienced does not satisfy the conditions of knowledge. Human experience is in flux, and hence the instrumentalities of sense-perception and of inference based upon observation are condemned in advance. Science is compelled to aim at realities lying behind and beyond the processes of nature, and to carry on its search for these realities by means of rational forms transcending ordinary modes of perception and inference.

There are, indeed, but two alternative courses. We must either find the appropriate objects and organs of knowledge in the mutual interactions of changing things; or else, to escape the infection of change, we *must* seek them in some transcendent and supernal region. The human mind, deliberately as it were, exhausted the logic of the changeless, the final and the transcendent, before it essayed adventure on the pathless wastes of generation and transformation. We dispose all too easily of the efforts of the schoolmen to interpret nature and mind in terms of real essences, hidden forms and occult faculties, forgetful of the seriousness and dignity of the ideas that lay behind. We dispose of them by laughing at the famous gentleman who accounted for the fact that opium put people to sleep on the ground it had a dormitive faculty. But the doctrine, held in our own day, that knowledge of the plant that yields the poppy consists in referring the peculiarities of an individual to a type, to a universal form, a doctrine so firmly established that any other method of knowing was conceived to be unphilosophical and unscientific, is a survival of precisely the same logic. This identity of conception in the scholastic and anti-Darwinian theory may well suggest greater sympathy for what has become unfamiliar as well as greater humility regarding the further unfamiliarities that history has in store.

Darwin was not, of course, the first to question the classic philosophy of nature and of knowledge. The beginnings of the revolution are in the physical science of the sixteenth and seventeenth centuries. When Galileo said: "It is my opinion that the Earth is very noble and admirable by reason of so many and so different alterations and generations which are incessantly made therein," he expressed the changed temper that was coming over the world; the transfer of interest from the permanent to the changing. When Descartes said: "The nature of physical things is much more easily conceived when they are beheld coming gradually into existence, than when they are only considered as produced at once in a finished and perfect state," the modern world became self-conscious of the logic that was henceforth to control it, the logic of which Darwin's *Origin of Species* is the latest scientific achievement. Without the methods of Copernicus, Kepler, Galileo and their successors in astronomy, physics and chemistry, Darwin would have been helpless in the organic sciences. But prior to Darwin the impact of the new scientific method upon life, mind and politics, had been arrested, because between these ideal or moral interests and the inorganic world intervened the kingdom of plants and animals. The gates of the garden of life were barred to the new ideas; and only through this garden was there access to mind and politics. The influence of Darwin upon philosophy resides in his having conquered the phenomena of life for the principle of transition, and thereby freed the new logic for application to mind and morals and life. When he said of species what Galileo had said of the earth, *e pur si muove*,[2] he emancipated, once for all, genetic and experimental ideas as an organon of asking questions and looking for explanations.

III

The exact bearings upon philosophy of the new logical outlook are, of course, as yet, uncertain and inchoate. We live in the twilight of intellectual transition. One must add the rashness of the prophet to the stubbornness of the partisan to venture a systematic exposition of the influence upon philosophy of the Darwinian method. At best, we can but inquire as to its general bearing—the effect upon mental temper and complexion, upon that body of half-conscious, half-instinctive intellectual aversions and preferences which determine, after all, our more deliberate intellectual enterprises. In this vague inquiry there happens to exist as a kind of touchstone a problem of long historic currency that has also been much discussed in Darwinian literature. I refer to the old problem of design *versus* chance, mind *versus* matter, as the causal explanation, first or final, of things.

As we have already seen, the classic notion of species carried with it the idea of purpose. In all living forms, a specific type is present directing the earlier stages of growth to the realization of its own perfection. Since this purposive regulative principle is not visible to the senses, it follows that it must be an ideal or rational force. Since, however, the perfect form is gradually approximated through the sensible changes, it also follows that in and through a sensible realm a rational ideal force is working out its own ultimate manifestation. These inferences were extended to nature: (*a*) She does nothing in vain; but all for an ulterior purpose. (*b*) Within natural sensible events there is therefore contained a spiritual causal force, which as spiritual escapes perception, but is apprehended by an enlightened reason. (*c*) The manifestation of this principle brings about a subordination of matter and sense to its own realization, and this ultimate fulfilment is the goal of nature and of man. The design argument thus operated in two directions. Purposefulness accounted for the intelligibility of nature and the possibility of science, while the absolute or cosmic character of this purposefulness gave sanction and worth to the moral and religious endeavors of man. Science was underpinned and morals authorized by one and the same principle, and their mutual agreement was eternally guaranteed.

This philosophy remained, in spite of sceptical and polemic outbursts, the official and the regnant philosophy of Europe for over two thousand years. The expulsion of fixed first and final causes from astronomy, physics and chemistry had indeed given the doctrine something of a shock. But, on the other hand, increased acquaintance with the details of plant and animal life operated as a counterbalance and perhaps even strengthened the argument from design. The marvelous adaptations of organisms to their environment, of organs to the organism, of unlike parts of a complex organ—like the eye—to the organ itself; the foreshadowing by lower forms of the higher; the preparation in earlier stages of growth for organs that only later had their functioning—these things were increasingly recognized with the progress of botany, zoology, paleontology and embryology. Together they added such prestige to the design argument that by the late eighteenth century it was, as approved by the sciences of organic life, the central point of theistic and idealistic philosophy.

The Darwinian principle of natural selection cut straight under this philosophy. If all organic adaptations are due simply to constant variation and the elimination of those variations which are harmful in the struggle for existence that is brought about by excessive reproduction, there is no call for a prior intelligent causal force to plan and preordain them. Hostile critics charged Darwin with materialism and with making chance the cause of the universe.

Some naturalists, like Asa Gray, favored the Darwinian principle and attempted to reconcile it with design. Gray held to what may be called design on the installment plan. If we conceive the "stream of variations" to be itself intended, we may suppose that each successive variation was designed from the first to be selected. In that case, variation, struggle and selection simply define the mechanism of "secondary causes" through which the "first cause" acts; and the doctrine of design is none the worse off because we know more of its *modus operandi*.

Darwin could not accept this mediating proposal. He admits or rather he asserts that it is "impossible to conceive this immense and wonderful universe including man with his capacity of looking far backwards and far into futurity as the result of blind chance or necessity."[3] But nevertheless he holds that since variations are in useless as well as useful directions, and since the latter are sifted out simply by the stress of the conditions of struggle for existence, the design argument as applied to living beings is unjustifiable; and its lack of support there deprives it of scientific value as applied to nature in general. If the variations of the pigeon, which under artificial selection give the pouter pigeon, are not preordained for the sake of the breeder, by what logic do we argue that variations resulting in natural species are pre-designed?[4]

IV

So much for some of the more obvious facts of the discussion of design *versus* chance as causal principles of nature and of life as a whole. We brought up this discussion, you recall, as a crucial instance. What does our touchstone indicate as to the bearing of Darwinian ideas upon philosophy? In the first place, the new logic outlaws, flanks, dismisses—what you will—one type of problems and substitutes for it another type. Philosophy forswears inquiry after absolute origins and absolute finalities in order to explore specific values and the specific conditions that generate them.

Darwin concluded that the impossibility of assigning the world to chance as a whole and to design in its parts indicated the insolubility of the question. Two radically different reasons, however, may be given as to why a problem is insoluble. One reason is that the problem is too high for intelligence; the other is that the question in its very asking makes assumptions that render the question meaningless. The latter alternative is unerringly pointed to in the celebrated case of design *versus* chance. Once admit that the sole verifiable or fruitful object of knowledge is the particular set of changes that generate the object of study, together with the consequences that then flow from it, and no intelligible question can be asked about what, by assumption, lies outside. To assert—as is often asserted—that specific values of particular truth, social bonds and forms of beauty, if they can be shown to be generated by concretely knowable conditions, are meaningless and in vain; to assert that they are justified only when they and their particular causes and effects have all at once been gathered up into some inclusive first cause and some exhaustive final goal, is intellectual atavism.[5] Such argumentation is reversion to the logic that explained the extinction of fire by water through the formal essence of aqueousness and the quenching of thirst by water through the final cause of aqueousness. Whether used in the case of the special event or that of life as a whole, such logic only abstracts some aspect of the existing course of events in order to reduplicate it as a petrified eternal principle by which to explain the very changes of which it is the formalization.

When Henry Sidgwick casually remarked in a letter that as he grew older his interest in what or who made the world was altered into interest in what kind of a world it is anyway, his voicing of a common experience of our own day illustrates also the nature of that intellectual transformation effected by the Darwinian logic. Interest shifts from the wholesale essence back of special changes to the question of how special changes serve and defeat concrete purposes; shifts from an intelligence that shaped things once for all to the particular intelligences which things are even now shaping; shifts from an ultimate goal of good to the direct increments of justice and happiness that intelligent administration of existent conditions may beget and that present carelessness or stupidity will destroy or forego.

In the second place, the classic type of logic inevitably set philosophy upon proving that life *must* have certain qualities and values—no matter how experience presents the matter—because of some remote cause and eventual goal. The duty of wholesale justification inevitably accompanies all thinking that makes the meaning of special occurrences depend upon something that once and for all lies behind them. The habit of derogating from present meanings and uses prevents our looking the facts of experience in the face; it prevents serious acknowledgment of the evils they present and serious concern with the goods they promise but do not as yet fulfil. It turns thought to the business of finding a wholesale transcendent remedy for the one and guarantee for the other. One is reminded of the way many moralists and theologians greeted Herbert Spencer's recognition of an unknowable energy from which welled up the phenomenal physical processes without and the conscious operations within. Merely because Spencer labeled his unknowable energy "God," this faded piece of metaphysical goods was greeted as an important and grateful concession to the reality of the spiritual realm. Were it not for the deep hold of the habit of seeking justification for ideal values in the remote and transcendent, surely this reference of them to an unknowable absolute would be despised in comparison with the demonstrations of experience that knowable energies are daily generating about us precious values.

The displacing of this wholesale type of philosophy will doubtless not arrive by sheer logical disproof, but rather by growing recognition of its futility. Were it a thousand times true that opium produces sleep because of its dormitive energy, yet the inducing of sleep in the tired, and the recovery to waking life of the poisoned, would not be thereby one least step forwarded. And were it a thousand times dialectically demonstrated that life as a whole is regulated by a transcendent principle to a final inclusive goal, none the less truth and error, health and disease, good and evil, hope and fear in the concrete, would remain just what and where they now are. To improve our education, to ameliorate our manners, to advance our politics, we must have recourse to specific conditions of generation.

Finally, the new logic introduces responsibility into the intellectual life. To idealize and rationalize the universe at large is after all a confession of inability to master the courses of things that specifically concern us. As long as mankind suffered from this impotency, it naturally shifted a burden of responsibility that it could not carry over to the more competent shoulders of the transcendent cause. But if insight into specific conditions of value and into specific consequences of ideas is possible, philosophy must in time become a method of locating and interpreting the more serious of the conflicts that occur in life, and a method of projecting ways for dealing with them: a method of moral and political diagnosis and prognosis.

The claim to formulate *a priori* the legislative constitution of the universe is by its nature a claim that may lead to elaborate dialectic developments. But it is also one that removes these very conclusions from subjection to experimental test, for, by definition, these results make no differences in the detailed course of events. But a philosophy that humbles its pretensions to the work of projecting hypotheses for the education and conduct of mind, individual and social, is thereby subjected to test by the way in which the ideas it propounds work out in practice. In having modesty forced upon it, philosophy also acquires responsibility.

Doubtless I seem to have violated the implied promise of my earlier remarks and to have turned both prophet and partisan. But in anticipating the direction of the transformations in philosophy to be wrought by the Darwinian genetic and experimental logic, I do not profess to speak for any save those who yield themselves consciously or unconsciously to this logic. No one can fairly deny that at present there are two effects of the Darwinian mode of thinking. On the one hand, there are making many sincere and vital efforts to revise our traditional philosophic conceptions in accordance with its demands. On the other hand, there is as definitely a recrudescence of absolutistic philosophies; an assertion of a type of philosophic knowing distinct from that of the sciences, one which opens to us another kind of reality from that to which the sciences give access; an appeal through experience to something that essentially goes beyond experience. This reaction affects popular creeds and religious movements as well as technical philosophies. The very conquest of the biological sciences by the new ideas has led many to proclaim an explicit and rigid separation of philosophy from science.

Old ideas give way slowly; for they are more than abstract logical forms and categories. They are habits, predispositions, deeply engrained attitudes of aversion and preference. Moreover, the conviction persists—though history shows it to be a hallucination—that all the questions that the human mind has asked are questions that can be answered in terms of the alternatives that the questions themselves present. But in fact intellectual progress usually occurs through sheer abandonment of questions together with both of the alternatives they assume—an abandonment that results from their decreasing vitality and a change of urgent interest. We do not solve them: we get over them. Old questions are solved by disappearing, evaporating, while new questions corresponding to the changed attitude of endeavor and preference take their place. Doubtless the greatest dissolvent in contemporary thought of old questions, the greatest precipitant of new methods, new intentions, new problems, is the one effected by the scientific revolution that found its climax in the *Origin of Species*.

NOTES

First published in *Popular Science Monthly* 75 (1909): 90–98, with the title "Darwin's Influence upon Philosophy," reprint, in MW.4.3–15.

1. Arthur O. Lovejoy, *The Great Chain of Being: A Study of the History of an Idea* (Cambridge, MA: Harvard University Press, 1936).
2. [Editor's note: Which translates to: "And yet it moves."]
3. [Dewey's note:] *Life and Letters*, Vol. I, p. 282; cf. 285.
4. [Dewey's note:] *Life and Letters*, Vol. II, pp. 146, 170, 245; Vol. I, pp. 283–84. See also the closing portion of his *Variations of Animals and Plants under Domestication*.
5. [Editor's note: Atavism refers to the tendency for an organism to revert to characteristics of a remote ancestor. Dewey is being clever in his word choice, noting the connection between holding to outmoded ideas and reversion to historical traits that are understood to be biological.]

35
Science, Belief and the Public

(1924)

EDITOR'S INTRODUCTION

In his writings, Dewey often expresses his faith in democracy. He believes in the positive potential for human intelligence to wisely direct public action. Given that faith, little could be of greater importance than the development of intelligence in the wider public. He argues that such growth depends on freeing minds and developing the scientific attitude in all citizens. These values and needs were threatened in Dewey's day, and in a way that continues today. In a May 2014 poll, for example, Gallup found that only 50 percent of Americans believe that human beings evolved, with or without God's guidance. And 42 percent said that God created humans in their present form.[1]

Dewey begins this essay by explaining that the traditional conflict between science and religion involved a tension among four factors: religion, science, public opinion, and general education curricula. While in Europe at the time the wider public with little understanding of the sciences was generally dismissed in an undemocratic or elitist fashion, in the United States, democracy meant that public opinion matters greatly and must be heard. What this implies, Dewey argues, is not some conclusion about the flaws of or need to defend democracy but rather that what is needed is the cultivation of the scientific attitude in all citizens. Citizens' minds must be freed and opened. Appeals to anti-intellectual sentiment, unreasoned bias, and prejudices all are destructive of the scientific attitude. The proper instilment of that attitude leads people to engage in scientific study or consideration, inclining them to believe what the best scientific evidence supports.

It is odd, according to Dewey, that the great antipathy toward Darwin's insights really only sprung up over thirty years after the dissemination of his findings. One likely explanation is that *The Fundamentals: A Testimony to the Truth*, a set of ninety essays published between 1910 and 1915, were collected and popularized as claims deemed fundamental to Christianity and played an important role in the fundamentalist Christian movement, which included beliefs deemed to be at odds with the findings of evolutionary science.[2] As Dewey points out, in the meantime a scientific revolution had taken place that cannot be undone, yet the public demonstrated the powerful need for greater education in the scientific attitudes. Dewey's insights and worries could not be more relevant today, when misunderstandings about vaccines, evolution, and threats from climate change abound.[3]

The old issue between science and religion, or as many preferred to call it between science and theology, has slowly but surely changed its aspect. The operation of four rather than two forces is clearly evident in the current fundamentalist controversy. Instead of an alignment of two opposing tendencies, there is now a quadrilateral situation. The "people" have been called in, so that public opinion and sentiment are a power to be reckoned with; because of this fact the state of general education is a new and decisive factor in shaping the course and outcome of the old struggle.

When a glance is cast upon the earlier conflict between the new science of nature and traditional dogmas, the mass of the people is seen to be indifferent and unconcerned; they are hardly even spectators of the combat. On one side there are a few scientific inquirers, men like Galileo, who in the course of their scientific investigations reach results, especially about astronomical matters and the place of the earth in the scheme of things, directly contrary to those contained in the official doctrines of the church. On the other hand, there are the official representatives of the church, aggrieved and insulted by the challenge of a few scientific heretics. Outside of these limited circles, few knew or cared about what was going on. But the printing press, cheap newspapers, mails and telegraph and the extension of schooling have changed all that.

Even in the few years since Darwin published his *Origin of Species* affairs have moved rapidly. The rise of Protestantism and the increased active participation of laymen in matters of religious beliefs had indeed aroused a much wider public concern about the new views regarding the development of life and a naturalistic interpretation of the Descent of Man, than had the older scientific heresies. The issue was no longer wholly between scientific men on one side and established official authorities of the church on the other. Hot debate took place in widely circulated books and magazines, and large numbers were stirred to passionate adherence and more passionate denunciations. But I should guess that the number of daily newspapers was small that concerned themselves with the issue beyond reviews in their literary columns; it would be, I fancy, a safe wager that the controversy did not make the first page of newspapers, with glaring headlines, nor cause anything approaching the stir excited today by a single sermon by a well-known clergyman. Certain it is that bills were not introduced in legislatures and parliaments. For geology and biology not being at that time regular parts of even higher schooling, except perhaps for a few, there was nothing for statutes to regulate, unless the state was to emulate the Inquisition in regulating the diffusion of all scientific notions about the world.

These considerations help explain, it seems to me, a fact which has puzzled so many. For a long time it looked as if the conception of continuity of organic development had, in some version or other, become about as firmly entrenched in science and as accepted from science by the public mind as Copernican astronomy. Many of us imagined that a serious attack upon evolutionary views with a revival of pre-Darwinian biology was as improbable as an attack upon the astronomy of Galileo, or a wide-spread and influential campaign in behalf of the Ptolemaic system. Certainly, from the specialized scientific point of view, the anti-evolutionary campaign comes about three centuries too late. If it were to affect seriously the course of scientific inquiries, a number of persons should have been strangled in their cradles some three hundred years ago. Nevertheless, the issue is for the public actual and vital today, in spite of the elapse of a generation in which we prided ourselves—just as we prided ourselves that a great war was henceforth impossible—upon the advance of the scientific spirit, and the accommodation of the public mind to the conclusions of scientific inquiries.

The moral is inevitable. The public, the popular mass that the enlightened could once refer to as canaille, has taken an active part; but the conditions which have enabled the public actively to intervene have failed in providing an education which would enable the public to discriminate, with respect to the matters upon which it is most given to vehement expression, between opinions untouched by scientific method and attitude and the weight of evidence.

This to my mind is the salient aspect of the present situation. In the large, the controversy between science and dogma in the old sense is over and done with. There are many individuals, believers and others, to whom the question of adjusting their religious conceptions to the conclusions of science is still a vital one. But as a technical and professional cause, science has won its freedom. Scientists in the field and the laboratory may be discommoded at times, individual inquirers and teachers may lose their jobs. But the scientific revolution is nevertheless accomplished; and it is one of the revolutions that do not turn backwards. Inquirers will go on inquiring, and the results of their inquiries will be disseminated at least among their fellow-workers, and will make their way—even if they are as revolutionary as are the discoveries of the last thirty years regarding the constitution of matter and energy, ideas more upsetting of older conceptions in many ways than were those of the intellectual pioneers of the seventeenth century. The real issue is not here. It concerns the growing influence of the general public in matters of thought and belief, and the comparative failure of schooling up to the present time to instil even the rudiments of the scientific attitude in vast numbers of persons, so as to enable them to distinguish between matters of mere opinion and argument and those of fact and ascertainment of fact.

Americans who have been abroad tell of the amused incredulity of educated Europeans over reports of the state of scientific and theological controversy in this country; the reports seem incredible except upon the basis of an almost barbaric state of culture. Yet it may be doubted whether if numbers alone were taken into account, there would not be a larger proportion of persons in this country who could give an intelligent statement of the scientific conceptions involved than in most European countries. The difference is that in those countries those who could not give an intelligent exposition hardly count at all. Here, owing to the spread of democracy in social relations and in education, they count for a great deal. They feel themselves concerned and have channels through which they can make their influence felt.

Naturally such a situation is sport for those hostile to democracy and to universal schooling. They are entitled to chuckle and to make the most of it in their indictments. But, after all, it is a condition and not a theory that confronts us. Defences of democracy are about as much out of place in any scheme of action as are attacks. No social creed produced the present situation. The consequences of the industrialization of affairs in such things as change of population from rural to urban, quick and easy transportation of persons and goods, cheap communications and the rise of cheap printing-matter, have created that state of society which we call democratic, and the democratic creed. Unless the movement of forces is radically altered, attacks upon democracy are about as effective as shooting paper-wads at a battle-ship—an occupation that may also conceivably relieve the feelings under certain conditions.

The realities of the situation centre about what can be done to ally the forces which create the democratizing of society with the mental and moral attitudes of science. The worst of the predicament is a tendency toward a vicious circle. The forces that compel some degree of general schooling also make for a loose, scrappy and talkative education, and this education in turn reenforces the bad features of the underlying forces. But it is some gain to know where the issue actually lies; to be compelled to face the fact that while schooling has been extended and scientific subjects have found their way into the regular course of studies, little has been accomplished as yet in converting prejudiced and emotional habits of mind into scientific interest and capacity.

This generic diagnosis of the disease may be specified in two particulars. There is a considerable class of influential persons, enlightened and liberal in technical, scientific and religious matters, who are only too ready to make use of appeal to authority, prejudice, emotion and ignorance to serve their purposes in political and economic affairs. Having done whatever they can do to debauch the habit of the public mind in these respects, they then sit back in amazed sorrow when this same habit of mind displays itself violently with regard, say, to the use of established methods of historic and literary interpretations of the scriptures or with regard to the animal origin of man. "Fundamentalism" might have been revived even if the Great War had not occurred. But it is reasonable to suppose that it would have not assumed such an intolerant and vituperative form, if so many educated men, in positions of leadership, had not deliberately cultivated resort to bitter intolerance and to coercive suppression of disliked opinions during the war.

Again, a man may be thoroughly convinced that the spread of certain economic ideas is dangerous to society; but if he encourages, even by passivity, recourse to coercion and intimidation in order to resist the holding and teaching of these ideas, he should not be surprised if others fail to draw the line of persecution and intolerance just where he personally would draw it. The statement that as we sow, so shall we reap, is trite. But there is no field of life in which it applies so aptly and fully as in that of belief and the methods employed to affect belief. Until highly respectable and cultivated classes of men cease to suppose that in economic and political matters the importance of the end of social stability and security justifies the use of means other than those of reason, the intellectual habit of the public will continue to be corrupted at the root, and by those from whom enlightenment should be expected.

The other point concerns the kind of education given in the schools, as that is affected by the temper of actual and professed pillars of society. There are at the best plenty of obstacles in the way of thinking in general, and in particular of using school instruction so as to further discriminating and circumspect thought. The weight of authority, custom, imitation, pressure of time, large numbers, the need of "covering the ground," of securing mechanical skill, of uniformity in administrative matters, of sparing tax-payers, all conspire to depress thinking. These extraneous obstacles are consolidated and held together by the fear entertained by many "best minds" lest the schools promote habits of independent thinking. Fundamentally, fear of the consequences of thought underlies most professions of reverence for culture, respect for quantity of information and emphasis upon discipline. The fundamental defect in the present state of democracy is the assumption that political and economic freedom can be achieved without first freeing the mind. Freedom of mind is not something that spontaneously happens. It is not achieved by the mere absence of obvious restraints. It is a product of constant, unremitting nurture of right habits of observation and reflection. Until the taboos that hedge social topics from contact with thought are removed, scientific method and results in subjects far removed from social themes will make little impression upon the public mind. Prejudice, fervor of emotion, bunkum, opinion and irrelevant argument will weigh as heavily as fact and knowledge.

Intellectual confusion will continue to encourage the men who are intolerant and who fake their beliefs in the interests of their feelings and fancies.

NOTES

First published in *New Republic* 38 (1924): 143–45, reprint, in MW.15.47–53.

1. Frank Newport, "In U.S., 42% Believe Creationist View of Human Origins," Gallup Politics, June 2, 2014, http://www.gallup.com/poll/170822/believe-creationist-view-human-origins.aspx.
2. I am grateful to Tibor Solymosi for pointing out this factor that neither Dewey nor I had recognized as one of the possible reasons for the timing of opposition to Darwin's insights. See R. A. Torrey and A. C. Dixon, *The Fundamentals: A Testimony to the Truth* (1917; Grand Rapids, MI: Baker, 2008). See also Eugenie C. Scott, *Evolution vs. Creationism: An Introduction* (Westport, CT: Greenwood, 2004).
3. See Sammy Roth, "Climate Change, Extreme Weather Already Threaten 50% of U.S. Military Sites," *USA Today*, January 31, 2018, https://www.usatoday.com/story/weather/2018/01/31/climate-change-extreme-weather-military-defense-department-trump-global-warming-wildfires-droughts/1079278001/; and Fortune editors and Reuters, "ExxonMobil Gives in to Shareholders on Climate Risk Disclosure," *Fortune*, December 12, 2017, http://fortune.com/2017/12/12/exxon-mobil-climate/.

36
Social Science and Social Control

(*1931*)

EDITOR'S INTRODUCTION

The year 1930 marked the start of the Great Depression. At that time of economic crisis, there was no dearth of views about economics and human behavior, whether communist or laissez-faire capitalist. When we begin with ideology and then try to apply it to present situations, Dewey explained, we are working backward.

Although the words "economics" and "economists" do not occur in this essay, Dewey understood them in terms of social science. At the time, people believed firmly in the physical sciences but doubted social sciences in general. In this essay, Dewey aimed to explain how people were misunderstanding the difference between social sciences and physical sciences and, in the process, how people were putting the cart before the horse with respect to the former.

Dewey makes a similar point in other works about ideas like social contract theory. That way of thinking imagined what would happen if people lived in some imaginary state of nature and came to an agreement about how to behave. Social contract theory has many intellectual proponents, but Dewey argued that the very orientation of its efforts was backward. If you start from the problems that ail society and the efforts that are already in place, if any, to address them, then social science can learn from how the world is functioning and theorize ways to bring about reform for the better. Reforms can then be tested and refined in further experimentation. The methods of the physical sciences in that sense have already been working in that more sensible way.

The aim in contexts like economics should not be to devise a first principle and then apply that knowledge to present circumstances. Both laissez-faire libertarianism and state communism make that mistake. Instead, the question is what are present circumstances, and how can we learn from them for the sake of social science and for creating hypotheses about how to achieve progress? Today we have witnessed many advances in social sciences, such as in psychology or political science, that have enabled explanations, predictions, and proposals for future decision making. In this essay, Dewey was advocating for a proper and sincere understanding of the methods of intelligent inquiry in application to the social facts studied in the fields of the social sciences. Just because physical and social sciences study different kinds of things does not mean that they cannot both make invaluable use of the experimentalist method of intelligence. In addition, it is a mistake to think that social science must be settled before efforts at social controls and planning can occur, for efforts at social control stimulate the social sciences and enable them.

It would require a technical survey, which would be out of place here, to prove that the existing limitations of "social science" are due mainly to unreasoning devotion to physical science as a model, and to a misconception of physical science at that. Without making any such survey, attention may be directly called to one outstanding difference between physical and social facts. The ideal of the knowledge dealing with the former is the elimination of all factors dependent upon distinctively human response. "Fact," physically speaking, is the ultimate residue after human purposes, desires, emotions, ideas and ideals have been systematically excluded. A social "fact," on the other hand, is a concretion in external form of precisely these human factors.

An occurrence is a physical fact only when its constituents and their relations remain the same, irrespective of the human attitude toward them. A species of mosquitoes is the carrier of the germs of malaria, whether we like or dislike malaria. Drainage and oil-spraying to destroy mosquitoes are a social fact because their use depends upon human purpose and desire. A steam locomotive or a dynamo is a physical fact in its structure; it is a social fact when its existence depends upon the desire for rapid and cheap transportation and communication. The machine itself may be understood physically without reference to human aim and motive. But the railway or public-utility system cannot be understood without reference to human purposes and human consequences.

I may illustrate the present practice of slavishly following the technique of physical science and the uselessness of its results by the present zeal for "fact finding." Of course, one cannot think, understand and plan without a basis of fact, and since facts do not lie around in plain view, they have to be discovered. But for the most part, the data which now are so carefully sought and so elaborately scheduled are not social facts at all. For their connection with any system of human purposes and consequences, their bearing as means and as results upon human action, are left out of the picture. At best they are mere physical and external facts. They are unlike the facts of physical science, because the latter are found by methods which make their interrelations and their laws apparent, while the facts of social "fact finding" remain a miscellaneous pile of meaningless items. Since their connections with human wants and their effect on human values are neglected, there is nothing which binds them together into an intelligible whole.

It may be retorted that to connect facts with human desires and their effect upon human values is subjective and moral, and to an extent that makes it impossible to establish any conclusions upon an objective basis: that to attempt inference on this point would land us in a morass of speculative opinion. Suppose, for example, all the facts about the working of the prohibition law and its enforcement were much more completely known than they are; even so, to establish a connection between these facts and the human attitudes lying back of them would be a matter of guess work. As things stand, there is much force in the objection. But if made universal, it would overlook the possibility of another kind of situation.

Wherever purposes are employed deliberately and systematically for the sake of certain desired social results, there it is possible, within limits, to determine the connection between the human factor and the actual occurrence, and thus to get a complete social fact, namely, the actual external occurrence in its human relationships. Prohibition, whether noble or not, is not an experiment in any intelligent scientific sense of the term. For it was undertaken without the effort to obtain the conditions of control which are essential to any experimental determination of fact. The Five Year Plan of Russia, on the other hand, whether noble or the reverse, has many of the traits of a social experiment, for it is an attempt to obtain certain specified social results by the use of specified definite measures, exercised under conditions of considerable, if not complete, control.

The point I am making may be summed up by saying that it is a complete error to suppose that efforts at social control depend upon the prior existence of a social science. The reverse is the case. The building up of social science, that is, of a body of knowledge in which facts are ascertained in their significant relations, is dependent upon putting social planning into effect. It is at this point that the misconception about physical science, when it is taken as a model for social knowledge, is important. Physical science did not develop because inquirers piled up a mass of facts about observed phenomena. It came into being when men intentionally experimented, on the basis of ideas and hypotheses, with observed phenomena to modify them and disclose new observations. This process is self-corrective and self-developing. Imperfect and even wrong hypotheses, when acted upon, brought to light significant phenomena which made improved ideas and improved experimentations possible. The change from a passive and accumulative attitude into an active and productive one is the secret revealed by the progress of physical inquiry. Men obtained knowledge of natural energies by trying deliberately to control the conditions of their operation. The result was knowledge, and then control on a larger scale by the application of what was learned.

It is a commonplace of logical theory that laws are of the "if-then" type. If something occurs, then something else happens; if certain conditions exist, they are accompanied by certain other conditions. Such knowledge alone is knowledge of a fact in any intelligible sense of the word. Although we have to act in order to discover the conditions underlying the "if" in physical matters, yet the material constituting the "if" is there apart from our action; like the movements of sun and earth in an eclipse. But in social phenomena the relation is: "If we do something, something else will happen." The objective material constituting the "if" belongs to us, not to something wholly independent of us. We are concerned, not with a bare relation of cause and effect, but with one of means and consequences, that is, of causes deliberately used for the sake of producing certain effects. As far as we intentionally do and make, we shall know; as far as we "know" without making, our so-called knowledge is a miscellany, or at most antiquarian, and hence without relevance to future planning. Only the knowledge which is itself the fruit of a technology can breed further technology.

I want to make the same point with reference to social prediction. Here, too, the assumption is generally made that we must be able to predict before we can plan and control. Here again the reverse is the case. We can predict the occurrence of an eclipse precisely because we cannot control it. If we could control it, we could not predict, except contingently; just as we can predict a collision when we see two trains approaching on the same track—provided that a human being does not foresee the possibility and take measures to avert its happening. The other day I ran across a remark of Alexander Hamilton's to the effect that instead of awaiting an event to know what measures to take, we should take measures to bring the event to pass. And I would add that only then can we genuinely forecast the future in the world of social matters.

Empirical rule-of-thumb practices were the mothers of the arts. But the practices of the arts were in turn the source of science, when once the empirical methods were freed in imagination and used with some degree of freedom of experimentation. There cannot be a science of an art until the art has itself made some advance, and the significant development occurs when men intentionally try to use such art as they have already achieved in order to obtain results which they conceive to be desirable. If we have no social technique at all, it is impossible to bring planning and control into being. If we do have at hand a reasonable amount of technique, then it is by deliberately using what we have that we shall in the end develop a dependable body of social knowledge. If we want foresight, we shall not obtain it by any amount of fact finding so long as we disregard the human aims and desires producing the facts which we find. But if we decide upon what we want socially, what sort of social consequences we wish to occur, and then use whatever means we possess to effect these intended consequences, we shall find the road that leads to foresight. Forethought and planning must come before foresight.

I am not arguing here for the desirability of social planning and control. That is another question. Those who are satisfied with present conditions and who are hopeful of turning them to account for personal profit and power will answer it in the negative. What I am saying is that if we want something to which the name "social science" may be given, there is only one way to go about it, namely, by entering upon the path of social planning and control. Observing, collecting, recording and filing tomes of social phenomena without deliberately trying to do something to bring a desired state of society into existence only encourages a conflict of opinion and dogma in their interpretation. If the social situation out of which these facts emerge is itself confused and chaotic because it expresses socially unregulated purpose and haphazard private intent, the facts themselves will be confused, and we shall add only intellectual confusion to practical disorder. When we deliberately employ whatever skill we possess in order to serve the ends which we desire, we shall begin to attain a measure of at least intellectual order and understanding. And if past history teaches anything, it is that with intellectual order we have the surest possible promise of advancement to practical order.

NOTE

First published in *New Republic* 67 (July 29, 1931): 276–77, reprint, in LW.6.64–69.

37

Education and Birth Control

(1932)

EDITOR'S INTRODUCTION

In "Education and Birth Control," published in the *Nation*, Dewey extends his outlook on the role of scientific and experimental inquiry to issues of democratic concern and public well-being. Dewey here argues that the quality of life is more important than its quantity in terms of family size. He also argues that more information, not less, enables greater wisdom for making choices about families.

Today, we find parallel concerns among those who wish to limit sex education to abstinence-only curricula, when comprehensive sex education curricula are available and demonstrably more effective at reducing STDs and unintended pregnancies.[1] The wish of some parents to control what their children learn is consistent with opt-out policies for sex education, whereas abstinence-only curricula face similar criticisms to those that Dewey raises in this essay—concerning the idea that people are choosing, and not only for their own children, ignorance and darkness over knowledge. In Dewey's day, lack of education about birth control meant large families. Today, similar lack translates into teenage pregnancy and consequent higher school dropout rates.

The opposition to the birth-control movement is not a unique or isolated fact. It is an expression of an ever-recurring struggle between darkness and knowledge. We are given to thinking that science has overthrown all enemies to its advance. This may be true of the technical aspects of science, those which have no clear social bearings. It is not true when newly discovered knowledge has important bearings upon the conduct of life. There is always a rearguard of ignorance, prejudice, dogma, routine, tradition, which fights against the spread of new ideas that entail new practices. It has been so in astronomy, physics, biology. It is not surprising that it is so in the case of medicine.

The line of battle changes. The particular ideas that are resisted change. But relatively the fight is constant. Men do not any longer, except a few cranks, strive against the Copernican astronomy. But some conflict between new truth and what is old and intrenched goes on, and probably will go on as long as man lives with a past behind him and a future ahead of him.

We forget how comparatively recent is any scientific knowledge concerning the processes of procreation and conception. It was only late in intellectual history that they were discovered to be chemical in nature, and that something of their mechanism was learned. Now, new knowledge always means the possibility of new control. With this particular scientific discovery there arose the possibility of intelligent control of blind natural processes. This is the logic of the birth-control movement. Just as expanding knowledge of electricity brought with it the electric light, telegraph, telephone, dynamo, so scientific knowledge of the transmission of life enables mankind to bring that process under human direction. Because knowledge always means increased control, there can be no doubt of where ultimate victory will lie in this particular conflict. The conflict between ignorance and knowledge becomes one between chance and control.

Meantime, however, individuals are prevented by law and by public sentiment from access to the knowledge which would give them more complete control of their conduct—laws and public sentiment that were formed when adequate scientific knowledge was lacking. How can anyone who believes in education and in enlightenment of the public through education fail to be opposed to this restriction on the flow of intelligence? The opposition to it should be all the stronger because what is proposed is only a legislation which places the source of this flow in the hands of scientists and physicians. There is always wholesome sanitation wherever there is free circulation of intelligence. We need light and circulation of air in intellectual and moral matters as in physical. Suppression and secrecy breed unfairness, mental and moral disorder. Our plea, from the side of education, is that there be removed arbitrary restrictions to that movement of knowledge and understanding which brings the action of the blind forces of nature under the control of intelligence.

The other point I wish to make is just as simple. All educators today attach great importance to the development of individual capacities. They are all opposed to merely mass education, to regimentation, the lock step, to uniformity imposed upon boys and girls, no two of whom are alike. But as long as multitudes of families have too many children and those children badly spaced, it is not possible for each child to have proper individual attention—physical, intellectual, moral. I have no hesitation in saying that no matter what educators may say and do in behalf of better development of individuals as individuals, their ideals cannot be realized unless there is intelligent control of the size of families. Mere mass and number will stand in the way with the great majority of families.

I can think of no change which would be more beneficial than one which would make us prize quality more and quantity less. Our American zeal for size is one thing that stands in the way of our giving proper attention to higher values. The exaggerated importance attached to size has affected our schools and the instruction they give. It stands in the way of a multitude of desirable improvements. If parents were in a position to make quality of life supreme in their own households, the larger problem of the schools would be taken care of.

NOTES

First published in *Nation* 134 (January 27, 1932): 112, repint, in LW.6.146–149.

1. John B. Jemmott III, Loretta S. Jemmott, and Geoffrey T. Fong, "Efficacy of a Theory-Based Abstinence-Only Intervention Over 24 Months: A Randomized Controlled Trial with Young Adolescents," *Archives of Pediatric Adolescent Medicine* 164, no. 2 (2010): 152–59.

38

The Supreme Intellectual Obligation

(1934)

EDITOR'S INTRODUCTION

On December 27, 1933, Dewey addressed the American Association for the Advancement of Science, which held a dinner in honor of James Cattell. Cattell was a professor of psychology at the University of Pennsylvania who contributed significantly to the advancement of psychology as a field and who edited a number of publications that were influential in the academy and beyond. In particular, he edited the journal *Science*, still one of the top scientific journals today, as well as *Popular Science Monthly*.

In Dewey's address, he notes the danger of academia's heightened specialization, through which the language of science becomes inaccessible to the wider public as well as more abstracted from practical value, at least in the public's understanding. The science education of his day, much like education today, was significantly focused on conveying information as facts or theories, but almost not at all on fostering in students the scientific attitudes and habits of mind that lead to knowledge and the resolution of problems. Dewey argues that the supreme intellectual obligation is essentially that scientific inquiry, understood broadly, ought to be employed for improving the lives of the masses of people. Esoteric and unintelligible discoveries not used to advance human ends fail to live up to this obligation. That does not mean that the public must or will understand all of what intellectual developments have to offer, yet the latter can be employed for public benefit and the public can be and ought to be educated sufficiently to be able to appreciate wisdom and to put it to use. Therefore, the supreme intellectual obligation demands consequently the development of the scientific attitude and habits of mind in the wider public through public education, including especially in elementary schooling.

Dewey's insights and argument are fresh today, as we witness the dismantling of the U.S. Department of Education.[1] In Dewey's day, information was not nearly so easily available as it is now, when the internet has exploded the availability of information, yet the problem he describes remains and is perhaps even more important: that what is needed now more than ever is the cultivation of intelligence and the scientific attitudes that enable people to make the wisest use of the mass of information that is today at our fingertips.

The central argument of Dewey's essay here draws from the philosophical tradition, especially from the lessons of Plato's allegory of the cave, which Dewey approaches democratically. Plato believed that the wise have an obligation to leave the cave, seeking the natural light of truth, and to reenter the cave for the sake of those left behind. Dewey adds the democratic push to empower everyone and to cultivate the scientific attitudes in all citizens. Today, it is reasonable to ask what effect the intense focus on standardized testing in U.S. public schools is having on the development of students' intellectual habits of mind and attitudes.

The scientific worker faces a dilemma. The nature of his calling necessitates a very considerable remoteness from immediate social activities and interests. His vocation is absorbing in its demands upon time, energy and thought. As men were told to enter their closets to pray, so the scientific man has to enter the seclusion of the laboratory, museum and study. He has, as it is, more than enough distractions to contend with, especially if, as so often happens, he is also a teacher and has administrative and committee duties. Moreover, the field of knowledge cannot be attacked en masse. It must be broken up into problems, and as a rule, detailed aspects and phases of these problems must be discriminated into still lesser elements. A certain degree of specialization is a necessity of scientific advance. With every increase of specialization, remoteness from common and public affairs also increases. Division of labor is as much a necessity of investigation into the secrets of nature and of man as it is of industry.

Nor does aloofness reach an end in this point. The language in use for common communication does not fit the needs of statement of scientific inquiries and results. It was developed for other purposes than that of accurate and precise exposition of science, and is totally unfitted to set forth comprehensive generalizations in exact form. The result is that the scientist speaks what for the mass of men is an unknown tongue, one that requires much more training to acquire than any living speech or than any dead language. He can speak directly about his own affairs and problems only to a comparatively small circle of the initiated.

These considerations define one horn of the dilemma. The other horn is constituted by the fact that the scientist lives in the same world with others, and a world that is being made over by the fruits of his labors. There is hardly a single detail of our common and collective life, whether in transportation of persons and goods, in modes of communication, in household appliances and conveniences, in medicine, in agriculture and all the varied forms of productive industry, that is not what it is today because of what science has discovered. The scientist may be aloof in his work and language, but the results of his work pervade and permeate, they determine, every aspect of social life. The inventor, the engineer and the business man are unremittingly occupied with translating what is discovered in the laboratory into applications of utensil, device, tool and machine, which have largely revolutionized the conduct of life in the home, the farm and amusement as well as industry. I could easily spend many times my allotted time in a partial cataloging of things unknown fifty years ago that are now everyday necessities.

These consequences of science extend their influence far beyond what anthropologists call material culture. They affect institutions and great modes of interest and activity. We have broken with the intellectual traditions of the past and the mass of men have not had the nature of the change interpreted to them, although science set the terms on which men associate together.

They transform life in ways that have created social problems of such vastness and complexity that the human mind stands bewildered. The intellect is at present subdued by the results of its own intellectual victories. It has become a commonplace to refer to consequences of chemistry in its application to warfare. High explosives, with their allies of steel and airplane derived from physics, are capable of destroying every city on the face of the earth, and we are even threatened with bacterial warfare. If the problems of peace and war have assumed a new and unprecedented form—which, alas, the nations are meeting for the most part only by increased expenditure for armament—it is because of applications of scientific knowledge.

I have selected but one aspect of the question. The economic problem which weighs so heavily upon us today affords another illustration of the new social impact of science. Here too it is a commonplace that mankind in advanced industrial countries and especially in the United States confronts the paradox of want in the midst of plenty. It is science, which through technological applications has produced the potentiality of plenty, of ease and security for all, while lagging legal and political institutions, unaffected as yet by the advance of science into their domain, explain the want, insecurity and suffering that are the other term of the paradox.

My title is the supreme intellectual obligation. But every obligation is moral, and in its ultimate consequences social. The demands of the situation cannot be met, as some reactionaries urge, by going backward in science, by putting restrictions upon its productive activities. They cannot be met by putting a gloss of humanistic culture over the brute realities of the situation. They can be met only by human activity exercised in human directions. The wounds made by applications of science can be healed only by a further extension of applications of knowledge and intelligence; like the purpose of all modern healing the application must be preventive as well as curative. This is the supreme obligation of intellectual activity at the present time. The moral consequences of science in life impose a corresponding responsibility.

As with almost everything in contemporary life, it is easier to diagnose the ill than to indicate the remedy. But there are some suggestions that occur to all who reflect upon the problem. The field of education is immense and it has hardly been touched by the application of science. There are, indeed, courses in science installed in high schools and colleges. That much of the educational battle has been won, and we owe a great debt to those who waged the battle against the obstacles of tradition and the inertia of institutional habit. But the scientific attitude, the will to use scientific method and the equipment necessary to put the will into effect, is still, speaking for the mass of people, inchoate and unformed. The obligations incumbent upon science cannot be met until its representatives cease to be contented with having a multiplicity of courses in various sciences represented in the schools, and devote even more energy than was spent in getting a place for science in the curriculum to seeing to it that the sciences which are taught are themselves more concerned about creating a certain mental attitude than they are about purveying a fixed body of information, or about preparing a small number of persons for the further specialized pursuit of some particular science.

I do not mean of course that every opportunity should not be afforded the comparatively small number of selected minds that have both taste and capacity for advanced work in a chosen field of science. But I do mean that the responsibility of science cannot be fulfilled by educational methods that are chiefly concerned with the self-perpetuation of specialized science to the neglect of influencing the much larger number to adopt into the very make-up of their minds those attitudes of open-mindedness, intellectual integrity, observation and interest in testing their opinions and beliefs that are characteristic of the scientific attitude.

The problem is of course much broader than the remaking of courses in science which is nevertheless requisite. Every course in every subject should have as its chief end the cultivation of these attitudes of mind. As long as acquisition of items of information, whether they be particular facts or broad generalizations, is the chief concern of instruction, the appropriation of method into the working constitution of personality will continue to come off a bad second. Information is necessary, yes, more than is now usually obtained. But it should not stand as an end in itself. It should be an integral part of the operations of learning that construct the scientific attitude; that are, indeed, a part of that attitude since the scientific inquirer is above all else a continuing and persistent learner. As long as intellectual docility is the chief aim, as long as it is esteemed more important for the young to acquire correct beliefs than to be alert about the methods by which beliefs are formed the influence of science will be confined to those departments in which it has won its victories in the past. I cannot refrain from saying that one great obstacle is that many scientific men still hold, implicitly if not expressly, that there is a region of beliefs, social, religious, and political, which is reserved for sheer acceptance and where unbiased inquiry should not intrude.

There is, moreover, a virgin field practically untouched by the influence of science. Elementary education is still a place for acquiring skills and passively absorbing facts. It is generally now admitted that the most fundamental attitudes are formed in childhood, many of them in the early years. The greatest indictment that can be brought against present civilization, in its intellectual phase, is that so little attention is given to instilling, as a part of organic habit, trust in intelligence and eager interest in its active manifestation. I take little interest in demonstrations of the average low level of native intelligence as long as I am aware how little is done to secure full operation of what native intellectual capacity there is, however limited it may be. Speaking generally, it is now everywhere subordinated to acquisition of special skills and the retention of more or less irrelevant masses of facts and principles—irrelevant, that is, to the formation of the inquiring mind that explores and tests. Yet childhood is the time of the most active curiosity and highest interest in continual experimentation. The chief responsibility for the attainment of a system of education in which the groundwork of a habit and attitude inspired and directed by something akin to the method of science lies with those who already enjoy the benefits of special scientific training.

I have spoken chiefly with respect to the education of the schools. But the problem and the responsibility of education go deeper. There are some signs of a rebirth of the educational interest that marked the Greeks who thought of it, as far as we can gather from the records, chiefly in terms of adults. The theme of adult education is in the air. There was never a time in the history of the world in which power to think with respect to conduct of social life and the remaking of traditional institutions is as important as it is today in our own country. There is an immense amount of knowledge available, knowledge economic, historical, psychological, as well as physical. The chief obstacle lies not in lack of the information that might be brought to bear, experimentally, upon our problems. It lies on the one hand in the fact that this knowledge is laid away in cold storage for safe-keeping, and on the other hand in the fact that the public is not yet habituated to desire the knowledge nor even to belief in the necessity for it. Hunger is lacking and the material with which to feed it is not accessible. Yet appetite grows with eating. The trouble with much of what is called popularization of knowledge is that it is content with diffusion of information, in diluted form, merely as information. It needs to be organized and presented in its bearing upon action. Here is a most significant phase of the obligation incumbent upon the scientifically trained men and women of our age. When there is the same energy displayed in applying knowledge to large human problems as there is today in applying it to physical inventions and to industry and commerce many of our present problems will be well on their way to solution.

I cannot close without reference to the pertinence of the theme discussed, however inadequate its mode of presentation, to the honored guest of the evening. James McKeen Cattell is himself an active scientific worker, one who has initiated in his own field of psychology many movements that have borne rich fruit. But he has found time, thought and energy to devote to the larger questions of the bearing of science upon life. He has given himself without stint to the better organization of scientific workers in all fields; he has striven valiantly for moral and financial improvement of the condition of academic workers; he has been the leader to the task of editing and diffusing the achievements of scientific inquiry. I do not need to press home the moral in connection with the intellectual obligation of which I have spoken. Laboring of the point is unnecessary as long as we have Cattell with us. He is a living example of the ways in which a scientific man can perform the supreme intellectual duty and as such we gladly greet and honor him this evening.

NOTES

First published in *Science Education* 18 (February 1934): 1–4, reprint, in LW.9.96–102.

1. See Randi Weingarten, "AFT President: Betsy DeVos and Donald Trump Are Dismantling Public Education," *Time*, May 3, 2017, http://time.com/4765410/donald-trump-betsy-devos-atf-public-education/; and Marta Baltodan, "Neoliberalism and the Demise of Public Education: The Corporatization of Schools of Education," *International Journal of Qualitative Studies in Education* 25, no. 4 (2012): 487–507.

39

The Revolt against Science

(1945)

EDITOR'S INTRODUCTION

In "The Revolt Against Science," published in autumn 1945, after the bombing of Hiroshima, Dewey challenges authors who at the time blamed the sciences for causing society's economic materialism and moral decay. Writing for the *Humanist*, a periodical still published today, he was not addressing those who resist scientific discovery because of reactionary motives. Instead, he was concerned about the practice in the fields of the humanities whereby humanists strongly differentiated themselves from scientists, as if their work did not also address profoundly important human concerns. In addition, whatever was the source of cynicism about the value of the sciences, Dewey worried about it. For a parallel today, consider those people who reject the insights of the sciences in the areas of vaccination, imagining vaccines to be the cause of autism, even though studies have clearly shown the worry to be unfounded.[1]

In the context of World War II, with the development and use of the sciences for unprecedented raw power, humanists and others worried about the sciences, thinking them to be part of the problem. Dewey was concerned about how scientific power was put to use, as well as about the forces of material consumerism, but he rejected the idea that science is to blame. While industrialists can apply the sciences for the sake of amassing wealth and material possessions, sciences can also be put to use for the development of mechanisms and practices for enriching the lives of the masses of people. The attention that the sciences pay in some quarters to material things does not limit them from applications that produce greater health and well-being for the many. Even if economic materialists and nations use some scientific advancements in troubling ways or for unjust ends, he explains that it makes no sense to be against science for the ways in which it is misused.

It would be a waste of time to argue that at the present time we are in the presence of a widespread revolt against science, for its presence is obvious in almost every field. In education it takes the form of setting the humanities up against the sciences, accompanied with the clamorous assertion that all the ailments and failures of the present school system—numerous and serious beyond a peradventure[2]—are the result of subordination of the "humanities" to the sciences. And if I place quotation marks about the word humanities it is because the attack which is made in this field proceeds from teachers of literary subjects and proceeds by identification of the humane with the linguistic and literary.

Upon the side of theory, of pseudo-philosophy, the attack rests upon calling the sciences "materialistic" while literary subjects are identified with whatever is idealistic and "spiritual" in our traditions and institutions. This position rests back upon belief in the separation of man from nature. Man is taken not only as Lord over Nature but as Lord in its oldest and most discredited sense—that of a despotic monarch supposed to rule by mere fiat. This separation, the most fundamental of all forms of isolationism, completely ignores the daily interests and concerns of the great mass of human beings which are bound up in the most intimate way with the conditions of nature they have to face—conditions which so largely affect their welfare and destiny as human beings. Any one who will allow himself to observe the spectacle offered to view by the great mass of human beings in the matter of making and having a decent living alone, will be aware of the monstrous insolence of identification of the humanities with linguistics and literatures.

The fact, however, that the identification is made and that the indictment of the sciences is then made to depend upon it is intensely illuminating. It spotlights the background of the revolt against science; it delineates the genuinely humane values and ends at stake, and points to the only road which leads to a genuine and not a sham, advancement of humanism. With reference to the background, with reference to the source of the revolt, it points straight to those who have "authority" against movements which threaten their supremacy by ushering in a new, wider and more humane order. Fundamentally, the attack proceeds from representatives of those who have enjoyed the power of control and regulation of other human beings because of the existing setup in political, ecclesiastical and economic institutions. Superficially and more vocally, it proceeds from teachers who find that their place and prestige in the educational system is being impaired, and who innocently, that is ignorantly, do the work of campfollowers.[3]

It will be found significant as well as interesting to compare the present revolt against science with the earlier movement that bears the name of "Conflict of Science and Religion." In that earlier warfare, attacks upon science hinged upon certain general conclusions reached by the sciences, first in astronomical and finally in biological science. The attacks centered upon the destructive doctrinal effect of the new conclusions upon beliefs that had been established in a primitive stage of human history, and that, in the course of intervening millennia, had become invested with all kinds of intellectual, institutional and emotional sanctions.

It can hardly be said that the scientific doctrines won a complete victory. "Fundamentalism" is still rife in both Roman Catholic and Protestant denominations. But upon the whole the climate of opinion became adjusted to the new views. Attacks upon them are now of sectarian rather than of general social importance. The present revolt against science goes deeper than the earlier one—and this in spite of victories won by scientific men in the intervening period. We no longer have a battle between a new set of beliefs in special matters and old ones which had endeared themselves to the human heart. The attack upon science is now an attack upon the attitude, the standpoint, the methods, which are science, with especial reference to their bearing upon human institutional problems, focussing on the supreme issue of who and what shall have authority to influence and to give direction to life.

I shall not attempt here to criticize the underlying philosophy used to provide justification for the attack upon science whenever anyone ventures to apply scientific methods and results beyond the technical "material" now so charitably allotted to it—provided of course it doesn't dare to trespass upon the moral domain of humane concerns. I want rather to point out some of the factors which confer a show of justification upon the attacks made upon science as "materialistic," and upon its materialism as hostile to the humane values. We are all familiar with the distinction commonly drawn between "pure" and "applied" science. I do not intend to repeat here a point which I have repeatedly made elsewhere—namely, that the sharp division which is made is an intellectual relic from the time when, in Aristotle's phraseology, "theory" had to do with things which were supreme because divine and eternal and "practice" had to do with things that were merely mundane, things at worst menial and at best earthbound and transient.

I want rather to call attention to the fact that however good may be the grounds a small class of intellectuals have for keeping pure and applied science apart, the great mass of people come in contact with "science" only in its applications. Science to them is what it means in their life day by day; the consequences it has on their daily occupations, the uses, enjoyments and limitations of use and enjoyment that mark their lives in homes, neighborhoods and factories; on their work and in failures to get work.

"Applied" science means, then, somewhat quite different to them from what it means to the philosopher who is engaged in making distinctions. It means something quite different from what it means to the inventor who is engaged in translating mathematical-physical formulae into machines and other power-devices. For it doesn't mean to him technology in the abstract; it means technology as it operates under existing political-economic-cultural conditions. Here and not in science, whether pure or abstract, is where materialism as the enemy of the humane is found; and here, not elsewhere, is where attacks should be directed.

When those who pridefully label themselves humanists, guardians of the moral and ideal interests of mankind, begin to attack the habits and institutions which cause the technological applications of science to work with harshness on such vast portions of the population, limiting alike their education and their other opportunities for a generous human life, transforming the potential instruments of security into devices for producing mass-insecurity, shall we have reason for believing that their concern for humane values is honest instead of a device, deliberate or innocent, for maintaining some form of institutionalized class interest. Human is as human does.

NOTES

First published in *Humanist* 5 (Autumn 1945): 105–7, reprint, in LW.15.188–192.

1. Luke E. Taylor, Amy L. Swerdfeger, and Guy D. Eslick, "Vaccines Are Not Associated with Autism: An Evidence-Based Meta-Analysis of Case-Control and Cohort Studies," *Vaccine* 32, no. 29 (2014): 3623–29.
2. [Editor's note: A "peradventure" here means a "doubt."]
3. [Editor's note: This term refers to the civilians and their families who follow armies, either as family members related to soldiers or as merchants or other military service providers not officially part of an army.]

PART VI
Philosophy and Culture

40

The Case of the Professor and the Public Interest

—

(1917)

EDITOR'S INTRODUCTION

Dewey was a constant advocate for freedom of inquiry, which he believed is vital for the "integrity and responsibility of the intellectual life of the nation." In 1914, he was named chairman of a committee to organize the American Association of University Professors (AAUP), which is still active today.

In "The Case of the Professor and the Public Interest," Dewey is concerned about the need for freedom in academic scholarship, the lack of shared governance in American universities, and the effects on professors' work of threats against their security in scholarship and employment. These concerns remain important today and still animate the AAUP's efforts. The cases that Dewey mentions in this essay, about Cornell University and the University of Pennsylvania, had to do with the United States' role in World War I. For example, President Schurman of Cornell delivered a report in which he proclaimed the importance of intellectual freedom, except to the point of "treason and sedition,"[1] language applied to pacifist opposition to entering the war. Recall that the charges against Socrates of impiety and of corrupting the youth were understood as treasonous and seditious. Bertrand Russell and Dewey both endured related attacks, and such trends continued through McCarthyism, which has been called a force against public philosophy, and to this day.[2]

Concerning public intellectualism, Dewey notes that professors' work becomes hyperspecialized and fills with jargon when scholars feel threatened. Through such means the faculty "speaks in tongues not understood by the public." He acknowledges that such practices develop as a matter of protection for inquiry, but they result in deeply troubling consequences. Scholars come to see their work as only meaningful if it is highly technical, jargon-filled, and either publicly impenetrable or irrelevant. Democracy and good leadership depend on intelligence not only of the elite classes but also of the wider public. Dewey is therefore deeply critical of the influence of powerful interest groups on university administrators, who often did not arise from the faculty.

We continue to encounter related problems today, when pressures cause conflicts over tenure and hiring, as well as severe cuts to major public research universities. Dewey's legacy endures not only in his writings but also in the AAUP, whose work remains relevant and important.

Newspaper comment on late academic events at the University of Minnesota and Columbia University reveals even more clearly than usual the split between the prevailing attitude inside and outside of university walls. To the general public practically every academic issue which gets upon the "front page" is one of freedom of teaching and speech. Reactions are condemnatory of administrative action if the editorial writer or the voluntary correspondent feels that there is danger of inquiry and discussion being stifled, especially if a vivid imagination sees universities being choked to death in the grip of capitalistic overlords. They are laudatory on equally general principles if the writer feels that teachers in universities are running amuck with political and theological radicalism, or even are trying to enlighten their students as to the drift of modern radical thought instead of confining themselves to inculcating well-established orthodoxies of interpretation. Show me one who, as Elihu Root said so naïvely about suffrage for women, "looked into the matter a great many years ago" and came to a conclusion which he has never found reason for reopening, and I will show you one who deprecates the tendencies of professors to adopt half-baked opinions and who rejoices at every curb placed by the firm hand of authority upon irresponsible licentiousness of thought. See, *passim*, the editorial columns of the *New York Times*.

Strangely enough, by contrast, one rarely finds the body of college teachers much excited about the free-speech issue. What it is concerned about is usually questions of procedure, which ultimately turn upon the relative authority to be exercised by the trustees as legal employers and guardians and the faculty as representing immediate educational interests.

The case of the faculty has never been better stated than by President Schurman of Cornell apropos of the resignation of Professor Beard. Consequently I make no apology for quoting him at length, especially as his official position protects his account from the charge of being an expression of unbridled professorial license.

The American professor is apt to chafe at being under a board of trustees, which in his most critical moods he feels to be alien to the republic of science and letters. Even in his kindliest moods he cannot think that board representative of the university. The university is an intellectual organization and the American professor wants the government of the university to conform to that essential fact. His indictment of the existing form of government is that it sets up and maintains an alien ideal, the ideal of a business corporation engaging professors as employees and controlling them by means of an absolute and irresponsible authority.

The professor's attitude is not so sensational as that of the public. It is less heroic than that of popular radicalism, which demands the thrill of combat, the plot of the oppressing villain and the martyrdom of the oppressed victim. It turns largely on formal and technical questions, questions of procedure—as may be seen in the report of the American Association of University Professors on the case of Scott Nearing at the University of Pennsylvania. There is a popular image of the association rushing to his rescue out of sympathy with radical views. As a matter of fact, the condemnation of the Pennsylvania authorities was based essentially upon prosaic details of failure to define grounds, failure to allow a hearing, upon details of time and method of dismissal, with presentment of collateral evidence that these irregularities of procedure were due to unacknowledged objections to the tenor of his economic doctrines. This case affords a reasonably fair symbol of the usual situation.

It is obvious that the professorial attitude is not one of itself to attain the dignity of the front page. It is too technical, not sufficiently dramatic and personal. It even readily lends itself to adverse and unsympathetic statement. The professors are represented as animated by a narrow class spirit, bound together to protect one another at all hazards, and setting themselves up as above the ordinary rules of responsibility to their superiors—that is, their employers. Sympathies that might easily be gained by the war cry of infringement of freedom of thought and teaching are dissipated or alienated when the case is rested so largely on formal grounds, when the struggle is revealed to be one for greater participation in university government. It may then be worth while to set forth the grounds on which teachers appeal for the sympathy and support of the public in what can readily be construed into a struggle for mere class privileges.

President Schurman stated the gist of the thing when he said that to the teacher the university is "an intellectual organization," and that he wants the actual government of the university to conform to this fundamental fact. If anything lifts the effort of the teaching body from an attempt to advance personal and class prerogatives up to that of a public interest, it is, of course, just this fact. If security and responsibility of intellectual organization are worth anything to the nation, then the professors' efforts to get a responsible share in college control form a public service. If guarantees of the independence of the higher intellectual life of the nation from alien and sinister influences are worth anything to contemporary America, then professors are entitled to every meed of public support in their battle against a situation which in the language of Professor Beard makes the status of the college teacher "lower than that of the manual laborer who, through his union, has at least some voice in the terms and conditions of his employment." For until this voice can be obtained, the calling of promotion of intelligence in the nation remains unassured, precarious, imperfectly responsible.

The case of the university teacher is simple. It is that the teaching body represents and embodies that function of scholarship and research which is the essential life of the university, while law and precedent, surviving from a day when economic and intellectual conditions were radically different from those of the present, confer control upon a body of men "alien to the republic of science and letters." He is only too well aware of the fact that legally the trustees (as in the words of the charter of Columbia University) "shall forever hereafter have full power and authority to direct the course of study and the discipline to be observed," and that he holds his position purely at "the pleasure of the trustees."

But he is also aware that these documents reflect the conditions of a century ago, when the modern university was as undreamed of on one side, as the modern big business corporation on the other. And when he is told that since he knew the conditions of his employment when he accepted his job, he is thereby estopped from complaint, his answer is not merely that trustees are far too wise to attempt to base their course consistently upon their legal authority, but also that his primary loyalty is to an idea, to a function and calling, to the advancement of learning and truth, and that it is his business as well as his right to struggle by every legitimate means to bring about a change in any situation which compromises the efficacy of his public calling.

Nothing is more desirable than that the change should come about by a voluntary devolution of authority on the part of its legal possessors. But events demonstrate that the past policy of holding, for the most part, these powers in tacit abeyance is rapidly becoming one of unstable equilibrium, and that the situation must be defined and clarified by an explicit conferring of authority upon the teaching body. If wisdom is lacking in high places to effect the change by voluntary abdication, then the question which the teaching body will have to face is how far it is willing to become a body of place-holders and technical specialists immune from interference because it speaks in tongues not understood by the public. I have written of the question as it affects the college teacher because I am familiar with the question from that angle. But the issue affects the entire teaching body of all our schools. The spread of the movement to federate public-school teachers with trade-unions cannot be understood except as a part of this larger issue. That portion of the public which deplores the fact that teachers resort to industrial unions for defense and support assumes, beyond all others, an obligation to recognize the concern of the public in the struggle of teachers to have a more responsible voice in the conduct of their work. In the end, it is the public, not the teachers nor their legal employers and regulators, whether in the university or in other schools, which will determine the settlement of the issue. It is not too much to say that the final issue is how much the American people cares about the integrity and responsibility of the intellectual life of the nation.

NOTES

First published in *Dial* 63 (1917): 435–37, reprint, in MW.10.165–168.

1. Editors, "Cornell to Uphold Academic Freedom, but Not Its Abuses," *Cornell Daily Sun* November 12, 1917, 5, http://cdsun.library.cornell.edu/cgi-bin/cornell?a=d&d=CDS19171112.2.41#.
2. John McCumber, *Time in a Ditch* (Chicago: Northwestern University Press, 2001); Robert Frodeman and Adam Briggle, *Socrates Tenured: The Institutions of 21st Century Philosophy* (Lanham, MD: Rowman and Littlefield International, 2016).

41

Social Absolutism

(1921)

EDITOR'S INTRODUCTION

Dewey was often an advocate for workers, but he was no absolutist. He was concerned both about the communist movement and about the opposing extreme proponents of unfettered capitalism. In "Social Absolutism," he offers a rich expression of the value of challenges to democracy, which force people to think through their beliefs and assumptions, rendering them live and meaningful. At the same time, he shows how vital it is to remain open in public inquiry and to avoid the undemocratic means employed in the Soviet movement, as well as the kinds of behavior that later arose as McCarthyism, around thirty years after this essay was published.

Friedrich Ratzel, mentioned in the essay, was a German ethnographer who is credited with first using the term *"Lebensraum,"* promoting expansionist imperialism. Both the Soviets and the extreme capitalists of the time were expansionist, as were the Germans—whom Dewey refers to as the "Teutonic" peoples. Dewey offers an important distinction in this piece between the idea of being state-minded versus socially minded. The Soviet Bolsheviks and the Germans were state-minded at the expense of the social.

Dewey frequently advocated for peace. He argued for openness and against the growth of extremism in politics and international affairs. Near the end of the essay, published in the *New Republic*, he refers to George Clémenceau and Alexandre Millerand, who were both French politicians influential in peace efforts. They joined with Woodrow Wilson to justify the fight against Germany in World War I. Wilson articulated "Fourteen Points" that served as the justification for the U.S. intervention in Europe, as well as a proposal for the eventual development of a League of Nations.

Among the most important lessons Dewey offers in this piece is the need to avoid extremes of belief that motivate persecution or expulsion of political or economic opposition. Ideologies that try to distill the complexities of the world down to one belief, principle, or way of thinking can cause great harm, Dewey explains, first of all by limiting the potential for intelligence. The United States today continues to see the extremism that Dewey warned against, which renders his message still fresh and important.

The writer's ignorance is such that he is unacquainted with the works of Ratzel. His curiosity was stirred and if the truth be told his wrath also, by a quotation from Ratzel he recently read. This said that a "philosophy of the human race worth its name must be charged with the conviction that all existence is one—a single conception sustained from beginning to end upon one identical law." It sounds rather metaphysical, and like a somewhat discredited Teutonic metaphysics at that. But it must have some immediate pertinence. For it is found (I regret to say it) in an advertisement of Wells's new world history published in the journal for which this article is written. Wells's book is inaccessible where this is written. It is accordingly impossible to tell how far the book agrees in spirit with the dictum of Ratzel. But Wells can hardly be wholly innocent. For the following words are quoted from him:—"History is no exception amongst the sciences; as the gaps fill in, the outline simplifies; as the outlook broadens, the multitude of details dissolves into general laws."

Now I make bold to say that this isn't science. It is the Victorian view of science which is the same as saying that it is the semi-literary, semi-sentimental, semi-moral, popular view of science, that was fashionable in the days when it was found necessary to appeal to science in order to repair the ravages wrought by science in popular beliefs. Historically it descends from the day when Sir Isaac Newton threw the mantle of deism about the physical universe. It required Spencer with his conception of evolution fully to domesticate the idea in the English mind. Or, rather, we may say it took the Tennysonian mind to rescue evolution from its bad repute, and to capture the doctrine and set it to work in behalf of popular credulous optimism. It is no wonder that in words omitted in the passage quoted from Ratzel, the latter says that the philosophy of the human race "must begin with the heavens and descend to earth." He perhaps was thinking of the astronomical heavens. But in fact the doctrine, even in its milder Wellsian form, began in the theological heavens, and then descended to mundane affairs.

However, we must not rely even upon the odium anti-theologicum. The doctrine might conceivably be true in spite of its origin, when it is applied to nature and history. But, oh, the remoteness of the doctrine that as we learn more facts, the outline simplifies: the vague remoteness of the plea that as science learns more facts, the multitude of details dissolves into general laws! That is precisely, according to the work of every existing living science, what doesn't happen. As known details multiply, we discover laws by which we formulate them and we also find laws by which to tie laws together. Some uniformity is conceivable for every discovered and discoverable detail. That much holds good. But such a statement is radically perverted when it is thought to mean that facts dissolve into general laws. We might as well say that when we find streets by which to find our way about in clumps upon clumps of houses, the houses dissolve into the streets; it is because the houses are obdurately there that we have to make streets; and it is because facts exist in such irregular thickets that we have to use every possible clew to introduce some kind of formulation, that is, of uniformity. If one wants a rough criterion for marking off the old popular view of science from the actual work of science he can find it here. Does exposition proceed on the assumption that concrete facts melt away into laws which then melt into more general laws? Then we are in the face of a period when thought was ruled by imported pre-scientific notions "which began in the heavens." Or do we find law treated as a descriptive formula for facts, so that there is a multitude of laws terminating in the same fact, according to the point of view from which it is described? Then science is speaking in its own voice.

This is dogmatically said, and it can hardly be proved without a long technical treatise quite out of place. But it is worth saying dogmatically if only to induce a reader to question that assumption which makes it easy for him to assume a unitary and absolutistic point of view when he approaches human history. It is, to speak moderately, a little unfortunate that such a saying as that of Wells is contemporary with the relativity doctrine of Einstein which substitutes for the neat, smooth, well-ordered world of Newton a world which is full of puckers and skews. Mechanics has always been the stronghold of the facts-dissolving-into-law notions, and it now appears probable that the science of mechanics has much more to do with our way of approaching and measuring facts than it has to do with nature.

We are interested, however, in the conception in its bearing upon human history and society. In this application, it appears that the doctrine is simply a "rationalization" of social monism, that is, of the attempt to impose a single movement upon history and a single law and rule upon man. One may sympathize with a longing for some state which shall reduce international anarchy to order, and enable harmonious intercourse to take the place of war. But even here it makes a mighty difference whether the super-state is something into which the multitude of nations is to "dissolve," or whether it is a descriptive formulation of conditions under which the multitude of local states, provinces, towns, villages, and other human groups may follow more securely their own careers, and voluntarily engage in undisturbed and fruitful conversation with each other. For the only conversation in which participants "dissolve" is the one in which some tyrant bore monopolizes discourse, while voices melt into monotony.

Mr. Wells long ago accused Americans of not being state-minded. He was right. We are (or were before the war seized us and we evolved a fair imitation of the British Dora) so far from being state-minded that we didn't even know exactly what Mr. Wells meant. It took the war and the Versailles project of a League of Nations to teach us; or we should have unanimously replied that the charge was not an accusation but a compliment. Not that the state isn't upon the whole a respectable and needed institution, but that to become state-minded instead of socially-minded is to become a fanatic, a monomaniac, and thus to lose all sense of what the state is. For a state which shall give play to diversity of human powers is a state in which the multitude of human groups and associations do *not* dissolve. It is a mechanism, up to the present a rather clumsy one, for arranging terms of interplay among the indefinite diversity of groups in which men associate and through active participation in which they become socially-minded.

There is no doubt that politics is a more reputable career than average American esteem makes it out to be, for the trained mechanic is needed in every pursuit. We have taken our cue too much from those untrained in political mechanics and skilled in personal preferment. But our depreciatory estimate of politics is nearer the truth than a glorification of a state of social unity and law in which concrete human beings dissolve. Such sayings are still dogmatism rampant. But they are intended to sharpen the issue, to make alternatives clear. For the alternatives are either variety and experiment or a single conception of life sustained from beginning to end upon one identical law. Those who like the latter kind of thing will go on liking it. But the average man is entitled to become clear upon what he likes, and to become aware of where a choice is taking him. What the average American has practically liked in the past is clear enough-in spite of our failure to make it clear to ourselves intellectually. We have believed in live and let live, in giving everything a show, in an easy toleration, in at least a passive good will. It was not hard to believe in those things and think we were living up to them as long as we had plenty of room in which to give everybody a chance. Now we awake to a discovery that we are crowded within and pushed from without. We find that if we are not to be hypocrites we must fight with intelligence and art for the things which in the past were given us by nature and fortune. We must become conscious of the principle upon which we have unconsciously acted. We have talked a great deal about democracy, and now for the first time we have to make an effort to find out what it is. We must, if you please, discover a social philosophy in order to clarify social activities.

We may choose a philosophy of unity of existence which exhibits a single conception borne up upon one law. We may search history for evidence of the one conception and law. But in that case we should know what we are doing. We are making a breach with all the impulses which have urged us in the past. We are turning to some form of social absolutism. The varieties of social absolutism are not exhausted in the divine right of kings nor in the Prussianism which we told ourselves we were fighting to destroy. The idea is capable of Protean forms. At the present time there is one militantly active form of this philosophy of one movement in history and one law in society entrenched in Russia. Foreign opinion has been so distracted by all kinds of minor issues and reports, largely lies, that it has failed to grasp the situation in its simplicity. The one end of history is the abolition of classes through the institution of communism by a dictatorship, not of the proletariat but of intellectuals representing a dumb and stupid proletariat. The one law of history is strife, internal conflict, civil war of classes. This is not any longer a theory of Marx expounded in manifestoes and books. It is a creed in action, a creed held with intense religiously fanatic fervor. The Marxian reading of Hegel in its monism, its absolutism and its conviction that all movement comes by internal strife, is embodied in Bolshevik Russia today. One does not have to meet Lenin; one has only to meet any intelligent Russian of the Bolshevist faith to know how ultimate, fierce and integral is this faith. For the Bolshevists know what they mean when they reserve their deepest contempt for democracy, even though they know even less than, say, we Americans what democracy really means, its essential pluralism, experimentalism, and consequent toleration.

It requires either hypocrisy, an innocence which is the dupe of hypocrisy, or else a faith equal to that of the Bolshevists and, informed by an opposite philosophy, to declare one's adherence to democracy, after the outcome of a war declared to have been a war in behalf of democracy. On the face of things the opponents of democracy, whether capitalistic or Bolshevistic or imperialistic have the best of the situation. Yet it may be that the best thing which can happen to the ideal of democracy is to be put on the defensive. For then it will no longer remain a vague optimism, a weak benevolent aspiration, at the mercy of favorable circumstances. It may become a compact, aggressive and realistic intelligence directing circumstance. Such an idea will recognize that its one great enemy is the hankering of men for unity of existence, aim and law in whatever form it may offer itself. It will recognize the infinite variety of human nature, and the infinite plurality of purposes for which men associate themselves together. It will recognize that progress is never in one line, but comes when a variety of things move along together. It will take its stand on the conviction that this movement comes about by many-sided interaction in which lee-way is given each force and principle for an experimental development. It will distrust every emancipation of the masses from above whether coming from a benevolent capitalism or a proletariat dictatorship.

These are generalities. A single specific illustration may be given. If one adopts the belief in unity of purpose and law in social matters but is opposed to the Bolshevist-Marxian gospel, then the policy of Clemenceau, Millerand and Wilson regarding Russia is right. It is the plain fact that this philosophy commits those who hold it to encouraging revolution and civil war in every country. The dictators of Russia are neither insincere nor cloudy-minded. They know and mean what they believe. Hence the rival social absolutist will declare for war on Russia; or, failing that, complete non-intercourse and blockade. He will declare for suppression, censorship and espionage at home; or, failing that, for a campaign of vilification and emotional terrorism. In so doing he is of course playing the Bolshevist game and illustrating the absolutism which underlies the Bolshevist philosophy. Sympathizers with Bolshevist ideas in America who deplore the blockade and the internal campaign against communistic ideas either lack the intellectual clarity of the real Bolshevists or are laughing in their sleeves. Otherwise they would welcome the confirmation these things give of the Bolshevist philosophy.

In other words, while there are no signs of conversion of America to Bolshevism, there are signs of decay of democracy and of unconscious adoption of some form of social absolutism. For if we believe in democracy we shall believe in the right of that vast group of human beings known as Russians to make their own experiments, to learn their own lessons in their own way. We shall be confident of their ultimate failure, at home and abroad, in just the degree in which we have an intelligent command of democratic ideas and methods, but we shall also believe that no group of human beings ever goes wholly wrong, and that along with the ultimate bankruptcy of Marxian absolutism there will develop many contributions of positive value to the problems of a better ordering of life, and we shall be anxious to learn and adopt these social lessons. Any other policy means that we are encouraging a capitalistic social absolutism in opposing a proletarian absolutism.

NOTE

First published in *New Republic* 25 (1921): 315–18, reprint, in MW.13.311–17.

42

Some Factors in Mutual National Understanding

—

(1921)

EDITOR'S INTRODUCTION

Dewey lectured in China in 1919 and 1920 and visited Japan as well. Both countries have changed radically since then, something to keep in mind while reading "Some Factors in Mutual National Understanding." He published this piece in the Japanese general-interest magazine *Kaizo*. While some of his remarks no longer apply, Dewey's central point is of enduring value. He offers guidance about how to achieve and enhance international relations through greater understanding across cultures.

Long before the practice was as common as it is today, Dewey offers many reasons to appreciate the value of travel abroad. Travel opens one's eyes and mind, but not inevitably. It takes the right attitude and outlook on travel to gain from it for the sake of international understanding.

Some of Dewey's terminology is outdated, such as in the use of the word "Oriental" in its singular and plural forms. What remains true today is the importance of study abroad. Regular forms of study-abroad programming in higher education were relatively new and rare at the turn of the twentieth century. For example, the University of Delaware, at the time a top-twenty research institution, launched America's first study abroad program with the "Junior Year Abroad" in Paris in 1923.[1]

Dewey captures important cultural concepts in differences between materialism and spirituality, as well as the recording and teaching of history. So often historical education was and sometimes today continues to be a matter of learning the names of people and events in the political story of a nation. Dewey notes that what is missing in such approaches is the story of a people, distinct from their state.²

Travel is known to have a broadening effect, at least if the traveller is willing to keep his mind open. The amount of enlightenment which is gained from travel usually depends upon the amount of difference there is between the civilization from which the traveller starts his journey and that of the country at which he arrives. The more unlike the two are, the more opportunity there is for learning. But at the same time this dissimilarity makes it difficult to learn. For we can understand any new experience only by means of our previous experiences. If the old one and the new one are too far apart, the new one will be a blank or else it will repel us. Consequently many travellers are offended by what they see which is different from what they have known at home. They use what is already familiar as their final standard or judgment, and criticize whatever departs from this standard. Fortunately however most persons have a natural liking for change and novelty and so are likely to be attracted by what is different from that which they are used to even if they do not understand it. So if the externals of nature are charming, and customs are picturesque, and towns are not repulsive with dirt and decay, most travellers enjoy what they see even if they get no great degree of new understanding from it.

Travellers are then often divided into two classes. Those who are not sensitive to new impressions and who have little esthetic taste go about criticizing what they see because it is unlike that which they are acquainted with and of which they have grown fond. Persons have even been known to blame the inhabitants of a foreign country because they could not speak or understand the native language of the traveller. Such persons are always discontented when they are abroad and feel when they return home that they have got back, as they say, to God's own country. But the other class goes in perpetual raptures over what is seen, and travel is a continual delight. But unfortunately this delight is more or less like the amusement which is taken in witnessing spectacles at the theater. It is a rather superficial emotion. The traveller treats the country as if it were a show provided for him to look at and makes no attempt to penetrate below the surface. Sometimes the natives of a country resent this attitude of a visitor even more than they do that of the grumbler and fault finder. They feel that they are not treated as reality but merely as something to look at and enjoy.

The first kind of visitor does not contribute anything useful to international understanding. He returns home more convinced than when he left it of the superiority of his own country to other nations. He returns with perhaps a positive contempt for other peoples and with all his native prejudices strengthened. The second type of visitor helps somewhat. He takes home an atmosphere of good-will and kindly feeling. He returns with a positive interest in the country to which he has been, a feeling that its people are also human and that they have many charming customs and picturesque ways. Emotionally he is broadened in outlook. This favorable disposition is, as far as it goes, a contribution to international good-feeling and makes for peace. But being chiefly a matter of sentiment, not of understanding, it does not go very deep, and if there is a period of strained relationships between his country and the other country, it readily gives place to another emotion, that of fear and dislike.

In short, we still have to face the question of how contact with another nation may become a real means of education, a means of insight and understanding. The case of the traveller is taken simply as an illustration or symbol of every kind of contact. Those who do not travel, those whose bodies stay at home, generally have some indirect contact with other peoples and so travel in imagination. They read books or newspapers and talk with persons who have greater acquaintance. Unconsciously even to themselves they are likely to form an attitude of like or dislike. They are attracted or repelled. They are curious, interested, sympathetic, or else are persuaded that there is nothing to be learned or gained from any further intercourse, except perhaps articles of trade. With all such persons also there is the question of how insight, understanding is to be furthered. And this question is one important to the peace and progress of the world. For while understanding will not guarantee mutual liking or even respect, while it will not be an absolute barrier to the development of strained relations, it will tend to create a belief in the possibility of an amicable settlement of all disputes and troubles, and will prevent a people being carried away by dangerous waves of resentment, floods of suspicion and panics of fear. For these flourish only because of ignorance and prejudice.

These general remarks are preliminary to a consideration of one special point which has to do with the general relations of the East and the West, and upon which a better intellectual comprehension would at least contribute a little to better relations. A visitor to the Far Orient from the West is struck by one idea about the Orient and Occident which he finds quite current in Japan and China. He finds it commonly believed that Eastern civilization is spiritualistic and Western is materialistic. The existence of such a belief is a surprise to him, even a shock, much more so than would be supposed by many Orientals who seem to think that the idea is almost an axiom and is accepted by Westerners as well as by themselves. The extent of the surprise may be indicated by saying that very many from the Occident would reverse the statement. They would say that the basis of their civilization at home is spiritualistic, while that which they see in their travels is materialistic. And they would cite many facts, or at least seeming facts, in support of their belief. My purpose, however, is not to argue the case or to take either side in the argument. I refer to the matter first as an illustration of some of the difficulties in the way of an international understanding, and secondly for the purpose of trying to show that there are certain ideal or spiritual elements within what at first sight seems to be the materialistic side of Western life, elements which are frequently ignored. This article will discuss the first of these two points.

In considering the statement that the respective qualities of Eastern and Western civilization illustrate the difficulties in the way of mutual understanding, there are two points I wish to make. The first is that there are different standards or measures used in the East and the West of the true meaning of spiritual and ideal. I do not profess to speak for these who represent the Oriental meaning, and should be very glad if some one from the East who is competent to speak would fully elucidate the matter. But I have heard one point frequently referred to, and will mention that. People in the West seem to be busy, active, and to prize activity above everything else. They do not seem to prize leisure and the cultivation of meditation, speculation, quiet, calm appreciation of the beauties of nature, literature and art. It is not denied, of course, that they have created fine art and excellent literature, but these things seem in the West to be incidents of civilization, rather than its most essential thing, and not to enter into the main current of life. For the mass, leisure when it is attained seems to present itself as an opportunity for another kind of activity. It is something to be enjoyed in an active, perhaps bustling and boisterous way. It is not an opportunity for a peaceful cultivation of the mind in meditation and contemplation. And for most people it is regarded as only a diversion not as a serious matter. It is aside from the main current of life, which is doing something, keeping busy. And apparently in the West keeping busy means primarily what is called business, buying and selling, making things to sell, dollar-chasing. These statements suggest, it seems to me, at least a part of what is meant by calling Western civilization materialistic. They also suggest at least a part of the idea of the meaning of spiritual or idealistic which is used as a measure in discriminating between the two civilizations. Refined cultivation and enjoyment of leisure, relief from direct activity, commercial, political, athletic, social meetings, is what is meant or at least so it appears to me. The esthetic element in its broadest sense, including a kind of metaphysical contemplation of the universal and meditation upon it, is prominent.

Now undoubtedly the Western measure for the ideal and spiritual is different. It does not wholly exclude the factor mentioned, but in the popular opinion this factor is quite subordinate. In it the ethical element is more stressed than the esthetic. Service of others, enthusiasm for social progress, for welfare of humanity, is regarded as ideal even by those who make no professions of it in their own lives. Sacrifice of personal enjoyment even of the refined enjoyment of leisure in behalf of service for the welfare of others is regarded as the important element in the spiritual. Having this measure more or less consciously in mind, many Westerners would reverse, as I have already said, the current Oriental opinion, and regard *their* civilization as the more spiritual. For they do not find as much of this public spirit and devotion as they suppose they find at home.

Now what we have here is somewhat flat contradiction of standards which makes mutual understanding difficult. The ideal of service is one of activity, of keeping busy. From the standpoint of leisure and its cultivation it would appear, accordingly, to be tainted with materialism, though a high quality of materialism. On the other hand, from the standpoint of the ethical ideal of service, esthetic appreciation and meditation appear to be tainted with materialism, although of an unusually high sort. For they seem to be colored with selfishness. Now how shall a choice be made between these two ideals? There is no common measure: there is no higher common standard to which both sides may appeal. There seems to be, as was said, a flat opposition in which each side is convinced of the inferiority of the other one. Consequently arguments leave the other side untouched. The most reasonable conclusion would be that a true ideal includes factors from both sides; that up to the present each point of view is one-sided and has something to learn from the other. But meantime the unlikeness of standards makes mutual comprehension difficult.

The other point is philosophically less fundamental, but psychologically and practically it is very important. Representatives of different civilizations tend to judge each other by external rather than internal facts, while in thinking of themselves they naturally include the internal phase as well. This way of judging is natural and to some extent inevitable. We are obliged to judge the character of a people as well as of a man by what can be seen and heard and touched. We have to start from the outside and work our way in. Now the first thing which attracts attention is outward differences, contrasts. The things which are similar are taken for granted and escape attention. But differences in natural scenery, in houses, clothes, articles of house furnishings, utensils, tools, machines, differences of color, of facial features, of language, at once strike the eye or catch the ear. It is very easy to judge the whole civilization by these outward things, the clothes, as it were, of civilization. It is almost impossible not to attach too much weight to them in comparison with the animating spirit of a people's life. So superficial and rather stupid persons can hardly imagine that a people is civilized at all whose visible manners of life, clothes, houses, etc., differ widely from those to which they are accustomed. And even for cultivated people it requires a long time and genuine sympathy to find their way into the spirit of which these things are the body. It requires extensive personal intercourse, knowledge of art and literature, acquaintance with history, with national heroes and festivals, national aspirations, popular beliefs and ways of judgment, standards of manners and courtesy and a multitude of other similar facts.

Now a native of a country is born into the things which mark the spirit of a civilization. He experiences them as a matter of course from early infancy. His feelings and ideas naturally gather about them. He is even more conscious of them than he is of the outward things which catch the eye of the visitor. Being brought up among them and educated largely by them, they form his idea of his own country and his own people. Unless a person has from early childhood taken part in the life of a people, including its plays and games as well as its worship and work, the spirit of that people can hardly mean to him what it means to those who have come to possess it by uninterrupted sharing in it from birth. Even if a foreigner admires a people intensely and is very enthusiastic about them, he is hardly likely to appreciate in them just what they esteem for themselves.

Unfortunately history which might be an aid in giving a background so as to enable a person to understand an alien civilization does not at present assist very much. In some respects, it hinders. The average person's knowledge of history is derived from the studies of his school days. During these days he has studied a good deal of his own history and not much of that of other peoples. The foreign history studied is more likely to be of ancient by-gone nations rather than of contemporary countries. At least in the United States we pay more attention to the history of Greece and Rome than we do to that of even contemporary European nations. The history of one's own nation is usually idealized and highly colored if not actually distorted. It is used as an instrument of fostering nationalistic patriotism. But aside from this fact which makes a bar to international understanding, the histories still give outward facts rather than the inner spirit and real life of a people. Hence even when they give correct information they do not give sympathy and understanding.

Most histories deal only or chiefly with the political life of a people. This is in many respects of chief external importance, but taken by itself it gives little insight into the life of the people. It centres about governments and rulers, and omits the life of the common people who constitute the great mass. Only recently have historians even for their own country begun to write the history of the people as distinct from that of the political state. Political history also omits the development of science, of art, of religion, and other matters which throw more light upon the spirit of a country than does the heaping up of great political names, wars, dynasties, etc. Generals and rulers play a large part, but little is heard of inventors, even those who have revolutioned industry, little of creators of art and literature, and probably still less of the men of science who have discovered the secrets of nature. It is for these reasons that I say that, upon the whole, history as now pursued is more of a hindrance than a help. It should give the background of existing outward facts so as to help us in penetrating beyond them to the sources of a country's aspirations, beliefs, standards and power. But mostly it only adds to the quantity of external facts that need to be understood.

The discussion may seem to have got a long way distant from the topic of the material or spiritual character of Western civilization. But a little thought will suffice to bring it back again. It is precisely the material phase of a civilization which is most evident to a visitor or foreigner, for it is the outward phase which strikes the senses forcibly. On the other hand, the person who has from early childhood been educated as a part of a civilization thinks of its idealized elements, and looks at the outward side much as he looks at works of nature. They are incidents, important in life in furnishing practical means but are not really life itself. Especially is it true of Western civilization that its outward material side is so extensive and prominent as to force itself upon the attention of an observer. No one can visit the United States, for example, without being struck by railway stations, the multitude of railways, of trains, of cars, the size of locomotives, the sky-scrapers in the cities, the huge smoking chimneys, the widespread use of telephones, the growing tendency to do by mechanical appliances what used to be done by hand, and a quantity of similar phenomena. What more is needed to prove that here we are dealing with a materialistic, a mechanical civilization? The visitor, unless he is a professional educator, is much more likely to be taken to see stock-yards than universities, stock-exchanges, banks, and factories than schools. If he does go to visit schools, the buildings and their equipment, rather than the spirit of teacher and pupil, are the things most readily seen. Unconsciously to himself, the native realizes that in a short time he can only impress externals upon the visitor. So he exaggerates the impression which would be made naturally upon the visitor by the things which he takes him to see. He feels that a visit to Concord to see the homes of Emerson and Thoreau or to Cambridge to see those of Longfellow and James would have little meaning. At most the visitor is likely, beyond commercial and industrial activities, to see only a show place or two, like Mount Vernon, the Library in Washington or in New York City or Boston. And they do no more than compete in grandeur or splendor with some of the railway stations and hotels.

The case is not so very different with the person who stays at home. The Western visitor especially the one from America to the Orient is struck over and over again with the fact that the two things about his own country which have really impressed those with whom he comes in contact are the battle-ship, with its symbolism of high explosives and mechanism applied to war, and machines as instruments of producing and distributing material commodities. This technical side of the activity of his own country, apart from missionary and educational activities, has alone impressed the inhabitants of the Orient. It seems to them the true manifestation of Western civilization. So far as China is concerned, one finds that up to comparatively a short time ago the great bulk of students who went abroad to study went to pursue technical studies, feeling that about all the East had to gain from the West was command of the machinery of production and distribution—engineering, agriculture, banking, the economics of industry and commerce, with the technical side of law, politics and diplomacy.

If he is judicious he will be more grieved than flattered by the estimate of the nature of Western superiority which this fact reveals. Reflection will show him however that it is natural. Trade and the implements of war are, aside from the missionary enterprises of Christianity (which many natives have also taken not to be as disinterested as they actually are, but as means of foreign extension of business and diplomacy), the aspects of foreign civilization which have forced their way in and which have impressed themselves upon observation and imagination. Art and science, letters and music, are not aggressive nor inherently expansive. They do not travel and seek foreign markets. Or, when they do, there is likely to be a commercial attachment. Foreign diplomacy even when it is peaceful is more likely to be concerned with trade and commerce, with economic questions, than with culture and literature. When one thinks of these things he will not be inclined to wonder at the current estimate of Western civilization as essentially materialistic; nor will he wonder that this estimate is contrasted with a consciousness of the spiritual character of the indigenous civilization.

I do not mean, of course, that there is no truth in this estimate. It is quite clear that comparatively speaking mechanical invention, physical science and its application to industry and trade, play a greater part in Western life than they have done, or do even yet, in Oriental. And along with this fact, there goes of course a certain preoccupation of life with business, with what is called practical activity, which gives real color to the current ideas about the West. Especially is it true of the United States that as yet its contributions to music, painting, literature and science (apart from applied science), do not equal those of the European West, while its contributions to applied science, to inventions in industry and transportation, relatively exceed those of the rest of the West. Only when we come to devotion to public welfare in philanthropy and to popular education, including the endowment of universities, museums, libraries, does the United States make any superior showing. The country is new and its original culture is correspondingly shallow even though it is comparatively wide-spread owing to means of dissemination and their constant use. I do not, therefore, mean to deny justice to the charge of a predominantly materialistic civilization. But there is even within this material aspect an ideal or spiritual phase which is usually overlooked and with which the genuine cultural achievements of the West are closely connected. I refer to the spirit and method of natural science, the *scientific spirit* as distinct from its technical applications, and to the *social phase* of industry and commerce, its use in cultivating public spirit and rendering genuine social services. To these two points, as embodying the ideal factors within the seemingly materialistic, mechanical civilization of the West, the next article will be devoted.[3] They seem to me to express the points at which the Orient has most to learn from the West, to mark contributions in comparison with which borrowing specialized technical application of science and industry may even do harm, especially if the latter are separated from the spirit of science and social service with which they are actually connected in their Western home.

NOTES

First published in *Kaizo* 3 (1921): 17–28, reprint, in MW.13.262–71.

1. Lisa Chieffo and Lesa Griffiths, "Large-Scale Assessment of Student Attitudes After a Short-Term Study Abroad Program," *Frontiers: The Interdisciplinary Journal of Study Abroad* 10 (2004): 166. A few examples date back to the late 1100s, but the idea of recurring and widespread study abroad programming as we know it now did not really launch until the twentieth century, according to William W. Hoffa, *A History of U.S. Study Abroad: Beginnings to 1965* (Carlisle, PA: Forum on Education Abroad, 2010).

2. Howard Zinn, who wrote on John Dewey at least with regard to the New Deal, is known for his book *A People's History of the United States: 1492–Present* (New York: Harper Perennial Modern Classics, 2005). There is no cause to believe that Zinn read or was influenced by this piece of Dewey's, but he certainly was aware of and appreciative of some of Dewey's philosophy. See Howard Zinn, *The Zinn*

Reader: Writings on Disobedience and Democracy (New York: Seven Stories, 2009), 209.
3. [Editor's note: The next article Dewey refers to is not included in the present collection. It was: John Dewey, "Idealism in Natural Science," *Kaizo* (April 1921): 198–208, reprint, in MW.13.433–435.]

43

The Basis for Hope

(1939)

EDITOR'S INTRODUCTION

Dewey published "The Basis for Hope" in December of 1939, a few months after Germany invaded Poland and two years before the United States entered World War II. In difficult times, hope staves off despair and Dewey felt the need to find cause for hope.

In 1939, the Soviets and Nazi Germany signed the Treaty of Non-aggression. While the Soviets and the Nazis were ideologically very different, they were both authoritarian. Given the United States' disagreements with both nations, Dewey saw inspiration for a renewed democratic spirit in America.

Dewey was prescient in this essay, especially as he hoped that Europe would gain from the conflict a sense of identity and unity that might lead to the United States of Europe. Twelve years later, six nations signed a treaty founding an initial cooperation important in history leading up to the establishment of the European Union. The treaty's aim was to manage the region's heavy industries so that "none can on its own make the weapons of war to turn against the other."[1]

Among Dewey's enduring insights in this essay is his challenge to the belief that war and physical force can or should be lasting sources for bringing about social changes. There were representatives of the opposite view in the lead up to the Iraq War, who believed that an invasion and removal of the dictator Saddam Hussein would prompt the quick development of democracy in the country. Now over a decade since the start of the war, critics are confirming Dewey's challenge, calling the billions of dollars spent promoting democracy in Iraq a "boondoggle" that was "all for nothing."[2]

Dewey also challenges false senses of liberalism. He refers to "genuine liberalism," by which he distinguishes the position sometimes called "liberal" from the traditional understanding of "liberalism." What he calls "genuine" refers to ideals of liberty, freedom of thought and expression, consent of the governed, and the defense of minority rights. In this sense of the term, Americans are liberals in general, even when they consider themselves conservatives.

Another lasting value of this essay is found in Dewey's ability to see opportunity in challenges. Democracy will often be challenged. As he argued in "Social Absolutism," it is when challenged that democracy ceases to be believed and accepted merely in the abstract. In the face of threats to democracy people must test it and appreciate its real meaning and implications.

I hesitate to predict anything whatever about the outcome of the present war. I am moved in my hesitation by something other than the fear of indulging in Pollyanna anticipations just by way of offset to the dire forebodings in which it has become customary to engage. For I believe that both pessimistic and optimistic expectations are likely to be based upon old data, while it is highly possible that the world is undergoing a crisis which makes precedents and old data irrelevant to forming an estimate of the future. Were past events an adequate ground for prognostication, I could easily fluctuate between anticipation of a Europe, and possibly a world, torn by another Thirty Years War, but leaving civilization in a state of greater ruin, and picturing a Europe which has at least started on the road of a Confederation which will end in a United States of Europe.

The most definite hope for the future which I am able to entertain, with any confidence, concerns not external political and economic results of the war, but a change which is already beginning in human attitudes, the factors which in the end influence external results. It may be that by the time these lines are published, the all but universal earlier predictions about destructive war waged against civilians will have begun to be realized. Even so, I think there are dependable signs that both abroad and in this country, belief in war and sheer force as the source of production for needed social changes has suffered greatly. There is even a possibility that belief in war as an agency for this end will have received a mortal wound by the time the war is over. In that case, if destructive wars continue to be resorted to—as they may be—it will be because of outright relapse into barbarism and not as an agency for advancing civilization and culture. In other words, I think there are grounds for belief that the world is passing from a pacifism which is mainly subjective to a realistic attitude based upon technological and scientific grounds—which diplomats and political leaders must henceforth take into account in making their plans.

Industrial and business interests, aside from stock-market speculators, have also changed their attitude about war. Upon the whole, although not absolutely, the old socialist charge of an intrinsic alliance between capitalism and militaristic adventure has lost its element of truth. It would seem as if, in time, this change would react upon imperialistic tendencies. As an offset, however, I cannot rid myself of the belief that the existing war situation strengthens a nationalistic spirit, which is already too strong. Representatives of the reactionary wing of the Catholic Church are, for example, just now vying with the Communists in wrapping themselves in the American flag.

The other hopeful sign of a change in attitude and morale is associated with the alliance of Soviet Russia with Nazi Germany. One must be aware of the dangers for the world that are involved in this alliance. But as far as human attitudes (which ultimately determine policies) are concerned, I think the effect of having the underlying principles of method common to the two brought out into the open is going to prove an encouraging healthful event.

For the last ten to fifteen years genuine liberalism—upon which we in this country have to depend—has been either arrested or deflected by ideology that won its prestige because of the Bolshevist Revolution. The seeming success of the latter had a hypnotic effect upon many in this country who had become impatient with the slow progress made in dealing by democratic methods with our serious economic ills. Discounting all the special criticisms that are passed upon Bolshevist Communism, it remains true that it operated in this country to divert attention and energy away from methods that are in harmony with American habits.

The hypnotic spell is now broken. I am willing to make one prediction, namely, that trust in panaceas and wholesale devices has received a shock from which it will not easily recover. We are now more prepared to realize that our reliance must be put upon intelligent human beings who bring their knowledge and their skill to bear in organized cooperation upon special problems that confront us. As the realization develops, democracy will take on a new significance and a new lease of life. As far at least as our own country is concerned, I do not think it utopian to believe that something of this kind is possible, and I am confident that the ground for the change has been provided by the chief event, so far, of the present War, the alliance of the two great totalitarian countries. As we appreciate the inherent connection existing between attempts at wholesale social change and the methods of dictatorship, we shall be made ready to employ genuinely democratic methods more systematically and more intelligently than we have in the past.

NOTES

First published in *Common Sense* 8 (December 1939): 9–10, reprint, in LW.14.249–252.
1. "A Peaceful Europe—the Beginnings of Cooperation: 1945–1959," in *European Union: How the EU Works,* http://europa.eu/about-eu/eu-history/1945-1959/index_en.htm.
2. Christian Caryl, "The Democracy Boondoggle in Iraq," *Foreign Policy,* March 5, 2013, http://www.foreignpolicy.com/articles/2013/03/05/the_democracy_boondoggle_in_iraq. I am grateful to Christine Dickason for pointing out the applicability here of Dewey's insight to the case of the Iraq War.

44

Art as Our Heritage

—

(1940)

EDITOR'S INTRODUCTION

In 1940, Dewey was invited to give a radio address at a banquet organized by the Section of Fine Arts in the U.S. Public Buildings Administration, a division of the Federal Works Agency. The FWA administered a variety of public works projects from 1939 to 1949, including construction, building maintenance, and other tasks authorized by the Reorganization Act of 1939. Dewey's speech was short and aired on WMAL. The text was published a few days later in the *Congressional Record*.

Today, public support for the arts, including in school curricula and in congressional appropriations, is shrinking. For example, in nonadjusted dollars, the National Endowment for the Arts was funded at a lower level in 2018—$153 million—than it was in 1980—$154 million.[1] When adjusted for inflation, support was cut by more than two-thirds since 1980—i.e., adjusted for inflation, $154 million in 1980 would be worth $466 million in 2018.[2] In addition, in 2017 the president called for eliminating the National Endowments for the Arts and the Humanities.[3] In the face of our present budgetary context, it is vital to revisit lessons that Dewey offers here regarding the role of the arts in the development of a democratic citizenry.

One of the crucial contributions not to be missed in this essay relates to Dewey's very democratic outlook on art. He challenged the idea that art is something acquired and housed in museums or that is only afforded by wealthy patrons for the poor to envy. Acquisition is no measure of greatness in art, but creation, he argues forcefully here, and the participation of the common person in the nation's arts is among the highly valued activities of a democratic society. People who champion wealth and conspicuous consumption and acquisition of beautiful objects are plentiful but, to Dewey, fail to appreciate the art available to all and created by their fellows.

In an earlier essay included in this volume, "Some Factors in Mutual National Understanding" (chapter 42), Dewey argues that art is not inherently expansive. In the present essay, "Art as Our Heritage," he says that art is universal. To understand Dewey, these concepts should not be conflated. "Expansiveness" refers to the process of expanding, such as in imperialism, evangelism, or the spread of capitalism or communism. Art is not necessarily expansive in that sense. Insofar as it touches human emotions, however, such as fear, joy, or love, it is universal for humanity since no society lacks such emotions.

In this essay, Dewey calls attention to the contribution that art makes to national identity even while the arts connect with emotions that are universal. Today we need to remember this lesson when we shape school curricula and our budgets for culture and the arts.

During the early years of the depression, when I was crossing the Atlantic, I fell into conversation with a fellow passenger. She was a gracious white-haired woman, and in telling her plans she said that since she had lost a great deal of her money because of bank failures and bad stock investments, she was now going to buy herself something nobody could take away from her. She was going to Athens to see the Acropolis and the Parthenon.

She knew what too few persons know, the difference between an investment in physical things that are perishable, at the mercy of external accidents, and an investment in something that is imperishable, because it enriches personal life and becomes a part of one's very self. But the incident has another face, a face which has a real bearing upon the cause that has brought us here together this evening. It was the art of Greece which was taking this woman on her pilgrimage just as the cathedrals and public buildings, the paintings, statues, and literature of Europe have taken countless thousands of Americans there. The art, the vision of which was an enrichment of her personal life, is that which has given Greece her enduring glory among nations. Material acquisitions and possessions have by themselves never given any people a sure place in the memory of mankind or an assured place in history.

It is by creation of the intangibles of science and philosophy, and especially by those of the arts, that countries and communities have won immortality for themselves after material wealth has crumbled into dust. What has been true of other peoples will be true of our own. Creation, not acquisition, is the measure of a nation's rank; it is the only road to an enduring place in the admiring memory of mankind.

There is a good reason why achievement in science and art is the criterion by which a nation's place in civilization is finally judged. In the case of material things, possession by one excludes possession, use, and enjoyment by others. In the case of the intangibles of art the exact opposite is the case. The more the arts flourish, the more they belong to all persons alike, without regard to wealth, birth, race, or creed. The more they flourish the less they are privately owned, and the more they are possessed and enjoyed by all. This is what is meant when we say that art is universal—more universal than is that other intangible, science, since the arts speak a language which is closer to the emotions and imaginations of every man. Accordingly, whether we like it or not, even whether we believe it or not, the question whether this country of ours is to be narrow and provincial, or whether it is to attain to that which is universal, will be finally decided by what we do and what we are capable of appreciating, and enjoying, in those intangible things of which the fine arts are the outstanding examples. It is on this account that I esteem deeply and gratefully the opportunity to be here this evening and to express, as best I can, not only gratitude as a citizen, to Edward Bruce for initiating and conducting the Section of Fine Arts in the Public

Buildings Administration, Federal Works Agency, but also my sense of the great significance of this work in the development of a worthy American civilization.

The work is significant both as a symbol and as an actual force in inspiring and directing activities, which will extend as time goes on far beyond what is done in post offices and other public buildings. As a symbol it is an acknowledgement from official sources, with the active encouragement of persons high in the government, of the importance to our Nation of the development of art and of ability to enjoy art products. Ned Bruce has shown me a letter from the postmaster of one of the smaller towns whose public building now has a mural upon its walls. In his letter of enthusiastic thanks for what has been done for his town, he included a sentence which might almost be a motto of the whole project: "How can a finished citizen be made in an artless town?" How indeed can an all-around and complete citizenry be developed without that development of creation and enjoyment of works of art to which the government, itself, must contribute?

Our public buildings may become the outward and visible sign of the inward grace which is the democratic spirit, while too often, especially in municipal halls and county courthouses, they have not even been kept clean.

As a symbol, the work carried on by the Section of Fine Arts is a service to democracy, so important, even in its present comparatively limited scale, that to starve it or allow it to lapse would be a defeat for democracy as genuine as one taking place on a physical battlefield. For the same reason, this governmental activity is more than a symbol. Hundreds of thousands of persons all over this broad land now have opportunities to see and enjoy works of art which they had not before. They are developing, within themselves, germs that were part of their being but which never had a chance, because of lack of nourishment, to grow.

If the arts come forth from museums to which they have retired, if they become a living part of the walk and conversation of the average man, and thereby parts of the legitimate heritage of a democratic people, a great debt will be owed to the stimulus provided by this governmental section in the buildings which belong to the common people and where they daily assemble.

Old World countries have been able to develop the fine arts by means of the patronage of the nobility and the wealthy. Their healthy development in our country will depend upon the active response of the civic consciousness of the common people. For this reason, I do not want to close without mentioning a fact which I could bring home to you only if television were at my command. For if you could see for yourselves reproductions of the murals which are now found in public buildings from Maine to the Gulf, from the Atlantic to the Pacific, you would see that the paintings combine the values of the arts which nourish the human spirit with the accomplishment of our past history which strengthens that legitimate pride, which enables one to say, "I am an American citizen!" Secretary Morgenthau, Mr. Carmody, and Mr. Bruce, may your work go forward to even greater triumphs.

NOTES

First published in *Congressional Record*, 76th Cong., 3d sess., April 29, 1940, 86, pt. 15:2477–78, from an April 25 radio address over WMAL, Washington, DC, reprint, in LW.14.255–58.

1. See National Endowment for the Arts, "National Endowment for the Arts Appropriations History," https://www.arts.gov/open-government/national-endowment-arts-appropriations-history.

2. According to the Bureau of Labor Statistics, "CPI Inflation Calculator," https://www.bls.gov/data/inflation_calculator.htm.
3. Sopan Deb, "Trump Proposes Eliminating the Arts and Humanities Endowments," *New York Times*, March 15, 2017, https://www.nytimes.com/2017/03/15/arts/nea-neh-endowments-trump.html/.

45

The Value of Historical Christianity

—

(1889)

EDITOR'S INTRODUCTION

Dewey was a young man of thirty years when he delivered and published "The Value of Historical Christianity." His mother, Lucinda, was a deeply religious Christian. Later in life, Dewey clearly rejects supernaturalism and values secular humanist approaches to communal life and government. At the same time, he holds firmly to democratic faith and takes faith to be meaningful and important.

We see in this early essay the germination of ideas that come to full expression later, in his book *A Common Faith*.[1] In that later work, Dewey calls people to look to what is common in everyone's religious experience of the world. There, he argues that the divine is best understood as an ideal of infinite moral value and that it is implicit in any and all people's experiences of value. The present essay reveals the roots of his later ideas about faith in democracy and about how he came to differentiate the religious aspects of experience, particularly in terms of adherence to faith, from institutional religions. His distinction illustrates that the experience of faith need not be tied to any particular historical religion, but can apply to the valuing of all of humanity.

In this piece, Dewey struggles against the common push to separate religious experience from nature or the world. In this 1889 essay, he argues that the value of historical Christianity is to be found in the connection between humanity and God. This view runs counter to the idea that God is fundamentally separate from the natural world. Young Dewey claims that God is found in human relationships and that Jesus was the ultimate example of the integration of God in humanity.

THE VALUE OF HISTORICAL CHRISTIANITY

Written long before *A Common Faith*, this essay calls the value of historical Christianity the encouragement of selflessness and the aim to advance the good of all of humanity. Dewey argues that the most important consequences of historical Christianity are found in appreciation for all human beings and in the connection between all experience and God. The themes of care for humanity, appreciation of the good of all, and devotion to experience and to learning from the sciences are all values that we see throughout Dewey's later work, including in his writings on humanism, one of the most famous of which concludes this collection of essays.

Religion, generally, has had for its aim the uniting of man to some force greater, more permanent, more real, than himself, to some power which underlies nature. Man has ever associated with such a unity the sense of reconciliation and peace, of a value in life which can find no justification save in peace. Man has ever been prone to find this unity with God, either in mere outward rites, dogmas, and events, or in his own consciousness. Teaching once incarnate with personal zeal and inspiration tends to harden into formal dogma. Deeds, once the spontaneous and necessary because the unforced expression of sympathy and devotion, become ceremonial rites without meaning. A community once bound together by common interests and love tends to become an outward ecclesiastical organization. When zeal and inspiration depart and give place to rites the life of the religion has departed. There remains but a skeleton—a source of fear and of bondage. The unity that was to unite man to God has somehow grown into an institution which with its dogmas, rites, sacred events, and sacred books keeps man from coming nearest to his God. The individual who thinks finds these forms all outside of himself. They touch him nowhere. It is either a burden he must bear or a bondage he must shake off. It is a dream imposed on him in his sleep: if he should awake, the dream, and with it his religious faith will vanish. Again, man seeks for that final peace, which only reconciliation with God can give in his own heart. His religion becomes a matter of moods and symptoms which the individual must watch as closely as the valetudinarian watches his bodily symptoms.[2] Religion is reduced to internal experiences of morbid and health-destroying introspection. The individual must watch his every thought and feeling to see if it please God or no. His life is one vast query. Have I the evidences of salvation? Religious activity becomes sentimentalism. Let the individual now awake to self-consciousness, and he is convinced that the realm of religion is a realm of cant; that there is no reality in it.

If the merely outward form of religion is a skeleton, the merely inward form is a fibreless and sinewless pulp, equally lifeless. It cannot be denied that Christianity has repeatedly assumed one or the other of these unspiritual forms. Whenever this has occurred, scepticism, social and individual has arisen as surely as human consciousness is sure to assert itself against everything which tends to bring it into bondage. But it cannot be denied that the great strength of Christianity has been in its power to overcome these onesided forms and to bind the historical and the internal, personal factors into a vital unity; and to bring the individual nearer to God through the uniting of these forces, in society and in history; and to make the historical expression of Christianity not dead dogma, traditionalism, ceremonialism, that happened 19 centuries ago; but to make this external side itself a manifestation of the unity of man with God, and an influence for its higher realization.

Christianity makes religion a social as well as an historical force, for it has its value in the power it has been to raise men out of their isolated individuality, and bind them into families and nations, and make them capable of higher social attainment in language, art and culture.

Christianity is unique, not in its unlikeness to other religions, but in the greater energy and fruitfulness with which it manifests and fulfills the essential elements of all.

The value of Christianity as an historical force in the world lies in the fact that there is a historical side, that Christianity is a principle which transcends all individualism; a principle which must find outward social expression in the world; and that it is a fact entering into that vast complexity of events we call history.

Men of philosophical tendencies have in the last hundred years repeatedly offered to compromise with the Christian community, expressing their entire willingness to recognize the truth of Christian ideas, if the Christian community would acknowledge Christian truth as only an idea, of which the historical facts are but imperfect symbols.

The Christian body have refused to surrender that which is its heart, but hold that Christianity is not only true as idea, but true also as a historic fact and force.

The historic side of Christianity is the growth it has had in history.

In order to teach and spread Christian truth and bring it home to the world, a certain amount of organization and machinery has been necessary. Christianity as a historical force means this and more. It means what Christ meant when he said, "He that hath seen me hath seen the Father." It means what St. John spoke: "That which was from the beginning, that which we have seen with our eyes; that which we beheld and our hands handled, concerning the Word of Life, declare we unto you."

Surely Christ did not mean that the man who had looked on him with bodily eye had seen the Divine Spirit. Surely St. John did not mean that he had actually seen and touched and heard, physically, the Eternal One—The Spirit of Life that was from the beginning. Both these are tremendous metaphors, the most tremendous and magnificent that have fallen from men's lips. They express in the only language which man can command that God is no remote Being away from the world, that He is no Force which works in physical Nature alone, but that He is an ever present fact in life, in history, and in our social relations. They express the fact that the Divine Spirit has touched our actual life so immediately, so directly and so certainly, that men have seen Him and touched Him. Surely only the vast meaning and reality that lie within the words save them from blasphemy. No, God is neither a far-away Being, nor a mere philosophic conception by which to explain the world. He is the reality of our ordinary relations with one another in life. He is the bond of the family, the bond of society. He is love, the source of all growth, all sacrifice, and all unity. He has touched history, not from without but has made Himself subjected to all the limitations and sufferings of history; identified Himself absolutely with humanity, so that the life of humanity is henceforward not for some term of years, but forever, the Life of God. Who can read the last talks of Jesus with His disciples, as recorded in John's gospel, and not feel that their one burden, surging for expression in all commands, entreaties, encouragements, instructions, revelations, promises and prayers, is that the unity of God and man is perfect, absolute, now, in the Christ who has made men realize the presence of God within them forever, in the Spirit, who shall guide them into all truth, and comfort them with all comfort and make them possessors of all God's riches.

Unless these are mere symbols, or at best experiences to be reached by a few choice spirits, but not the common vantage of man, they must mean that the Spirit of God has entered into history, and that the Spirit is not a mystery working only in miracles, in revivals, etc., but is the intelligence present in all man's science, is his inspiration for whatever is better than himself.

Such is the meaning of the historical aspect of Christianity. What is its value in practical life? All men, right-minded and serious, have questioned. What is the purpose, the function of my life, and how shall I fulfill it? There has been but one answer—though in form it has varied from the almost inarticulate babble of childhood in primitive religion, to the clear triumphant utterance of a St. Paul—likeness to God, unity with Him.

How shall this unity be attained? The value of what has been termed the historical force of Christianity lies in the answer that it gives to this question. Union with humanity and humanity's interests, and surrender of individual desire.

Consciousness that the purpose of one's life is to be like God gives no help in the attainment of that likeness so long as it shuts the individual within his own interests. Such consciousness but weighs man down with the feeling of his utter impotency and the entire hopelessness of his case. But man is not thus isolated, and hence he does not have to deal with God face to face, but through the mediator of that corporate humanity of which he is a member, and Jesus, the head. Man thus feels that in his weakness he is strong. It is not that his consciousness of responsibility to God is diminished; not that he feels his individual powerlessness now that he has found shelter in the righteousness of another. It is because he knows that the God who has laid the claim upon him is Himself working in and through humanity to realize its highest good.

The individual has but to surrender himself to the common interests of humanity in order to be freed from the claim upon him as an individual. He stands no longer isolated, but a member of that humanity whose living spirit is God Himself.

If a man, forgetting the historic force of Christianity; forgetting that God is not some remote supernal being, but a present fact and force in historic and social life, attempts to realize what the words of Jesus, Paul and John mean, without realizing their nature, he will impose upon himself one of two things; either he will decide that the words can have no reality back of them, unless they be exaggerated expressions of experiences of some unusual souls, and will reject them as mere cant, or unconscious self-deceit; or he will attempt to realize their truth in his own experiences and feelings as an individual, which is impossible, for they are not the expressions of the experiences of an individual in his isolated relations to God, but rather of a man who has lost his individuality in his identification with humanity's interests, in the family, in the community, of interest in the better self.

The person who thus attempts to realize these things gradually divorces himself from reality, and begins by living a life of unreality of word, then of thought, and too often finally of deed.

The chief danger after all, in our practical religious life, is the tendency for the religious life to become a sphere by itself, apart from the interests of life and humanity. The healthy religious life knows no separation of the religious from the secular, which has no Sunday or week-day divisions in it, which finds in every daily duty, whether in study or business, or recreation an approach to God as surely and truly as in the retirement of the closet. This frame of mind can never be attained unless we realize that God is in history, is in the social state of life, reconciling men unto Him. He who finds in every true and pure relationship in life a bond of union with God, has his religious life built upon a rock which cannot be shaken by the storms of life, nor undermined by the subtleties of temptation.

NOTES

First published in *Monthly Bulletin* 11 (November 1889): 31–36, from an address delivered October 27, 1889, before the Students' Christian Association of the University of Michigan, reprint, in LW.17.529–33.

1. John Dewey, *A Common Faith* (New Haven, CT: Yale University Press, 1934), reprint, in LW.9.1–58.
2. [Editor's note: A person unduly concerned or focused on his or her health.]

46

What Humanism Means to Me

―

(1930)

EDITOR'S INTRODUCTION

In this short essay, Dewey explains the historical development of humanism as a return to the study of classic Greek and Roman literature. Various versions of humanism were adopted and defined, most notably by Francis Bacon, who believed in the potential of putting science to work for human benefit. A divergence from this way of thinking was adopted in the negative humanism of authors like Irving Babbitt. Babbitt saw humanism as a matter of separating human beings from nature. Dewey's humanism calls for a return to Bacon's kind of humanism but with emphasis on seeing the connection between human beings and nature, such that nature and our knowledge of it can be put to use for the sake of human flourishing.

Dewey's humanism places great importance on science, in a way that many romantics associated with the label "humanism" do not. Given the kind of continuity and connection that Dewey sees between human beings and nature, he accordingly identifies science with moral values and inquiry with human progress. Such humanism resists the thinking that treats humanity's nature as base and to be rejected, suppressed, or denied. Instead, it is in human beings' nature to have the potential for the development of intelligence and values. For Dewey, that development is not inevitable but can come with effort. In 1933, Dewey was a signatory on the first Humanist Manifesto.[1]

Humanism is a portmanteau word. A great many incongruous meanings have been packed in it. Words mean what they are made to signify by those who use them. Otherwise, it might be said that the proper use of the word is its historical one. At least it designated originally a phase of the revival of learning which occurred in the latter part of the Fifteenth and the early part of the Sixteenth Centuries. Applied to this movement, Humanism signifies the activity of a group of men of letters who were intensely interested in the literature of Greece and Rome. They strove to use Latin and Greek as living languages; they had an immense zeal for the propagation of ancient literature; their contempt for the vernaculars of Europe was such that, while they did a great amount of translating, it was from Greek into Latin.

In view of the peculiar meaning assigned the word Humanism by a group of contemporary American literary critics, it is worthy of note that no less an authority than Saintsbury says that the Humanists of that earlier day were in violent rebellion against all authority.[2]

The scope of Humanism widened. It passed from interest in classic literature to concern for all that related to human action and feeling. It made human life in the present and in the past the centre and source of all that is most important, as the Middle Ages had fastened itself upon the supernatural.

Humanitas was the opposite of *divinitas*. The humanities were put in opposition to theology and theological interest. A beautiful if somewhat idealized picture of this phase of Humanism is given by Walter Pater. He said:

> The essence of humanism is the belief that nothing which has ever interested living men and women can wholly lose its vitality—no language they have spoken, nor oracle beside which they have hushed their voices, no dreams which have once been entertained by actual human minds, nothing about which they have ever been passionate, or expended time and zeal.

This Humanism is also far removed from the doctrine of restraint and negation that Paul Elmer More and Irving Babbitt have baptized by the same name.[3]

The next phase of Humanism is that initiated by Francis Bacon and his successors, especially the great Frenchmen of the Eighteenth Century, notably Condorcet. Its essence was the conviction that all knowledge and all scientific inquiry should be organized about an ideal of human well-being for the "amelioration of the human estate." Bacon did not deny the reality of the divine and supernatural, but relegated it wholly to a realm of faith sharply marked off from that of knowledge. With his successors, the human element came more and more to the front. Auguste Comte, with his conception of a religion of humanity and the unification of all the sciences about humanity as its central theme, was greatly influenced by Condorcet.

In contemporary thought, there is an echo of this meaning in the new religious movement that calls itself Humanism. However, it does not propose to worship humanity, much less set up a system of rites which are to do for this worship what the sacraments did for mediaeval Christianity. It finds its conceptions of God and of other religious ideas of the past in the realm of human ideals and aspirations, and would yoke the religious emotions of mankind to the promotion of the ideal phases of human life.

Then there is also a philosophical development of pragmatism to which Schiller, the Oxford thinker, has given the name Humanism. He has taken for his motto the saying of Protagoras: "Man is the measure of all things." He has applied this conception to the rejuvenation of logic, ethics and metaphysics, making the conception of value central in philosophy, and finding the source of value in human desire, purpose and satisfaction. Even this brief survey shows the variety of meanings conveyed by the term "Humanism." None of them has any close resemblance to the movement signalized in the recent book *Humanism and America*.

Many persons attached to the older and better established meanings will regret that some other name could not have been found for the gospel according to More and Babbitt. Its chief claim to the title of Humanism is negative. It is not only anti-romantic, but also anti-naturalistic. The significance it gives to the "human" can be understood only in antithesis to the view it holds of nature. In philosophical terms, its philosophy is thoroughly dualistic. It holds to a complete gulf between nature and man in his true being, and finds in the irruptions of nature into human life the source of all the evils and all the woes that beset mankind.

This fact accounts for its distinctly negative temper. It attacks a philosopher[4] who, to most readers, is a type of genuine Humanist merely because he has tried to include man and nature in a way which sends the mechanistic aspect of it to the rear. This negative character would seem to doom the new movement to sterility.

Its creed enables it to attack many things in contemporary life which others also find undesirable. But in an age like our own, any philosophy which sets off man from nature, and which condemns science as a foe to higher human interests cannot, it is safe to predict, become productive.

It has much more in common with the romanticism it condemns than it is aware of. Its ethics are essentially those of Kant; its idea of a reason and rule that are divorced from all natural basis and natural positive use is the expression of a "transcendental imagination." If it follows its own logic to its conclusion, it will terminate, like the earlier romanticism, in the bosom of the church.

There remains intact another Humanism. The problem of integrating science in its bearings upon life, and of rendering it the servant instead of the master of human destiny, has grown only the more pressing since the days of Francis Bacon. It was then a possibility; it is now a necessity, if the dignity of human life is not to be submerged. Social life itself demands this integration, and science invites to the task. A Humanism of this type will endure long after the much advertised "Humanism" of a present group has found its way into a paragraph in a chapter on early Twentieth Century American letters.

At all events, what Humanism means to me is *an expansion, not a contraction, of human life, an expansion in which nature and the science of nature are made the willing servants of human good.*

NOTES

First published in *Thinker* 2 (June 1930): 9–12, reprint, in LW.5.263–67.
1. You can find the document on the American Humanist Association's website: http://americanhumanist.org/Humanism/Humanist_Manifesto_I.
2. [Editor's note: George Saintsbury (1845–1933) was a British literary historian who authored works of criticism on French literature.]
3. [Editor's note: Dewey is referring to More's and Babbitt's version of "humanism" which called for restraining human impulses, expecting self-control over behavior and the denial, negation, of baser instincts.]
4. [Note from the editor of *Thinker*:] Alfred North Whitehead, English scientist, metaphysicist, and mathematician, author of *Science and the Modern World*, etc.–Editor.

References

THE ELECTRONIC EDITION OF *THE COLLECTED WORKS OF JOHN DEWEY*

For this project, I am principally indebted to the Center for Dewey Studies at Southern Illinois University in Carbondale, IL, and especially to Dewey's collected works. The citation for those works has been abbreviated in this text with reference to the portion of the collection, namely the early works (EW), the middle works (MW), or the later works (LW).

Boydston, Jo Ann, ed. *The Collected Works of John Dewey, 1882–1953: The Electronic Edition*. Carbondale: Southern Illinois University Press, 1996.

ORIGINAL SOURCES OF THE TEXTS INCLUDED IN THIS COLLECTION

References for the first published versions of John Dewey's public writings, before their inclusion in *The Collected Works of John Dewey*, are listed here in the order of the chapters of this book.

Chapter 1: "Democracy Is Radical." *Common Sense* 6 (January 1937): 10–11, reprint, in LW.11.296–300.
Chapter 2: "Address to National Negro Conference." *Proceedings of the National Negro Conference, 1909* (New York: National Negro Conference Headquarters, n.d.): 71–73, reprint, in MW.4.156–58.
Chapter 3: "A Symposium on Woman's Suffrage." *International* 3 (1911): 93–94, reprint, in MW.6.153–54.
Chapter 4: "The Challenge of Democracy to Education." *Progressive Education* 14 (February 1937): 79–85, reprint, in LW.11.181–91.
Chapter 5: "America in the World." *Nation* 106 (1918): 287, reprint, in MW.11.71–73.
Chapter 6: "Our National Dilemma." *New Republic* 22 (1920): 117–18, reprint, in MW.12.4–8.
Chapter 7: "Pragmatic America." *New Republic* 30 (1922): 185–87, reprint, in MW.13.306–11.
Chapter 8: "The Basic Values and Loyalties of Democracy." *American Teacher* 25 (May 1941): 8–9, reprint, in LW.14.275–78.

Chapter 9: "Creative Democracy—the Task Before Us." In *John Dewey and the Promise of America*, Progressive Education Booklet No. 14. Columbus, Ohio: American Education Press, 1939. 12–17, reprint, in LW.14.224–31.

Chapter 10: "Politics and Culture." *Modern Thinker* 1 (May 1932): 168–74, 238, reprint, in LW.6.40–48.

Chapter 11: "Intelligence and Power." *New Republic* 78 (April 25, 1934): 306–7, reprint, in LW.9.108–112.

Chapter 12: "Force, Violence, and the Law." *New Republic* 5 (1916): 295–97, reprint, in MW.10.212–16.

Chapter 13: "Why I Am Not a Communist." *Modern Monthly* 8 (April 1934): 135–37, reprint, in LW.9.91–96.

Chapter 14: "Dualism and the Split Atom." *New Leader* 28 (November 22, 1945): 1, 4, reprint, in LW.15.199–204.

Chapter 15: "Is There Hope for Politics?" *Scribner's* 89 (May 1931): 483–87, reprint, in LW.6.182–190.

Chapter 16: "A Liberal Speaks Out for Liberalism." *New York Times Magazine*, February 23, 1936. 3, 24, reprint, in LW.11.282–89.

Chapter 17: "Future of Liberalism." *People's Lobby Bulletin* 4 (February 1935): 1–2, reprint, in LW.11.258–61.

Chapter 18: "What Is a School For?" *New York Times*, March 18, 1923, reprint, in MW.15.189–93.

Chapter 19: "Dewey Outlines Utopian Schools." *New York Times*, April 23, 1933. Education section,

Chapter 20: "Industrial Education—A Wrong Kind." *New Republic* 2 (1915): 71–73, reprint, in MW.8.118–123.

Chapter 21: "Why Have Progressive Schools?" *Current History* 38 (July 1933): 441–48, reprint, in LW.9.147–58.

Chapter 22: "Can Education Share in Social Reconstruction?" *Social Frontier* 1 (October 1934): 11–12, reprint, in LW.9.205–10.

Chapter 23: "Nationalizing Education." *Journal of Education* 84 (1916): 425–28, reprint, in MW 10.202–11.

Chapter 24: "The Teacher and the Public." In *Vital Speeches of the Day* 1 (January 1935): 278–79, from a speech broadcast January 16, 1935, over radio station WEVD, New York City, as part of the NBC *University of the Air* series, reprint, in LW.11.158–62.

Chapter 25: "Democracy and Education in the World of Today." Pamphlet, Society for Ethical Culture. New York, 1938. 15 pp., reprint, in LW.13.294–304.

Chapter 26: "Capitalistic or Public Socialism? The Fourth Article in Professor Dewey's Series, 'Individualism, Old and New,'" *New Republic* 62 (March 5, 1930): 64–67, reprint, in LW.5.91–99.

Chapter 27: "Does Human Nature Change?" *Rotarian* 52 (February 1938): 8–11, 58–59, reprint, in LW.13.286–94.

Chapter 28: "The Ethics of Animal Experimentation." *Atlantic Monthly* 138 (September 1926): 343–46, reprint, in LW.2.98–103.

Chapter 29: "Ethics and International Relations." *Foreign Affairs* 1 (1923): 85–95, reprint, in MW.15.53–65.

Chapter 30: "Dewey Describes Child's New World." *New York Times*, April 10, 1932, reprint, in LW.6.137–42.

Chapter 31: "The Collapse of a Romance." *New Republic* 70 (April 27, 1932): 292–94, reprint, in LW.6.69–75.

Chapter 32: "The Economic Situation: A Challenge to Education." *Journal of Home Economics* 24 (June 1932): 495–501, reprint, in LW.6.123–31.

Chapter 33: "The Jobless—A Job for All of Us." *Unemployed* (February 1931): 3–4, reprint, in LW.6.153–56.

Chapter 34: "The Influence of Darwinism on Philosophy." Originally titled "Darwin's Influence Upon Philosophy." *Popular Science Monthly* 75 (1909): 90–98, reprint, in MW.4.3–15.

Chapter 35: "Science, Belief and the Public." *New Republic* 38 (1924): 143–45, reprint, in MW.15.47–53.

Chapter 36: "Social Science and Social Control." *New Republic* 67 (29 July 1931): 276–77, reprint, in LW.6.64–69.

Chapter 37: "Education and Birth Control." *Nation* 134 (January 27, 1932): 112, reprint, in LW.6.146–49.

Chapter 38: "The Supreme Intellectual Obligation." *Science Education* 18 (February 1934): 1–4, reprint, in LW.9.96–102.

Chapter 39: "The Revolt against Science." *Humanist* 5 (Autumn 1945): 105–7, reprint, in LW.15.188–92.

Chapter 40: "The Case of the Professor and the Public Interest." *Dial* 63 (1917): 435–37, reprint, in MW.10.165–68.

Chapter 41: "Social Absolutism." *New Republic* 25 (1921): 315–18, reprint, in MW.13.311–17.

Chapter 42: "Some Factors in Mutual National Understanding." *Kaizo* 3 (1921): 17–28, reprint, in MW.13.262–71.

Chapter 43: "The Basis for Hope." *Common Sense* 8 (December 1939): 9–10, reprint, in LW.14.249–52.

Chapter 44: "Art as Our Heritage." *Congressional Record.* 76th Cong., 3d sess. April 29, 1940. 86, pt. 15: 2477–78, reprint, in LW.14.255–58.

Chapter 45: "The Value of Historical Christianity." *Monthly Bulletin* 11 (November 1889): 31–36, reprint, in LW.17.529–33.

Chapter 46: "What Humanism Means to Me." *Thinker* 2 (June 1930): 9–12, reprint, in LW.5.263–67.

OTHER WORKS BY DEWEY

Dewey, John. *A Common Faith.* New Haven, CT: Yale University Press, 1934.

———. *The Correspondence of John Dewey, 1859–1952.* 2nd ed. General ed., Larry A. Hickman. Ed. Barbara Levine, Anne Sharpe, and Harriet Furst Simon. Charlottesville, VA: InteLex, 2001.

———. "Democracy and Educational Administration." In LW.11.217–26.

———. "Idealism in Natural Science." *Kaizo* (April 1921): 198–208. Reprint, in MW.13.433–35.

———. "The Reflex Arc Concept in Psychology." *Psychological Review* 3, no. 4 (1896): 357–70. Reprint, in EW.5.96–110.

Index

academia: "The Case of the Professor and the Public Interest" (1917), 277–81; "The Supreme Intellectual Obligation" (1934), 6–8, 263–69
Addams, Jane, 4, 225
"Address to the Negro Conference" (1909), 24–26
Adler, Felix, 161, 163
aesthetics, 70, 75. *See also* arts, the
Affordable Care Act, 98
African Americans, 6; "Address to the Negro Conference" (1909), 24–26; and beliefs about hereditary conditions, 24–26; and education, 161; intolerance toward, 57–58, 168. *See also* National Association for the Advancement of Colored People; racism
agriculture: and economic depression, 178, 233; farmer as the backbone of society in the early U.S., 167; farming and individualism, 173, 179; government intervention in support of, 173, 178–79; and tariffs, 179
"America in the World" (1918), 40–43
American Association for the Advancement of Science, 263
American Association of University Professors, 277, 279
American Commonwealth (Bryce), 33
American Federation of Teachers, 55, 160
American Teacher (periodical), 55
anger, and warfare, 188
animals: adaptation and evolution of species, 237–38, 240–41; "The Ethics of Animal Experimentation" (1926), 193–99; and laws of nature, 204
anti-Muslim sentiment, 56
anti-Semitism, 55–57, 168
Aristotle, 187, 189, 241
"Art as Our Heritage" (1940), 303–7
arts, the: "Art as Our Heritage" (1940), 303–7; creation vs. acquisition, 303–5; and education, 117–18, 303; in Europe, 297, 306; low standards for media, 73–74; "Politics and Culture" (1932), 69–77; and poverty, 75; public support for, 303, 305–6
atavism, 245, 248n5
atomic bomb: "Dualism and the Split Atom" (1945), 93–97
authoritarianism: "Why I Am Not a Communist" (1934), 88–92. *See also* dictatorships; Germany; Naziism; Soviet Union

Babbitt, Irving, 314, 315
Bacon, Francis, 50–54, 79, 314, 315
Baldwin, Roger, 144, 145
Barnard, Henry, 165, 170n4
"Basic Values and Loyalties of Democracy, The" (1941), 55–58
"Basis for Hope, The" (1939), 299–302
Beard, Charles A., 280
belief: avoiding extremes of belief, 182–88; "Science, Belief, and the Public" (1924), 249–54; and scientific habits of mind, 267
Bentham, Jeremy, 108, 206

birth control: "Education and Birth Control" (1932), 260–62
Black Panthers, 2
Bloomberg, Michael, 161
Bruce, Ned, 305, 306
Bryce, James, 33

"Can Education Share in Social Reconstruction?" (1934), 144–47
capital gains tax, 174
Capital in the Twenty-First Century (Piketty), 174
capitalism: and "bourgeois" democracy, 20; "Capitalistic or Public Socialism?" (1930), 173–84; capitalist social absolutism, 282; "The Collapse of a Romance" (1932), 8, 217–22; and communist view of history, 90; and democracy, 20–21; and democratization of industry, 90; and free enterprise in Europe, 20–21; and government intervention in support of corporations, 173–82; and government regulations, 145; and humanitarian vs. laissez-faire liberalism, 108–10; industrial/business interests and warfare, 301; legislation aimed at owners of capital, 156; and liberty, 109; morality of living upon interest, 157; the Right's prioritization of commercial interests, 19; and romanticism in the U.S., 218–22; and "rugged individualism" doctrine, 109, 144–46, 217, 228; and safety nets (*see* social welfare); the wealthy as a favored class, 156–58, 160. *See also* commerce; commercialism; economics and economic justice; industrialization; laissez-faire liberalism
"Capitalistic or Public Socialism?" (1930), 173–84
Carlyle, Thomas, 218, 222n2
"Case of the Professor and the Public Interest, The" (1917), 277–81
Catholic Church, 202–3, 272, 301
Cattell, James McKeen, 263, 268
causes, secondary vs. first, 238, 241, 243–44
"Challenge of Democracy to Education, The" (1937), 30–39
charity, 231–33
charter schools, 78
Child and the Curriculum, The (Dewey), 5
children: behavior problems, 139; *The Child and the Curriculum*, 5; child health, 213; curiosity and interest in experimentation, 267–68; "Dewey Describes Child's New World" (1932), 211–16; Dewey's concern with, 5 (*see also* education); "Education and Birth Control" (1932), 260–62; education and individual psychology of the child, 136–37, 140; and labor reforms, 108; learning styles, 136–37; and mental illness, 212, 214; and "The Reflex Arc Concept in Psychology," 5; *School and Society*, 5. *See also* education
Children's Charter, 215–16
China, 33, 289, 291–92, 296; British-American cooperation in, 47; Dewey in, 5, 289
Chipman, Harriet Alice, 3
Christianity, 6; conflict among science, religion, public opinion, and general education curricula, 249–54, 272; and ethics, 202–4; fundamentalism, 250, 253, 272; and humanitarian liberalism, 105; missionaries, 296; "The Value of Historical Christianity" (1889), 3, 308–13; Wesleyan movement, 105–7
Christian Science, 181, 184n15
citizenship: education and intelligent citizenship, 34, 118, 164–65. *See also* democracy; education: purposes of
civics, study of, 34
civil liberties, 56–57, 60, 88, 89, 103. *See also* freedom
Clémenceau, Georges, 45, 48n1, 282, 287
Cochran, Thad, 28
"Collapse of a Romance, The" (1932), 8, 217–22
collective thinking, 228, 229
collectivism, 145
Columbia University, 5, 8, 278, 280
commerce: and European liberal political parties, 108; and the physical sciences, 296–97; talent and brainpower channeled into industry and profit rather than democratic culture, 69–70. *See also* capitalism; economics and economic justice; laissez-faire liberalism
commercialism, 11; and European heritage, 53; and low standards for media, 73–74; and pragmatism, 49, 50–54
"Common Core" curriculum, 149
Common Faith, A (Dewey), 4, 308
communication: barriers to, 7, 60, 63, 71–72, 76; jargon, 7, 277–78; loyalty of democracy to, 56–57
communism, 2, 19, 20, 36, 60, 287; capital "c" vs. "small-c" communism, 88–89, 92; philosophy of history, 88, 90, 286; and suppression of civil

liberties, 89; and Treaty of Non-aggression between Soviet Union and Germany, 301; and violence, 105, 111; "Why I Am Not a Communist" (1934), 88–92
Comte, August, 316
Condorcet, Marquis de, 315–16
conservatism, 27–28, 187. *See also* Republican Party; Right, the
cooperation: cooperation among democratic nations, 168; and democracy, 64; and humanitarian vs. laissez-faire liberalism, 105–6
Cornell University, 277
corruption, 102, 179
"Creative Democracy—the Task Before Us" (1939), 10, 59–65
credit, 189–90, 220–21
criminality, 85–86, 157, 191
critical thinking, 223, 227, 229; and the obligations of intellectuals, 264, 266–67; "Science, Belief, and the Public" (1924), 249–54; scientific habits of mind, 263–64, 266–67
"cultural lag," 95
culture: "Art as Our Heritage" (1940), 303–7; and brutalizing effects of industrialization and profit motive, 76; "Does Human Nature Change?" (1938), 185–92; and intellectual and artistic capacity of human beings, 75–76; low standards for media, 73–74; "Politics and Culture" (1932), 69–77; and poverty, 69, 75, 77; as province of the elite, 76; reverence for culture and fears about independent thinking, 254; "Some Factors in Mutual National Understanding" (1921), 289–98. *See also* arts, the
Current History (periodical), 133

Darwin, Charles, 4, 10, 59; and conflict between science and religion, 250–51; "The Influence of Darwinism on Philosophy" (1909), 237–48
Darwin, Emma, 238
democracy: "America in the World" (1918), 40–43; and the arts, 303–7; and avoiding extremes, 282–88; and barriers to free communication (hatred, fear, etc.), 60, 63; "The Basic Values and Loyalties of Democracy" (1941), 55–58; "The Basis for Hope" (1939), 299–302; "bourgeois" democracy, 20; "The Challenge of Democracy to Education" (1937), 30–39; and civility, 10; and communism, 19, 20; and cooperation, 64; cooperation among democratic nations, 168; "Creative Democracy—the Task Before Us" (1939), 10, 59–65; "Democracy and Education in the World of Today" (1938), 161–70; democracy as a way of personal life, 62–65; "Democracy Is Radical" (1937), 10, 19–23; democratic attitudes, 2, 9, 10, 32–33, 55–58, 60–65, 148–49, 162–71, 299–302; democratic ends requiring democratic means, 2, 19–23, 89, 113, 114; democratic values, 3–4, 55–58, 60–65; democratizing economies, 98–99, 144, 175; Dewey's democratic approach to education, 9, 164; and diversity, 10; dynamic nature of, 32–33, 166, 169; and economic individualism, 58; and economic insecurity, 167; and education, 30–39, 64–65, 161–70; effect of challenges to, 300–302 (*see also* "Social Absolutism"); exploitation by special interests, 111; and faith in human potential, 57, 60, 62–63; and fascism, 19, 20; and foreign policy, 45–46; and handling differences and conflicts, 64; and human experiences, 64–65; and industrial/commercial interests, 21; as key element of the American spirit, 148–49; and nationalizing education, 154–55; necessity of asking people what they want and need, 163; and new political parties, 98–104; "Our National Dilemma" (1920), 44–48; and public opinion, 249–50; "Social Absolutism" (1921), 282–88; and social control, 111, 163; "A Symposium on Woman's Suffrage" (1911), 27–29; and voter apathy and cynicism, 99–101, 180; and women's suffrage, 27–29
Democracy and Education (Dewey), 5, 238
"Democracy and Education in the World of Today" (1938), 161–70
"Democracy Is Radical" (1937), 10, 19–23
democratic liberalism, 7, 106, 111
Democratic Party, 100, 176–77
democratic socialism, 174
Derbyshire, John, 27–28
Descartes, René, 242
Dewey, Archibald, 3
Dewey, Gordon, 5

Dewey, John, 185; background, education, and career, 3–9; belief in adapting/letting go of past habits of thought and practice, 6, 9, 10 (see also "Does Human Nature Change?"); belief in the obligation of the intellect to act for the benefit of humanity, 6, 10, 51, 74–75, 263–71, 314, 317; birth and death, 2; death of sons, 4, 5, 194; as humanist, 4, 6, 8, 314–17; James and, 4, 13n18, 54n2; marriage, 3; overview of life and works, 1–11; and philosophy (see humanism; philosophy; pragmatism); and public engagement, 6–8; and religion, 3, 6, 8, 308–13; scientific outlook of, 4, 9, 10 (see also science); and testing abstract ideas in the real world, 4, 6

Dewey, Lucina, 3, 308

Dewey, Morris, 4, 194

"Dewey Describes Child's New World" (1932), 211–16

"Dewey Outlines Utopian Schools" (1933), 121–26

Dickens, Charles, 106

dictatorships, 2, 22, 91, 111. See also communism; fascism; Germany; Soviet Union; totalitarianism

"Does Human Nature Change?" (1938), 185–92

dogmatism, 52, 80, 113–14, 251–52, 284, 285

"Dualism and the Split Atom" (1945), 93–97

DuBois, W. E. B., 24

economics and economic justice: brutalizing effects of profit motive, 76; "Capitalism or Public Socialism?" (1930), 173–84; and causes of modern wars, 188; changing attitudes toward interest and credit, 189–90; and changing industries, 166–67, 178; "The Collapse of a Romance" (1932), 8, 217–22; concentration of wealth, 175, 178; and confidence, 220–21; and corruption, 102, 179; and critical thinking, 227, 229; democratizing economies, 98–99, 144, 175; distribution of income, 176; economic origin of political questions, 103; "The Economic Situation: A Challenge to Education" (1932), 223–30; economic stimulus, 178; effects of economic insecurity, 167; and equality of opportunity, 154, 228–29; and global interdependence, 41; and humanitarian vs. laissez-faire liberalism, 105–11; income inequality, 174–75, 177, 179; industrial/business interests and warfare, 301; and insecurity and uncertainty in business, 219–22; "The Jobless—a Job for All of Us" (1931), 8, 231–34; laissez-faire policies, 101; and magical thinking, 181; overcapitalization and overproduction of industries, 178–79; and participation in culture/the arts, 69–77; and political power, 103; and Republican Party, 173–74, 176–78; Republican support for government intervention in support of corporations, 173–74, 178–79; the Right's prioritization of commercial interests, 19; and romanticism in the U.S., 218–22; and "rugged individualism" doctrine, 109, 144–46, 217, 228; "Social Science and Social Control" (1931), 255–59; and the Soviet Union, 182, 257; and the status quo, 144–45; stock market crash of 1929, 181; talent and brainpower channeled into industry and profit rather than democratic culture, 69–70, 77; tariffs, 109, 178–79, 207. See also capitalism; commerce; commercialism; Great Depression; poverty and the poor; wealthy, the

"Economic Situation: A Challenge to Education, The" (1932), 223–30

education: adult education, 268; and breaking down class divisions, 169; "Can Education Share in Social Reconstruction?" (1934), 144–47; "The Challenge of Democracy to Education" (1937), 30–39; and connection of knowledge, information, and skills with social action, 34–38; and critical thinking, 223, 227, 229, 249–54; and culture/the arts, 72–73, 117–18; current debates, 78; current practices, 10, 11, 30, 121, 128, 133, 149; and democracy, 30–39, 64–65, 154–55, 161–70; "Democracy and Education in the World of Today" (1938), 161–70; democratic approach to, 9, 164 (see also progressive schools); "Dewey Outlines Utopian Schools" (1933), 121–26; diminished quality during the Great Depression, 157, 159; dropouts, 75; "The Economic Situation: A Challenge to Education" (1932), 223–30; "Education and Birth Control" (1932), 260–62; education for children's private interests vs. social duties, 32; emphasis upon economic form of success, 146; and equality of opportunity, 154; and faith in human capacity for intelligent judgment and action, 63, 125; funding for, 120; history education, 294–95;

history of education in the U.S., 135–37; and improving public conditions, 223–30; and individual psychology of the child, 136–37, 140; "Industrial Education—A Wrong Kind" (1915), 127–32; and intelligence and power, 81–82; intermediary between aimless education and inculcation/indoctrination, 38; isolation of school from life, 34, 36; learning by doing, 9, 123; lifelong learning, 11; Mann and, 31–32; "Nationalizing Education" (1916), 148–55; National School Lunch Program, 69; and peace, 169; and plasticity of human nature, 190–91; purposes of, 117–20, 123–24, 134–35, 163–65, 214–15, 224–26; and the renewal of civilization, 214; science education, 7, 35–36, 253, 263, 266–68; social studies education, 30, 34–35; and the status quo, 144–45; "The Teacher and the Public" (1935), 156–60; testing, 30, 121, 124, 223, 264; and third-party movements, 103–4; tracking, 127–28, 130; and travel abroad, 289–98; utopian schools, 11, 121–26; vocational education, 30, 36–38, 127–32, 154; "What Is a School For?" (1923), 117–20; "Why Have Progressive Schools?" (1933), 133–42; and women, 25. *See also* schools; teachers

"Education and Birth Control" (1932), 260–62

Einstein, Albert, 284

Eliot, Charles W., 117, 119

emotions: and the arts, 304, 305; and human nature, 188–89; and pacifism, 86; and presidential elections, 176–77; and warfare, 188. *See also specific emotions*

employee stock ownership plans (ESOPs), 175, 183n14

ends and means: and communism and fascism, 91; democratic ends requiring democratic means, 2, 19–23, 89, 113, 114; democratic methods of social change, 111; and force, 84

entertainment: low standards for entertainment media, 73–74

equality of opportunity, 36, 62, 154, 228–29

ESOPs. *See* employee stock ownership plans

ethics. *See* morality and ethics

"Ethics and International Relations" (1923), 200–210

"Ethics of Animal Experimentation, The" (1926), 193–99

Europe: and the arts, 297, 306; European Union, 299; force used by authoritarian states, 169; and liberalism and free enterprise/commercial interests, 20–21, 108; and nationality and citizenship, 42; as place of old habits and practices, 10, 53; political parties, 20–21; politics in, 38; propaganda in anti-democratic states of, 164–65

evolution, 10, 283; and conflict between science and religion, 250–51; and *Human Nature and Conduct*, 5–6; "The Influence of Darwinism on Philosophy" (1909), 237–48; teaching of, 145

Farm Relief Board, 178

fascism, 2, 19, 20, 36, 60, 91, 105, 168

fear: as barrier to free communication, 60, 63; and human nature, 188; and independent thinking, 254; and international relations, 291; and presidential elections, 176–77; and vocational education, 128–30; and warfare, 188–89

Federal Reserve Board, 178

Federal Works Agency, 303, 305–6

feudalism, 50, 53, 54, 90, 107

Fitzmaurice, Andrew. *See Humanism and America*

force: and authoritarian states of Europe, 169; and discipline in schools, 140; "Force, Violence, and the Law" (1916), 83–87

"Force, Violence, and the Law" (1916), 83–87

Ford, Franklin, 4, 6

foreign policy: "Ethics and International Relations" (1923), 200–210; "Our National Dilemma" (1920), 44–48

France, 45, 46; French Revolution, 55, 58

Franks, Robert A., 117

fraternity, 55–56, 58

freedom: freedom of assembly, 56, 60, 103; freedom of speech, 56, 60, 103, 277–81; freedom of the press, 56, 103; "Future of Liberalism" (1935), 112–14; Lippmann and, 112, 113; workers' lack of freedom, 113, 144. *See also* liberty

French Revolution, 55, 58

Friedman, Thomas, 40

Fries, General Amos, 224

"Future of Liberalism" (1935), 112–14

Galileo Galilei, 242
George, Henry, 110
Germany, 20, 58; fascism in, 91; injustice/intolerance in, 55, 58; invasion of Poland, 59; and political ethics, 207–8; propaganda in, 56; racial intolerance in, 168; as state-minded rather than socially minded, 282; Treaty of Non-aggression with Soviet Union, 299, 301. *See also* fascism; Naziism
Gilman, Charlotte Perkins, 28
God: and chance vs. design, 238, 243–45; and laws of nature, 203; Spencer and, 246; "The Value of Historical Christianity" (1889), 308–13
government intervention: and aid to the poor, 108–9 (*see also* social welfare); and freedom, 109–10, 113; and private industry/corporations, 109–10, 145, 173–74, 178–79
Graves, Frank P., 117
Gray, Asa, 238, 244
Great Britain: and foreign policy, 46–47; and liberalism and free enterprise/commercial interests, 20–21, 108; liberalism in, 106–7; U.S. alliance with, 46–47
Great Depression, 8, 19, 59, 78; "The Collapse of a Romance" (1932), 8, 217–22; Hoover and, 181; and humanitarian vs. laissez-faire liberalism, 105; "The Jobless—a Job for All of Us" (1931), 231–34; legislation aimed at owners of capital, 156; safety nets created during, 144, 156–57, 218, 232; "Social Science and Social Control" (1931), 255–59; stock market crash of 1929, 181; support for corporations, 173–74, 181; tax rates, 174; unemployment during, 156, 217, 231; worsening working conditions for teachers, 157–59
Greek and Roman literature, 314, 315
Greek philosophy and ethics, 76, 207, 240
Grotius, Hugo, 202, 203, 210n1

habits, changing, 6, 9, 10, 185, 187, 190. *See also* status quo
Hamilton, Alexander, 167, 258
happiness: and education, 134, 150, 215; and utilitarianism, 108, 200, 205–6, 208
Harvey, Alexander, 28
hatred: as barrier to free communication, 60, 63; and hypocrisy, 62; and nationalism, 150; as obstacle to democracy, 10, 60; and warfare, 188
health care, 98

Hegelian moral theory, 200, 205, 207–8
heredity, 24–26
Herrick, Robert, 28
Hiroshima, 270–73
history: communist view of, 88, 90, 286; recording and teaching history, 289, 294–95; and social absolutism, 285, 286; "The Value of Historical Christianity," 308–13
History of Western Philosophy (Russell), 49
Hitler, Adolf, 38
Hobbes, Thomas, 52; Hobbesian moral theory, 200, 207
Hogben, Lancelot, 35, 37
Holt, Hamilton, 28
homosexuality, 6, 185
Hook, Sidney, 88, 92n1
Hooker, Sir Joseph Dalton, 239
Hoover, Herbert, 109, 177, 181
Hubbard, Elbert, 28
human beings: belief in human equality, 62–63; "Does Human Nature Change?" (1938), 185–92; needs of, 186; religion and the betterment of humanity, 308–13; science and the betterment of humanity, 51, 74–75, 263–71, 314, 317. *See also* public, the; workers
humanism, 4, 6, 8; Humanist Manifesto, 8, 314; negative humanism, 314, 315, 316; and science, 270–71, 273, 314, 317; "What Humanism Means to Me" (1930), 8, 314–17
Humanism and America (Fitzmaurice), 316
Humanist Manifesto, 8, 314
humanitarian liberalism, 105–11
human nature: "Does Human Nature Change?" (1938), 185–92
Human Nature and Conduct (Dewey), 5–6, 185
Hume, David, 52, 80
Hussein, Saddam, 299
Huxley, Thomas Henry, 239
hyphenism (e.g., Irish-American), 151–52

immigrants, 41, 46, 161, 168
income inequality, 174–75, 177, 179
India, 47
Indiana school laws, 127–32
individualism: democracy and economic individualism, 58; and education and social reconstruction, 146; and government intervention in support of corporations, 173–74, 180; and laissez-faire liberalism, 105;

and progressive schools, 140; "rugged individualism" doctrine, 109, 144–46, 217, 228; and socialism, 175; and social responsibility, 181–82

Individualism, Old and New (Dewey), 173

"Industrial Education—A Wrong Kind" (1915), 127–32

industrialization: brutalizing effects of, 76; and laissez-faire liberalism, 107; and unemployment, 232. *See also* capitalism; economics and economic justice

inflation, 178, 220–21

"Influence of Darwinism on Philosophy, The" (1909), 237–48

information: and distinction between knowledge and understanding, 33–34; isolation from action, 34; and the obligations of intellectuals, 263–69

inquiry: and experimentalist method of intelligence, 256; freedom of inquiry in academia, 277–81; and jargon as defensive measure, 277–78; and obligations of intellectuals, 6–7; and science education, 7

instincts, 186, 188, 204

intellectuals. *See* academia; "The Supreme Intellectual Obligation"

intelligence: and class interests, 81–82; defined/described, 79; democracy and the freedom to develop intelligence, 57; education and critical thinking, 223, 227, 249–54; and education and democratic engagement, 31, 164–65; faith in human capacity for intelligent judgment and action, 63; "Intelligence and Power" (1934), 78–82; intelligent citizenship, 34, 118, 164–65; and pacifism, 86; public intelligence and democratic ends, 22–23; "Science, Belief, and the Public" (1924), 249–54; and social change, 30, 113–14; as a type of power, 81–82; understanding and intelligent action, 33–34, 38. *See also* education; knowledge; understanding; wisdom

"Intelligence and Power" (1934), 78–82

intelligent design, 238, 243–45

internationalism, 148–52

international relations: "Ethics and International Relations" (1923), 200–210; "Some Factors in Mutual National Understanding" (1921), 289–98

Interstate Commerce Commission, 178

intolerance, 52, 55, 57–58, 63, 168, 253

Iraq War, 299

"Is There Hope for Politics?" (1931), 9, 98–104

Italy, 55, 56, 91, 168

James, Alice Howe Gibbens, 13n18

James, William, 4, 13n18, 49–53, 54n2, 189

Japan, 5, 56, 289, 291–92

jargon, 7, 277–78

Jefferson, Thomas, 167

Jewish Americans, 161

"Jobless—a Job for All of Us, The" (1931), 8, 231–34

Johns Hopkins University, 3, 226

Josephson, Matthew, 156

journalism, 4, 49

Journal of Home Economics, 223

Kaizo (Japanese magazine), 289

Kallen, Horace, 59

Kandel, Isaac Leon, 147, 147n3

Kant, Immanuel, 316

Kellog-Briand Pact of 1928, 201

knowledge: distinguished from understanding, 33–34; free circulation of, 71, 76 (*see also* communication); and intelligence, 79 (*see also* intelligence); isolation from action, 34

laissez-faire liberalism, 105–11, 113, 145

land ownership, 189–90

law: and animal experimentation, 196–97; and change and human nature, 190; force as, 84, 86; "Force, Violence, and the Law" (1916), 83–87; Indiana school laws, 127–32; "Industrial Education—A Wrong Kind" (1915), 127–32; labor reforms, 108, 156; laws of history, 283, 284, 286; laws of nature, 202–5, 258; legislation aimed at owners of capital, 156; and liberalism in the U.S., 108; outlawing war, 200; positive laws, 205; unemployment insurance laws, 232

leadership, 228, 278

League for Industrial Democracy, 231

League of Nations, 48, 283, 285

learning styles, 136–37

Left, the: and Dewey's critique of mismatched ends and means, 19–23; "Why I Am Not a Communist" (1934), 88–92. *See also* communism; Democratic Party

legalism, 54

Levinson, Salmon, 209
liberalism: and cooperation vs. violence, 105–6; democratic liberalism, 7, 106, 111; and dogma of natural rights of the individual, 54; false vs. genuine liberalism, 300, 301; and free enterprise in Europe, 20–21; humanitarian vs. laissez-faire branches, 105–11; "A Liberal Speaks Out for Liberalism" (1936), 105–11; and radicalism, 109–11, 114; and social change, 110–11, 113–14; and the U.S., 21
"Liberal Speaks Out for Liberalism, A" (1936), 105–11
liberty: and dictatorships, 111; and government intervention in private industry, 109–10; and humanitarian vs. laissez-faire liberalism, 105, 109–10; public's fatigue with the responsibilities of political liberty, 162. *See also* freedom
life, right to, 232
Lincoln, Abraham, 162
Lippmann, Walter, 112, 113
literature, 72, 106, 292, 314–15
Locke, John, 52
loyalty: "The Basic Values and Loyalties of Democracy" (1941), 55–58
Lyell, Sir Charles, 239

Machiavelli, Niccolò, 207
Making of Citizens, The (Merriam), 226–27
Malthus, Thomas, 218, 222n2
Mann, Horace, 31–32, 161, 165, 167, 170n4
marriage, 122, 126n2, 238
Marx, Karl, 38, 89, 92n1, 113, 175–76, 286, 288
materialism, 11; cultural concepts in difference between materialism and spirituality, 289, 291–93, 295–97; and science, 270–73
Matthison, Edith Wynne, 28
McCarthyism, 277, 282
McReynolds, Phillip, 13n11
Meaning of Marx, The (Hook, ed.), 88
Medicare and Medicaid, 174
medicine: child health, 213; "The Ethics of Animal Experimentation" (1926), 193–99
Mencken, H. L., 102
mental illness, 212, 214
meritocracy, 228–29
Merriam, Charles E., 226–27
Method of Freedom, The (Lippmann), 113
Meyer, Annie Nathan, 28
Mill, John Stuart, 25, 27, 206

Millerand, Alexandre, 282, 287
morality and ethics: "The Basic Values and Loyalties of Democracy" (1941), 55–58; and Christianity, 202–4; "Does Human Nature Change?" (1938), 185–92; "Dualism and the Split Atom" (1945), 93–97; "Ethics and International Relations" (1923), 200–210; "The Ethics of Animal Experimentation" (1926), 193–99; Greek political ethics, 207; Hegelian moral theory, 200, 205, 207–8; moral frontier in the U.S., 60–61; natural law tradition, 200–205; "The Revolt against Science" (1945), 270–73; and suffrage, 29; "The Supreme Intellectual Obligation" (1934), 263–69; utilitarianism, 200, 205–7; "The Value of Historical Christianity," 3, 308–13
More, Paul Elmer, 315
Mussolini, Benito, 38, 114, 162

NAACP. *See* National Association for the Advancement of Colored People
name-calling, 63
Napoleonic wars, 208
National Association for the Advancement of Colored People (NAACP), 5, 6, 59
National Endowment for the Arts, 303
nationalism: different aspects of, 149–50; "Nationalizing Education" (1916), 148–55; role in producing totalitarianism, 58; and World War I, 148
"Nationalizing Education" (1916), 148–55
National School Lunch Program, 69
Nation (periodical), 260
natural law, 218; and ethics and international relations, 200–205
Naziism, 2, 20, 58, 62, 299, 301
Nearing, Scott, 279
New Republic, 8, 46, 173, 282
news media, 60, 81
Newton, Isaac, 283, 284
New York Society for Ethical Culture, 161
New York Times, 117, 121, 161, 211
Niebuhr, Reinhold, 80, 81, 82n2
"noble savage," 106

Obama, Barack, 174
On the Origin of Species (Darwin), 4, 59, 239, 242, 248, 250
"Our National Dilemma" (1920), 44–48

pacifism. *See* peace and peace movements
parenthood: "Education and Birth Control" (1932), 260–62; education and health of parents, 214; and quality of life, 260, 262; and teachers, 122, 126n2
Paris Peace Conference, 48n1
Pasteur, Louis, 74–75
Pater, Walter, 315
patriotism, 155, 225
Pax Americana, 41
Pax Romana, 208, 210n3
Peabody, George Foster, 28
peace and peace movements: and education, 169; and ethics and international relations, 201, 208; and human nature, 187; pacifism, 83–86, 189, 277, 301; and World War I, 282
Peirce, Charles Sanders, 49, 51, 52
Philippines, 47
philosophy, 13n11; and the betterment of humanity, 51; and Dewey's scientific outlook, 4, 9; importance of philosophy for life and policy, 9; "The Influence of Darwinism on Philosophy" (1909), 237–48; reconstruction of, 9, 13n11; Rorty and, 13n11; Scholastic tradition, 237–38; school of philosophy at the University of Chicago, 5; "Social Absolutism" (1921), 282–88; "The Value of Historical Christianity," 308–13; "What Humanism Means to Me" (1930), 314–17. *See also* humanism; morality and ethics; pragmatism; utilitarianism
Piketty, Thomas, 174
Plato, 237, 264
pledge of allegiance, 168
plutocracy, 111
political parties, 9; and education and intelligent citizenship, 35; independent voters, 102; "Is There Hope for Politics?," 98–104; "liberal" parties in Europe, 20–21; and minority activism, 104; third-party movements, 98–104
politics: and corruption, 102; economic origin of political questions, 103; and education and intelligent citizenship, 34–35; in Europe, 38; "Future of Liberalism" (1935), 112–14; "Intelligence and Power" (1934), 78–82; "Is There Hope for Politics?" (1931), 9, 98–104; "A Liberal Speaks Out for Liberalism" (1936), 105–11; "Politics and Culture" (1932), 69–77; and public apathy and cynicism, 99–101, 104; "Why I Am Not a Communist" (1934), 88–92. *See also* democracy
"Politics and Culture" (1932), 69–77
Pollock, Sir Frederick, 203, 210n2
Popular Science Monthly, 237
poverty and the poor: and culture/the arts, 69, 75, 77; and government intervention, 108–9; and humanitarian liberalism, 107–9; income inequality, 174–75, 177, 179. *See also* social welfare
power: and democratic ends requiring democratic means, 22; "Force, Violence, and the Law" (1916), 83–87; "Intelligence and Power" (1934), 78–82; power of privileged minority in the U.S., 144; types of, 81
"Pragmatic America" (1922), 49–54
pragmatism: Bacon and, 50–54; and commercialism, 49, 50–54; James and, 49–53; and love of truth and love of neighbor, 50–52; Peirce and, 49, 51–52; "Pragmatic America" (1922), 49–54; Russell's critique, 49–51
pregnancy, 126n2
Principles of Psychology, The (James), 4
Pritchett, Henry S., 117, 118
Progressive movement, 108
progressive schools, 133–42
Prohibition, 100–101, 257
propaganda, 56, 164, 168, 188, 230
property, 189–90
Protagoras, 316
Protestantism, 202, 250, 272
psychology: education and individual psychology of the child, 136–37, 140; "The Reflex Arc Concept in Psychology," 5. *See also* "Does Human Nature Change?"
Psychology (Dewey), 3
public, the: necessity of asking people what they want and need in a democracy, 163; and obligations of intellectuals, 6–8, 263–69; public's fatigue with the responsibilities of political liberty, 162; "Science, Belief, and the Public" (1924), 249–54; and science education, 7; and scientific habits of mind, 263–64, 266–67; support for the arts, 303, 305–6; voter apathy and cynicism, 99–101, 104, 180. *See also* democracy; education; human beings; workers

public engagement: and Dewey's humanism, 8; "The Supreme Intellectual Obligation," 6–8, 263–69

quality of life, 106, 260, 262

race: "Address to the Negro Conference" (1909), 24–26
racism, 55–58, 62, 148, 168, 238
radicalism, 109–11, 114, 190, 278, 279
Ratzel, Friedrich, 282–84
Reconstruction Finance Corporation, 109
"Reflex Arc Concept in Psychology, The," 5
religion, 8, 82n2; conflict among science, religion, public opinion, and general education curricula, 249–54, 272; and Darwinism, 239–40; and humanitarian liberalism, 106–7; and intolerance, 253; "The Value of Historical Christianity" (1889), 308–13. *See also* Christianity
Republican Party, 21; identification as the party of prosperity, 173–74, 176–78; and Prohibition, 100; support for government intervention in support of corporations, 173–74. *See also* conservatism; Right, the
Retreat from Reason, The (Hogben), 35
"Revolt Against Science, The" (1945), 270–73
Ricardo, David, 218, 222n2
Right, the, 19, 27–28. *See also* conservatism; Republican Party
risk, and business, 219–22
Robinson, James Harvey, 120
romanticism, 316–17; "The Collapse of a Romance" (1932), 8, 217–22
Root, Elihu, 278
Rorty, Richard, 3, 7, 13n11
Rousseau, Jean Jacques, 106
Royce, Josiah, 13n11
"rugged individualism" doctrine, 109, 144–46, 217, 228
Russell, Bertrand, 13n11, 49–51, 88, 89, 277
Russia: and appreciation of the arts, 73; and communism, 90–92 (*see also* communism); Russian Revolution, 111, 301; and social control, 111; weak middle class in, 92. *See also* Soviet Union

Sanders, Bernie, 174
Schiller, F. C. S., 316
Scholastic tradition, 237–38
School and Society (Dewey), 5
schools: current practices, 133; "Dewey Outlines Utopian Schools" (1933), 121–26; discipline in, 133, 139–40; earliest types of schools in the U.S., 135, 165; and experimentation, 138, 141–42; and social reconstruction, 144–47; traditional schools, 133, 138; "Why Have Progressive Schools?" (1933), 133–42. *See also* education; teachers
Schroeder, Theodore, 28
Schurman, Jacob Gould, 277, 279, 280
science: and the betterment of humanity, 51, 74–75, 263–71, 314, 317; conflict among science, religion, public opinion, and general education curricula, 249–54, 272; costs and benefits, 6–7; Dewey's scientific outlook, 4, 9; "Dualism and the Split Atom" (1945), 93–97; "Education and Birth Control" (1932), 260–62; and equality of opportunity, 36; "The Ethics of Animal Experimentation" (1926), 193–99; and humanism, 270–71, 273, 314, 317; "The Influence of Darwinism on Philosophy" (1909), 237–48; and intelligence and power, 80; jargon, 265; and materialism, 270–73; misconceptions about, 258; "pure" and "applied," 272–73; "The Revolt against Science" (1945), 270–73; "Science, Belief, and the Public" (1924), 249–54; science education, 7, 35–36, 253, 263, 266–68; scientific attitudes, 3, 4, 7, 9, 10, 80, 241–48, 249–54, 256, 258, 263–68, 272; "Social Science and Social Control" (1931), 255–59; "The Supreme Intellectual Obligation" (1934), 6–8, 263–69; Victorian view of, 283; and warfare, 265, 270; in the West, 296–97
"Science, Belief, and the Public" (1924), 249–54
Scribner's (magazine), 9
Scudder, Vida D., 28
sexuality, 6, 185
Sidgwick, Henry, 245
Sinclair, Upton, 28
slavery, 90, 108, 187
Smith, Adam, 107
"Social Absolutism" (1921), 282–88
social change: "Can Education Share in Social Reconstruction?" (1934), 144–47; democratic methods needed for, 111 (*see also* ends and means); "Does Human Nature Change?"

(1938), 185–92; "The Economic Situation: A Challenge to Education" (1932), 223–30; and education, 223–30; and intelligence and power, 82; and intelligent action, 113–14; and liberalism, 110–11; and warfare, 299–302
social class: class conflict, 153, 286; and Dewey's skepticism about communism, 90–91; education and breaking down class divisions, 169; and intelligence and power, 81–82; power and class interests, 78, 81, 111; rejection of classism, 148; weak middle class in Russia, 92
social contract theory, 255
social control: "Can Education Share in Social Reconstruction?" (1934), 144–47; democratic methods needed for, 111; of economic forces, 145; of industry, 180; and necessity of asking people what they want and need in a democracy, 163; "Social Science and Social Control" (1931), 255–59
socialism: "Capitalistic or Public Socialism?" (1930), 173–84; and communist view of history, 90; democratic socialism, 174; and humanitarian liberalism, 109; and individualism, 175; misconceptions about, 175; women and, 27–28
social justice. *See* economics and economic justice; humanitarian liberalism; poverty and the poor; social welfare; workers
social science: and "fact finding," 257, 259; and the physical sciences, 256–57; social prediction, 258; "Social Science and Social Control" (1931), 255–59
"Social Science and Social Control" (1931), 255–59
Social Security, 144, 174, 217
social studies curricula, 30, 34–35
social welfare: and humanitarian vs. laissez-faire liberalism, 110; "The Jobless—a Job for All of Us," 231–34; lack of safety nets prior to the Great Depression, 173; and morality and ethics, 205; safety nets created during the Great Depression, 144, 156–57, 218, 232; and unemployment, 179, 231–34
Socrates, 277
Solymosi, Tibor, 254n2
"Some Factors in Mutual National Understanding" (1921), 289–98
Soviet Union, 20; economics in, 182, 257; Five Year Plan, 257; injustice/intolerance in, 55; propaganda in, 56; Russian Revolution, 301; and social absolutism, 282, 286–87; as state-minded rather than socially minded, 282; suppression of civil liberties, 57; Treaty of Non-aggression with Germany, 299, 301; and "Why I Am Not a Communist," 89. *See also* communism; Russia
Spencer, Herbert, 246, 283
Spinoza, Baruch, 207
spirituality vs. materialism, 289, 291–93, 295–97
status quo, 144–45; and human nature, 187; and social function of education, 225–26; and teachers, 145–46, 223, 225–26
Stearns, Alfred E., 117, 118
stock market crash of 1929, 181
Subjection of Women, The (Mill), 27
suffrage, 6; of nonwhite people, 28; and property qualifications, 29; "A Symposium on Woman's Suffrage" (1911), 27–29; women's suffrage, 27–29, 59, 278
"Supreme Intellectual Obligation, The" (1934), 6–8, 263–69
"Symposium on Woman's Suffrage, A" (1911), 27–29

tabula rasa, 5
tariffs, 109, 178–79, 207
taxation, 174, 179
"Teacher and the Public, The" (1935), 156–60
teachers: as agents of improving public conditions, 223–30; "The Case of the Professor and the Public Interest" (1917), 277–81; discrimination against female teachers, 126n2; and freedom of speech and inquiry, 277–81; and revolt against science, 272; and social reconstruction, 144–47; and the status quo, 145–46, 223, 225–26; "The Teacher and the Public" (1935), 156–60; teaching critical thinking, 223; teaching of democratic attitudes and respect for differences, 149, 152, 155; unions, 157, 160, 281; in utopian schools, 122; as workers, 156–60, 280–81; worsening working conditions during the Great Depression, 157, 158–59
technology: changing industries, 178; costs and benefits, 6–7; "Dualism and the Split Atom" (1945), 93–97; and obligations of intellectuals, 6–7; and profit motive, 74

testing: high-stakes testing, 121, 223, 264; and utopian schools, 124
totalitarianism, 57, 58, 63. *See also* dictatorships
tracking in education, 127–28, 130
travel, 289–98, 304
truth, 10; Bacon and, 51; love of truth and love of neighbor, 50–52, 54; and religion, 82n2; Russell and, 49–51

understanding, 30–38
Unemployed (periodical), 231
unemployment, 8, 19–20; "The Jobless—a Job for All of Us" (1931), 8, 231–34; unemployment statistics (1932–1933), 217
unions, 157, 160, 281
United States: "America in the World" (1918), 40–43; and being state-minded vs. being socially minded, 282, 285; benefits and pitfalls of alliances, 44–48; changing conditions for children in, 211–16; chief traits of American people, 153; and communist view of history, 90; current polarized state, 60, 98; as diverse/multicultural society, 10, 40, 42–43, 148–52, 155; and federation, 42; as frontier society, 60–61, 73; history of education in the U.S., 135–37; isolation/end of isolation, 40–42, 44–48, 150; liberalism in, 108–9; and nationalism and internationalism, 148–55; nationalism in, 58; "Our National Dilemma" (1920), 44–48; Pax Americana, 41; as place of experiment in the world, 10, 40, 42–43, 53; pledge of allegiance, 168; "Pragmatic America" (1922), 49–54; separation of nationality and citizenship, 42; and social absolutism, 287–88; social system and "high culture"/the arts, 69–77; and the struggle against nature, 153; support for the arts in, 303, 305–6; talent and brainpower channeled into industry and profit rather than democratic culture, 69–70, 77; toleration in, 42; want in the midst of plenty, 266; and World War I, 40–45, 83–87, 150–51; and World War II, 299–302. *See also* democracy
University of Chicago, 4–5
University of Delaware, 289
University of Minnesota, 278
University of Pennsylvania, 277, 279
utilitarianism, 200, 205–7
utopian schools, 11, 121–26

"Value of Historical Christianity, The" (1889), 3, 308–13
values, 3–4; "The Basic Values and Loyalties of Democracy" (1941), 55–58; democracy as a way of personal life, 60, 62–65; and education, 164
violence, 2; and achieving democratic ends by democratic means, 113; and communism and fascism, 91–92, 105, 111; force as, 84, 114; "Force, Violence, and the Law" (1916), 83–87; and handling differences and conflicts in a democracy, 64; and liberalism, 105; minimum of intelligence used with, 114; and social change, 192; as a type of power, 81. *See also* peace and peace movements
vocational education, 30, 36–38, 127–32, 154

warfare: "The Basis for Hope" (1939), 299–302; causes of modern wars, 188; "Dualism and the Split Atom" (1945), 93–97; "Force, Violence, and the Law" (1916), 83–87; and human nature, 187–89; illegitimate/unjust wars, 201; and industrial and business interests, 301; and military preparedness, 224; and morality and ethics, 206–7; outlawing war, 200, 209–10; propaganda, 188, 230; and science, 265, 270; and social change, 299–302; as a type of power, 81
wealthy, the: capitalistic socialism protecting the interests of the few, 173–82; concentration of wealth, 175, 178; and corruption, 179; and income inequality, 174–75, 177, 179; indifference to education of the masses, 165; and social responsibility, 181–82; taxes on, 174, 179
Wells, H. G., 283, 284, 285
Wells-Barnett, Ida, 24
Wesleyan Protestant Christianity, 105–7
West, the: "Some Factors in Mutual National Understanding" (1921), 289–98
"What Humanism Means to Me" (1930), 8, 314–17
"What Is a School For?" (1923), 117–20
"Why Have Progressive Schools?" (1933), 133–42
"Why I Am Not a Communist" (1934), 88–92
Wilson, Woodrow, 48n2, 282, 287
wisdom, 11, 264, 281
women: Derbyshire and, 27–28; discrimination against female teachers, 126n2; and education, 25; and independent voters, 102; and labor

reforms, 108; Mill and, 27; and suffrage, 27–29, 59, 278; "A Symposium on Woman's Suffrage" (1911), 27–29

workers: accidental selection of jobs by the young, 130; changing workplaces, 166–67; fear-driven voting in presidential elections, 176–77; and humanitarian liberalism, 108; "The Jobless—a Job for All of Us" (1931), 231–34; and labor reforms, 108, 156; lack of control over their work, 96, 167; lack of economic freedom, 144; Marx and, 175–76; teachers as workers, 156–60, 280–81; unemployment, 156, 179, 228, 231–34; unemployment statistics (1932–1933), 217; unemployment statistics (2019), 174–75; vocational education, 30, 36–38, 127–32, 154

World War I, 40–45, 48nn 1,2, 148, 282; and emotions, 188; "Force, Violence, and the Law" (1916), 83–87; and intellectual freedom in academia, 277; and nationalism, 148, 150–51

World War II, 19; "The Basis for Hope" (1939), 299–302; beginning of, 59, 299; "The Revolt against Science" (1945), 270–73; tax rates, 174

Zinn, Howard, 297n2

CPSIA information can be obtained
at www.ICGtesting.com
Printed in the USA
JSHW022213250321
12947JS00004B/23